Another Tale to Tell

V

Contents

Acknowledgements

The pieces collected here originally appeared, in print or as public address, and often enough in a slightly altered state, in the following places: *College English* ("Icons for Clowns"); *Fiction International* ("Aesthetics and Politics," "Fiction after History"); *the minnesota review* ("The Aesthetics of Disappointment," "Consumer Projections"); *The Nation* ("Popular Expressions," "Policiers Noirs," "Down the Beanstalk"); *Socialist Review* ("Postmodernism and Our Discontent"); *Social Text* ("Plot Devices in the Occupation"); *The Village Voice* ("Beating the Odds"). "'Makin' Flippy-Floppy'" was first published in *The Year Left* Volume I, ed. Mike Davis *et al.* (London: Verso, 1985); "Potholders and Subincisions," in *Postmodernism and Its Discontents: Theories, Practices*, ed. E. Ann Kaplan (London: Verso, 1988). "Marxism, Feminism, and Postmodern Culture" was given as a talk at the first Socialist Scholars Conference in New York City, April 1983; "Plot and Patriarchy in the Age of Reagan," at the annual Institute for Culture and Society sponsored by the Marxist Literary Group, Pittsburgh, June 1986; "Montage Dynasty," at the Center for the Humanities, Wesleyan University, March 1988; and "These Disintegrations I'm Looking Forward to," at the Humanities Institute, SUNY-Stony Brook, May 1988.

My gratitude to those who invited me to talk or printed what I wrote, for both the original occasions and for this opportunity to publish or reprint.

Plate 1 is reproduced by permission of *Esquire*, and courtesy of the Hartford Public Library; Figures 1, 3, and 7 are reproduced courtesy of the University of Massachusetts, Amherst; Figures 2, 4, 5, and 6 are reproduced by permission of *Esquire*, and courtesy of Wesleyan University.

The Haymarket Series

Editors: Mike Davis and Michael Sprinker

The Haymarket Series is a new publishing initiative by Verso offering original studies of politics, history and culture focused on North America. The series presents innovative but representative views from across the American left on a wide range of topics of current and continuing interest to socialists in North America and throughout the world. A century after the first May Day, the American left remains in the shadow of those martyrs whom this series honours and commemorates. The studies in the Haymarket Series testify to the living legacy of activism and political commitment for which they gave up their lives.

Already Published

BLACK AMERICAN POLITICS: From the Washington Marches to Jesse Jackson *by Manning Marable*

PRISONERS OF THE AMERICAN DREAM: Politics and Economy in the History of the US Working Class *by Mike Davis*

MARXISM IN THE USA: Remapping the History of the American Left *by Paul Buhle*

THE LEFT AND THE DEMOCRATS *The Year Left 1*

TOWARD A RAINBOW SOCIALISM *The Year Left 2*

RESHAPING THE US LEFT: Popular Struggles in the 1980s *The Year Left 3*

THE LEFT AT THE DOORSTEP: The Radical Politics of Place in America *The Year Left 4*

CORRUPTIONS OF EMPIRE: Life Studies and the Reagan Era *by Alexander Cockburn*

FIRE IN THE AMERICAS: Forging a Revolutionary Agenda *by Roger Burbach and Orlando Núñez*

Introduction

I backed into the project of this book as I now edge backward into this introduction, with some anxious suspicions as to the overall value and coherence of the works assembled here. These essays and reviews were, after all, written at various points over twelve years which at least in retrospect seem characterized by nearly constant, and constantly shifting, political and intellectual challenge. They are, moreover, almost all site-specific to the diverse journals, audiences, and occasions for which they were written; none, save "The Flâneur at *River's Edge*," was written to be part of this book. Throughout most of these past twelve years, I have thought of myself as a fiction writer primarily, albeit one who occasionally, almost helplessly, emits a bit of criticism or theory now and then, as a sort of spin-off to the main task of writing politically charged and efficacious narratives, within the conditions and against the current of my own culture and time. So I begin this introduction with something like the same sense of part-terrifying, part-hilarious masquerade that has gripped me every time I have stood up to deliver a talk on some aspect of current cultural politics before some assembled group out there shifting its haunches in ranked hard chairs.

On the other hand, I have also to acknowledge by now the extent to which this pose itself constitutes its own masquerade, shrug off the costume of my discomfort, and affirm the actant that I have become. So let me admit that over the past few years in particular, I have come to think of my project as a writer as a dual one, encompassing not only the construction of politically explicit stories and novels which draw from the left and feminist currents of my time, but also the task of intervening in those theoretical currents themselves, and seeking to direct their flow, however slightly, in paths that might be useful to the challenge of constructing a socialist and feminist culture. Less grandiosely, I could say that these articles and essays record my sortings through various

1

models for mapping contemporary culture, in the search for methods and insights I could use to critique and strengthen my own artistic and political practice as a white male writer and activist, a member of the American professional-managerial class, and a socialist and (would-be) feminist, struggling within the boundaries of a nation whose dominant political practices lead me still to think of it, for all the economic dominance of Japan, as the capitalist heart of the Death Star.

This sorting-through itself has in turn taken place on various levels, and towards separately distinguishable ends, as the divisions of this volume suggest. Beginning with the first, and earliest, essay, "Icons for Clowns"—a piece so old its target is a mode of modernist *macho* in American fiction that is now for the most part long surpassed in white male writing by post-feminist self-pity on the one hand, and the shallow fast-food fiction of Jay McInerney, Bret Easton Ellis and other assorted u.m.c. "brat-packers" on the other—I have tried to clear, clarify, and enlarge the space for left political and artistic practice and, in so doing, to sort out some lessons for my own practice along the way. The first section of this book thus includes, in addition to "Icons," a selection from the review-essays on various books I have written over the years for *The Nation, The Village Voice,* and *the minnesota review,* the left-feminist literary magazine I have helped to edit throughout most of the eighties. Such attempts at a highly specific, left-feminist form of "practical criticism" might then be read in the more general context established for them by the longer essays that follow in the last two sections of the book. These, in their separate ways, attempt both a larger historical mapping of the cultural terrain on which we find ourselves, and an intervention in several of the left and left-feminist discourses which, like my own, both emanate from that terrain and seek to critique it—a terrain which I, like a horde of other commentators, left, right, and center, have called "postmodernism." Part II consists of essays which, as it were, "fly over" both that terrain itself and the overlapping airspaces of the political debates and theoretical discourses that swarm above it. They both conduct a search for the *social location* of that terrain and airspace on the class/race/gender map, and attempt to wrest from its gnarly and noisy entanglements some shadow traces of a potentially progressive sensibility which might somehow be mobilized into a collective political will. Part III continues such investigations, in admittedly eccentric readings of various middlebrow, modernist and postmodernist texts. These readings tend to pursue what I find to be the texts' curious and instructive relationships with contemporary critical and theoretical arguments, particularly within left-poststructuralism and psychoanalytic feminism, and seek to draw political lessons from the encounter between the two.

These forays into postmodern culture might generally be distinguished from the current rush of such studies in three ways. First, they do not take "postmodernism" to be the general or universal condition or definition of culture within the First World metropole; rather, from "'Makin' Flippy-Floppy'" onward, they argue that "postmodernism" is the distinctive cultural expression or "structure of feeling" of a largely white professional-managerial class produced by the social formations (and, in this book, particularly the North American social formation) of the developed world. Secondly, they are often disrespectful of the privileged relationship ordinarily assumed to exist between critical theory and those "merely" fictional or imaginative narratives which that theory may feel free either to "operate on" or ignore. No doubt in part because I write both fiction and criticism, and have come to find them overlapping and reciprocally illuminating kinds of work, such a hierarchy of practices seems increasingly dubious to me; so much so, indeed, that I am not entirely happy with my own "airspace" metaphor (another lesson in just how hard it is to pull one's own practice away from the hegemonic norm). In any case, what nearly all the essays in Part III insist on, tacitly or explicitly, is that theoretical discourses themselves are but so many other social texts to be set alongside and not above "creative" ones, so that a given film or novel may be said, and seen, not only to "flesh out" or "re-present" a given ideological or theoretical discourse, but, as it were, to cast that discourse in a critical light, to *talk back to it*, intentionally or not. And finally, this collection takes its distance from other works on the nature of postmodern culture in the frankly didactic and utopian notes I have tried to strike in it. Even—and, alas, perhaps especially—within many putatively left, "post-leftist" and/or feminist works on postmodernism, including most of the nouveau-canonical ones (Jameson, Hutcheon, Lyotard, Baudrillard, etc.—most readers of this introduction will already know the list), postmodernity is either taken to be the disaster that has already occurred, leaving us utterly resourceless and without hope, walking zombies under perpetual erasure wandering aimlessly through an endless mall; or else it is just as unproblematically celebrated as a disintegration of old hierarchies and an explosion of new cultural and political practices, from "subversive readings" to the "new social movements," which together constitute a new carnival of freedom, somewhere out beyond the old orthodoxies, including Marxism itself. What both sides have in common is both their universalist starting point, in which postmodernism, like Pascal's God, is everywhere and nowhere at once, and their fatalistic conclusion, in which, for better or for worse, there is nothing to be done but more of the same. In the essays which follow here, though readers will find borrowings enough from theoreticians in both camps, they will also find, I hope, a refusal of the apocalyptic cast of mind that deforms and disables their best insights.

Instead, while insisting on the specific history and social location of postmodernist culture, indeed precisely *by* insisting on it, I hope to have opened up a space for specific political calculation and assessment, for strategy as well as for critique. That, as Stuart Hall once pointed out in the course of his own work on the concept of the "popular," is what we ought to be doing with the concepts we work with; otherwise, I would say of postmodernism what he says of any depoliticized conceptualization of his chosen term—"I don't give a damn about it."[1]

On the other hand, I must confess the extent to which I do give a damn about postmodernism, indeed about all the cultural practices described in this book, and say something briefly about the history of my approach to them. In a real sense, that history begins for me in the fall of 1967, as with my mother and sister I drove around the Amherst college quad searching for my freshman dorm, a scholarship kid from a remote factory town in the Allegheny Mountains of northwest Pennsylvania, and felt my heart beat faster and my head grow light at the sound of the blaring, wacky strains of *Sgt. Pepper's Lonely Hearts Club Band* streaming out to me from several dorm windows at once. The joy I felt at that moment was literally an uncanny one: for all that summer, back home after work, I'd been playing that album over and over for myself alone; no one, not even my closest friends, liked its polymorphous weirdness but me; and here at this new place, this impossibly alien landscape with its prim brick buildings, with rich kids all around, here *everyone* was playing the music I liked. I was home, in effect, but not home—and have remained so ever since, a "stranger in paradise," as exiles from the working class like me are called in the poignant testimonial volume South End Press has published about our experience of academe.[2] A good deal of my intellectual labor since then, and a good deal of this volume, beginning with the self-destructive *macho* writing lifestyle described in "Icons for Clowns" and ending with the poststructural sublime limned out in "Potholders and Subincisions," has consisted in negotiating a difficult relationship with various cultural artifacts, practices, sensibilities which at first I could neither take nor leave alone. The downside of such hard-wired homelessness, in the volatile, constantly reversing action of affinity and alienation it effects, makes for a certain amount of permanent discomfort, it is true; but I cling to the hope that there is some value in the position I have willy-nilly come to occupy. As Brecht once said, exiles make the best dialecticians, and at least my historical situation and vexed class position have always required me to keep in mind that even within my own society, postmodernism is far from the only game in town.

And yet here, too, I want to reverse position again, and register my partial agreement with some of those who have argued for postmodern-

ism as a sensibility and style that stretches across the whole cultural field
of First World capitalist society. For it is now well-nigh indisputable that,
within and across the older national boundaries of capitalist production,
and against the concessions and coercions of an earlier "Fordist"
relationship between capital and labor, a new "post-Fordist" regime of
accumulation is rapidly under construction. This latter can be characterized, as Stuart Hall has written, by

> a shift to the new "information technologies"; more flexible, decentralised
> forms of labour process and work organisation; decline of the old manufactur-
> ing base and the growth of the "sunrise," computer-based industries; the
> hiving-off or contracting-out of functions and services; a greater emphasis on
> choice and product differentiation, on marketing, packaging and design,
> on the "targeting" of consumers by lifestyle, taste and culture rather than by
> the Registrar General's categories of social class; a decline in the proportion
> of the skilled, male, manual working class, the rise of the service and white-
> collar classes and the "feminisation" of the workforce; an economy
> dominated by the multinationals, with their new international division of
> labour and their greater autonomy from nation-state control; the "globalis-
> ation" of the new financial markets, linked by the communications
> revolution; and new forms of the spatial organisation of social processes.[3]

Obviously, such transformations are nationally inflected in significant
ways—as will be evident to anyone who has read, for example, Mike
Davis's authoritative account of the rise to power of the American
"sunbelt," driven by the deranged engines of military spending and
aerospace.[4] But the analyses of the French "regulation school" in the
1970s, and, more recently, of Lash and Urry in their important work,
The End of Organized Capitalism, make it clear that a general, epochal
shift in the directions described above appears to be underway throughout the developed world.[5] The emergence of postmodernism as a "period
style" must somehow be related to this epochal transformation in the
mode of production—not as any cultural "essence" or "superstructural"
secretion, but as a new and evolving set of cultural practices and
possibilities flowing from the radical expansion of both "subject-posi-
tions" and always-already-commodified "lifestyle choices" churned out
by this new transnational machine. In this general sense, postmodernism
thus bears the same relation to "post-Fordism" or "disorganized capitalism" that modernism bore to Fordist mass production; and, indeed, the
old but unresolved debates around the political valence of modernism,
most recently rehearsed in the debate between Marshall Berman and
Perry Anderson, are well under way around the new "P-word" as well. In
such debates, as that between Berman and Anderson illustrates, the real
stakes center finally on a question of method and definition: on whether

the given period style is to be understood as a broad social phenomenon, or as a set of cultural practices and pleasures with a quite specific social location and history.[6] On this question, then, in relation to postmodernism, readers will find that I have been something of a gadfly, flitting from one position to another, taking up the first, for example, in "Marxism, Feminism, and Postmodern Culture" and "The Flâneur at *River's Edge*," and the second in " 'Makin' Flippy-Floppy' " and elsewhere. Yet, at the risk of repeating an earlier point, and for all my genial tolerance on the question in general, I must urge here the necessity of adopting the more specific and conjunctural mode of analysis for the purpose of reading out of cultural texts some strategic sense of the problems of political organization and agency that confront us as socialist-feminists in our place and time, if only because it seems to me that for whatever reasons (academicization? simple fear of being "vulgar" or flat wrong?) far too little work of this kind is being done.

That said, however, I will climb down off the pedestal I've ascended, and cop to a few of my own dissatisfactions and discomforts with the rest of this book—starting with my diffuse but persistent sense of something like shame at even practicing cultural critique. For all my bold, self-approving protestations of commitment to strategic analysis, there is something suspect about using visual art, novels, music, TV and film—the stuff I take in as entertainment, the stuff I *like*—as my raw material or starting point for thinking about politics. Just as surely, my ability to do so—to slog my way through contemporary theory, to stuff in and meditate on all these "texts"—rests on a high, plush platform of what Pierre Bourdieu calls "cultural capital," a far higher fund than most people in my society ever possess.[7] I have no doubt that there are some trenchant ready-made responses to my nagging suspicions as to the value of this kind of work (perhaps having to do with the "naive" opposition between work and play, between going to a movie, going to a political meeting, and going to work—since to "read" a text, after all, is precisely to work on it, *n'est-ce pas?*), and no faith whatsoever that any of them could assuage my anxiety and sense of illicit privilege. I can only say, crude as it sounds, that nearly all of these pieces were written in conjunction with my continued, and continuing, involvement in left and left-feminist political organizing, and that I hope ongoing activism has exerted its pressure and left its mark on them.

A more localizable but equally serious problem comes up, however, around my protestations about the putatively feminist character or tendency of these essays. There are, after all, good reasons, and a dreary track record, behind any feminist woman's suspicion of any male critic's claim to be really on her side. Already, within this introduction, I have felt a twinge of anxiety every time I have invoked "feminism," hyphenated with "socialist" or not, as a term to describe the positions taken in the essays that follow, and not least because the vast majority of the works they take up for consideration have been authored by men. My anxiety is in some part a result of an arguably excessive desire not to be seen as sitting anywhere near the judgment seat on women's work. But I have also felt rather strongly that it was my place, if not my obligation, to think through contemporary male-authored texts using the terms and insights of feminist theory, which of course has inevitably never been just about women—nor can it just be for them, if our present sex/gender system is ever to shift lastingly towards freedom and equality. Accordingly, readers will find, perhaps to their consternation, that I not only draw on various strands of feminist theory throughout much of this volume, but have felt free here and there (and especially with regard to some contemporary French feminist work) to point to what I see as certain of its limits or drawbacks. Some feminist critics may also object to my unabashed willingness to cross boundary lines within feminism, drawing, for example, from both Lacanian feminism and from the far more orthodox (and, I think, properly materialist) object-relations-derived socio-psychoanalytic modelings of Dinnerstein, Chodorow, and Benjamin. Be that as it may, I hope it will become clear to any reader of this text not only that feminist theory can do much to illuminate the character of our present cultural moment, in which, to paraphrase Gramsci, an old sex/gender system is slowly collapsing and a new one is not yet born, but that thanks to feminism our whole way of thinking questions of collective agency, organization, and utopian goals has changed, and must continue to change.

But this collection exhibits yet another defect, a more blatant and unredeemable one, which I can only admit to, not defend. Looking back over this work, I am ashamed to see how glancingly and inadequately the reviews and essays included here have treated questions of race. A single review of one black writer's work, a brief reference to the "postmodernism" of hip-hop culture, a few remarks on racial otherness in *Fiskadoro* and racism in *Back to the Future*—these are surely not enough for any collection which hopes to capture even partially the character and political valence of contemporary cultural production in the United States. Here, too, as with feminist works by women, I might plead my reluctance to take up the role of critic and commentator on Afro-American cultural production, as well as my lack of credentials for doing so; but in a moment in which, for reasons themselves entirely deriving from American racism, the number of Afro-American cultural critics and theorists remains disgracefully small, and the arena in which their voices may be heard even smaller, I am at best only admitting my own criminal ignorance and complicity. (I focus on Afro-American culture here, moreover, only insofar as the black/white color line remains the central axis of American racism; the same truth, and the same self-criticism, apply with regard to the cultural productions of Chicanos, Puerto Ricans, Asian-Americans, Native Americans, and others.) As any history of the American working class and any analysis of the shortcomings of the American left amply demonstrate, racism has been at least as constitutive of the politics and culture of this country as the class exploitation with which it has been consistently and poisonously fused. And the occasionally positive obverse of this fact is equally true: no American cultural production ever comes to us unmarked by racial difference, whether that difference be registered by exclusion and silence or by inclusion in Bakhtinian dialogue. The collection that follows is seriously weakened by my failure to consider, adequately and systematically, these basic historical facts of life; but here I can only apologize for that failure, and promise to correct it as best I can in what I write in future.

To these self-criticisms, finally, I would attach one further note, one simultaneously critical and approving. I have already spoken of my desire throughout this work to press my readings towards conclusions both political and didactic; yet even (or perhaps especially) readers who agree with much of what I have to say in what follows are likely to find themselves, at the conclusion of various essays and the book as a whole, with far more problems than solutions on their hands. That comes partly out of a personal predilection for getting myself stuck, rather than reciting what I think I already know: so much so, indeed, that the one long essay on postmodernism I have written which most clearly places its political bet on a theoretical line (in this case, on feminist materialism, and deliberate changes in child-rearing practices towards co- and collective parenting) seems now so flawed by its monotheistic enthusiasm that I have chosen not to include it here.[8] But my willingness to get stuck, to push toward the edges of what is currently available is something more, I hope, than just a personal tic. "Historic risks, historic opportunities," as old socialist warhorses like to say; but the slogan has never seemed more poignantly apt than at the present moment, when so much of what has called itself socialist staggers under the weight of its past and present crimes, while in the capitalist world feminists, environmentalists, and people of color engage in struggles in which, at the present moment at least, they find the categories and emphases of Marxism almost by definition irrelevant or outright pernicious. In this context—to which must be added, moreover, the epochal shift within capitalism from Fordism to post-Fordism briefly sketched out above—I want to underscore my continuing allegiance to the project of constructing a democratic socialism, in the United States and around the world. But the essays in this volume attest to my equally strong conviction that both the fundamental definition of that utopian term and our strategic thinking and struggle to reach it must now be transformed almost beyond recognition. To do so, to take account of our past failures and present fears and hopes, will inevitably require us to go beyond, *though not without*, the standpoints and insights of Gramsci, Althusser, and Marx. I will stick my head out even further, and offer it up to both orthodox Marxists and anti- or "post-" Marxists alike, by saying that, while a democratic socialism (that is, for those who may have forgotten it, an egalitarian society in which both production and consumption are primarily controlled by popular will, and political and economic decisions are democratically made) provides no guarantee of an end to exploitative divisions of gender and race or a turning away from ecological disaster, within our own national culture those ends are inconceivable without it. Accordingly, the feminist, anti-racist, and environmental utopian projects must all also be socialist, whether they be called so or not. Either that, or they—and we along with them—will all go down.

As for what the socialist project will look like, retooled and altogether redesigned by feminists, people of color, ecologists and the like—that is here, as with Marx's comments on "class" in *Capital*, where the manuscript breaks off. But not before these essays issue their calls for help to socialists and non-socialists alike, to participate in what can only be the *collective* project of imagining new ends, and coming together in new ways to reach them. To do so of course is no less than to construct a new collective narrative, "another tale to tell." That is the point of the short piece of deconstructive fiction which ends this collection, and one of my reasons for lifting the title of this book from the old, apocalyptic Dylan song "Wheels on Fire." Yet another level of resonance, however, emerges from the whole sentence from which I take this phrase: "No man alive will come to you / With another tale to tell." These lines have taken on a peculiar, if unintended pungency for me, in the light of the poststructuralist critique of "dominant" or "bourgeois" narrative that emerged in the writings of Barthes, Kristeva, and others in France in the late 1960s and early 1970s, was echoed and amplified in *Screen* and other British books and journals in the mid-to-late 1970s, and began to show up in American theory and criticism from the late 1970s on. For such leftist and feminist cultural theorists, too, "No [oedipal] man will come to you with another [dominant, bourgeois] tale to tell"; or if he does, you should throw him out. But while I have learned much from the post-structural critique of bourgeois narrative, as the following pages will attest, I have also been skeptical of some of its directions, particularly when its critique turns into a denunciation of any and all attempts to represent difference, the embrace of either an intransigently esoteric and exclusive avant-gardism or an ever-less-critical embrace of the commodified, mass-mediated heteroglossia that is, combined with a more or less explicit abandonment of the project of radical social change, in favor of, at best, a "war of position" without end: an aesthetic of esoteric works and minuscule audiences, combining with a purely theoretical politics to compose what is finally no more than a rictus of privileged despair.

Against such elitist cultural practices and apolitical politics and against their opposing other, the view that finds no possibilities within postmodern culture at all, these essays begin with the "bad new days" we are in, insisting that even within them we may find hints of the alternatives to strive for, fragments of "another tale to tell." To be sure, that tale, when constructed through cultural and political practice alike, will be something other than bourgeois-oedipal narrative in either its realist or modernist versions, and markedly different from the heroic narratives of traditional Marxism as well. Its political forms and activities may look more like those of ACT UP or the Greens than those of the Communist Party or (god help us) DSA; its cultural forms more like those of *Pee-Wee's Playhouse* or *Cloud Nine* than *Mother Courage* and *To Die in Madrid*. But that is because the other tale we have to tell must necessarily come out of the culture—or, more accurately, cultures—we have if it is to work within them. In the title of this volume, then, the verb is meant to work both ways: to suggest that there *is* another tale to tell out there, elusive though its presence may be, and to urge us, again in both senses of the verb, to enact it.

Though the words of this book, like those of most tales in the telling, come from only one person, the end-product is like all books and tales collectively-authored. My debts to Jessica Benjamin and Stuart Hall are obvious and frequently acknowledged in the following pages; but I mention them here anyway because their contributions to my critical thinking, teaching, and political practice have been so large. Likewise, despite the divergences from his thinking that show up here and there in this work, I must express my gratitude for the enabling example of Fredric Jameson, who has inspired and challenged a generation of younger critics like me to think dialectically and "always historicize." Other thanks must go to Trinity College, the Rockefeller Foundation, and the Center for the Humanities at Wesleyan, for giving me the time I needed to write much of this book, and to the people at and around Wesleyan's Center in the winter and spring of 1988 for their challenging and generous fellowship. In New York City, Maria Margaronis has been a stalwart friend and a brilliant editor, pressing my thinking forward and trimming my verbosity to equally good effect, first at *The Nation* and now at *The Village Voice*; while closer to home, Ann Augustine, John McClure, and Jim Miller have supplied criticism, called me on jargon, and offered many new insights and lines of investigation along with their love and unconditional support. For this book, however, my greatest thanks and deepest gratitude must go to Michael Sprinker. Throughout the past ten years, as my co-editor, sometime colleague, and unstinting pal, the example of his energy, intelligence, and commitment have been as indispensable to me as his friendship. Without his encouragement, many of these essays would never have been written, and certainly this book would never have appeared. My respect and gratitude are all the greater for the fact of our ongoing differences in matters of both politics and theory, which, far from standing in the way of our friendship or stalling this work, have consistently enriched both. Indeed, in the making of this book, he has functioned as more than a good editor; here, as in the rest of my life, he is, in the old, strong sense of the term, a comrade as well.

Hartford, Connecticut
July 1989

NOTES

1. "Notes on Deconstructing 'The Popular'," in Raphael Samuel, ed., *People's History and Socialist Theory* (London: Routledge and Kegan Paul, 1981), p. 238.

2. Jake Ryan and Charles Sackrey, *Strangers in Paradise: Academics from the Working Class* (Boston: South End Press, 1984).

3. Stuart Hall, "Brave New World," *Marxism Today* (October 1988), p. 24.

4. See the second part of his *Prisoners of the American Dream: Politics and Economy in the History of the US Working Class* (London: Verso, 1986), especially "The Political Economy of Late-Imperial America," pp. 181–230.

5. See Michel Aglietta, "World Capitalism in the Eighties," *New Left Review* 136 (November–December, 1982), pp. 5–41; Alain Lipietz, *Mirages and Miracles: The Crisis of Global Fordism* (London: Verso, 1987); and Scott Lash and John Urry, *The End of Organized Capitalism* (Madison: University of Wisconsin Press, 1987).

6. See "Modernity and Revolution," Anderson's critique of Berman's *All That Is Solid Melts Into Air*, and Berman's reply, "The Signs in the Street," *New Left Review* 144 (March–April 1984), pp. 96–113 and 114–23, respectively.

7. *Distinction: A Social Critique of the Judgement of Taste*, trans. Richard Nice (Cambridge MA: Harvard University Press, 1984).

8. See "Postmodernism as a 'Structure of Feeling'," in Larry Grossberg and Cary Nelson, eds., *Marxism and the Interpretation of Culture* (Urbana: University of Illinois Press, 1987), pp. 381–404. Or better yet, don't.

PART I

Icons for Clowns:

American Writers Now

On the desk in front of me rests the October 1973 special issue of *Esquire* commemorating its fortieth anniversary, revised by David McKay as a textbook reader in the same year. The cover title reads:

ESQUIRE
The Best of Forty Years

and under this banner thirty-nine people, most of them writers, are flocked.

The faces of these writers have been scrupulously painted from photographs, so that they seem, at first glance, to be strikingly realistic. But this "realism" is not quite true, not real. A certain flat consistency of color has been applied to each face, each of whose few special lines and curves of mouth seem engraved, stamped into an essential smoothness. So if you examine any one face closely, or stare at them all together long enough, the faces of these American writers will seem like JFK's on a half dollar, FDR's on a quarter coin: icons on a commodity simultaneously identifiable as modern American writing and *Esquire* magazine. Then each of these figures, these thirty-nine icons, has a white number placed on it, and his or her name listed in an index at the bottom of the picture which extends, mural-like, to the back cover of the magazine.

I am an American writer, and I feel as though I have been carrying such icons of American writers in my head for a long time, along with the mythology of writers and writing they express. And I am quite certain that all the American writers I know must contend with the same bag of craven images, which in their turn hold such a heavy weight of mythic dreams; so that we all felt a thrill, and shock of recognition, and a darker ripple of guilt or even shame when we first saw this issue with its cover. And many of us bought the magazine.

This issue is four years old now, but I have not been able to forget this cover; it haunts me as much as a perfectly achieved work of art. Yet its

Plate 1

0-679-30264-6

21. Irwin Shaw
22. Richard H. Rovere
23. Truman Capote
24. Vladimir Nabokov
25. Peter Bogdanovich

26. Garry Wills
27. Richard Joseph
28. Leon Trotsky
29. Ralph Ellison
30. Tennessee Williams

31. Malcolm Muggeridge
32. Sinclair Lewis
33. Gore Vidal
34. John Sack
35. Arnold Gingrich

36. John Dos Passos
37. Thomas Berger
38. John Cheever
39. Laurence Stallings

effect is the opposite of art's: it does not purify my dreams, it concentrates them, it flaunts their cheapness and co-option in its perfectly unexamined form.

I think that by looking hard enough at these images of writers, by imagining and recreating the process by which they reached the cover of this particular magazine in this peculiar form, we can know a lot about the writer's real position in this country, as well as his imagined, desired one: positions dictated by the corruption of power and fear of the imagination in America, positions *Esquire* itself, in its small way, helps to create and uphold.

Who are these thirty-nine writers? How does *Esquire* show them? Thirty-seven of them are men (beneath *Esquire*'s cover title the inscription, "The Magazine for Men," usually appears). Thirty-five of them are white men. Thirty-four of the thirty-seven men are wearing suits, and all the men are dressed up. The two women shown seem to be wearing somewhat formal dresses.

I showed this cover picture to a friend of mine who is not a writer, and asked what he thought of it. He stared at it for a moment and said, "They look like businessmen." And so they do. They have the dark-hued conservative garb of businessmen, the stiff postures and inexpressive, unfocused intensity in the eyes and all about the face; the even-toned pinkish skin or alcoholic ruddiness of most of their faces, this even-castedness that I just called unreal, does after all exist somewhere in the real world—on the faces of business executives who spend so much time indoors, under artificial light.

But why does *Esquire* make writers look like businessmen?

Look at the five men who are not in business suits: Ernest Hemingway, William Faulkner, Tom Wolfe, Truman Capote, Tennessee Williams. Their current "recognition factor" soars above all the rest combined. They are celebrities. The average magazine reader (someone must have known) would recognize *these* images instantly, could spot Hemingway's African hunting outfit, Wolfe's ice-cream suit, the open braying jaws of Tennessee's raucous face a mile away on the racks. In fact it would not do at all for these figures to be cast as businessmen; Tom Wolfe *is* that dandy's outfit, that prim weirdness *makes* Capote what he is, Faulkner's collar must be open in that casually, mildly raffish southern way. We may not have read these men's work, we need not have read it; we know these images through the mass media, the news magazines and talkshows that can show us only trappings, the celebrity aura, safari suit, the laugh. So we know these people must be powerful, and good writers to boot—even though (precisely because) they cannot be shown in anything but the costumes that now possess them.

But those others, the pallid, more-or-less anonymous businessmen in their suits—we do not recognize them. We can guess that they're writers—they are, after all, in the same space with Hemingway et al.—but how can we tell that they're good writers? That they matter?

To supply an aura of power commensurate with Capote's, Wolfe's, Williams's, Faulkner's, Hemingway's powers as celebrities, all the rest have been given the costume and facial mask of power in this country: the businessman's suit, the professionally anonymous face. These writers, the cover tells us, are as successful and powerful as a clutch of rich corporate execs. And the *Esquire* reader will know how powerful that is, for he is likely to be such a man.

(As for the two women, they could, I suppose, be businesswomen. Or secretaries. They are in the background anyway.)

Esquire does—or would—have a certain problem in presenting writers visually *as* writers. Writers affect no particular style of clothing, have no special uniform or cast of face. A writer can look like anyone else. Anyone can be a writer. Yet we need to believe that writers are special, that they have unique appearances and effects—and no one wants to think so more than the writer himself.

I went to get a haircut a few years ago, and told the barber in the middle of our formally idle conversation that I was a writer. He got very excited, told me he was a writer too, hauled out a few of his stories from a drawer beneath the barber's mirror, and shot a stream of questions at me about publishing—was I published, how could he publish, where did you start? I acted as though I had been published a lot—in fact only one piece had ever been printed, in an undergraduate magazine—and tossed out my hazy answers with blithe arrogance. Meanwhile, I was running my eyes over one of his short pieces, a pathetically clichéd, virtually illiterate animal story—a dog who made friends with some cute little squirrels.

In fact I felt an embarrassment so great it amounted to a fury that this man with his greasy hair, stupid face, and maudlin earnestness dared to call himself a writer and I could do nothing to distinguish myself from him, show nothing to prove even to myself that I was one and he wasn't.

And even if I had published five books, had been able to brandish a Nobel Prize in his face and shout that he was a fool not a writer, just a dumb barber whose stuff was crap, even if he cringed then and repented—I would have been wrong.

At least when he was writing that story he was a writer.

But we want to believe that we *are* writers, essentially, platonically writers, those of us who write. If everyone who writes anything is a writer, it makes my identity as a writer less unique. I am no longer set apart.

A horror of not being special. I want to be set off and engraved on the cover too, where no one can get me, no one can efface or blur my absolute once-and-for-all uniqueness, my claim to fame.

(Yet in all their "uniqueness" the faces on the cover look so much alike.)

Shelley said that poets were "the unacknowledged legislators of the world." Later another poet, W.H. Auden, pointed out that it is really the secret police, not the poets, who are the unacknowledged legislators. It was also Auden, I think, who said that a person is a writer when writing, a shopper when shopping, a reader when reading, etc.

Marx argued that Milton wrote *Paradise Lost* for the same reason that a silkworm spins silk. A misleading analogy, I think. Writing is one of the most deliberate acts in the world, even when (or especially when) those deliberations issue from an otherwise unused and fuzzy patch in the writer's consciousness. And yet writing is no more deliberate than, say, heart surgery either. What Marx was perhaps trying to demythologize was the presumed "holiness" of what we call "the creative act"; what he was reaching for was a sense of the writer as an organism bound up in a process of production: a worker.

We cling to this hoked-up, mystical sense of ourselves as Writers, of writing as a special oracular priestly activity and secret rite, precisely because writing, at least in this country, has so little effect. And because it is obviously not enough in this country to be just another human being. We must be special, absolutely unique.

An ordinary human being writing at a desk in America is not special; like most other Americans, he has very little power. Yet he is, at that moment, a writer.

Most of the writers I know share a half-explicit assumption that the primary test of a good writer is his ability to write a good line of verse, or a good sentence in prose. This quality of goodness will have little or nothing to do with what the sentence or line says, or how it connects with the next, or the arguments of real existence which are being raised in its utterance.

Once I was at a party that included two writers, a strong-armed Southerner and a great shaggy hulk from Montana nicknamed "Buffalo." The Southerner had just lost an arm-wrestling match, and since his arm-wrestling was an important proof to him of his uniqueness and power, he was shaken and mad. Still at the table, the scene of his defeat, he said loudly, to everyone, "I write the best sentence in America."

The Buffalo reared off the refrigerator he had been leaning on, out of his stupor. "What's that bullshit? You saying you—"

"I'm saying, you drunk animal, I write the best sentence in the United States."

Buffalo lurched forward, jowls swaying. "You shit too, *I'm* the best goddamn sentence writer in the *world!*"

The Southerner let out a carefully composed laugh of malicious condescension. "Aw, Buffalo, come on now—"

And eventually they had to go off and each get a story and sit at the Southerner's kitchen table with their stories in front of them, reading to each other out loud, one sentence at a time. But before the duel was settled, they passed out.

Yes, they were both drunk, they are both alcoholics. But that should not smear the shape of what I am trying to say. If anything, it should clarify it.

I wasn't there when the two of them held their sheaves of paper in their thick fingers and strained to focus on the page, but I know them and their tastes well enough to tell you what made one sentence better than another for them. It was mostly a matter of sound, rhythm, diction. Startling turns of phrase, abrupt bounces in or out of iambic pentameter (neither one of them would have called it that), closed stops when a paragraph concludes. A kind of prosody of prose. What the stores were about, what the sentences said, was entirely separate from how good they were. Meaning had nothing to do with it.

Other people know and can tell you much better than I how writing and most other art has come to be so judged by most artists and critics, on the basis of its formal qualities alone.[1] Here I will only mention two famous representative quotations. They come from the late nineteenth and early twentieth centuries, respectively, when the estrangement of the artist from capitalist society was made, by mutual agreement, virtually complete. Then aesthetic formalism came into flower; Walter Pater said that all the arts "aspire to the condition of music," and Ezra Pound backed up Mallarmé's contention that it is the purpose of poetry "to purify the language of the tribe."

Now at the mention of either name, Pater or Pound, I know the Southerner would roll his eyes up, the Buffalo would snort out another "Shit." But there at the kitchen table they are chewing their ancestors' words just the same. For what has issued from such statements, and the poetic practice they buttress, is a notion of the value and purpose of literature of which the New Criticism, still alive (or dead) and well, is only the proverbial iceberg tip. Language, like paint or musical pitches, is seen to be a self-enclosed, fanatically guarded medium. Its ability to perceive or to express perception of the world is secondary or immaterial; the desired end of the act of writing is a closed, autonomous, self-referential body of well-shaped, beautiful language.

In the latter stages of capitalism art has developed in a similar way to science and other branches of knowledge. On one hand specialization has become more and more intense; on the other hand, the results of the pursuit of specialized knowledge have become more and more difficult to apply for the benefit of society as a whole.[2]

So the writer becomes a Joyce-like priest of language; his separation from his world approaches infinity as the reality or perception explored in his work approaches zero.

So much may seem—may really be—tired ground. (Then why doesn't it change? Because the texture of contemporary life is so numbing, painful, and incomprehensible? Because the writer's estrangement from society rocks nobody's boat?) What has not been pointed out so often, and what is very odd to me, is the way this total aestheticism literary critics proudly call Modernism has been embraced by many of the writers I know as a kind of *toughness*, a proof of virility. The Southerner often arm-wrestled at that same kitchen table where the sentences fought it out that night. And just the other day another writer (also alcoholic) said to me of the Buffalo: "Line for line old Buffalo's the best writer I know."

Compare that line with "Pound for pound, he's the best boxer in the ring." But the joke is that pantywaists like Pater and that snob Ezra are historically behind it all. An odor of violets on the round brown Everlast gloves.

Look again at Ernest Hemingway on the *Esquire* cover, number four in his safari suit, the largest figure of them all.

Hemingway really is the seminal character of American twentieth-century writing—or at least of its mythology. It is Hemingway who enables the Southerner and the Buffalo to look back through the years for the source of their devotion to "clean" sentences, "good" writing, without finding some horrifyingly limp-wristed dink like Pater there. Hemingway gets into the ring and you don't even notice Stein and Pound and Eliot in the corner as trainers and managers. He blots them out. He's that big, that tough. A man's man.

Hemingway wanted to knock Tolstoy out of the ring (he said so). Hemingway said what mattered was writing good and true, and made good writing all bound up with tough he-man things like fishing, hunting, fighting wars, bullfighting, heavy drinking, fucking, going on when your balls were shot off (ultimate test number one), being tough while you died (ultimate test number two). Hemingway shot his head off in Ketchum, Idaho; big country, man's country, good hunting there. So even the defeats were tough, taken toughly all the way, good and true.

He had destroyed his talent by not using it, by betrayals of himself and what he believed in, by drinking so much that he blunted the edge of his perceptions, by laziness, by sloth, and by snobbery, by pride and by prejudice, by hook and by crook.

The sentence comes from "The Snows of Kilimanjaro," first printed in *Esquire*, reprinted in the fortieth anniversary issue. It is a sentence I must admire because it is true, one of the most relentless catalogues of abuse of talent ever written. But it is also, you will notice, good and clean, beautifully scraped bare, and it is made to fit in a context that takes it almost all back. Because by the end of the story we have been powerfully convinced that the writer-character is tough and good and true despite all that, and Hemingway the Writer is, too. The man dies by disappearing into Nature, who is even better and cleaner and truer than he himself, up snow-capped Mount Kilimanjaro; it is apotheosis, not loss. And Hemingway, of course, has not been lost either; he has come back to write this good and true story, right? He is still in there fighting Tolstoy.

I find it incredibly hard to write about Hemingway, even painful. Again I know that I am dealing with matters everybody is familiar with: Hemingway's cult of manliness and death, and the good clean writing. But these two hackneyed cartoon creeds, these diseased atoms, are fused with such force in Hemingway's writing and life that every male American writer I know, including me, carries the disease that is the fruit and fallout of his sickness in our bones.

One night I was with another writer, a man much more well-known than I, who has published much more work. We were drinking, of course, and I began to feel my own "inferiority" to him so sharply that I started to rag him about his chic San Francisco dress and styled hair—his lack of "toughness"—until finally he snapped back: "Listen, Fred, you know damn well you'd have to beat the bushes a long time to find a more Hemingway guy than me."

Hemingway has been justly praised as the creator of a style that presents to us the flat, shimmering juxtapositions and joinings that appear in the painting of Braque and Cezanne. Yet his writing presents none of the widening of perspectives, dazzling simultaneities, flooding sense of the possibilities of totalized vision, that issue from the same canvasses Hemingway so admired in Paris. Why not? Because this style is used to craft the same vision of manhood and courage and toughness that appears on the Marlboro billboards looming over our freeways, or comes off the pages of *Argosy* magazine. A pathetic misuse: as if the laser had been invented to slice Velveeta cheese.

But when a literary technique that is the analogue of Cezanne's is used to consecrate *macho*, the technique comes to seem *macho* too. And Hemingway will be (and was) praised by Arnold Gingrich, editor of *Esquire* (the Magazine for Men) for seeing reality as Cezanne had seen it. And seeing like Cezanne will come to seem as tough and wonderful and necessary to one's whole selfhood as staying up all night arm-wrestling— like my friend the Southerner, or Hemingway's Old Man.

So Hemingway's style of writing was ruined almost beyond any possibility of cure by his Style of Life; and the style, the writing style, was made safe, stigmatized; and Hemingway was crowned King of Writers by *Esquire* and, later, *Life* magazine.

Good writing has nothing to do with being tough. It does have a great deal to do with seeing. There is no intrinsic reason why Hemingway's famous stripped style cannot be freed of the objects and encrustations that fouled it and killed Hemingway himself. There is no reason why that style cannot show us ourselves. In fact, I know a writer who has made use of something like Hemingway's style in stories that display our desolation, our inability to grasp our experience, the way this culture blocks and spoils our experience in the instant we perceive it. I wrote a review of this man's book, praising it in these terms; but the review hurt his feelings after all, for I had not found his writing tough, not good and true in the Hemingway mold. And he needed to hear that he was tough, for he was and is a frightened man.

Hemingway is the largest figure on the cover of the magazine, and he is in his safari suit as if he were going or had just gone hunting. His lip is curled in a smile or snarl; he is that tough, he is that much a Man, a Man's Man. All these facts have far too much to do with writing in America.

I stood there, watching the friend I have just mentioned reading my review of his new book. He was having some trouble already, though it was only about eight at night. I could see his eyes sliding off the page, tracking back over the same lines.

We were in the apartment of a mutual friend, another writer, who sat off in the kitchen, watching TV and smoothing out his grass-high with his nth cold beer of the day.

In the room between the kitchen and the front room where I stood is hung a black and white advertisement from back in the fifties sometime, carefully framed. About half the ad is taken up by a photograph of Ernest Hemingway in loose summery clothes, leaning back in a chair with a Ballantine ale; the other half of the ad is a letter Hemingway wrote for Ballantine, which tells, more or less, how Ballantine is his kind of ale, i.e., a Man's ale, a good ale and true.

The writer who was reading the review is an alcoholic. The writer who was our host that night is an alcoholic. Both of them drink enough to sink them into incoherence or unconsciousness nearly every day.

On the *Esquire* cover most of the writers have drinks. It is as if they have come together to drink. It is as if *Esquire* likes, perhaps even admires, the writers' drinking. It is as if these people can be identified as writers because they all drink.

Why is alcoholism the occupational disease of American writers?

There is something obsessive and asocial about writing. As I sit here at my desk directing this trek of words across the page, it is impossible for me to avoid feeling that I am at a real remove from the woman walking to her job at Pacific Telephone, the cars sweeping past each other on the street—from action, life. My engagement with the world and other people seems indirect, incomplete, filtered through this premeditated skein of words, a process by which what I do now, writing the words, loses the name of action.

So far, though, writing seems no lonelier or more abstract than, say, computer programming; yet computer programmers, so far as I know, are not known for their attachment to booze. Nor is the writer necessarily any more sensitive to his alienation than the programmer (though the claim is often made, to mystify the mystery away, and make the writer's job seem special—made by writers, of course). The writer is not a special human being; what makes him especially likely to be a drunk?

The programmer is certain of the effect and efficacy of his or her work. The American writer is not—is, in fact, radically uncertain, or despairing, of its effect. And this uncertainty and/or despair exists or is possible at every step of the process by which these words reach your mind, as that process appears to me. For starters, I do not know—I probably never will know—whether you catch my tone, or accept it. I do not know how much you know about Hemingway, whether you recognize Everlast gloves, whether the *macho* mystique of Hemingway is a revelation to you or old hat. I do not know who would be interested in printing this piece, or reading it. Who am I talking to now? Who will listen to me? I am afraid—

A parable drawn from bourgeois life, or a Buñuel movie. I am giving an elaborate dinner party. Everything is ready, the invitations were sent out months ago, the fanciest foods (imagine them yourself) have been bought and lavishly prepared—but the appointed hour arrives and no one comes. And it does not take very long for my initial protective anger to drop away, for me to try to think what can have gone wrong. Is the postal service still working, did my invitations get through? No, maybe everybody's just a little late, they'll come along. . . . Then I start to worry about the menu. Did I overlook some course essential in the formal feed, couple two dishes together in some inexcusably tasteless way—or is the whole meal too rich? Nobody comes. I invite them all for the next night, spend my last cash on a whole different plan—simpler dishes, or spicier, paper hats, favors by each plate. Nobody shows up. I invite them all again, borrow money for a meal that features all my favorite food, to hell with them (maybe they'll spot my sincerity). No one comes. I break down and break out the cooking sherry, rotten stuff, but it does the trick. And maybe just before I pass out my guests will stroll in and sit down, laughing:

"Hey man, listen, they had this incredible three-part series on CBS the last couple nights. All about food, you know? But this stuff you got here, it tastes great, you—look out, man, watch the—"

Too late. I pass out face down in my plate. They eat fast and run off, leaving a lot of expensive food untasted; the news will be on soon, they have to catch it—

My friend's new book has all the best imprimaturs on it. Gordon Lish himself, influential Fiction Editor of *Esquire*, helped place the book with a publisher and wrote a dustflap for it. *The New York Times* and *New York Review of Books* have praised and blessed it movingly, against the choral background of other writers, most more famous than I, all hymning Laudamus Te in various journals. So much the book deserves; it is fine, and my friend spent many years inching his way up the quarterlies, straining to place stories in those magazines that only other writers read, to finally get a book published, to finally get enough clout to get *read*.

But now he is a very severe alcoholic; and anyway, short story collections aren't really expected to sell more than 500 copies, no matter how well they are reviewed. So the cream that never quite rises to the top, because there is no top, is spoiled anyway.

W.H. Auden described American poetry once as "a plane over Wyoming at night." We read these words and smile, thinking of the beauty of the image, the breadth of the land, its mystery and muteness. But see the ignorance too, and lack of connection: the plane's isolation from all that happens beneath it, its suspension in a black void, while the earth and its people lie below asleep, unaware of the distant droning that scarcely rustles their private dreams.

Black writer and Random House editor Toni Morrison predicts that by the end of this century all the major New York houses will be part of larger media conglomerates; that within those houses, only the work of a dozen or so already-established fiction writers will be aggressively promoted as serious literature; and that the rest of what is now called "quality fiction" in the trade will gradually be dropped.

And if the guests have left the dinner party for the nightly news on television, if we do not hear the plane pass overhead because we are sitting up in bed engrossed in *Time*, how can you blame us? You writers who do not want to be praised for anything other than the tough beauty of your art, its thrilling manly linguistic risks—if we cannot be transformed (and do not know art can transform us), we will get informed; if we can't get informed, we'll get sedated. If your art is just stunt-flying in the dark, who needs you? I can see more thrilling daredevils on "Wide World of Sports" and get more truth from Walter Cronkite.

But if the glasses in the writers' hands are badges of their loneliness, isolation, lapsed communication and fear, why is the drinking celebrated on the cover of *Esquire*? How is the drinking made to appear a positive affirmative act?

Consider Hemingway again; look at the glass in his hand; remember the Ballantine advertisement framed on my friend's wall.

Once I was trying to convince this same friend that he was drinking too much, that he should cut down. First he just denied it; I only saw him when he was with other people (by definition), that was the only time he drank. Then his voice grew lower, gruffer; he didn't care that much; the important thing was to be able to say that you'd had a good life when you went, lots of friends, played it hard and fast all the way, written some good stuff. And finally, the capper: he leaned forward on the table across from me, his voice smeared with more than alcohol: Besides, it was the way Hemingway and Scottie—

It is so hard to believe that you are a writer, that you have the right to call yourself one, that you are special in that way. You want to show that your every move is a writer's, that Writer is a special being you just *are*.

Hemingway, F. Scott, whom *Esquire*'s cover also prominently displays, and Faulkner, just above Scottie's face—they are the men we think of when we think of Famous Modern American Writers, and they all drank conspicuously hard. In fact, their drinking is what we commonly remember of all three of them; they rise to mind with glasses in hand. And their drinking was part of what we imagine were their hard-lived, rough-tough lives; they went the whole way, stopped at nothing, burnt themselves up, by God.

So drink, drink hard, court the fires that gut the brain. So then the public that no longer reads can look at the flames shooting against the sky, the newest monument to immolation undertaken out of loneliness and fear and self-doubt, and say, "Look Marge, must be there goes another writer." So then *Esquire* can put you, too, on the cover with a drink, and you'll be recognized. Besides, if hard drinking is (in the absence of women to fuck or wars to fight or frontiers to mow down) the only proof of our Manhood, and Manhood the compensation for our impotence as writers in a society which does not listen and to which we do not speak—then we will drink, hard. It must be great, too, if Papa and Scottie and Faulkner went that way; maybe (who can tell?) it was the flames themselves, shooting up to the sky, that showed them, the cracking up that unloosed—

No. No.

A writer is anyone who writes. A man is anyone with a penis. No one should accept the drinks *Esquire* offers; they are a death, a silencing and admission of failure. Writing must be an act of communication from the whole living self to the world.

Some of the writers shown on the cover, I am sure, are not hard drinkers; certainly we do not know whether they drink hard or not, or whether their manhood is important to them or in doubt. Many of them are clearly concerned with using language as a vehicle as much as an end. Some of them are even interested in showing us our world and transforming our perception of it. And some of them are not primarily known as writers at all, but as journalists (Rovere, Sack), economists (Galbraith), famous Communists (Trotsky).

All of these figures are given power, made to signify, by being dressed in business suits, and pressed into service of the myth of writing/manhood by the drinks painted into their hands.

Writing should demand we see. Seeing should demand we change.

For a second just now I thought with envy of women and black writers, to whom the white male American writing myth need not or cannot apply; they at least have a far greater chance to resist the infection.

Now I think of the oppression of blacks and women in this country. I think of the economic and psychic weapons ranged against them that they may never speak at all, never act. I see the two women on the cover, the two blacks. Out of thirty-nine. *Esquire*—the Magazine for (White) Men.

In the center of the cover, a white man in red serving dress is offering James Baldwin a drink. The gesture must appear even more liberal and emancipated to those who know that the servant is Lee Eisenberg, an Associate Editor of the magazine. *Esquire* does not mind appearing even more liberal to itself than it does to you.

Thank god I am not a black or a woman in this country.

I often wish I were not a white man.

I have perhaps done *Esquire* an injustice. They did not create the conditions that made the act of writing a test of "goodness," the "goodness" a proof of manhood. Nor is their commitment to writing primarily an aesthetic one.

Esquire's editor, Arnold Gingrich, himself number thirty-five on the cover: "Our only touchstone, or divining rod, in assembling the contents of *Esquire* has always been the homely rule of looking for a 'good story, even if it *is* Literature'."[3]

Underneath the pious humility of "homely," behind the coy disclaimer of extra quotes for "'good story ... Literature'," hides a sharp operator who knows his market cold. Who reads *Esquire*? Its core audience is a group of young to middle-aged white men in the upper middle class who are, presumably, more or less satisfied with their sizable lot of the world's goods, and therefore with their perception of the world. Many of them have no doubt been to the best schools, so they know about "Literature." "Literature" is "good" writing, beautiful useless arrangements of language; some may even understand that this same "Literature" occasionally makes so bold as to challenge their perception or their rule. This second kind of "Literature" is of course unacceptable (unless of course we can understand that whatever it says, it is only "Literature"). But the first is acceptable, as long as it's a good story; in fact, a little touch of "style" may make the tale more piquant, give the *Esquire* reader the extra *frisson* of recognizing in himself a tasteful, sensitive soul.

As long as it's a good story; something we men like to read.

Imagine how pleased Gingrich must have been to receive and print "The Snows of Kilimanjaro." You've got this guy, see, a real Hemingway he-man successful writer out hunting with his sexy wife in the wilds of Africa and he gets wounded and gets to think back over all the tough living he did and be a shit to his wife and you're wondering all the time whether he's going to live or not—*and* it's so well-written, it's "Literature" to boot! It is no small thing to find an opportunity when one's professional demands and private interests merge. Look at Gingrich, number thirty-five, the professional litterateur, friend of Scott and Papa. Think how pleased he must have been.

But today, of course, things are better. Today's reader of *Esquire*, the well-to-do young white man is far more hip to "Literature" than his dad, more titillated by it; he has learned to take neat even the wonderful wordplay of Joyce, Beckett, Proust, to roll "Literature" like good whiskey on his palate, savoring perhaps the additional refinement of reflection on how goddamn tough it is to really "be" a writer (he knows about Hemingway, Fitzgerald, Faulkner too).

Which is more thrilling to this reader, the beautiful (though manly) writing or the rough life it takes? It's hard to tell. Here is Gordon Lish,

the present Fiction Editor, introducing an anthology of contemporary
Esquire stories:

> It is my ardent proposition that the writers presented here, in the works of
> fiction shown, have each discovered something not commonly known. I also
> propose that these writers went through some bad times to find out, which
> opinion is the organizing principle of this collection, in case you were
> wondering.[4]

Which opinion is "which opinion"? Hard to tell. Think of what you
know about writing, what Gordon knows, that spectacle: the sweat of all
the rough tough life that must be lived, and then the second sweat of
putting it all down in safe clean words, "Literature"; the existential
anguish and abysses (we're all hip to existentialism now too); the
craziness of hanging out in this crazy USA; the drinking—wow! It
must be so great for Gordon to get a story that makes him think of
all that.

Some of my rough, tough, hard-living alcoholic Writer friends know
Gordon. I asked them what kind of guy he is: "Oh Jesus, hell of a guy,
hell of a guy, right out there on the edge, boy, I'm telling you. . . ." Does
he drink? "Oh, jesus, *drink*? Does he *drink*? I'll tell you, when you're
with that sonuvabitch you really get into it. Why that guy's a total
alcoholic—"

So the circle of the mythology is closed, and ideology talks to itself,
and we are all—writer, editor, *Esquire* reader—greatly entertained by
ourselves.

But Lish deserves his due. He does print stories every so often that are
about "something not commonly known," or not often faced—some
piece which seems to imply that day-to-day life in this country is seriously
disturbed or diminished, and that our common perceptions are perhaps
not quite right, when the "something not commonly known" is not just
something about how pretty language looks when patterned a certain
way.

It is not Lish's fault that such a piece will be nestled in the plush body
of a sleek magazine lined with and financed by advertisements for
expensive liquor and clothes and cars (and women)—all the rewards for
not listening to the piece, reminders that essentially everything is all
right, a stream of voices cooing soothing noises in our ears. It is not
Lish's fault that such a piece will be read by affluent white men, college-
trained in the "art" of reading "Literature," with no regard for its
potential seriousness (for "Literature," we all know, cannot advise or
change anyone, "A poem must not mean / But be"), who will end the

story and walk, refreshed, back into life with at most a bittersweet sense that life in this age is particularly crazy and sad.

I went to a BBC film on the Arts in Cuba. A Cuban novelist was interviewed. The interviewer was concerned about the possibility of censorship in Cuba, where writers are to some extent subsidized by the state. The writer agreed that a writer who wrote books totally hostile to the Revolution might find his work suppressed. But he argued that a writer's freedom in the United States (where he had lived for twelve years) was only the freedom not to be taken seriously. What the American says does not matter to anyone except himself, said the Cuban writer; the artist in the United States is a clown.

Look again at the *Esquire* cover: many of the writers are talking. Who are they talking to? There is no one else in the space they inhabit but them. Yet they are not looking even at each other. Their jaws are flapping, they are laughing at jokes, smiling at, talking with, responding to air, to the empty air.

Look at the *Esquire* cover, at the space that surrounds the figures shown. The flat light grey behind them could be a wall, close by or far off. Or it could be the same empty space spreading out to infinity. So they stand drinking in a closed bare room or in a void.

There is a Buñuel movie in which a dinner party of upper middle class people dressed like these figures finds itself mysteriously trapped in the drawing room after dinner. They are unable to get out for days; some even die. In the meantime, outside, the people of the town are trying to get in; but they too find themselves unable to cross the invisible barrier at the entrance to the house.

So the writer in America. So his audience.

The writer in America is trapped in that room. The writer in America is a clown. The writer in America—especially if he is a white man—blinds himself to his isolation and impotence by dreaming the most tawdry and abusive dreams of power and manhood, by drinking to verify that cheap dream and to numb his sense of solitary worthlessness, by subscribing to the most sterile, impotent aesthetic of what literature should be and do, and the cheapest notions of what it should be about; and by equating that notion and aesthetic with virility. And it is this mythology, this useful and pathetic lie, that *Esquire* of necessity has helped to create and sustain. It is this mythology that *Esquire* presents in visual form on the cover of its fortieth anniversary issue. It is this lie that has become truth.

Esquire is one of perhaps twenty mass-circulation magazines that print "quality" fiction reaching a large audience. The core market for most of these magazines is the upper middle class, more or less satisfied with its sizable share of the world's goods. The work published in these magazines will therefore continue to be necessarily safe, on the whole; or else it will not be listened to, it will be drowned out in the context of the rest of the magazine.

Yet every writer wants to reach an audience. Imagine, then, the evisceration the writer must practice on his or her art; imagine the acceptance of the lie; imagine the absurdity of saying that there is no censorship in the United States.

To write this piece I have abused the privacy and trust of friends I love, of writers whose work I admire. If they forgive me, I hope it will be not merely because they know I am ensnared in the same cheap dreams of writing and have followed the same spiral of self-destruction, but because they know, with me, that we can change. We can write to try to change perception, to transform ourselves and the world, to make it stop making us lie.

Then no one, man or woman, who writes in America, will be shown indexed by number, safely catalogued, painted flat against a flat empty background, drinking, looking at no one, dressed in businessman's clothes, talking in empty space to no one at all.

But then the United States would have to be a very different place.

(1977)

NOTES

1. Raymond Williams, *Culture and Society, 1780–1950* (Harmondsworth: Penguin, 1965) is still probably the best place to begin.

2. John Berger, "Problems of Socialist Art," in Lee Baxandall, ed., *Radical Perspectives in the Arts* (Harmondsworth: Penguin, 1972), p. 126.

3. Arnold Gingrich and L. Rust Hills, eds., *The Armchair Esquire* (New York: Putnam, 1958), p. 18.

4. Gordon Lish, ed., *The Secret Life of Our Times: New Fiction from Esquire* (Garden City NY: Doubleday, 1973), p. xiv.

Writing and Politics:

Eight Notes

INTRODUCTORY NOTE

In the fall of 1983, the new editors of Fiction International *sent an opening statement and set of questions on the relationship of imaginative writing to political commitment to various writers, whose responses were then printed in the Spring 1984 issue of the magazine. The text of their mailing, authored by Harold Jaffe and Larry MacAffery, read as follows:*

> *1984 is upon us. If it is not precisely the realization of Orwell's daemonic vision, it is perilously close to it: history altered and falsified; the ruling class constructing and deconstructing reality through their manipulation of language and dissemination of information. Compounding our chronic oppressions of classism, racism, sexism, poverty in the midst of plenitude, despoliation of the environment—we have nuclear mania, with its increasing prospects of "accident" or apocalypse.*
>
> > *Given such conditions, what is the writer to do? Is the writer obligated to use his/her medium as an instrument of social betterment? Or can the writer still invoke (in Tom McGrath's words) "the privilege of alienation"? What strategies (if any) can best serve both the writer's allegiance to aesthetics and social change? For example, is the post-modern emphasis on formal refinement and self-reference a "luxury" that needs to be modified? Or can these intrinsic strategies also be viewed as in some sense serving committed ends? Finally, have developments in technology significantly diminished fiction and poetry as vehicles for social change?*

The response printed below ignores several of these questions, as the reader will soon see. Instead, it takes up the question of political commitment in writing largely to weight in against the current theory-driven and sociologically ignorant tendency towards elitist avant-gardism evident at that moment (and still) in much self-styled radical cultural production. I wanted to remind those drawn towards such strategies of some of the brute realities any would-be political artist faces today, and of the inevitable gaps and connections between most artistic or literary production and other, more obvious and direct forms of political work. And finally, at the risk of sounding nostalgic or even reactionary in the face of the current critical indifference to fiction and poetry, I felt the need to affirm the distinct and literally ongoing value of words on the printed page.

* * *

For some years now, I've thought of myself as a political artist. At the same time, I've written some criticism and a fair number of reviews dealing with the politics of various kinds of writing and other forms of art; and for the last couple of years, I've co-edited *the minnesota review*, "a journal of committed writing." What comes out of all this, then, in response to your questions is a collection, in no particular order, of truisms I've come to accept; quotations I've agreed and argued with; problems I run up against again and again in my own and others' work; some central hopes and fears—and here and there a few stray things I have learned that might be true.

1. First, last, and always, any art offers its audience certain kinds of pleasure, most *but not all*, of whose elements are historically variable, socially determined, audience-specific, etc. In that sense, all art, including all imaginative writing from *Portrait in a Convex Mirror* to *Princess Daisy*, is political. And yet there are certain patterns, moments, combinations within any piece of imaginative work that aim to please in ways so old and elemental they lie outside the political as well: primary relationships of forms and colors and sounds, the delights of the medium itself; primary designs of expectation, resolution, and surprise; a basic vertigo in the face of any even indirectly representational work that puts us in the presence of a scene or set of objects which is not actually there. Any would-be political artist who forgets, discounts, or refuses these blandishments in the name of politics turns out bad—that is, ineffective—work, if only because nobody else but at most a few hard-core political intellectual types will want to have anything to do with it.

2. Every person who engages in imaginative work is a political artist. But the politics of that work may be more or less apparent, depending on how natural, ahistorical, socially *un*specific its forms and shapes and emphases have come to seem to us. What we mean when we say B. is a political writer is that we *recognize* the political in her work. Today, all Vietnam fiction, all fiction about non-white people's lives, most fiction written by women in which women are the central characters, are recognized as more-or-less political by definition; whereas most fiction dealing with the private lives and personal problems of upper-middle-

class white folks is not. What little fiction one can find dealing with the lives of working-class whites is generally given a place in the DMZ between these two zones. For the most part, though, perhaps because such fiction is so hard to situate, the white working class is left in peace.

3. It is of course possible for a writer to treat an apparently non-political subject—the private lives of the white upper middle class, say—in a way that effectively politicizes it. But it is just as possible, and far more common, for an entire network of publishers, reviewers, critics, and reading audiences to collude in suppressing the political focus of even the most explicitly committed work. My own favorite case in point is *One Hundred Years of Solitude*, a novel whose urgent recuperations and insistences have in this country been quite satisfactorily muffled by the cries of "imaginative triumph" and "great novelistic art." But one could just as well speak of any number of paperback bestsellers that explicitly endorse, batten onto, and extend the newest versions of the Cold War, the glories of counter-revolution, and/or the excitement of the military fix. "In God's name," Agee wrote at the beginning of *Let Us Now Praise Famous Men*, "don't think of it as Art." But if his work had been digestible as the newest "riveting thriller" destined for the airport racks, recognition of its political intents and effects would have been just as safely blocked.

4. Some politically committed writers have chosen more-or-less deliberately to write in popular genres and styles. Marge Piercy's somewhat pulpy novels might be one example of such work; the Wahloos' Swedish police novels of a few years back might be another. Other committed writers, myself included, have chosen to work the "quality-lit" game. Either way has its failures built in, and not merely because the predominant conventions and formulae attendant on each kind of writing have hardly been constructed by writers and audiences bonded together by a progressive political stance. Mass-market fiction, whatever its political explicitness and slant, works a lot like a fast-food milkshake—an industrial product whose primary ingredient is nondigest-ible plastic, produced to be consumed and shat straight out. But Carol Duncan's bleak prognosis of the probable fate of political work within the high-art world can be applied with only minor modifications to political writing within the quality-lit scene as well:

> some artists are very intent on expressing their beliefs, ideas, and experiences
> as human beings beyond the art world. But if they want to say those things *in*
> the high-art world, they must also demonstrate sufficient amounts of "purely
> artistic" intentionality or keep the life experience very personal, "universal,"
> or ambiguous. Or they must build into their work certain strategies: critical
> bypasses around the "non-art" content or clever "aesthetic" resolutions in

which the art part subsumes the rest. ("Who Rules the Art World?," *Socialist Review* 70 [July–August 1983], p. 107)

5. Yet this latter comparison can be pressed too far. The norms of what constitutes good writing on the quality-lit scene will probably never become as purely formalistic as they are for visual art, if only because of language's inherent referentiality, its continuing capacity to tell and to point. Then, too, there is the matter of our love of narrative, of the dips and rises and clinch-points of stories themselves—a love which is shared and played upon, albeit in perverse forms, even by the most dandified postmodern *littérateurs*. At the present moment in this country, what seems to me to be the cultural norm in quality lit which complements formalism itself—which, you might say, helps with its police work—is the artistic and critical validation of an intensely anomic, alienated vision of human life. This vision is centered, of course, on the private individual consciousness—once again, upper-middle-class, college-educated, white, etc. more often than not—whose life is unfulfilling, whose past is a lost blur, whose desires are disconnected and random, whose relationships can't work out. Again and again, in those few major magazines that still print "quality fiction" and in our foremost literary quarterlies, we see this poor subject rendered through a language of scrupulous precision, delicate evasions, a bell-tolling sense of muted, elegiac loss. What is left of the great dialectic of nineteenth-century bourgeois fiction between social determination and the individual self is only these lovingly perplexed murmurs of self-pity, coupled with the refusal to know more, or to believe more can be known. One of the foremost practitioners of such high literary art, a man whose work has been praised from coast to coast, thus solemnly mutters to his interviewer, "What are insights? They don't help any. They just make things harder." It must, I suppose, be the way a lot of upper-middle-class white folks feel—which might be why they choose to read this stuff over again and again; and why a newsletter I recently received advertising a forthcoming all-fiction issue of one of our country's most touted literary mags makes the following appealing claim: "There is a striking unity to this issue, across its variety of authors, styles and subjects, in its basic vision of the anarchy of lives (an anarchy which isn't anyone's fault)." Working as a political artist in a context in which such "apolitical" visions are so hegemonic that they seldom even have to be articulated, one learns to treasure such gems of rare wisdom, to take them to one's galvanized heart with a bitter laugh.

6. For the politically committed writer, mass-market fiction versus the quality fiction scene seems less like a choice than a pincer movement, a squeeze play, a pair of nicely matched claws. But these snapping claws are not just to be found or felt within the field of literary production;

rather, their movements within that field are symptomatic instances of the general interplay of high and mass, modernism and industrialized mindlessness throughout our culture. Even radical politics itself, as a cultural field in this country, is mutilated by an analogously symptomatic gap between a hothouse, hypertheoretical discourse on the one hand and undirected or at best single-issue activism on the other. Think of the relationship between the Polish intellectuals and artists of KOR and the Solidarity movement; or, for that matter, of the progressive Latin American intellectual or artist and his relationship to revolutionary politics there. Then look back at our country, and you'll see what I mean. The politically committed writer in the United States may be able to devise local and temporarily successful expedients (formal devices, new subject matters, even new mechanisms of publication and distribution) to position his or her work outside the constantly encircling, depoliticizing embraces of high and/or mass culture. Yet as matters stand, that success will inevitably turn into failure; at the moment of its success as political art, that work will be either canonized or consumed.

7. It follows that in the long run the chances for a lasting politically progressive art of any kind do not depend on the individual sensibilities of the artists themselves, or even on the political climate within the sets of groups and institutions through which that art is produced, distributed, and received, but on the possibility of constructing a progressively politicized and mobilized American culture across the board. Accordingly, the politically committed writer who argues that his writing *is* his politics makes no sense to me. Nor can I understand where that writer's politics come from, what they matter to him, how he is able to stay in touch with his own commitment if all he does is write—how he preserves himself and his work from either slack acceptance or despair. To sustain themselves such writers, I suppose, must have some other form of collective nurturance and support outside activist politics—but how long, even then, can their commitment survive? And finally, do they really believe that their writing alone can make any short-run difference—in this moment when the short run counts so much? To choose just one example: as I write these words, 100 political assassinations per week are being carried out on civilians by government-assisted death squads in El Salvador—100 a week, every week. Which will do more to stop that in the short run, a fresh short story or some door-to-door leafletting, imploring people to write their Congressfolk and tell them to cut off aid to that nightmare regime, and/or to hit the streets?

8. Yet for all I have said here—for all the bleak probabilities, all the urgent non-aesthetic tasks—writing still counts. Words can go deep; stories can last. Such propositions are frankly theological, matters of faith, and I admit I am as astonished as anyone to find I continue to

believe them. I will even go further and confess my inability to extend such professions of faith to video or film, perhaps because, impressive as works in either medium can be, they do not seem to offer the same possibilities for re-reading and reflection; for absorption to the bone; for a permanence of neither truth nor experience but of the movement of the words themselves, the beautiful sounds of their beating in pursuit of knowledge and life. I write these lines and feel not only distressingly unhip but downright un-American; to profess such a faith in this country, at this moment, seems more ridiculous and humiliating than declaring myself a democratic socialist. Better, then, to turn to the words of another democratic socialist and believer, whose eloquence and foreignness together may render this faith in words and their powers more distinct and credible. What follows is the last paragraph of Czeslaw Milosz's novel, *The Seizure of Power* (1955; reprinted by Farrar, Straus, Giroux in 1982): Gil, a Polish professor discredited by the new Soviet regime, has just completed his translation of Thucydides.

The summer sky was blue, with white clouds, and the darting flight of swallows. In the distance the sound of a brass band mixed with the rattling of streetcars. Gil put the finished pages in order. He straightened them and squared the pile with the palms of his hands. In spite of everything, a man was given a chance to get a little peace. He allotted himself a task and, while performing it, realized that it was meaningless, that it was lost among a mass of human endeavors and strivings. But when a pen hung in air and there was a problem of interpretation or syntax to solve, all those who once, long ago, had applied thought and used language were near us. You touched the delicate tracings warmed by their breath, and communion with them brought peace. Who could be so conceited as to be quite sure that he knew which actions were linked up and complementary; and which would recede into futility and be forgotten, forming no part of the common heritage? But was it not better, instead, to ponder the only important question: how a man could preserve himself from the taint of sadness and indifference.

(1983)

The Aesthetics of Disappointment*

Since the publication in this country of John Berger's prize-winning novel G. in 1972, his reputation here among leftists, and leftist artists especially, has grown steadily—and with good reason. Today, the example of his work over the last twenty-odd years (beginning, significantly enough perhaps, from around the time of his departure from Britain's stifling CP) constitutes, in effect, the first major set of standards for Marxist literary practice, and creative cultural practice in general, in the English-speaking world.

Of this achievement and this set of standards at least two elements seem particularly distinctive, both of which are amply in evidence in the two works under review. First, the example of Berger's openness to a variety of cultural practices, a willingness to open *out* to radical possibility, which manifests itself not only in the range of Berger's work—he has written, to date, four novels, three "photo-texts" or documentary essays (with Jean Mohr), four collections of essays on art, culture, and politics, three film-scripts (with Alain Tanner), and *Pig Earth*, a well-nigh unclassifiable work of fiction, poetry, and commentary—but in his rare commitment to finding moments of such possibility outside those places where they are conventionally expected to be. Thus, in his classic essay, "The Moment of Cubism," he describes that movement not as a slide into modernist, elitist decadence on the part of a few terminally alienated, apolitical painters, but as a literally revolutionary moment in the history of western consciousness whose innovations, thanks to the failure of political revolution in the west and its petrifaction in the east, still await our full understanding and assimilation. Thus, in a character like G.'s Beatrice, the wife of a proto-sadistic military officer in the midst

*A review-essay on John Berger, *About Looking* (New York: Pantheon, 1980) and *Pig Earth* (London: Writers and Readers Cooperative, 1979).

of the Boer War, he is able to find and describe an understanding of herself in relation to imperialism that is enacted wholly privately, even wordlessly.

> She is aware that there is another way of seeing her and all that surrounds her, which can only be defined as the way she can never see. She is being seen in that way now. Her mouth is dry. Her corsets constrain her more tightly. Everything tilts. She sees everything clearly and normally. She can discern no tilt. But she is convinced, she is utterly certain that everything has been tilted. (G. [New York: Viking Press, 1972], pp. 102–3)

Secondly, as this quotation suggests, there is the matter of Berger's rootedness in what can now be called a tradition of overlapping radical and phenomenological concern. It is this concern that makes Berger's art criticism so accessible and vital, combining a dual emphasis on both the artist's and the viewer's perceptions with a sensitivity to the historical fields in which both operate. And it is this attention to the politics within the smallest, most apolitical actions, and the most private perceptions, that may well be Berger's most enduring contribution to the practice of radical literature, as in this excerpt from his essay on the European industrial migrant:

> He looks for the photo among the over-handled papers stuffed in his jacket. He finds it. In handing it over, he imprints his thumb on it, almost deliberately, as a gesture of possession . . .
> The photo defines an absence. Even if it is ten years old, it makes no difference. It holds open, preserves the empty space which the sitter's presence will, hopefully, one day fill again. (A Seventh Man [New York: Viking Press, 1976], p. 16)

Yet readers of this piece so far will probably be aware of something odd in my choice of quotations from books other than those under review. And if they sense a certain reluctance to confront these two new works by Berger—a reluctance, at any rate, to take them up outside the context of his previous work—they are right. For the first thing that must be said of both Pig Earth and About Looking is that both are perplexed and weakened by Berger's current mood of political and cultural despair.

> During the second half of the 20th century the judgment of history has been abandoned by all except the underprivileged and dispossessed. The industrialized, 'developed' world, terrified of the past, blind to the future, lives within an opportunism which has emptied the world of justice of all credibility. (About Looking, p. 54)

Normalization means that between the different political systems, which share the control of almost the entire world, anything can be exchanged under the simple condition that nothing anywhere is radically changed. (*About Looking*, p. 127)

Such apocalyptically bitter statements occur regularly in the essays collected in *About Looking*, serving usually as the contextual setting for Berger's perception of the object that is being looked at. The problem with such observations, however understandable they may be at the present time, is that they are not really observations at all, even invalid ones, but fears; for out of despair nothing but fears issue. And the result of these fears is a slackening in the perceptual focus of Berger's critical attention. One senses too often, reading these essays, that Berger's critical judgments are both too thin and too fast, as when he concludes that *the* theme of the painting of working-class artist Ralph Fasanella is its "protest against . . . impersonal ahistoricity" (p. 102), which latter is, in its turn, said to be *the* primary experience of contemporary urban life in the west; or when he endorses the conventional opinion of the English painter Lowry's secondary importance by stating that "the mainstream of twentieth-century art . . . is concerned in one way or another with interpreting new relationships between man and nature," a view which, if taken up seriously, would allow us to relegate much of the work of Picasso (about whom Berger himself, in *The Success and Failure of Picasso*, has had far more trenchant and liberating things to say), much of Matisse, most of Rauschenberg, Johns, Judy Chicago—indeed, practically all serious contemporary American art—to the dustbin.

The deepest and most disturbing result of Berger's new, fearful pessimism is the same split between phenomenology and radical praxis, history and perception, that came to characterize the later, anti-political work of Merleau-Ponty, a philosopher from whom Berger has obviously learned a good deal. Unlike Merleau-Ponty, Berger by no means has reached the point of condemning radical actions; yet in *About Looking*, he appears to approve most fully of only that contemporary work which, like Lorquet's sculpture, or (in a very different and somewhat less absolute sense) Giacommetti's work, is founded on the ground of "pure," ahistorical being, outside a contemporary cultural dialectic which is written off as collapsed.

It is not surprising, then, to find Berger turning to the margins of our culture in his newest work of fiction, *Pig Earth*, in an attempt to escape the hopelessness he finds here by entering a world still heavy with the density of Being. One cannot deny the urgency and rightness of his claim in the book's "Historical Afterword," that "the remarkable continuity of peasant experience and the peasant view of the world, acquires, as it is threatened with extinction, an unprecedented and unexpected urgency" (p. 212). One cannot disavow both the rich power of these assembled stories and poems of French peasant lives in a town where Berger now lives and works, and the distance of those lives from our own. Yet both the writing itself and our position with regard to it are regularly disturbed and, finally, vitiated by the unresolved difficulties of Berger's own position in the book.

These difficulties are two-fold—or rather, they can be discerned in at least two ways. First, and most immediately, they can be felt in the difficulty of *trusting* these stories and poems, of understanding where they come from and how we are to take them. Near the beginning of *Pig Earth*, Berger tells us, rightly I think, that "as the stories succeed one another ... they ... look more deeply into the subjectivity of the lives they narrate" (p. 13); and it must be added that as Berger continued to write these stories (they are arranged chronologically, in order of composition), he becomes more and more wonderfully adept at the *modus operandi* of peasant and folk narrative, its ability to tell one story within another within another, to move from tale to tale as naturally as breath. Yet it is equally true that at various moments in each story we are brought up against phenomenological "moments" which, as peasant subjectivity, peasant consciousness, simply do not ring true.

> On his way home snow was blowing into Marcel's and Gui-Gui's eyes. He said afterwards that, as he rode in the cart, all explanations escaped him. All he could see was his next action drawing closer and becoming larger. (*Pig Earth*, p. 92)

This is a moment of pure being, all right; but it is all John Berger's, not Marcel's. Such recurring moments, together with the poems that follow each story—poems whose ghostly "natural" voices and imagistic concision remind me more of W.S. Merwin than of any peasant life—put us in an odd quandary. They are marvelous but inauthentic; we want more of them, but somewhere else; for they are unmistakably the products of a highly *self-consciously* phenomenological mind.

It is a mind, moreover, which stands on the verge of abandoning its most complex and open stances of the past. If in *Pig Earth* we yearn for the full allusiveness and flexibility of Berger's richest fictional work, yet recognize its inappropriateness here when it appears, we can also see that he is close to a position in the "Historical Afterword" that is quite literally indefensible, in his implicit endorsement of the peasant's "culture of survival" in which time, lived from season to season and act to act, opens out to justice only in the past. Such a culture may indeed be preferable to the alternative Berger describes, the "culture of progress" which, in opening out continually towards an illusory future, numbs the present and destroys the past. Yet if these really are the only choices for us—and for Berger—liquor is quicker. The culture of survival, however valuable it may be in itself and to us, is hardly a real option; even Berger, finally, cannot fit his sensibility into it.

One wants to argue with John Berger about these choices; surely, radicals will want to say, this is not inevitably, irrevocably the way our historical moment is stacked. Indeed, Berger's own best work, as I have suggested, is an invaluable example of how a unity of consciousness and practice can be forged from the culture of survival (and phenomenology, its intellectual descendant) and the culture of progress (and its offspring, radical action and hope). Yet it would be foolish to blame Berger alone for the flaws and weaknesses of these troubled—and often brilliant— works. One must also blame the paralysis of the western left since 1969, and its crippling effects:

When I look around at my friends—and particularly those who were (or still are) politically conscious—I see how the long-term direction of their lives was altered or deflected at that moment 1969 just as it might have been by a private event: the onset of an illness, an unexpected recovery, a bankruptcy. I imagine that if they looked at me, they would see something similar. (*About Looking*, p. 127)

And we do. Readers unfamiliar with the significance and power of John Berger's work should go first to *G.*, the collection of essays *The Look of Things*, the photo-text *A Seventh Man*, and to any of the Berger–Tanner films. Those readers who take up these two new disturbing, flawed, yet important and beautiful works, *Pig Earth* and *About Looking*, may well find they want something from them that John Berger is unable to supply us with now: a sense of our own political and cultural vitality and possibility. But it is precisely this something which, in 1980, we must rediscover and extend, for Berger's sake and the sake of his work, and for the sake of our lives.

(1980)

Consumer Projections*

At first glance, the three books under review here—a work of cultural criticism, an interview-style biography, and a collection of short fiction—may seem oddly, even randomly grouped; yet in one major respect, their subject matter is the same. Each finds its own possibility in the cultural-political situation Marxists and other leftists are wont to describe as "the society of the spectacle": a society in which images, texts, and signifiers seem to have both conquered and disengaged themselves from any prior material reality or referents to which they once appeared to be subordinately attached. In such a relentlessly textualized social landscape, Marx's poetic description of the enormous energy of capitalism as a dematerializing force takes on a newly extended literalness: now, paradoxically, the sense that "all that is solid melts into air"—or has always already done so—constitutes one of the most basic experiences of our daily lives, a sort of ground bass of the quotidian. The Ewens' book seeks to analyze and historicize this situation, while *Edie* and *Shiloh* re-create and dramatize it as lived out by a hapless member of a particularly kinky branch of the American ruling class on the one hand, a wide collection of rural working-class Kentuckians on the other. Each book thus offers us a more-or-less explicit projection of the textualization and spectacularization of American society, from the origins of these processes in the nineteenth century to their "great leap forward" in the sixties, and on up to the present day.

---

*A review-essay on Stuart and Elizabeth Ewen, *Channels of Desire: Mass Images and the Shaping of American Consciousness* (New York: McGraw-Hill, 1982); Jean Stein and George Plimpton, *Edie: An American Biography* (New York: Knopf, 1982); and Bobbie Ann Mason, *Shiloh and Other Stories* (New York: Harper and Row, 1982).

Unfortunately, though, the book at least some of this review's readers might expect to contain the most adequate and cogent rendition of life in consumer society turns out to be the most flawed and disappointing of the three. Elizabeth and Stuart Ewen have both worked long and well for *Radical America*, arguably the best general access leftist magazine in this country. Stuart Ewen, moreover, is the author of *Captains of Consciousness: Advertising and the Social Roots of Consumer Culture*, a pioneering work of social history on advertising as a more-or-less deliberate political strategy in the first half of the century. Yet the same manipulation thesis which in that earlier work proves irrefutable from the point of view of bourgeois elites and the advertising industry, turns into a serious mystification in a book devoted to the dialectical relationship between the mass image and its American working-class audience. The Ewens' stated project is to chart the history of the subjection of "channels of popular sensibility and desire" to the exploitative "encroachments of a marketable vernacular" (p. 27). Yet the perspective implicit in such a formulation simultaneously scrambles and predetermines its results in advance. The fatal move here is the separation of desire from its object—a move we can no more make in any field of collective psychohistory, leftist or not, than in the analysis of any particular troubled psyche. Only by means of such a move, however, can the Ewens uphold the essential meritoriousness of working-class sensibilities, and thus condemn the absolute perfidy of the image industry; yet the toll exacted by their strained adherence to such a crudely melodramatic scenario is high. On a formal level, it turns their book into a structural shambles: discontinuous, wildly unequal sections and chapters enact an incoherent shuttle between quasi-empiricist study (for example, the history of the department store, or the rise of the fashion industry) on the one hand, and macro-generalization on the other. The Ewens tell us that "a new way of life" for American working-class immigrants "did not arrive merely as a cold economic structure ... its evolution was wrapped in the history of mass imagery and need" (p. 70). But for the most part that "wrapping" is represented to us as an enforced psychic exploitation applied entirely from without. Any sense of the working-class immigrant audience as *co-creator* of mass imagery, as an active if unequal *participant* in the struggle over that imagery's meaning and form is largely absent. Thus, inevitably, on the level of content, *Channels of Desire* carries a consistent undertone of nostalgia for pre-capitalist society close to nature, a "genuine" community bound by kinship; and thus it ends with an explicit assertion of sad bewilderment over where we can go from here. For the Ewens, capitalism has been a virtually unmitigated disaster from first to last, a purely external imposition on the chaste yet supine body of the working class. One can only hope their confessed inability to come up with "coherent alternatives" (p. 282) to its depredations may lead them and the left in general away from such an essentialist/economistic pornodramatic scenario, and towards a more functional political theory and practice for the eighties and beyond.

To turn from the Ewens to *Edie* is, of course, to come to a rather different melodramatic formula, that of the girl who had everything going for her but who lived too hard, too fast, too much and too soon, and so came to an early, unhappy end. The brief life and career of Edie Sedgwick—from "privileged background" to Warhol superstar to burnout and death—thus seems most properly an occasion for a mini-series of lurid articles for the *New York Post* or the *National Enquirer*, not for plush treatment by Knopf. But Jean Stein and George Plimpton (that seasoned expert in the art of making mass culture high) have hit upon a novel way of repackaging this familiar plot and its low-class satisfactions for a "quality" audience. Far from being delivered to us through the shrieking monotone of gutter journalism, Edie's story comes to us through artful snippets of interviews, scattered voices of all the great and not-so-great, the hip and not-so-hip who knew her and/or the other significant players in her life: from Henry Geldzahler to the biker Preacher Ewing, Norman Mailer and Truman Capote to poor zonked-out Billy Name. Edie herself as a presence is sublimated, repressed, redispersed; and a gossip-sheet scandal of rather modest proportions, thanks to modernist technique, has been recuperated as a legitimate, civilized pleasure for those with genuine taste.

Yet *Edie* offers another level of interest as well, beyond its appeal as mass culture/high culture changeling, in the paradigmatic relationship Edie's life enacts between cultural revolution (that is, the newly extended hegemony of the image-world) and psychic revolt. It is indeed this relationship, far more than the famous voices or the gossipy details of Warhol, Dylan, the druggy life of Max's Kansas City and the Factory, that makes *Edie* work dramatically, and justifies at least in part the otherwise wholly absurd and offensive claim that, in the words of interviewee Joel Schumacher, "she was the total essence of the fragment-ation, the explosion, the uncertainty, the madness that we all lived through in the Sixties" (p. 295). Edie's rebellion seems to have been against her father, Francis, a brutal strutting bully haunted by fears and doubts of his own real prowess, with little external authority in any extra-familial social realm. This simultaneously deauthorized yet omnipotent father ultimately helped to provoke the suicides of Edie's older brothers, and eventually her own flight to the counterauthority of an appositely demonic, deauthorized father-lover counterpart: Andy Warhol, who only liked to watch. This flight from a degraded, eroded, abusive oedipality into the center of an overheated image society became a paradigmatic movement in the sixties, standing behind all other white social and cultural movements from Pop Art to feminism; insofar as the deoedipalization process brought on by late capitalism continues apace (we now have such a strutting pseudo-father in the White House) it remains paradigmatic today. In that sense, behind its high culture gloss and beyond its scandal-sheet appeal, *Edie* is a primally ambivalent fairy tale in which the princess can only escape from her father's kingdom because his rule is already decayed—and then only into the purely spectacular world of junk.

Such a fairy tale, despite its obligatory princess, is of course much less characteristic of the American ruling class in general, where the rule of the Father is still relatively intact, than of the lower orders from the middle classes on down, where deoedipalization holds increasing sway. Moreover, in its traditional, conservative concern for resolution and retribution, this tale's apparently predetermined ending and strong closure must be bracketed and left open to doubt. Is the passage from the traditional, oedipalized class patterns of an earlier stage of capitalist development into the bewildering society of the spectacle inevitably to be seen and dramatized as a tragic fall? Bobbie Ann Mason's first collection of fiction, *Shiloh and Other Stories*, suggests that the answer to this question is not necessarily Yes. The immediate surface of Mason's stories will be almost monotonously familiar to readers of Ann Beattie, Ray Carver, and the like: present-tense, short sentences, a *mise-en-scène* stripped down to brief spurts of narration between bouts of extended, oblique yet vernacular dialogue. But where the work of those other, more sleekly despairing authors deals primarily with the greedy angst of one or another order of white-collar professionals, and works through strategies of subtraction—details of scene and situation withheld, connections and recognitions refused—Mason's rural blue and pink-collar characters are skilled *bricoleurs* who work hard at connecting up and thinking through whatever images drift their way or bombard them into their own kind of sense. Leroy, the main character of the title story, is an out-of-work independent trucker whose marriage to Norma Jean, clerk at the local Rexall, is sliding towards the rocks. But even when, on the battle ground of Shiloh, Norma Jean finally tells him she wants out, his realization of how far short his efforts at reconciliation have fallen, including his proposal to buy and assemble a log cabin kit for them, only makes Leroy think harder over what has happened: for he cannot afford to despair.

Leroy knows he is leaving out a lot. He is leaving out the insides of history. History was always just names and dates to him. It occurs to him that building a house out of logs is similarly empty—too simple. And the real inner

workings of a marriage, like most of history, have escaped him. Now he sees
that building a log cabin house is the dumbest idea he could have had. (p. 16)

Leroy's doggedness in the face of what seems certain loss here is not the
badge of an extraordinary valor or stupidity, but the symptom of a kind
of life in which both nostalgia and self-conscious alienation are useless
and hopelessly expensive luxuries. Robert Towers, reviewing *Shiloh* in
The New York Review of Books (December 16, 1982), describes Mason's
stories as enacting a "clash" between "the once meaningful old and the
mindless new"; but these terms, like those implicitly proposed by the
Ewens, are loaded in a class-biased way both Mason's own characters and
the rural working-class men and women I grew up with in northwestern
Pennsylvania would almost certainly reject. The "mindless new" may be
junk, but it is junk that can and must be made to *mean* new things, as
good or better than the old. So Cleo Watkins, in "Old Things," not only
watches the TV but thinks through watching, activating the images with
her thoughts for herself, her recently separated daughter Linda and
Linda's children, and her hope that all will yet be well:

> Cleo ... watches the *10 O'Clock Report*. She tells herself that she has to wait
> up to unlock the doors for Linda. She has put a chain on the door, because
> young people are going wild, breaking in on defenseless older women. Cleo is
> afraid Linda's friend Shirley is a bad influence. Shirley had to get married and
> didn't finish school. Now she is divorced. She even let her husband have her
> kids, while she went gallivanting around. Cleo cannot imagine a mother
> giving her kids away. Shirley's husband moved to Alabama with the kids, and
> Shirley sees them only occasionally. On TV, Johnny Carson keeps breaking
> into the funny dance he does when a joke flops. Cleo usually gets a kick out
> of that, but it doesn't seem funny this time, with him repeating it so much.
> Johnny has been divorced twice, but now he is happily married. He is the
> stay-at-home type, she has read. (pp. 80–1)

Shiloh is not a perfect collection. A few of its sixteen stories read as
weak or strained versions of her strongest work; and her endings tend to
clutch all stray details together into an implausibly epiphanic totality. But
at its best—in "Shiloh" and "Old Things," "The Ocean," "A New Wave
Format," and "Detroit Skyline, 1949"—Mason's fiction portrays a truth
about life in the image society of late capitalism which neither glossy *Edie*
nor the addled *Channels of Desire* seems able to admit or suggest. At the
elite level of image production and distribution, it is certainly quite
deliberately exploitative; at the level of consumption it is often a
bewildering, dazzling mystification at best. But for many working people
the same images and free-floating signifiers that fill white-collar Marxists
and intellectuals with despair constitute a new language and set of

options for thinking and action—a new kind of freedom, in effect. Until we learn to understand this positive, even utopian component of the society of the spectacle as thoroughly as its much more frequently analyzed negativity, we cannot know how to move politically from here.

(1983)

Fiction after History*

I chose to consider these two apparently quite incongruous recent novels because, for a variety of reasons, I hoped to like them: Garrett's novel of late Elizabethan England, since like many other writers who earn their living in and around the faintly sleazy yet by now quite complex and well-established institutions of "Creative Writing" in the United States—the writers' workshops, degree programs, writers' conferences, little magazines, grant agencies, etc.—I have met and liked George Garrett, an eminently sunny, decent man who has rattled around the scene for years; Cantor's fictional life of Che, because of my own engagement in writing politically committed fiction, and my delight that Knopf, for whatever reasons, had chosen to publish and push even one example of such work.

Unfortunately, this hope was unfulfilled; in my capacity as the relaxed and (I hope) receptive reader in the armchair, I found both novels basically unsatisfying "reads." But their troubles, their lacunae and contradictions are not just a function of bad intentions or simple mistakenness. In some small and not so small ways, their failings are symptoms of a larger crisis of mimetic narrative and representation within what we recognize, under a variety of names and labels, as a new moment in capitalist culture: consumer society or the society of the spectacle; late or multinational capitalism; or, more commonly and apolitically, the perceptual universe we now almost casually designate as the *postmodern*. That crisis of narrative is the more obvious in these two texts as they offer themselves specifically as *historical* novels. For whatever else the historical novel may have been or yet become, it surely

---

*A review-essay on Jay Cantor, *The Death of Che Guevara* (New York: Knopf, 1983), and George Garrett, *The Succession* (Garden City NY: Doubleday, 1983).

represents the mimetic-realistic impulse of fiction in its most ambitious and complex form, insofar as it offers (or purports to offer) us no less than the inner experiential feel of times, spaces, and perceptual modes far different, decisively Other, from our own; and in so doing, to represent if only penumbrally the experience of History itself. In a prefatory note to *The Succession*, moreover, Garrett provides us with a classical description of how this triumphant imaginative act of historical recuperation is traditionally supposed to take place:

> what happened ... was that in trying to contemplate two splendid characters [Queen Elizabeth and King James], I was forced to summon up many others to help me, ghosts from that time, some of them "real" (Sir Robert Cecil, Sir Robert Carey, the Earl of Essex) and some of them "imaginary"—a messenger, a priest, a player, some Scots reivers, etc. And very soon it was clear that if they were to bear witness, they must be allowed to tell their own tales also. They jostled each other for places in the story. And so, finally, here they are in a story which has changed its shape and form many times before it settled into this one, a story which surely took its own sweet time to become a book. (pp. vii–viii)

This is not the place to mount an exhaustive analysis of the entire nest of paradigmatic assumptions nestled in such a statement; let us merely note promises. One does one's research and then, in the midst of one's patient, will-less, transparently receptive meditations on a central character or characters, other presences quite naturally appear and press character or characters, other presences quite naturally appear and press forward, insisting on their "places" and thereby themselves *producing* the novel, presumably just as their analogous "real-life" counterparts produced their own historical Real. The aesthetic ideology here invoked is, of course, that curious late Romantic mixture of self-exaltation and abnegation enshrined in Keats's letters as "negative capability". The larger historiographic paradigm which that ideology projects and through which it achieves legitimacy is that equally blithe, equally nineteenth-century vision of historical production most succinctly and famously formulated in Engels's 1890 letter to Joseph Bloc:

> History proceeds in such a way that the final result always arises from conflicts between many individual wills, and every one of them is in turn made into what it is by a host of particular conditions of life. Thus there are innumerable intersecting forces, an infinite series of parallelograms of forces, which give rise to one resultant—the historical event. This may in its turn again be regarded as the product of a power which operates as a whole *unconsciously* and without volition.[1]

As History, then, so historical fiction—with the anonymous, automatic
Dialectic replaced by the equally omnipotent and involuntary Imagination as ghost in the works. We may leave aside the question of whether
such a model of History and/or historical fiction was ever the truth in
either case (though surely, insofar as these models are distilled conceptual expressions of the experience of space and time in classical bourgeois
society, they cannot be merely dismissed as "mystification" or "false
consciousness"). What is most striking and significant for our purposes
about Garrett's invocations of such notions here, at the beginning of a
novel on which he has labored for twelve years, is how extraordinarily
misleading they are—as misleading as the chorus of nearly unqualified
praise which has greeted his book, describing it as "a world in itself," "the
only contemporary novel I know that takes me into the lives of those
survivors in the stone-cold corridors of power," and (of course) a novel
which "succeeds admirably" in demonstrating (once again) "how close
we are in our humanity, our virtues and vices, to those personages great
and small who have been for centuries in their graves."[2]

In the face of so many mystificatory plaudits and misdescriptions—the
product, one must suppose, of a still-hegemonic literary-humanistic
ideology on a blind rampage of praise—I can only throw up my hands
and appeal to the willing reader to take a look at what is actually on the
page. It is true that historical events enable *The Succession*—the riven
factionalisms and power plays of the last thirty-five or so years of
Elizabeth's reign, culminating in the difficult, delicate uncertainties of
the Succession itself. It is also true that the novel's sixteen separate
dechronologized sections, ranging from eight to nearly one hundred
pages apiece, are nominally organized around a multitude of presiding
consciousnesses or narrative perspectives, from lowly actor (and double
agent) to persecuted Catholic priest, from Scots reivers sitting around a
fire on a wet night in the borderlands telling stories to pass the time, to
King James himself, fretting and chafing in the wings. And yet the novel,
with occasional and quite brief exceptions, remains stalwartly detached
from any truly interiorized, individuated evocation of character, and for
the most part avoids any direct scenic rendition of dramatic events. The
adventures of the Priest come to us through the letters and documents
found on his person when captured; the Queen's Secretary peruses and
meditates on the correspondence which has passed between Elizabeth
and James; even the novel's most vividly realized character, Essex, and
his doomed rebellion, the most dramatic and compelling action in the
book, come to us obliquely, through a set of astonishingly novelistic
notes taken by the Player in his capacity as double agent, confiscated and
perused by yet a third agent of another group of nobles (and perhaps
James himself) eager to cover their tracks.

Finally, though, what most effectively subverts any sense of classically totalizable dramatic action in *The Succession* is the uniform performance of Garrett's style itself, which effectively transforms every "referent" it touches, whether meditation, document, or dramatic action itself, into yet another delicate figuration in a uniformly two-dimensional tapestry or set of tableaux. It is not just that all voices sound alike, that every utterance and scrap of writing is as fulsomely turned out and richly worded as every other; the problem is the extent to which each situation and every character is merely a subordinated pretext for the release of yet more of the same gorgeous decorative prose. Nowhere is this more clear than in those five sections of the novel devoted to the passage on horseback of a secret messenger from Edinburgh to London, to inform his master, the Queen's Secretary Cecil the elder, of James's birth; with each successive section, the point and urgency of the journey itself, as well as the individual character of the Messenger, are more and more attenuated, smothered by the ravening exigencies of Garrett's prose:

> If only he still had his little Scots mare and time to spend. Then he would linger long enough to relieve some Yorkshiremen of their prosperity. But he must be gone. First through sandy country to the village of Bawtry. A poor place with a few shabby half-timbered houses set close to a little pond. Lying low and swampy next to River Idle. Then farewell to Yorkshire and welcome to Nottingham. Road running through flat red-clay fields. To Scrooby (a mere hamlet only) with its large moated manor house for the Archbishop of York. (p. 267)

Admittedly, such a passage represents *The Succession* at its antiquarian-guidebook worst. But in its verbless, heavily-cadenced flow and faintly formal echoes of Elizabethan diction it does legitimately suggest something of the degree to which the novel's dramatic and historical referents are enveloped and overcome by the sheer static blanketing weight of a style which is itself, one comes to realize, the novel's main attraction, a kind of sumptuous, exhaustively researched, culinary pastiche.

At this point, with our arrival at the concept of pastiche, we find ourselves looking out from Garrett's novel to find it and ourselves once again on the terrain of the postmodern as a perceptual mode, within whose solipsistic and spectacularized boundaries "we seem condemned to seek the historical past through our own pop images and stereotypes about that past, which remain forever out of reach."[3] And it is to Jay Cantor's credit that in *The Death of Che Guevara* he seems, unlike Garrett, doggedly, even painfully conscious of the terrible baffled mess of commodified language and pop imagery, the cul-de-sacs of postmodern pastiche and modernist self-reflexivity, plus the sheer cultural and historical distance which lies between his authorship and its object, the real historical Che Guevara, revolutionary martyr-emblem to the world. The process of recovering/recuperating an aesthetically whole and politically useful representation of Che necessarily entails for Cantor not the discovery of some magical empathetic end-run around these barriers but an engagement with them, a dialectical passage into and through these networks, image clusters, aesthetic and political positions—not in the illusory hope of discovering the "real" Che somehow on the other side of them, but in the hope of reproducing a vertiginous, inherently unstable "dialectical image," as Benjamin would have it, out of such scandalously heterogeneous, incompatible materials.

Yet for all its self-consciousness and fine serious intention, *The Death of Che Guevara* seems to me a large failure—one which seems, moreover, to founder in ways which bear some symptomatic relation to the problems of Garrett's far less self-conscious and more retrograde work. In a novel which purports to present us with a veritable babble of different speakers, writers, and points of view, there is once again the omnipresence of a leveling, homogenizing voice. For starters, such a voice, whose characterization I will hold off for a moment, is perhaps minimally justifiable throughout most of the book's first half, which consists of a long, scattered, self-reflexive set of autobiographical writings presumably set down by Che while separated from Fidel at the Isle of Pines—a fragmentary criticism/self-criticism, in effect, written while in soft detention, accompanied by his guard, friend, and fellow guerrilla Walter, a.k.a. Ponco. In the book's second half, presumably a collage-narrative of Che's final doomed adventure in Bolivia composed by Ponco out of the journals of Che and their fellow guerrillas, now all fallen, plus additional dramatic/narrational/confessional/meditative material supplied by himself, the nearly uniform persistence of the same voice running through each writing or utterance effectively destroys any illusionistic sense of differentiated character, multiperspectivity, and even finally any sense of dramatic authenticity itself.

Yet the reader will have no doubt noticed that my complaint here seems at least in part an apparently contradictory one: was it not for his very eschewal of any intention to capture the "real" Che that I was praising Cantor a moment ago? Just so; yet despite this eschewal, it is not I but Cantor himself who refuses finally to make a clean break with the whole problematic of representational authenticity and characterological attribution in his novel. Here again, given limitations of space and time, I must limit myself to only one instance of the unsatisfying effect of this particular contradiction in intention, by referring more specifically back to the problem of Ponco's purported "authorship" of the novel's second half. A justification for and defense of this authorship is laboriously planted throughout the text: we are carefully informed, again and again in the first half of the book, what a voracious literary reader Ponco has become now that (thanks to the Revolution) he can read; we are carefully informed how and when it is that each separate journal comes into his keeping when its author dies. Ponco is even shown to exhibit his own self-doubts over his authorship, his own immersion in a properly Bloomean "anxiety of influence," both resisting and merging with, memorializing and excoriating the beloved, despised political-spiritual-linguistic Father Che by whom he was loved and betrayed. Yet the more Cantor explains, covers up, and rationalizes, the more flagrantly the result appears as a paradigmatically modernist collage of unattributable utterances, a montage of filmscript, playlet, quotation, meditations, poetry and dramatic scene cut and pasted together by an unseen and anonymous author who, in this case unlike Joyce, refuses to acknowledge his own modernist stance "behind or beyond or above his handiwork, invisible, refined out of existence,"[4] up until the novel's brilliantly deconstructive close. Then such acknowledgement comes very late indeed, when we have for hundreds of pages been effectively asked to play a quite different game, believing Che and Ponco's fellow guerrillas to be the separate subauthors of their own subtexts despite the recurrence of identical phrases ("walnut-sized bumps" as a description of insect bites inflicted; the sound of Che's asthmatic breathing seemingly by one and all compared to the clanking of a machine) and the even more outrageous eruption of literary quotations (in the case I am thinking of, from Charles Olson's *Call Me Ishmael*) in the middle of journal entries and dramatic scenes. The recurrence of such scandalous verbal automata, when combined with Cantor's equally strong up-until-the-last-instance insistence on characterological distinction and attribution, ask of us a kind of reading which is, I think, literally impossible. We are, to invoke Barthes' useful distinction, to read *The Death of Che Guevara* at one and the same time as internally coherent, self-enclosed "work" and as heterogenously produced, fissured "text," even though— for now at least—such ways of reading are antithetically opposed: you truly can't have the book both ways.

Aside from this relatively complex aesthetic-literary dilemma, moreover, there is the problem of that single, undifferentiated voice as well, to which we may now return for a closer look. What is the nature of this voice which runs through virtually every character, scene, and type of utterance? What effects and representations does it enable or foreclose? Of what "idiolects" is it composed? Here are two brief quotations, taken quite randomly from widely separate places in the novel. The presumptive author of the first is Che himself, working on his criticism/self-criticism, remembering the sight of Indian peasants in Bolivia about to

be sprayed by the government with DDT; the second passage is
presumably part of a journal authored by Coco, one of Che's band in
Bolivia fourteen years later.

> I tried to fix the old man's gaze as he went by me. But he walked past as if I
> weren't there; or he weren't. Anyway, someone had died. The mestizo put
> the hose down the boy's back; waited for eyes to close; sprayed his neck and
> hair; world without end. No one asked for an explanation. Someone pushed
> your child's head underwater; someone doused you with this evil-smelling
> acid. The event required of you as much or little faith as baptism; and it was
> plainly, just as inevitable. (p. 144)

> 8/14/67: The time in the jungle was hard for me—for all of us. The
> chloroquine Mora gave me helped, but the jungle still made my tissues so
> watery that I could hardly stand. And the heat turned the watery flesh to
> steam; my face melted away; now I'm so thin that I look as dour and lean as
> Inti. The Revolution has made us into brothers! (p. 473)

What makes these utterances indistinguishable is not merely the strong
similarities of their syntax and grammar—the accumulating clauses
stapled into series with semicolons, the emphatically straightforward
rhythm and regular order of the words—but the same identical movement within each short passage from an accretive description which
builds up the image to a requisite pitch of vividness, to a sudden and, as
it were, "on the spot" allegorical exegesis of the image's meaning, an act
of instant reading which in effect "spends" the vividness and drama just
accreted in a single profligate rush of local significance.

In Cantor's other published work, a thin book of meditative essays on
literature and politics entitled *The Space Between*,[5] the same circuit is
travelled again and again; only there the object so read is of course the
literary quotation itself, a bit of shimmer in which to find one's own
reflection and pass on. There, too, the immediate derivation of this
seemingly compulsive stylistic habit is more unmistakably clear, especially
if one notes the glowing preface to the work by Stanley Cavell, Harvard's
foremost contemporary philosopher-aesthete, along with Cantor's
equally warm thanks to his former mentor in his own acknowledgements.
For Cavell's own work—and, one might add, the entire present
aesthetic-intellectual climate of Harvard itself—is characterized by
precisely such instant and untotalizable allegorical clevernesses, such
quick, smart readings and spend-thrift analyses.

Yet to name Cantor's idiolect so narrowly as a product merely of the
hothouse climate of the brahmin herd in Harvard Yard would be to miss
its wider significance as the symptom of a more general cultural crisis or
impasse. For what is this compulsion to scan, interpret, and pass on from

one vivid sign to the next but a rarefied intellectual form of that far more basic quotidian reading we must do every day in a culture which subjects us to a steady stream of unassimilable information and "hot" imagery, the instant and instantly analyzed newsbreak, the instant replay and quick-stat of the sports event, the flash of the billboard and electric-prod jolt of the thirty-second commercial on TV? Such a habit of mind and stylistic signature in Cantor's work may thus be taken as an instance of a far more widespread defensive reaction against the incessant assaults of consumer society, against the psychic bombardment of the spectacular in nearly every aspect of our present cultural life. Yet when reproduced as literary style, the cost exacted by such bombardments and by our very defenses against them becomes all too clear; in Cantor's novel they destroy the possibility of any sustained build in dramatic tension or development, any sense of character or story line, and finally any sense of coherent literary or historical intelligibility at all.

It is in this bleak sense that the two novels under review here most resemble one another, despite all their marked differences in style, subject matter, and stated or implicit intention: in their failures to find or fall back on any narrative form or figure for historical emplotment, development, or action; in their substitution of other pleasures—rich phatic pastiche or local shock-readings—for any new or old narrative totalizations which could connect the individual, existential experience with the larger and more abstract structural determinations of Historical time. We may read in these novels and ourselves the presence of a constricting historical limit here at the center of the late capitalist empire and dream machine which we shall have much work to do to overcome—not merely so that some new and as yet unimaginable historical novel might be written, but so that History itself (once again? for the first time?) might be *made*.[6]

(1984)

NOTES

1. As quoted in Lewis S. Feuer, ed., *Marx and Engels: Basic Writings on Politics and Philosophy* (New York: Doubleday, 1959), p. 399.

2. The first two of these quotes are from O.B. Hardison and Mary Lee Settle, respectively, and may be found on the back of *The Succession*'s dustjacket; the third is from Walter Sullivan's review of the novel in *The Sewanee Review* 92, 2 (Spring 1984), p. xxii.

3. Fredric Jameson, "Postmodernism and Consumer Society," in *The Anti-Aesthetic* (Kennikat WA: Bay Press, 1983), p. 118.

4. *A Portrait of the Artist as a Young Man* (New York: Modern Library, 1928), p. 252.

5. (Baltimore: Johns Hopkins University Press, 1981.)

6. For further consideration of the relationship between postmodernism and the

contemporary American novel, see Fredric Jameson's review article on De Lillo and
Yurick in the Spring 1984 issue of *the minnesota review* NS 22, pp. 116–22; and Ray
Mazurek's "Ideology and Form in the Postmodernist Historical Novel," in *the minnesota
review* NS 25 (Fall 1985), pp. 69–84.

Popular Expressions*

A few years ago, at a group show in SoHo co-sponsored by *The Village Voice* on visions of 1984, I stood staring at a photograph of skulls assembled into perfect tetrahedrons, perhaps twenty-five skulls wide at the base of each side. The shot was one of three or four depicting the results of the Khmer Rouge's zeal for purification through extermination, and, like the rest, was accompanied by explanatory notes. Alongside me, a sparkling young couple stood gazing at the same photograph. The young man wore an elegantly antiquated suitcoat from the 1940s and a thin leather tie; his companion looked much more conventional, in a beige wool sweater and crisp burgundy jeans. We stared in silence for a while; then a flash of wit lit up the man's face. He leaned over to the woman and murmured his clever one-word metaphor: "Grapefruit." She smiled and chuckled; they turned their smiles toward one another and moved on.

Now, one can draw from such an anecdote any number of lessons about yuppies, SoHo galleries and the New York art scene; or, if your taste runs to high theory, the episode might make a neat parable of the divorce of sign from referent in the landscape of late capitalism. But I would rather use my story here as grounds for two other observations. The first is that cultural transmission and reception are always site-specific; no cultural document comes with its political meaning neatly wrapped inside its content or form. The second point, which extends from and complicates the first, has to do with the distance—historically created, to be sure, but no less real for that—which separates politics from art in our lives. What is "Grapefruit," after all, except a playfully expert affirmation of the pleasures of composition, texture and sensuous

*A review-essay on Guy Brett, *Through Our Own Eyes: Popular Art and Modern History* (Philadelphia PA: New Society Publishers, 1986), and Douglas Khan and Diane Neumaier, *Cultures in Contention* (Seattle WA: The Real Comet Press, 1985).

form over the quickly exhausted surface meaning of this particular photographic text? Or, to reverse the question, how can we, why *should* we, take a photograph of Cambodian skulls as art?

Such issues kept coming up as I read these two books on radical art. Guy Brett's *Through Our Own Eyes* offers us five examples of what he calls "vernacular art": the *arpillera* patchworks of Chilean women, recording their suffering, faith and struggle through the dark days and nights of Gen. Augusto Pinochet; the paintings of commune life created by the members of the Huxian commune in the People's Republic of China; the historical-mythological paintings produced by the people of Shaba Province in neocolonial Zaire; the drawings and paintings made as testimony and warning by the survivors of Hiroshima; and the perform-ance pieces, collages, drawings and happenings produced by the women's antinuclear settlement at Greenham Common in Britain. Kahn and Neumaier's *Cultures in Contention* is an even more mixed bag, an anthology of twenty-four articles by radical artists and cultural workers of many different stripes. There are pieces on Sistren, a Jamaican women's theater, and on Buga Up, an Australian group of "billboard activists"; there are articles on gallery works in downtown Manhattan, lesbian art in Los Angeles and poetry workshops in Nicaragua; contributions by Sweet Honey in the Rock's Bernice Reagon, high-art nose thumber Hans Haacke and jazz musician Archie Shepp.

Both books are generously larded with illustrations of the works and activities discussed; and at best the discussions exhibit a blend of commitment and sophistication which is beyond reproach. Take, for example, Brett's discussion of the "Mamba Muntu" genre of Shaba paintings, which depict a large light-skinned mermaid looking straight out at the spectator as her arms enfold a small, dark-skinned man. These are the most popular Shaba paintings among their Zairean working-class audience; they may also be found in western shows of contemporary African art, though usually with no accompanying explanation to obstruct our aestheticizing glance. Yet as Brett makes clear, the meaning of such images within their own culture is as complex and ambiguous as any formalist reading could make them. Mamba Muntu is, it turns out, a "generic being which is said to live in many lakes and rivers of the country. The one who is lucky enough to obtain a lock of her hair, or any object associated with her, and promises absolute fidelity to her, may expect to suddenly become very rich." In the context of the shattering urbanization visited on the Shaba peoples, in which a few may become dazzlingly rich while the rest are exploited, this icon has a special significance: it looks back toward traditions in the process of being effaced, and forward to the embrace of an alien, exciting but potentially lethal, white-dominated world.

Of course, there is more to say about such imagery—among other things, about the way in which the fear and allure of the new world is projected onto a male fear of and desire for the giant mother/lover. Still, Brett is at his best when reconstructing historically specific contexts and connecting them to other aspects of community life—as when, in this same essay, he goes on to link the Shaba paintings with other practices, from barbershop sign-painting to children's play. Similarly, the most valuable pieces in *Cultures in Contention* are those that define their subjects most concretely in terms of situation, audience and intent. Honor Ford-Smith of Sistren defines the group as "a collective/cooperative structure within which its members educate themselves through drama, and later, through drama and theater, share their experiences with others," and describes how the group moves between consciousness-raising workshops in "Drama for Problem Solving" and major commercial productions. Peter Dunn and Lorraine Leeson, two British graphic artists, have put their talents at the service of various progressive causes in East London, producing, among other works, an extraordinary billboard series depicting what developers plan to do to the Docklands area and showing how the neighborhood can unite to push them back. And there are several other essays—those by Fred Lonidier, Hans Haacke, Suzanne Lacy and Leslie Labowitz come to mind—in which one can find equally clear examples of political commitment, strategic intelligence and artistic creativity at work.

Yet, for all their virtues, these books also reveal much that is threadbare or just plain wrong in traditional left notions of progressive culture and radical art. One of the oldest and least satisfactory habits is that of designating as "people's art" any number of quite distinct cultural practices in which oppressed people are engaged, and proclaiming them equally good, wise and politically correct. Despite all that is best and most specific in his individual readings, Brett's *Through Our Own Eyes* is often guilty of this sort of mumbo jumbo. Perhaps because the complex relationship of these works to their political and cultural situations seems insufficiently inspiring to him, he must instead convert them into parts of an international upsurge of "vernacular art" that is not only unified, but uniformly progressive. So the Shaba paintings are fused with Chilean *arpilleras*, Chinese commune paintings, art by Hiroshima survivors and the activities at Greenham Common—even though, in the process, each loses the specific coloration that Brett had just restored to it. "The popular expressions in this book," he writes, "are the embryonic images of *a movement* by groups of people all over the world to make themselves visible *in their own terms*, to represent themselves." (my emphasis.)

It is not hard to hear in such formulations the echo of old assumptions about the innate wisdom of the people which will shine forth once the bourgeois mystifications that have obscured it are peeled away. "The people" here may be redefined as you like or need—as workers, women, blacks, etc.—in which case the authors of the mystification are redefined accordingly. But what happens if we substitute for this Manichaean theology, the more complex concept of cultural struggle put forth by British Marxist Stuart Hall, in his contribution to *People's History and Socialist Theory*?

> Cultural domination has real effects—even if these are neither all-powerful nor all-inclusive. If we were to argue that these imposed forms have no influence, it would be tantamount to arguing that the culture of the people can exist as a separate enclave, outside the distribution of cultural power and relations of cultural force. I do not believe that. Rather, I think there is a continuous and necessarily uneven and unequal struggle, by the dominant culture, constantly to disorganise and reorganise popular culture.... There are points of resistance; there are also moments of supersession. This is the dialectic of cultural struggle. In our times, it goes on continuously, in the complex lines of resistance and acceptance, refusal and capitulation, which make the field of culture a sort of constant battlefield.

This expanded view of cultural politics not only sharpens and enriches our judgments of what Brett calls "popular expressions"; it also opens up more sides of the street for radical artists to work. Under the old definition of progressive culture the people were always wise by definition, so the artist's only job was to serve as a conduit for their inherently correct sensibilities, while staying clear of bourgeois institutions like galleries and museums at all costs. But in "Working with Unions," Fred Lonidier's contribution to *Cultures in Contention*, the author argues for the importance of adding his own analyses and historical accounts to his photos of and quotations from union workers, in terms that support Hall's view of what cultural struggle is about. "To represent things as they are," he writes, "without indicating *why* they are this way—that is, how they came about—is to reify causation and reinforce the contention that the status quo is immutable. My own contribution[s] to the pieces ... are efforts to intervene in the discourse of the trade unions (and art world) and insert that which is needed but absent." Note the inclusion, albeit in parentheses, of "art world." For artists like Lonidier and Hans Haacke, the ordinary norms and practices of the high-art scene need to be contested within as well as outside that world. As Haacke puts it in his interview with Catherine Lord in this same volume, "I am a bit afraid of what is purported to be an irreconcilable opposition between working inside or outside the institutions of art. In both areas, consciousness is being shaped, and it is useful to participate in this process wherever one sees a promising opportunity. The rest is sectarian bickering."

There are, of course, real dangers in working exclusively within a high-art context, just as there are risks in working exclusively within the Democratic Party. In each case, without a larger political community and context, the drift toward some sort of reformist co-optation is, I think, nearly inescapable. Several of the contributors to *Cultures in Contention* speak of the ways in which their work helps to construct, educate and encourage the political community in which it is situated. My problem with the collection as a whole, however, is the opposite of my problem with Brett's book: *Cultures in Contention* suffers from its lack of focus. Some of its offerings are no more than brief introductions to various practices and groups (such as Buga Up, Paper Tiger TV, Free Radio in Japan); others are slender evocations (Holly Near on Uruguayan women's song) or puff pieces (García Márquez on *Alsino and the Condor*, Abbie Hoffman on himself). One, by Günter Wallraff, is a straight-forward piece of investigative journalism; another, by Richie Perez on the Committee Against *Fort Apache*, is a report on the successful boycott of a racist film by a group of activists in the South Bronx. Confronted with such diverse materials, even the most simpatico reader eventually tunes out.

At the beginning of his contribution to this book, Fred Lonidier says, "What we need more and more, as oppositional work achieves wider dissemination, is writing which itself compares and contrasts and interrogates our works. When we are invited to group shows and anthologies, the host must see to it that the political and formal issues are laid out in some way; otherwise we have lettuce and tomatoes but no salad." It's too bad that the editors didn't heed his advice. This collection is an uneven and at times contradictory mix, but I don't think the fault lies with the editors and contributors alone. When it comes to radical art, the left has a way of celebrating as "rich diversity" what is actually a jumble at best; either that, or select bits of that jumble are stuffed into the bottomless hole of "people's culture," in the manner of Brett. Both approaches are fundamentally dismissive; what they really tell us about is the scant attention paid by the rest of the left to radical artists and to the construction of an alternative culture. If silence and/or patronizing acceptance are all the left can offer to counter my SoHo yuppies' wit, it is no wonder that the voices in this collection are in such disarray; and no wonder even the strongest of them sounds a little isolated, a little desperate. *Cultures in Contention* cries out for a conversation within the left, between artists, activists and intellectuals, a conversation that has scarcely begun.

(1987)

Policiers Noirs*

In the summer of 1948, Chester Himes delivered an address titled "The Dilemma of the Negro Novelist in the United States" to a mainly white audience at the University of Chicago. Himes was thirty-nine: he had worked as a bellhop, day laborer, small-time hustler, gambler and crook; served more than seven years of a twenty-to-twenty-five-year sentence for armed robbery; and published numerous short stories and two novels, *If He Hollers Let Him Go* in 1945, and *Lonely Crusade* in 1947. The first novel was acclaimed as an honest and effective work of "social protest," still a reviewer's category in 1945. The second, despite its implausibly affirmative ending, contained within its sprawling canvas enough portraits of racist and/or fascist whites, psychopathic and/or Tomish blacks and unscrupulous and/or double agent Communists to offend everyone—black and Communist reviewers as well as white establishment ones. In 1948, Himes's wounds from the flaying *Lonely Crusade* had received were still fresh; even so, on that summer afternoon in Chicago he hoped his words might yet be taken seriously in his native land.

Himes had three main points to make that afternoon. Any one or perhaps even two of them might have secured his reputation within either the black community or the white establishment. The three of them together, however, made a message which still sends most people, white and black, scampering for the exits. To begin with, Himes proclaimed that his "negro novelist" and indeed all American blacks were *Americans*: "the face may be the face of Africa, but the heart has the beat of Wall Street," He next insisted that, given white racism, all

---

*A review-essay on Chester Himes, *If He Hollers Let Him Go*, and *Lonely Crusade* (New York: Thunder's Mouth Press, both 1986), and *Cotton Comes to Harlem, The Crazy Kill, The Heat's On, A Rage in Harlem*, and *The Real Cool Killers* (London and New York: Allison and Busby, 1985, 1985, 1986, 1985, 1985).

American blacks "must, of necessity, hate white people ... at some time.... [There] are no exceptions. It could not possibly be otherwise." And finally, he argued that any honest exploration of the condition of the black American psyche would have to admit to and describe the damage at its core.

> If this plumbing for the truth reveals within the Negro personality homicidal mania, lust for white women, a pathetic sense of inferiority, paradoxical anti-Semitism, arrogance, Uncle Tomism, hate and fear and self-hate, this then is the effect of oppression on the human personality. These are the daily horrors, the daily realities, the daily experiences of an oppressed minority.

The reaction to such total honesty was utter silence, in response to which Himes stayed drunk for the better part of the next five years. During this time two more novels were accepted for publication: *Cast the First Stone*, a prison novel for which Himes resentfully supplied his publishers with a white protagonist; and *The Third Generation*, a thinly fictionalized account of Himes's family history and early life. Still, his literary reputation continued to fade; he was once again supporting himself mostly as a porter, janitor and bellhop; his marriage fell apart; and he entered into a ruinously self-destructive affair with an equally troubled white woman from the New York literary world.

Yet Himes was finally able to pull himself out of the depths to which his rage, fear and despair had brought him. At what one feels must have been the eleventh hour, he found the cash to leave the country. Like Richard Wright before him, Himes discovered a literary reputation awaited him in Paris. It was in Paris, too, that Himes's French publisher, Marcel Duhamel, first suggested Himes knock out some detective fiction to make a little money. The first such book, *For Love of Imabelle* (republished as *A Rage in Harlem*) won Himes the 1958 Grand Prix Policier; the eleventh and last, *Blind Man With a Pistol*, appeared in 1969 to a flurry of favorable publicity in the United States and abroad. Indeed, it is not too much to say that Himes's reputation today (he died in 1984) rests mainly on these slim, commercial *policiers noirs*.

We know by now, or ought to know, that what gets us off as entertainment is rarely simple and never innocent. All the more so, then, when the subgenre in question is concerned with illegal versus official violence; when the scene is Harlem, and both the criminals and good guys are black; and when the author is a black man with an analysis of white racism's power to provoke within blacks not only an answering hatred but paranoia, self-doubt and self-contempt. Reading the five Harlem thrillers recently republished is, properly undertaken, something like submitting to a special kind of Rorschach test: your reactions to the lurid images, actions and characters they hurl forth reveal at least as much about you as about Harlem or Himes.

Take, for example, the opening sequence of *The Crazy Kill*, which flaunts its energy and virtuosity as brazenly as the first long take of any Orson Welles film. Our attention is turned from a small-time thief stealing a bag of change from a Plymouth double-parked outside an A&P to a man leaning out of the window overhead watching the ensuing chase, leaning so far out that he falls from the window, landing on a soft, warm pile of newly baked bread stacked outside the store. Cut back to the apartment from which the man has just fallen—a raucous, bleary wake is under way, attended by a cast of characters with enough lust for power, money and sex to fuel the next five seasons of *Dynasty*: in walks the man who fell from the window, now revealed as one Reverend Short. Short recounts in slightly crazed terms his brush with death, his salvation in and through the basket of bread; the other characters run to the window to look down; and there in the basket below lies another friend of the family—only this one has a knife in his chest.

Likewise in *Cotton Comes to Harlem*, a con man's back-to-Africa barbecue and rally is ripped off by two white men in a meat delivery truck which in turn is chased at breakneck speed by the con man and his two guards through a spray of machine-gun bullets; in *The Real Cool Killers*, a large, greasy white man, who has been attacked in a bar by a drunken black man with a knife (subsequently literally disarmed by an ax-wielding bartender), is chased through the Harlem streets by a hopped-up hipster firing blanks from a pistol, then shot dead in mid-stride by someone else in the gawking, leering crowd. If it is almost always steamingly hot in these novels, that is because Himes's Harlem is a volcano in constant eruption, a desperate, sordid *Walpurgisnacht* without end:

> An effluvium of hot stinks arose from the frying pan and hung in the hot motionless air, no higher than the rooftops—the smell of sizzling barbecue, fried hair, exhaust fumes, rotting garbage, cheap perfumes, unwashed bodies, decayed buildings, dog-rat-and-cat offal, whiskey and vomit, and all the old dried-up odors of poverty.

> It was too hot to sleep. Everyone was too evil to love.... The night was filled with the blare of countless radios, the frenetic blasting of spasm cats playing in the streets, hysterical laughter, automobile horns, strident curses, loudmouthed arguments, the screams of knife fights. (*The Heat's On*)

Against such a landscape, the violent opening of each novel constitutes less a crime to be solved than an overture promising more mayhem to come. If you wanted to be trendy, you could say that the "hermeneutic" function of the standard crime novel is systematically downplayed in these books in favor of regular moments of "semic excess" like the following:

> One slug caught Sister Heavenly in the left side below the ribs and lodged in the side of her spine; the other went wild. She fell sideways to the pavement and was powerless to move, but her mind was still active and her vision was clear. She saw Benny Mason slide quickly across the seat, leap to the sidewalk, and aim the pistol at her head.
>
> Well now, ain't this lovely? she thought just before the bullet entered her brain. (*The Heat's On*)

> He slapped her with such savage violence it spun her out of the chair to land in a grotesque splay-legged posture on her belly on the floor, the red dress hiked so high it showed the black nylon panties she wore.
>
> "And that ain't all," he said. (*A Rage in Harlem*)

Only those postmodernists most fully loosed from "the tyranny of the referent" will be able to savor without qualm the *jouissance* such passages offer. On the other hand, especially when they are placed in their helter-skelter context, it is hard to deny completely the appeal of their twisted energy. It is not incidental that Himes's detectives are named Grave Digger Jones and Coffin Ed Johnson; or that the latter's acid-scarred face is frequently compared to a zombie's; or that they contribute at least as much shocking violence to these narratives as they prevent. Grave Digger and Coffin Ed are in fact not so much crime-solvers as priests of violence; the swirling, brutal action over which they preside and to which they contribute is a voodoo celebration of black America, a black mass indeed.

And then there is the problem of Himes's women. In the Harlem novels there is almost always one grotesquely fetishized compound of male desire and dread like Imabelle of *A Rage in Harlem*: "She was a cushion-lipped, hot bodied, banana-skin chick with the speckled brown eyes of a teaser and the high-arched, ball-bearing hips of a natural-born *amante*." This *femme fatale*, who will before the story's end get slapped around by one or both of our detectives, is also invariably "high-yellow," and for more than one reason. She is yellow because she is a blend of the two mythic women that black shipworker Bob Jones oscillates between in Himes's first novel, *If He Hollers Let Him Go*: his fiancée, the beautiful black-bourgeois Alice, and Madge, a blond redneck co-worker who "looked ... ripe but not quite rotten," and whose alarm and excitement at the sight of him fill Bob with an angry lust "like an electric shock." And she is yellow-skinned because so was Himes's mother, Anna Bomar Himes, a woman whose neurotic love and rage overwhelmed his early years. Himes's mother doted on him for his own light skin; she oiled and brushed his hair every night to straighten it, and let him brush her hair and file her nails; she was morbidly sensitive to racial slights from whites and to the encroachment of those blacker in color or manner than she, including her husband, whom she viewed with resentment and disgust.

Not surprisingly, then, throughout *If He Hollers Let Him Go* Bob Jones treats most of his fellow blacks with a contempt almost equal to his fury at white people; his single, obsessive concern is to stand tall as a black *man*. Thus too the gross sexist sadism of the Harlem novels. Yet the male hysteria that pervades Himes's work, and the Oedipal pathology behind it, are themselves just two more symptoms of the widespread violence wrought by a racist culture, intertwining love and aggression, rage and fear, hatred and self-hatred in the soul of the oppressed. In an interview conducted relatively late in his life, Himes told fellow black novelist John A. Williams, "I would like to see produced a novel that just drains a person's subconscious of all his attitudes and reactions to everything. . . . Since [the black writer's] reactions and thoughts will obviously be different from that of the white community, this should create an entirely different structure of the novel." And, from the same interview: "That's one of the saddest parts about the black man in America—that he is being used to titillate the emotions of the white community. . . . I want these people to take me seriously. I don't care if they think I'm a barbarian, a savage, or what they think; just think I'm a serious savage." The first quotation tells us how, intentionally or not, he wrote his Harlem novels; the second, how we ought to read Chester Himes.

(1986)

Down the Beanstalk*

In 1969, when John Nichols moved with his wife and two children from New York City to Taos, New Mexico, he was known in East Coast literary circles as a promising young author. Then as now, stories of wacky, bittersweet love affairs and comings-of-age exerted an extraordinary hold over the collective imagination of the agents, editors and reviewers who select and endorse what counts as quality fiction—especially, for some strange reason, if those stories portrayed the young, white upper middle class of the northeastern United States in a compassionate light. So *The Sterile Cuckoo* (1965), an account of the goofy and sad romance of Jerry and Pookie, and *The Wizard of Loneliness* (1966), a look at the tenth year in the life of one Wendell Oler of Stebbinsville, Vermont, seemed to suggest that a modest success for Nichols lay ahead. Certainly no one looking at those books could have predicted the sometimes wonderful, sometimes godawful, always excessive books to come, or the strange combination of cult appeal and critical neglect they would draw in their wake.

For what those early, conventional books did not reveal was that by the late 1960s, thanks to a brief, eye-opening stay in Guatemala and to the Vietnam War, Nichols was already something of a leftie. So, shortly after moving to Taos, he volunteered his services to a muck-raking journal called *The New Mexico Review*. As he covered the escalating struggles over land and water rights between Hispanic smallholders and Anglo developers, Nichols himself became a player on the side opposing what he would later call the "Anglo Axis," in the name of a rich, multiracial culture that is both traditional and oppositional. When *The*

---

*A review-essay on John Nichols, *American Blood* (New York: Henry Holt, 1987), *The Magic Journey*, *The Milagro Beanfield War*, and *The Nirvana Blues* (New York: Balantine Books, 1983, 1976, 1983).

New Mexico Review collapsed in 1972, Nichols set to work on a novel about the community of endurance and resistance he had joined.

The Milagro Beanfield War, published in 1974, drew mixed reviews. The *Times* critic, in a typical notice, called Nichols to task for failing to provide the reader with a central protagonist, adequately (that is, psychologically) motivated characters, or a sufficiently graceful prose style. The publisher remaindered the book on schedule; and Ballantine, without much enthusiasm, put out a modest paperback run, which sold out, sold out again, and has been doing so ever since.

By now *Milagro* is certifiably a cult classic—a book, that is, whose enduring popularity is neither assisted by nor saddled with any imprimatur from the officials of the literary world. In this respect, it resembles other triumphs of popular pleasure over gatekeeping convention—like, say, *Pickwick Papers* or *Gargantua and Pantagruel*. Like Dickens and Rabelais, too, Nichols writes an exuberantly overloaded prose whose shifting tones draw from the diverse community it depicts, from Milagro's Charley Bloom, liberal lawyer and East Coast dropout, to Amarante Córdova, ancestral Hispanic who refuses to die. And just as in Dickens or Rabelais, *Milagro*'s plot proceeds through and against a centrifugal energy which spins off any number of digressions, sub-plots, characters and tales within tales, and runs the gamut of causality from pure coincidence to individual and collective intention to divine, mythic fate.

As an example of Nichols's multiaccented prose, take the following passage, which dips and slides through virtually all the diction pools and dialects of Milagro to describe Joe Mondragón's awakening to solidarity:

> Just like that, something tender he had never felt before took over his bones and seeped into his guts like a golden molasses, making him want to cry.
>
> Which was a hell of a spooky thing to happen to Joe, because about the only time he ever cried was when he chopped onions to sprinkle on Nancy's enchiladas, or when he ate a real hot jalapeño.
>
> No getting around it, though: suddenly he held a profound tenderness for his people, that's what it was. His people. His gente. His bunch of inbred, toothless, tubercular, flea-bitten, illiterate vecinos, sobrinos, primos, cuates, cabrones, rancheros, and general all-around fregado'd jodidos.
>
> Suddenly he loved the people he lived with, he cared about their lives. And this feeling, this *tenderness* oozing through his body, made him almost weak.

Similarly, though this same Joe has unintentionally started the war of the book's title by illegally opening up an old irrigation ditch, he remains no more significant than a dozen or so other citizens of Milagro. Gradually the community stumbles and blunders ("United we flounder," says

Benny Maestas, "divided we flounder") toward more or less unified opposition to the coolly rational machinations of the water commissioners, state engineer, state troopers, Forest Service, special agents, governor, real estate dealers and rancher-developers, all working toward the seizure and "development" of the land. Nichols's diffuse narration and rambling plotting beautifully convey the feel of a war that in one sense is always going on yet in another never really begins. If the community does come fitfully to resist the greed that rules it from outside, it's also true that its greatest moment of triumph is triggered with perfect serendipity by Joe Mondragón's shooting of his sweet old neighbor Seferino Pacheco and Pacheco's much-beloved wandering pig. Nor, at the novel's end, does Nichols suggest that the townsfolk's victory settles anything once and for all. As Bernabé Montoya, Milagro's ambivalently positioned, smart-but-stupid sheriff, thinks to himself:

> To be sure, life wouldn't return to what it was yesterday, but neither could it continue to be what it is today. The people had been apart for a long time, and now he sensed a small coming together—although who knew what those who had survived could do with a future nobody had defined?

When the film of *The Milagro Beanfield War*, directed by Robert Redford, is released this fall, the publicity will no doubt fuel some new interest in this cult book and in the two novels that followed it, *The Magic Journey* (1978) and *The Nirvana Blues* (1981). Unfortunately, though, with the latter two books, the good news about Nichols's writing slowly turns sour. Although both are set in Chamisaville, a medium-sized town not far from Milagro, and both offer readers scads of characters and buckets of hijinx, it is impossible to read through what Ballantine has boxed together as "The New Mexico Trilogy" without noticing that the road from Milagro leads steadily downhill.

For one thing, both *Journey* and *Nirvana* have a darker story to tell: the story of what *Journey* bitterly labels the "betterment of Chamisaville" by Anglo business and government over the past forty years, right down to what is described in *Nirvana* as its "pizzafication" in the present. Moreover, as that bleak chronicle unfolds, some funny things happen to the collective focus and carnivalesque energy of Nichols's earlier work. The current that in *Milagro* ran through the community of the oppressed seems in *The Magic Journey* either to have been taken over by the Anglo Axis in all *its* variety (including Junior Leyba and J.B. LeDoux, two exceptionally well-drawn traitors to class, race and *causa*), or to have been displaced onto a single protagonist, the irrepressibly gorgeous, bawdy radical April Delaney, rebellious daughter of the town's leading capitalist. Nichols's title phrase refers, in fact, both to Chamisaville's

"progress" from sheepherders' village to resort-town nightmare, and to
April's headlong plunge through life as, among other things, a peasant
fisherman's wife in France, a bullfighter in Spain, a black radical's wife in
New York City and, finally, the upstart editor of *El Clarín*, a muck-raking
paper back in Chamisaville. Outside these events, there is not much juice
to spare for stories of Chamisaville's oppressed. So when we do turn from
the evil schemes of the Anglo Axis or the flamboyant exploits of the
marvelous April to drop in on the suffering natives, we generally find
them stuck in the same rut they were in last time we looked: Espeedie
Cisneros retelling the same fable about the perfidy of the Anglos the
pueblo once took in, lawyer Virgil Leyba toiling through the night on his
endless pile of defense briefs and countersuits, the armed ghostriders of a
more militant resistance disappearing back into the mountains and sky.

What results from all this is problematic in terms of pleasure and
politics alike. Even when the ever-feisty, politically correct April finally
returns to town to sound *El Clarín*, the war we expect to heat up never
quite takes center stage. Instead, having subordinated the community to
April, Nichols now lets the story of her part in the struggle be upstaged—
first by a subplot about her psychic and sexual healing of a childhood
friend, whose romantic aspirations lie stifled under a life of married
middle-class respectability until they are unleashed by April's larger-
than-life example, earnest sermonizing and obligingly male-pleasing
sexual appetite ("'Come on, god dammit!' she hollered, 'Stuff it up me,
bang me, screw me! Hey, I love that cock! It's so hard! It's so BIG!'"),
then by the story of her struggle against cancer. In *Milagro*, too, there are
some dumb, cartoonish characterizations, several inert stretches and a
smattering of big-boobed-buckaroo sex fantasy that seems compounded
of equal parts of *Playboy*, *Rodeo World* and *Outdoor Life*, but they are
fewer and the earlier book's insistently collective focus and irrepressible
high spirits make them seem forgivable. Because *The Magic Journey* lacks
that collective, carnivalesque will to struggle buoying everything up, such
defects eventually sink the book.

And in *The Nirvana Blues* the problems are worse still. It is the end of
the 1970s, the forces of reaction are gathering throughout the land, and
Chamisaville has been wholly lost to the developers and their nouveau-
countercultural clientele. Only a single plot of land still belongs to a
native smallholder, the indomitable Eloy Irribarren, and now he must let
it go to cover his debts. Eloy would like to sell the land to Joe Miniver, a
former East Coast advertising man, socialist and freelance garbage
collector, but to make the $60,000 he needs to buy it, Joe has to put
through a deal involving some five pounds of uncut cocaine. *The Nirvana
Blues* is the story of his woefully unsuccessful attempts to score and sell
the dope, resist the blandishments of a string of big-breasted New Age

women, patch together his disintegrating marriage, keep his conscience minimally quiet and nail down that last 1.7 acres of farmland before one of the town's several professional land-sharks can gobble it up.

All this might have made for an entertaining read from a writer with more conventional gifts, but in Nichols's hands, despite some fine low comedy and high political commitment, the result is a longwinded, tedious mess. For well-nigh 600 pages Joe bounces haplessly from dope deal in town, into bed with one woman or another, to his troubled home, to Irribarren's land. And every time, at every point in the circuit, the punch line is the same: for all his lofty socialist ideals, Miniver is too complicit with all he despises to do anything real or right. This joke gets old long before the book is done, especially since the carnivalesque and multiaccentual qualities of Nichols's writing are simultaneously degraded—intentionally or not, I cannot guess—into a bloated parody of their former selves. Nirvana pelts us with hundreds of ephemeral characters, the hungry hustlers and New Age narcissists that make up the pseudocommunity Chamisaville has become; it babbles and protests at such wearying, maddening length that when at last Joe Miniver stands dying in the field he wanted to own, we may feel justified in reading his final outcry as an expression of Nichols's own aesthetic frustration and political near-despair:

Why oh why had he been unable to articulate a revolutionary consciousness, dying ... as a valuable martyr to compassionate causes? Instead, what little memory of him endured on earth would be tainted by the foolishness of his final days, the irresponsibility of his slipshod sexual quest, the absurdity inherent in the last defiant gesture of robbing the bank.

It is this wail, the cry of a man without a community or movement to join, that brings us at last to Nichols's new novel. American Blood purports to be one Michael Smith's first-person account of his redemption from the evil, pornographic nightmare of American violence, in Vietnam and back home again, through the love of—you guessed it—a feisty, bra-bursting single-mother waitress named Janine. In other words, it's a classic romance, in which the damaged quester moves through a ravaged landscape in search of psychic wholeness, and finds it finally through love. But romance is the diametrical opposite of the novel of collective liberation Nichols once wrote: its enabling assumptions foreclose the possibility of any salvation beyond the personal. Moreover, it is a form for which Nichols's talents are particularly ill-suited. From the first page on, it's apparent that what we're hearing is not a single character's voice but a cramped, awkward version of the old freewheeling Nichols narrator. "When I awoke at dawn," Nichols has his Michael

Smith say, "it was not with any sense of consolation that the war at last had ended. But rather, I greeted the day in a sweat-drenched terror, convinced that the sadism and horror would permanently torment my new life in the world." Or, from later in the book, when his dreaded *doppelgänger* and former comrade-in-arms, Thomas Carp, shows up to tempt him back to the sex-and-violence of his darkest memories and desires: "No words could I summon up for this lumpy, sniggering man who had me hog-tied in the devil's breathless ozone."

The book is loaded with such clunkers—and it's worth noting that the editor who waved them through also lets Michael pass out on some steps at the top of page 119, have a dream, and come to at his desk at work on page 120. But what is even more distressing than such ugly, implausible sentences and sloppy editing is the desperate muddle of *American Blood*'s terribly earnest, garbled plot. Michael is cured, thanks to a 1000cc. dose of wild sex and nurturance from tough-but-tender Janine; then he must see her through her own dark time, after some horrible monster—Carp, of course—has raped, tortured and murdered her teenage daughter. Once Michael has revealed his suspicions of Carp to Janine, she herself becomes a monster of vengeance and forces him to help plot Carp's execution. But when the two finally track Carp to his banal suburban lair, they discover he has already done the job for them, with a gun in the mouth. Lest the significance of this event, and Janine's virtually instant return to *caritas*, seem confusing to the reader, both Janine and Michael hasten to spell out its rather surprising lesson. She tells him: "You really *are* a saint, Michael. Some kind of bumbling, awkward angel who's been placed on earth to save me." And in the middle of the dream that closes the book, Michael exclaims, "By gum, I really *was* an angel sent earthward to mend all my friends and enemies alike!"

I'm sorry Nichols wrote *American Blood*, and sorrier still that Holt let it out. But I also think its faults are not just chargeable to Nichols and his editors. For all his flaws and failures, here is a writer whose radical vision we must admire, whose best work was enabled by the upsurge from below that swept through northern New Mexico and every corner of this country in the late 1960s and early 1970s, and whose decline as a writer corresponds to the recession of those same tides. So I read the melodramatic excess and skewed, didactic exhortation of *American Blood* as the symptoms of a forced retreat from a vision of collective struggle to a fantasy of private redemption. And I hope, for Nichols's sake and ours, that there will be another, larger upsurge sometime soon.

(1987)

Beating the Odds: The Brechtian

Aesthetic of Russell Banks*

Twenty years ago, a frustrated college teacher of mine broke the mysterious silence he had held towards me and the short stories I had been handing in to him for the past four or five months with a sudden splutter: "Why do you *write* about these people?" he said, sliding my newest piece towards me across the surface of his darkly gleaming desk with a massive flick of his hand. And ten years ago, the woman who was at the time my frustrated agent echoed the sentiment one night when the two of us were out having dinner with her brother, who asked over coffee and dessert what my work was about. "It's about ordinary people," my agent said—and then cast down her eyes and gave out a hopeless, involuntary sigh: "Ordinary, ordinary, ordinary . . ."

By "ordinary" here, by "these people," read white working class—the kind of people I grew up with in the factory town I'm from. And I rehearse these anecdotes not to show my scars, but to point up an obvious fact about the lit-business today. We can have a certain limited number of feminist writers and novels around now; and there remains a smaller, but equally distinct quota for "minority voices" as well. But virtually no one within the institutions and apparatuses of literature-land who is in a position to promote, publish, and affirm or canonize the quality of "quality fiction" in this country gives a shit about narratives focused on the pathologies and resistances that result from the violence we neutrally call "social class."

So the writer who would make narratives out of working-class (or poor people's) experience tends to find him- or herself in a tightening box from which there are not many exits. One might, like Raymond Carver in his earliest and best work, write so obliquely and sparely of such

---

*A review-essay on Russell Banks, *Affliction* (New York: Harper and Row, 1989).

marginalized and exploited lives that the social location of their angst
gradually disappears, and the trauma at its core can be consumed instead
as a bleak, existential metaphysic. Or one might, like Bobbie Ann
Mason, write about such lives in an idiom whose relentlessly bouncy
present-tense simplicity, combined with regular doses of pop-culture
cues, allows upscale readers to savor the narrative as a virtual transcrip-
tion of likeable, down-home stupidity. One might take up such strategies
without being fully conscious of them as ways of "getting over" to an
audience from another class, but rather as ways of dealing with the pain
and anger within oneself—or as the results of a desperate striving to get
published, to be read and heard. One might, indeed, be required *not* to
know or understand what one's work means (as Carver, by his own
admission, did not), or how easily and with what patronizing voyeuristic
pleasure any Mason story nestled in *The New Yorker*, just across from the
Tiffany ads, can be misread. Or one might, with the same not-quite-
consciousness, merely learn to write about some other subject; or learn
not to write at all.

I sketch this stunted landscape and lay out the dim possibilities it
presents, however, not to lament them, but to celebrate the wonder of
Russell Banks's achievements against the dismal odds. For beginning
with *Trailerpark* in 1981, and continuing through his stunningly ambitious and achieved *Continental Drift* (1985), the collection *Success Stories*
(1986), and this new novel, he has ever more clearly emerged as a writer
from the white working class, writing explicitly about the rage and
damage, the capitulations, self-corruptions, and small resistances of
subordinated lives. *Affliction* tells the story of the final two weeks of self-
and-other destruction in the life of one Wade Whitehouse, a 41-year-old
well-driller, snow-plower, and small-town cop in his decrepit hometown
of Lawford, New Hampshire. There the mill that once justified the
town's existence is long since shut down, leaving Wade's father Glenn to
early retirement back at the dilapidated family homestead with Wade's
faded mother and a secret stash of Canadian Club tucked throughout the
house and barn. Wade, however, doesn't get by to see the folks that
often. His worklife is spent in resentful double fealty to Gordon
LaRiviere, Lawford's only success story, a beefy, sleazy entrepreneur and
town selectman to whom Wade is indebted as both employee and town
cop. His life outside work is a smear of alcohol, depression, and rage that
stretches from his trailer south of town through the bars and back roads
to the sad but amiable bed of divorced diner waitress Margie Fogg, and
all the way down to Concord, where his scornful ex-wife Lillian lives in
her middle-class home with her middle-class husband and Wade's
daughter Jill, who doesn't want to see him any more.

At forty-one, in other words, Wade's real daily work is the management of an unstable and ever-enlarging fund of pain and fear. He has lost the woman he loved, who once loved him; he has lost his youth, the promise of a better job, perhaps as a state trooper, that commands more respect; he is now losing his child. Worst and most frightening of all, however, is the constant sense of "this particular kind of fragility" in every encounter, even something as simple as a stop for coffee at the local diner, whenever and wherever he is reminded of his own failure to connect with or understand the world:

> One minute he was moving securely through time and space, in perfect coordination with other people; then, with no warning, he was out of time and place, so that the slightest movement, word, facial expression or gesture contained enormous significance. The room filled with coded messages that he could not decode, and he slipped quickly into barely controlled hysteria. (p. 108)

Behind all such fears and doubts and dislocations, at their base and as their horizon line, there is always the child who is being beaten, the *Ur*-spectre of Wade's drunken, crazy-mean father fissuring into violence, punching the mother, smacking the boy down on to the floor until finally the mother calms him down, waits for him to start whining "'When I say do something, I mean it,'" (p. 102) then soothes him and leads him off to bed.

Affliction is thus most centrally a representation of that terrible cycle in subaltern lives in which powerlessness breeds self-loathing breeds hysterical violence, and the beaten child is not only father to but identical with the beaten, beating man. Banks avoids the twin dangers of a mere "sociological" accuracy on the one hand, and a voyeuristic sensationalism on the other, through a wise combination of elevating and distancing techniques. For one thing, he has constructed a plot for this novel which is as tragic as that of *Oedipus Rex*, and in the same way. Wade Whitehouse, like the old original child-man, does not simply suffer his fate, but rather fulfills it precisely in the attempt to transcend it and transform himself. In the various plot lines braided through the book, Whitehouse tries to win his daughter back, to bury his mourning for his marriage and make a new life with Margie, to reconcile with his father in the aftermath of his mother's pathetic death, and to find justice and punishment in the public realm for LaRiviere and his cohort, the rich union official whose father-in-law Wade believes they have killed to increase their own corrupt power and wealth. But all these efforts only result in that nightmarish moment in which, out of work, utterly discredited and desperate, he strikes his daughter, draws blood, and receives at last the terrible blessing of the father looking on, triumphant athlete, warrior, thief, a man who had come through harrowing adversity and risk with his bitterness not only intact but confirmed, for it was the bitterness that had got him through, and the grin and the crackled laughter was for the confirmation, a defiant thanksgiving gloat. The son finally had turned out to be a man just like the father. (p. 340)

Thus the novel's title, taken from a Simon Weil quotation distinguishing between "suffering" and "affliction," between the hard-wired contradictions which we must endure, and the constructed fate—constructed by the gods in one era, by history and society in our own—against which we struggle and by which we are struck down.

This same distinction is, from a different angle, that between melodrama, which provokes our complicit tears, and tragedy, which encourages our understanding, invites us to draw conclusions, imagine alternatives, to think (and, just possibly, act) otherwise. I'm talking Brecht here, not Aristotle—or, rather, not the standard bourgeois purgation-catharsis model of Aristotle that gets peddled in Drama 101. And so is Banks, knowingly or not, whenever he pulls one of the several distancing maneuvers that do so much in and of themselves to heighten and enlarge *Affliction* beyond case study or grotesquerie. To tell Wade Whitehouse's story (as for Bob DuBois's, in the half of *Continental Drift* that belonged to him), Banks elects a studiously detached point of view, an expository near-omniscience you can already see in the quotations above, which follow easily from the middle of ongoing dramatic scenes which they then as easily rejoin. He has made a style, in other words, that openly "tells" as much as it "shows," against the pinched advice of every creative writing primer and 95 percent of all the "quality fiction" published in the United States over the past forty years. A style which, moreover, largely works by eschewing style as it is ordinarily conceived, in favor of the steady-sighted, straightforward additive sentence, scrupulously naming as it goes, growing not more excited but merely somewhat longer when thoughts and feelings get busy and/or the action heats up— as here, in the midst of a passage about Wade's ex-wife Lillian's feelings, as a young woman, towards her dead alcoholic working-class dad:

Her father was weak and sweet, and he had not frightened a soul. The most alarming moments she had endured with her father came on those rare occasions when she realized that, if he was not drunk, he was thinking about getting drunk and so was not in fact present to her, did not actually see or hear her in the room. Those moments made her feel as if she did not exist and so lonely that she got dizzy and had to sit down and babble to him, make him lift his head and smile benignly at her, a big sleepy horse of a man, while she chattered on about school, about her sisters and her mother, making up events and whole conversations with neighbors, teachers, friends, madly filling with words the hole in the universe that he made with his presence, until, at last, her father rose from the kitchen table, patted her on the head and said, "I love you a whole lot, Lily, a whole lot," and went out the door, leaving her alone in the kitchen, a speck of bright matter whirling through a dark turbulent sky. And now her father was dead, and she believed that she did not feel that pain anymore, because she missed him so. (p. 194)

Banks's depiction of his female characters is not always up to this mark; the women in his novels are at times more uncertainly observed than understood—as with *Affliction*'s somewhat sentimentalized Margie Fogg. Yet in this passage the timing is as unobtrusively precise as the words themselves. By choosing recounting over representation, sober translation over the standard mimetic attempt to "reproduce" the character's "voice," Banks evinces his respect for his working-class characters, and his sensitivity to the problem of representing them to an alien readership from another class. And he also gains an enormous freedom to *move*, from character to character, across an array of splendidly sketched small-town types, between the present and the past, and, perhaps most distinctively and fruitfully, from individual experience to the wider net of social and material circumstances in which that experience is enmeshed. Thanks to its steady, sober detachment, Banks's narration is capable of delivering to us the geologic and social history of the region in which Wade Whitehouse makes and meets his fate, or halting the plot to describe the savage and demotic mysteries of the annual deerhunting ritual, which in its unfoldings this year will include the shooting death, by design or accident, that propels Wade's over-determined rage for justice. Banks accomplishes all this without ever making us feel that we are wading through yet another intrusive digression. What we get, rather, is a demonstration of the terrible truth of Marx's insight no American writer has ever seen, or transmitted, with such clarity before: that "Men [sic] make their own history; but they do not make it just as they please; they do not make it under circum-stances chosen by themselves, but under circumstances directly encoun-tered, given and transmitted by the past." And we also get the revolutionary lesson Marx draws from this principle—that for the sake of human freedom, those circumstances themselves must be changed. To this novel, too, then, we might properly attach the wish with which Banks ended *Continental Drift*, in all revolutionary seriousness: "*Go, my book, and help destroy the world as it is.*"

How Russell Banks has taken this stance, and attained commercial success with it, would probably make an interesting and instructive story in itself. I remember reading some of his early work (*Searching for*

Survivors and *The New World*) back in the seventies, and finding it oblique in its concerns and pointlessly obsessed with narrational experiment. Yet it may be those same works, formalistically hollow as they seemed to me then, were actually groping towards that Brechtian combination of directness and estrangement he now employs with such triumphant success—and that the commendation those early works received gave him a position within the quality-lit marketplace which now ensures that works like *Affliction* must be taken seriously. But whatever ruses of authorial and institutional history secured Banks's initial reputation, we must be grateful for them, and for Banks's presence on the American scene. He has become, I think, the most important living white male American on the official literary map, a writer we, as readers *and* writers, can actually learn from, one whose books, like *Continental Drift* and now *Affliction*, help us to grow and urge us to change.

All this said, however, I still have to cop to a few dissatisfactions with this new work, at least one of which is sure to be echoed by other, less admiring reviewers. For in *Affliction* Banks tries to convince us that all his splendid narration issues from one of the novel's characters, specifically from Wade's younger brother Rolfe, an escapee from Lawford, New Hampshire, and to some extent—he's a history teacher now, down in the Boston suburbs—from his class fate. The problem is that I simply never believe Rolfe can know all he's saying or execute this masterful narration; nor do I believe in or care about him as an individual character whenever he is roped into the plot. In fact, *Affliction*'s only systematic lapses occur at those points, usually at the opening of a chapter, when Banks has to reintroduce him (since for the most part, thankfully, we can forget he's supposed to be the source of what we read). Suddenly, the beautifully pitched detachment of the rest of the novel turns into portentous, unpersuasive flailing, including, at worst, swatches of the very self-pity that lies underneath so much white male writing in this post-feminist age, and that it is otherwise part of *Affliction*'s greatness to refuse—as when Rolfe confesses, for example, that he is telling us all this because

> finally I could stand the displacement no longer and determined to open my mouth and speak, to let the secrets emerge, regardless of the cost to me or anyone else. I have done this for no particular social good but simply to be free. Perhaps then, I thought, my own story and, at last, not Wade's will start to fill me, and this time it will be different.... Will I marry then? Will I make a family of my own? Will I become a member of a tribe? Oh, Lord, I pray that I will do those things and that I will be that man. (p. 49)

The best that can be said of such passages is that they are mercifully self-contained and utterly inimical to the rest of the book. We can easily do as we read what Banks should have done as he wrote and excise whiney Rolfe from the text.

The other problem I have with *Affliction* is more fleeting but more troublesome; it is with those few yet central moments in the novel when Banks's painstakingly detailed account of the historical determinations in class and gender of Wade's working-class masculinity gives way to a revved-up rhetoric that portrays the roots of the syndrome in terms of a ghastly, ahistorical mythology. Appropriately enough, it is Rolfe himself who pushes this wrongheaded point most explicitly near the end of the book, when he describes the ruin that has been Wade's life as "a paradigm, ancient and ongoing." (p. 339) But the same slippage from history to myth occurs shortly thereafter, in Banks's own depiction of that climactic moment when, having lost everything, Wade is down on the ground looking up at his terrifying, vengeful, drunken father,

> a man compelled to perform a not especially pleasant task, the decision to do it having been made long ago in forgotten time by a forgotten master, the piece of iron pipe in his meaty hands a mighty war club, a basher, an avenging jawbone of an ass, a cudgel, bludgeon, armor-breaking mace, tomahawk, pick, maul, lifted slowly, raised like a guillotine blade, sledge-hammer, wooden mallet to pound a circus tent stake into the ground, to slam the gong that tests a man's strength, to split the log for a house, to drive the spike into the tie with one stroke, to stun the ox, to break the lump of stone, to smash the serpent's head, to destroy the abomination in the face of the Lord. (p. 341)

Such a passage has, of course, its own awful power, a persuasiveness based in the persistence of patriarchy and male violence throughout many long epochs and across many cultures. Yet that is all the more reason why we should resist the urge to collapse their various manifest-ations into one intractable mythic image, and insist instead on their present determinations in the here and now. *Affliction* at its best does just that; it names the parts and shows how they function with an unerring precision and a terrible, compassionate detachment that will not yield to the despairing comfort of myth. Here, for example, against the passage just quoted, is Banks's quite different, and for me far superior, description of Wade's first beating at the hands of his old man:

> There was no time to hide from the blow, no time to protect himself with his arms or even to turn away. Pop's huge fist descended and collided with the boy's cheekbone. Wade felt a terrible slow warmth wash thickly across his face, and then he felt nothing at all. He was lying on his side, his face slammed against the couch, which smelled like cigarette smoke and sour milk, when there came a second blow, this one low on his back, and he heard his

mother shout, "Glenn! Stop!" His body was behind him somewhere and felt hot and soft and bright, as if it had burst into flame. There was nothing before his eyes but blackness, and he realized that he was burrowing his face into the couch, showing his father his backside as he dug with his paws like a terrified animal into the earth. He felt his father's rigid hands reach under his belly like claws and yank him back, flinging him to his feet, and when he opened his eyes he saw the man standing before him with his hand cocked in a fist, his face twisted in disgust and resignation, as if he were performing a necessary but extremely unpleasant task for a boss. (p. 101)

Affliction is full of such passages and such knowledge. However Banks has survived and grown to write it, and however it has been published, we should read this work, forgive its lapses—and be thankful, even astonished, that it exists.

(1989)

These Disintegrations I'm Looking

Forward to: Science Fiction from

New Wave to New Age

As we know the seemingly endless line of period histories coming out these days in both book and talkshow form, one constitutive aspect of the "best of times, worst of times" constellation of forces and feelings which were the sixties was the explosive upward mobility of previous depreciated cultural forms. The emergence of "Pop Art" would be the most famous and readily grasped example of this process at work, I suppose. Yet alongside and together with it, we might place the example of science fiction, and the phenomenon of the relatively swift critical acceptance of a whole generation of SF writers—Ursula LeGuin, Joanna Russ, Philip K. Dick, Thomas M. Disch, and Samuel Delany, to name only the most well known today—whose cultural legitimacy must seem, from any pre-1960s point of view we can remember or evoke, nearly as aberrant as that of pale-faced, straw-haired Andy himself.

Or, for that matter, from the point of view of the eighties as well, insofar as one mark of our contemporary moment is precisely the process, begun in the late seventies and gathering speed and force throughout this decade, of the redlining and ghettoization of precisely such emancipatory cultural open space. There are many conjunctural factors at work in the shutdown—certainly too many for me to attempt an exhaustive list or analysis here. On one level, the crisis of declining readerships that struck the entire publishing industry in the mid-1970s, combined with the devastating effect of the Supreme Court's decision on the value of inventories in the Thor Power Tool case, and the corporate conglomerization of publishing in the last half of the seventies, have all contributed to the decline of the power of the editor, the rise of the marketing folks, and the increasingly rigid application of all received generic categories and established narrative formulae, especially within the branch of publishing devoted to fiction. Moreover, the shift of younger intellectuals, perhaps especially progressive intellectuals, away from a concern with contemporary literature, "high" or "low," towards newer and more massified cultural forms like film, television, and popular music, has also helped chill the climate for crossover work. Yet beyond these dynamics and the Big Chill of the *Zeitgeist*, we can also mark the internal shifts in style and thematics that go along with SF's return to its subcultural ghetto. For the 1980s SF of William Gibson, Bruce Sterling, Vonda McIntyre, and Octavia Butler is a very different thing from the New Wave SF of the 1960s; it is at one and the same time "trashier," "pulpier," and far more sophisticated, even more liberatory, than those earlier writings in ways it is my purpose here to describe and explore.

To see that difference clearly, it will be helpful to spend a minute or two situating that earlier work within the SF tradition from which it sprung—from which, indeed, it had to spring. For by the 1960s, the utopian mapping and dystopian exorcism which had always been, in effect, SF's official, serious business (as opposed to those prepubescent technotwit satisfactions supplied by a whole other branch of SF, from Jules Verne to Heinlein and Asimov, through great dollops of masculinist space-jockeying adventure and "amazing" technogadgetry for sexually terrified twelve- and thirteen-year-old boys of all ages) had long since run aground. Or rather, that utopian mapping had run aground, had become impossible—and dystopian exorcism had supernova'd and become a black hole. All this, insofar as the ideological core around which the projects of celebration and/or critique were gathered in traditional SF from Bellamy and Morris on the utopian side to Shelley and Zamiatin on the dystopian (with Wells oscillating uncertainly from one pole to the other) was an ideal type of instrumental rationality and social engineering which, after fascism, two world wars, Stalinism, and the sight of the first mushroom clouds, was open to virtually nothing else but doubt, if not outright contempt. When I place *A Canticle for Leibowitz*, Walter M. Miller's brilliant, reactionary critique of this tarnished and repudiated ideal, as the American tombstone of this tradition, I hardly mean to say that all celebrations of technocratic problem solving and social rationality within American SF ceased from 1959 on; I only mean that such celebrations ceased to be interesting, or seem serious, except of course to a sizable group of largely white twelve- and thirteen-year-old boys, for whom it continued to come with the territory—and even they, or a good many of them, soon found that you could get just as much fun and confirmation from the nostalgic-whimsical, vaguely liberal and literary fictions of a Ray Bradbury. And writing yet another SF novel to flay the excesses and delusions of the technorationalist ideal—another book in which machines conquer humanity, or in which human faith in reason and perfectibility leads to totalitarianism or Armageddon—had come to seem as easy, and about as useful, as beating a dead horse.

So in the sixties we come to the moment of J.G. Ballard—the moment of his discovery, I mean, by a new generation of American SF writers, of the relevance of his example for them as the author of an unprecedentedly *literary* SF, one full of brilliant impressionistic imagery and psychological insight. Fredric Jameson seems here to have read the "political unconscious" of Ballard's work with perfect accuracy when he declares that Ballard's "world dissolutions" are paradigmatic of "the ways in which the imagination of a dying class—in this case the cancelled future of a vanished colonial and imperial destiny—seeks to intoxicate itself with images of death that range from the destruction of the world by fire, water, and ice to lengthening sleep or the berserk orgies of high-rise buildings or superhighways reverting to barbarism."[1] What I want to suggest that New Wave SF writers found, however, either through Ballard's work or from some other prompting, is the aestheticizing principle itself as a way to work what we might, following Benjamin, call the "allegorical ruin" of a now collapsed and bankrupt utopian/dystopian dialectic. That, at any rate, is how I understand the otherwise inexplicable, hothouse florescence and sudden significance of that whole host of autotelic language practices, experimental forms, and, strictly speaking, inadequately motivated but luxuriant image play which is the SF New Wave: the splendid, simultaneously exhilarating and horrifying excess of wacky ornamental detail chunked into virtually any sentence of a Philip K. Dick novel; the decadent, syncopated elegance of Thomas Disch's unrepentant slides from high sublimity to ad- or comix-speak; the graceful, limpid style and craft-object feel of LeGuin's poetic work; or the high-flying generic miscegenation and ostentatious brilliance of the performances of Joanna Russ, whose early masterpiece *The Female Man* symptomatically concludes with an "Envoi" whose very "literariness" is guaranteed to scuttle the normalizing fate it announces for the book it concludes:

> Take your place bravely on the book racks of bus terminals and drugstores.... Do not complain when at last you become quaint and oldfashioned, when you grow as outworn as the crinolines of a generation ago and are classed with *Spicy Western Stories*, *Elsie Dinsmore*, and *The Son of the Sheik*; do not mutter angrily to yourself when young persons read you to hrooch and hrch and guffaw, wondering what the dickens you were all about. Do not get glum when you are no longer understood, little book. Do not curse your fate. Do not reach up from readers' laps and punch the readers' noses.[2]

In my view, then, the moment of New Wave SF in the 1960s and early 1970s is characterizable as one in which science fiction briefly *becomes modernist,* just as European bourgeois literature had done a half century earlier, when it too found itself caught in crisis between an "old"—including, of course, an old set of narrative thematics and plots—which was dying, and a "new" which could not yet be born. In both cases, the escape route, the strategic displacement of anxiety and desire, lay in the direction of aesthetic self-consciousness and autotelic form. What then becomes most striking about the practice of a new generation of SF writers, by contrast, is the signal absence of formalist interests and concerns. To turn from even the most recent New Wave production—say, Disch's *The Businessman* or Joanna Russ's *(Extra)Ordinary People*—to the newest William Gibson or Octavia Butler novel is to move from a kind of capital-L Literature we have all been trained to delect and decode to a type of non-literary narrative which I am tempted to say has no "political unconscious": a kind of writing in which, instead of delving and probing for neurotic symptoms, we are invited to witness and evaluate a relatively open acting out.

By "acting out," in this case, I mean that much contemporary science fiction in effect means what it says—or, more precisely, that as in traditional SF, the SF organized around the old utopian/dystopian poles of the debate on the rationally engineered society, this new SF hardly requires the literary analyst's ingenuity in order for us to find or fathom its real social content; the collective anxieties and desires that fuel it are relatively openly evoked and worked through. And this shift from formal and aesthetic experimentation back to experiments in social thought itself suggests that in at least some senses and sectors we have indeed moved on from that earlier humanist debate on freedom, power and order to some new or at least mutated social and ideological ground, which is once again open and fresh enough to be explicitly tried on and explored.

With contemporary mainstream SF, then, the old modern or Enlightenment or oedipal-capitalist questions of freedom versus order, irrationality versus rationality, selfhood versus society have now been superseded by a whole new set of postmodern, post-oedipal (though hardly post-capitalist) non-binary questions concerning what, following Deleuze and Guattari, we might call the complex "rhizomatics" of difference and filiation: the same questions, in effect, that get asked within both poststructuralist and feminist theory, as well as across the whole spectrum of progressive political activity in the 1980s, from the Rainbow Coalition and the Jackson campaign to the Central America solidarity movement—the questions that appear, in effect, whenever we begin to try to think and move "beyond the fragments," towards a hitherto unthinkable unity-*in*-difference for our lives and work.

Moreover, as this new SF tries out and works through these questions, it also tries *on* the new post-industrial, cybernetic sensorium in which all the old certainties about self/other, inside/outside, body/world are increasingly decentered and dissolved. Indeed, we might well begin our explorations of contemporary SF by noticing the extent to which, in works like Bruce Sterling's *Schismatrix* and William Gibson's *Neuromancer* and *Count Zero*, as in *Blade Runner* and the *Alien(s)* films, the rushing forward movement of the relentless, pulpy plot, swift as it is, is nonetheless constantly impeded to the edge of dissolution by what we might call our "lateral" fascination with the novels' ceaselessly shifting and absorbing decor:[3] in *Schismatrix*, both the tide-pool-like eco-social systems of the various planets and colonies in which the diplomat-hero Abelard Lindsay finds himself, and the vastly different world-historical epochs in whose altered and alien-ruled powergrids he must find or construct a place for himself; in *Neuromancer* and *Count Zero*, the landscape of cybernetic "simstim" in which, as in Cronenburg's film *Videodrome* but minus the horror, questions of a given character's "reality" and "authenticity" are gradually dissolved in the power-discourses of apparent and effective computer-generated simulacra, along with the multiple implants and interactive interfaces of and with a new cybernetic technology of perception and operation which is literally jacked and programmed *into* the main characters in a world in which the megalopolis of the East Coast is as formidably, materially perceptible in towering heaps of information and communication as it is in buildings, bridges, and streets:

> Home.
> Home was BAMA, the Sprawl, the Boston-Atlanta Metropolitan Axis.
> Program a map to display frequency of data exchange, every thousand megabytes a single pixel on a very large screen. Manhattan and Atlanta burn solid white. Then they start to pulse, the rate of traffic threatening to overload your stimulation. Your map is about to go nova. Cool it down. Up your scale. Each pixel a million megabytes. At a hundred million megabytes per second, you begin to make out certain blocks in midtown Manhattan, outlines of hundred-year-old industrial parks ringing the old core of Atlanta...[4]

Within such modelled and modelling landscapes it seems virtually beside the point to look down through the breakneck, baroque plotting of Gibson or Sterling in order to focus on the minimally enabling, liminal oppositions which first or finally set the characters in motion—even when, as is the case in Gibson's two novels, the ultimate bad guys turn out to be the Usheresque electronic (dis)embodiments of the great dynasties of capitalist wealth, now coiled in their incestuous off-planet lairs somewhere in outer space. What counts, what satisfies and fascinates, is

the blurred and elided edge of character, action, and setting where you
are, the edge where the distinction between plot and *mise-en-scène*, like
the the oppositions between human and machine, self and other,
body and world, begin to dissolve. This contemporary SF is about trying
on this new situation of boundary breakdown, this new ontology in
which all "identities seem contradictory, partial, and strategic"[5]—the
ontology, as Donna Haraway would have and celebrate it, of the
interactive cyborg, with its fluid and shifting boundaries between animal,
human, and machine. In the interactions, interfacings, and affiliations
the male main characters of Sterling's and Gibson's novels must make
with machines, with non-human and/or alien others, and with equally
programmed, implanted and "jacked-in" women, in order to survive and
achieve their goals; in these novels' plotted emphasis "on boundary
conditions and interfaces, on rates of flow across boundaries—and not
on the integrity of natural objects" or given, essentialist characterological
identities; this new SF with all its complex, even frenzied tryings-on of a
new, cybernetic sense of identity constitutes on the level of narrative
representation a contribution to what Haraway calls "the theoretical and
practical struggle against unity-through-domination or unity-through
incorporation." This struggle, she says, "not only undermines the
justifications for patriarchy, colonialism, humanism, positivism, essential-
ism, scientism, and other unlamented -isms, but *all* claims for an organic
or natural standpoint."[6]

What Haraway both sums up and sloganizes throughout her influential essay is no less than an epochal paradigm shift separating the
progressive social thought and imaginary of the 1980s from that of the
1960s, and from Enlightenment- and organicist-driven thought and
struggle *tout court*: a struggle whose enabling conditions and energies are
largely derived from the interaction of the new forces and relations of
production we call "post-industrial" with the new non-essentialist,
post-Enlightenment visions, practices, projects and energies which have
come to us primarily out of contemporary feminism. Because it constitutes a break from those older norms and seemingly exhausted practices,
the new paradigm necessarily involves the construction of a new non-
totalized vision of politics, and a radical critique and revalencing of the
old, essentialist categories of alienation and selfhood, which now appear
in mutated form in the new poststructuralist emphases on deconstruction, decentering, *différance*.

But before I move on to demonstrate in some detail the presence of
these concerns and emphases in the work of one of the most interesting
of the new SF writers, Octavia Butler, I want to point first to some ways
in which much of the new SF written by men, for all the boundary erosions
and breakdowns it dramatizes, remains stuck in a masculinist frame. In

Gibson's work, the inflection is unmistakable: if, on the very first page of his newest novel, Count Zero, the corporate mercenary Turner is literally blown up (by a "slamhound" with a "core" which "was a kilogram of recrystallized hexogene and flaked TNT") then reconstructed, thanks to a "good contract," by a Dutch surgeon and his team (who "cloned a square meter of skin of him, grew it on slabs of collagen and shark-cartilage polysaccharides" and "bought eyes and genitals on the open market"),[7] he nonetheless remains identifiable for us throughout the novel as the familiar macho figure of the insider-turned-rebel, using all the natural and programmed ingenuity at his disposal to clear a path through a maze of lethal cybernetic enemy systems which more or less constitute the world. Similarly, in Gibson's award-winning debut novel Neuromancer, despite his close working partnership with cybernetic samurai Molly, console cowboy Case remains the star attraction as, jacked-in, he rides wildly up against and through the giant walls of corporate-conglomerate "ice" to the secret lairs, simultaneously located in cyber-space and the material world, where the darkest secrets and powers are hid. And in Sterling's Schismatrix, too, though perhaps less explicitly, we can find the same masculinist video-game paradigms at work: though, as he is literally deconstructed and reassembled and reprogrammed throughout the novel, Abelard Lindsay's goal is not to rebel or to penetrate but simply to negotiate new coalitions across competing or alien orders and simply survive. Yet even though, as in videogames, the question is no longer "who am I?" but "where am I?" as Gillian Skerrow notes,[8] the drama nonetheless remains focused on the struggle of the male protagonist (through a series of universes and social orders in which, significantly enough, all female characters, however intelligent, dynamic, and ingeniously programmed, remain in place within their worlds) to wend his lonely way through the worlds.

Against such dramas, for all their fascinating depictions of late capitalism (in Gibson) and epochal historical shifts (in Sterling's Schismatrix), the example and evolution of Octavia Butler's SF forms a strik-ing and instructive contrast in its quite different essaying of the dialectics of otherness, affiliation, and difference. In Butler's work—all of it writ-ten, by the way, in an extraordinarily styleless style, a "writing degree zero" as far in its transparency and unobtrusiveness from the literary pyrotechnics of New Wave SF as one could imagine—such questions of difference, connection, and power are explicitly posited as the questions which generate the plot and around which all subsequent dramatic action devolves.

In Butler's first novel, Kindred (1979), the protagonist Dana, a black woman writer living in contemporary L.A. (like Butler herself) is catapulted backwards in time to the antebellum Maryland plantation in which she must protect the life of Rufus, the psychologically damaged, self- and other-loathing son of the plantation's patriarchal master, so that he can survive long enough to engender on the slave named Alice the slave-child from whom she herself will ultimately descend. The somewhat schematic and repetitive action that follows from this premise is complicated in two significant ways: first, through Dana's relationship in the present with her white husband Kevin, who, by deliberately holding on to her as she is seized by one of her disappearing convulsions, travels back with her at one point, only to find that within the new/old world in which they have landed they must take on the roles of master and slave to survive; second, and more centrally, through the complex mutual dependence and connection the enslaved Dana and the em-powered young master Rufus must feel and work out with one another if either or both of them are to survive. Already, as Dana thinks to herself early on in the novel, the liminal horizon towards which the novel's dramatic action works is some new relationship of self and other, beyond the connections of blood, race, or sex, and past the nihilistic self- and other-destroying dialectics of master–slave: "Not," she thinks, "that I really thought a blood relationship could explain the way I had twice been drawn to him. It wouldn't. But then, neither would anything else. What we had was something new, something that didn't even have a name. Some matching strangeness in us that may or may not have come from our being related."[9] Late in the novel, as Dana meditates once again over how and when she can return to her contemporary life, she has to ask herself, "But how do I come home? Is the power mine, or do I tap some power in him?"[10] The latter question is left significantly unanswered; and the new relationship-without-a-name is shown to be unrealizable within the social relations of the time. "A slave is a slave," thinks the despairing Dana at the novel's climax, as she advances towards Rufus with the knife in her hand. "And Rufus was Rufus—erratic, alternately generous and vicious. I could accept him as my ancestor, my younger brother, my friend, but not as my master, and not as my lover."[11] But with Rufus's death, and their inevitable shared failure to transcend the power-riven contradictions in which he and Dana are enmeshed, there comes a price: by murdering him, Dana is at last literally set free from history, but she returns to her contemporary world and marriage less than whole, minus an arm that has been ripped away from her body and sucked back into the literal and figurative wall through which she re-emerges, free at last.

In this early novel the price of failure to deconstruct power, to bridge and connect, is clearly thematized as mutilation. In her subsequent fiction, however, Butler has not shrunk from depicting the full measure of terror, repulsion, and dis-ease that must be felt and worked through as the self mutating towards Otherness becomes Other to itself. In *Clay's Ark* (1984), that measure is figured as the sickness engendered by the invasion of a virus-like alien agent brought back in the contaminated exploratory spacecraft of the novel's title, and spread by the crew's lone survivor, Eli. Such a familiar enabling premise evokes a wide run of 50s SF films and literature, with their thinly disguised paranoia over the contaminating power of hostile foreign ideologies (chiefly the bad C-word) from beyond. Yet in *Clay's Ark* both premise and subsequent drama are mutated, in the same way as the virus-figure is; in Butler's novel, as one infected character explains to another fresh "convert," the invasive agent is a "symbiont" which "doesn't use cells up the way a virus does. It combines with them, lives with them, divides with them, changes them just a little."[12] And those who survive the initial onslaught of their permanent disease, far from suffering the de-eroticized zombification of the folks in *Invasion of the Body Snatchers*, find their needs for food and for contaminating touch and sex as heightened as their newly sharpened night-creature senses. Indeed, for the small desert community comprised by Eli and those he has infected—a community described in ways that brilliantly fuse our memories of the organic-communalist experiments of the sixties (for example, Steven Gaskin's Farm, with its blend of Old Testament gender division and New Age collectivism) with our current nightmare-images of the feverish, wasted bodies of those with AIDS— the problem becomes precisely how to negotiate the tension between the need for touch and connection and the horrifying prospect of spreading the infection through the world. As Eli himself reminds a member of the group, "We've lost part of our humanity. We can lose more without even realizing it. All we have to do is forget what we carry, and what it needs."[13] The shaky compromise this infected New Age community reaches with itself is to stay out in the desert and limit themselves to nabbing, contaminating, and absorbing the fewest number of hapless road travellers possible. As another member of the group explains to another new convert, "If not for people like you—people we have to catch and keep, I could never control myself enough . . . With no outlet it gets . . . painful and crazy, sort of frenzied when there are a lot of unconverted people around. I have dreams about suddenly finding myself moving through a crowd—maybe on a big city street. Moving through a crowd where I have no choice but to keep touching people. I don't even know whether to call it a nightmare or not. I'm on automatic. It's just happening."[14]

Given the limits of a short essay, I'll forego a summary and analysis of *Clay's Ark*'s plot; suffice it to say that by the novel's end the liberal-progressive Dr. Blake has failed in his attempt to spare himself and his daughters from capture and contamination; Keira, his one remaining daughter, has more-or-less "voluntarily" (insofar as any "infected" action undertaken is voluntary, if you know what I mean) joined the group; and the "symbiont" has escaped and is being spread around the world, with results as unforeseeable as the nature and fate of the strong, feral, and faintly visionary children who have already been born to the group.

Having modelled a new world of partial identities, of the kind of linkage to both animality and alien complexity which is, in effect, an embodied definition of Haraway's liberatory cyborg, Butler's open ending, with all its horror and promise, marks "that boundary or limit beyond which thought cannot go," as Jameson asserts of SF endings in general.[15] What I want to point to here, however, is the very explicitness with which it does so in Butler's work, and the extent to which that limit is not just one of thought but of political and social practice as well. *I don't know whether to call it a nightmare or not*—that sentence and that sentiment might well stand as the boundary line or warning track of our own collective postmodern project, and as the honest emblem of our own horrors and hopes in what Jane Flax calls "our transitional state" as we seek in thought and practice "how to understand and (re-)constitute the self, gender, knowledge, social relations, and culture without resorting to linear, teleological, hierarchical, holistic, or binary ways of thinking,"[16] and as at least some of the old boundary lines, to our terror and delight, begin to give way. For the "problem of dealing with difference without constituting an opposition," which Jane Callop once speculated "may be what feminism is all about,"[17] is increasingly what progressive politics and possibility is about across the board. We see it in the struggle against racism as the project of constructing what Stuart Hall recently called "a difference that matters, but does not need to will itself to power ... an ethnicity which is situated without needing to stand in a position of authority";[18] in the various peace and Central America movements as the struggle to move beyond a world-vision founded on a Manichaean polar opposition to one based on interdependence and equality; in the environmental movement as the struggle to shed the increasingly destructive view of Man (*sic*) versus Nature for a responsibly lived sense of humanity *within* it; and even in traditional left-marxist politics and theory as the problem of "contradictions among the people," that is, of the post-Leninist construction of an effective counter-hegemonic bloc across the manifold divisions of stratum and class.

Let me begin to bring this chapter to a close, then, by summarizing what I have tried to argue: that, first of all, the very efflorescence of a highly literary science fiction in the 1960s was itself paradoxically the sign of a certain exhaustion of content, of the bankruptcy of the utopian/ dystopian dialectic on which virtually all serious SF was based for the first hundred years of its existence; and, secondly, that much of the best and most interesting SF being written today is acting out the anxious yet queasily hopeful energies of a historically new paradigm of self as cyborg, living out a non-essentialist set of identities which are always understood as "contradictory, partial, and strategic," and engaging in equally new political struggles to construct an unprecedented unity-with-difference. Thus the interest of the work of Gibson, Sterling, Butler, and a small host of others (such as Kim Stanley Robinson, Vonda McIntyre, and Lucias Shepard) for us today—an interest which might well reward our attention even more than do those complex and fashionable SF films like *Alien(s)*, *Blade Runner*, *The Terminator*, or *Brazil*, on which we have to date spilled so much ink. For, as many theorists writing on these films have noticed, from Robin Wood to Constance Penley and Barbara Creed,[19] the logic of their aesthetic practice always seems to reach an ideological sticking-point along the route of a postmodern politics of difference beyond which they cannot go, except to hit the wall of conservative recuperation and containment. That sticking-point is well to the right of those limits of embodiment and representation reached in the print SF I have been describing here, if only by virtue of the far greater capital-intensiveness of mass-market film, compared to book publishing.

But let me leave you now with a challenge to see for yourself. Try reading the politics of (post)modernity and (post)maternity of *Aliens'* Ripley against those of Lilith in Octavia Butler's newest novel, *Dawn*; or read *Blade Runner* against *Count Zero*, or *Schismatrix* against *Brazil*. But no—no, really, do Butler's *Dawn* first. It's actually a weird sort of complicated and redeemed slave narrative, in which Lilith, the main character, and a whole bunch of other people have been preserved after the destruction of the Earth and kept alive by these, well, *beings* called Oankali, who have this really different sex/gender system, and who are now tampering with the people's genes, and who are sort of their masters and sort of not, so the question becomes are they human or not, are they enslaved or not, do they want to and how can they escape, and which disintegrations *do* we look forward to, anyway?

But I really should stop here; the last thing I want to do with this stuff, after all, is give away how it all comes out.

(1988)

NOTES

1. Fredric Jameson, "Progress Versus Utopia: or, Can We Imagine the Future?" in *Art After Modernism: Rethinking Representation*, ed. Brian Wallis (Boston: David R. Godine, 1984), p. 245.

2. Joanna Russ, *The Female Man* (1975; rpt. Boston: Beacon Press, 1986) pp. 213–14.

3. Janet Bergstrom draws our attention to this aspect of *Blade Runner* and other contemporary SF films in "Androids and Androgyny," *Camera Obscura* 15 (Fall 1986), pp. 38 ff.

4. William Gibson, *Neuromancer* (New York: Berkley Publishing Group, 1984), p. 43.

5. Donna Haraway, "A Manifesto for Cyborgs: Science, Technology, and Socialist Feminism in the 1980s," *Socialist Review* 80 (1985), p. 72.

6. Ibid., p. 81.

7. William Gibson, *Count Zero* (New York: Arbor House, 1986), p. 1.

8. Gillian Skerrow, "Hellivision: An Analysis of Videogames," in Colin McCabe, ed., *High Theory/Low Culture: Analysing Popular Television and Film* (New York: St. Martin's Press, 1986), p. 130.

9. Octavia Butler, *Kindred* (Garden City NY: Doubleday, 1979), p. 29.

10. Ibid., p. 247.

11. Ibid., p. 260.

12. Octavia Butler, *Clay's Ark* (New York: St. Martin's Press, 1984), p. 37.

13. Ibid., p. 104.

14. Ibid., p. 50.

15. Jameson, p. 241.

16. Jane Flax, "Postmodernism and Gender Relations in Feminist Theory," *Signs* 12, 4 (Summer 1987), p. 622.

17. Jane Gallop, *Feminism and Psychoanalysis*, as quoted in Laura Mulvey "Changes: Thoughts on Myth, Narrative and Historical Experience," *History Workshop* 23 (Spring 1987).

18. Stuart Hall, "Rethinking Popular Culture," talk presented at the Center for the Humanities, Wesleyan University, Middletown, Connecticut, April 11, 1988.

19. See Robin Wood's reading of *Blade Runner* in *Hollywood from Vietnam to Reagan* (New York: Columbia University Press, 1985), Barbara Creed's remarks on *Aliens* in "From Here to Modernity: Feminism and Postmodernism," *Screen* 28, 2 (Spring 1987), and Constance Penley's carefully hedged argument for *The Terminator* in "Time Travel, Primal Scene, and the Critical Dystopia," *Camera Obscura* 15 (Fall 1986).

PART II

"Makin' Flippy-Floppy":

Postmodernism and the

Baby-Boom PMC

Fredric Jameson's "Postmodernism, or the Cultural Logic of Late Capitalism" seems to be the last word on the subject of postmodernism, and/or on the postmodern subject.[1] Ranging magisterially over a wide array of aesthetic practices and terrains from Pop Art to poetry, from contemporary "retro" films to L.A.'s Bonaventure Hotel, Jameson provides us with a stunning phenomenology of the postmodern: what, he asks, is it like to be in the presence of this object, to watch this sort of film or read this book, to stand or move in this peculiar architectural "hyper-space"? His answers are a *tour de force* of existential description, which in turn underwrites the credibility of his larger claim that the common characteristics he has discovered in these works—their depthlessness, ahistoricity, and centerlessness in particular, with all their associated effects—together compose what he calls the "cultural dominant" of late capitalism *tout court*.[2] For Jameson, the postmodern sensibility is essentially the effect or reflection of the deep structure of the latest stage in the capitalist mode of production, which, having reconstituted itself on a new, even more multinationalized and penetrative basis, is seen to be all ready to catch the next Kondratieff wave.

Jameson's Postmodernism thus takes its place alongside Lukács's Realism: the former stands in relation to multinational or late capitalism in the same way the latter stands to the "golden age" of industrial capital, as an aesthetic expression of the mode of production as totality, and as a part of that totality itself. It is not my purpose in the present chapter to dispute this claim nor to enter the long lists of those engaged with the totality question, that philospher's stone (along with ideology) of Marxist theory. What I want to argue instead is simply that the totalizing power of such a Lukacsian depiction, in its bid to offer itself not only as final word but as full story, ought to be resisted. For underneath the apparent naturalness and inevitability of "postmodernism" and "late capitalism" as what Gramsci calls "organic movements" lies another level of unnatural, willed and contingent reality—the reality of the "conjuncture."[3] Such a distinction is crucial for us as cultural and political agents; for the "organic" in all its achieved naturalness is always the effect of innumerable conjunctural struggles won or lost, on the cultural, political, and economic levels alike. The organic, the totality, may set its limits above us, demarcate our moving space; but it is only on the level of the conjunctural that we in turn can act and move to change the space's shape and trajectory.

What follows is an analysis of postmodernism not as the inevitable extrusion of an entire mode of production but as a cultural-aesthetic set of pleasures and practices created by and for a particular social group at a determinate moment in its collective history. Specifically, I will be arguing that postmodernism is preeminently the "expressive form" of the "social and material life-experience" of my own generation and class,[4] respectively designated as the "baby boom" and the "professional-managerial class," or PMC.[5] To make this argument, I will need to describe that "life-experience," or at least its main determinants, at some length, if still too sketchily to qualify as a full treatment; only then will we return to postmodernist works themselves, at which point some of their most distinctive features may become legible in new and newly salient ways. This chapter's main value will stand or fall on the extent to which it states the obvious—beginning with the obvious fact that most postmodern culture is first and foremost a production of and for a numerically large and privileged generation, the majority of whom is placed in a uniquely ambivalent relationship to, that is to say, on the very hinge of, the capital–labor contradiction which both underwrites and undermines capitalism as much as ever, albeit in new, more complex and elaborate ways.

Before proceeding to this task, however, it is probably necessary to establish quite firmly a fact which stands behind and enables all that will follow here: namely, that the generation of the baby boom is also generally describable as a class. For if it be accepted that what Stanley Aronowitz has called the "technical intelligentsia," the Ehrenreichs the "PMC," Albert and Hahnel the "coordinators,"[6] is by any or all of these names a class—or class fraction, if you will—we must also come to grips with the reality that the overwhelming majority of those United States citizens who in 1980 were between 25 and 35 years of age were members of that class, at least occupationally. Of the 37.4 million citizens between those ages, 22.2 million were employed in 1980 in managerial and professional specialty occupations (engineers, architects, computer scientists, systems analysts); health diagnosing occupations (primarily dentists and doctors); in health assessment and treating (licensed nurses and therapists); as teachers, librarians and counselors; and in technical, sales, and administrative support occupations (lower-level managerial—not including salesclerks in stores).[7] That's 59 percent of all 25–35 year olds, 82 percent of all those employed.[8] Clearly, such amazing statistics are rife with implications, chief among which must be their effects on our reading of the recent history of class struggle in the U.S. On the one hand, they lend credence to theories of the *embourgeoisement* and massification of the U.S. working class, whose children, we may well surmise, have been groomed and encouraged to fly the coop outward and upward, at the expense of old class traditions, networks and ties. Yet they also suggest a degree of successful class struggle as well, insofar as upward mobility for the next generation in terms of work status, if not actual remuneration, was an implicit but very real political demand of the 1950s and 60s—a demand which had already brought up to "a quarter of the sons of skilled blue-collar workers and close to a fifth of the sons of semi-skilled workers . . . into the PMC" by the mid-sixties, according to one study noted by the Ehrenreichs,[9] and which emerged explicitly in the "open university" and "open admission" struggles of the 1960s and early 70s. The statistics attest to a striking convergence of middle- and working-class trajectories in the post-war period as, through the 1950s, 60s, and 70s, the bulk of the baby boom was funneled into the professional-managerial class by pressures from above and below. It is this common experience we must now examine, albeit necessarily in schematic and abstracted form—for it is this specific experiential matrix from which postmodernism draws its life.

I

FROM BABY BOOM TO PMC: A SOCIAL HISTORY

The private sphere

And you may find yourself
  in a beautiful house
  with a beautiful wife,
And you may ask yourself—
  Well . . . how did I get here?

(Talking Heads, "Once in a Lifetime,"
    Remain in Light [1980])

So hold me, Mom, in your long
arms.
In your automatic arms. Your
electronic arms. In your long
arms.

(Laurie Anderson, "O Superman,"
    Big Science [1982])

By the private sphere, I mean those spaces and experiences set off and against the public realms of economy and the state—chiefly, in other words, those networks of kinship and collectivity which we call friends and family, those experiences we group together as our private or personal lives.[10] Yet the most striking transformation in this private sphere for both middle and working classes in post World War II America is precisely the invasion and colonization of its hitherto sacrosanct territory by new economic and political exigencies and concerns. Here I am referring first and foremost to that network of politico-economic strategies and decisions which underlay the mass movement out of the cities and into the suburbs in the 1940s and 1950s.[11] Suburbanization, not affordable urban public housing, was the combined reply of business and state interests to the potentially dangerous popular demand for affordable space in the post-war years; and it proved a most effective solution. All those Levittowns and census tracts, loosely tied together by federally funded expressways and beltways, those interminable circuits of "living units" splayed out around the cities' decaying cores, not only made a fine living for whole hosts of speculators and developers—much of it, of course, on federally guaranteed low-interest mortgages and loans—by literally distancing both blue- and white-collar workers from their place of work, by snapping the nuclear family out and away from wider networks of neighborhood, kin and clan; they also boosted consumption while simultaneously shrinking both the private and public sphere. Workplace and neighborhood cultures effectively dried up and disappeared; now the attenuated family "unit" stayed home in its own private living room and watched TV.

By breaking up these old communal networks and cultures, suburbanization thus paved the way for the commodification of daily life on a newly expanded scale. For wives and mothers in particular, as Ehrenreich and English have made stunningly clear, hordes of commodities and experts offered themselves in exchange for those cheaper, friendlier, more socialized functions and services of the past—and offered dire prophecies of what would come if the whites weren't white enough, the car not new enough, the house not kept pretty and picked up.[12] The official goal of all this spending and striving was a level of privatized consumption and attainment exaggerated even by previous middle-class standards; yet it was, to a very real extent, the only goal or life-model in town. And one consequence of these new quantitatively higher standards of consumption was, paradoxically enough, that more and more women sneaked out of their gilded cages, found paying jobs, and went (back) to waged work in the public sphere.

Yet this movement in turn coexisted uneasily with a whole different set of expectations, also brilliantly evoked in For Her Own Good, for childrearing.[13] Even as the state took over more responsibility for the child's formal socialization through increased public schooling, and even as the television, that most effective and anonymous of all informal socializers, reached more greedily and precisely for the child's attention span, mothers were saddled with increasingly exclusive responsibility for the proper, scientifically guided and tested formation of the infant self. Insofar as the child is seen as a possible candidate for PMC status, and PMC status as the nearest thing to a guarantee of the good life, the importance of proper childrearing becomes paramount; for if this status is viewed as attainable through individual merit, rather than by inheritance, and it is further agreed that "a child's future achievement is determined by the nuances of its early upbringing,"[14] then the science of childraising is everything. It is, in fact, far too important to be left to women themselves, who must be cautioned and advised at every turn, lest they either suffocate the child in too much love, stunt it permanently with maternal deprivation, or ruin its chances in yet some other way.

For Her Own Good plausibly locates one source of contemporary "second-wave" feminism in the impossible double-bind dilemmas that suburbanized and/or middle-class mothers and housewives were forced to live during these Cold War years of the Great Barbecue: confined to a space simultaneously more privatized and more colonized than ever before, at once pushed out toward the (waged) workworld for that oh-so-useful second income, and pressed back into the atomized home to fulfill her rightful role as full-time mother under the watchful eye of distant experts from Dr. Gesell to Benjamin Spock.[15] For our purposes, however, it is more important to sum up all the transformations described so far within the private sphere in terms of their cumulative effect on the traditional oedipal "family romance" of engenderment and individuation. The extreme separation of working life from hearth and home, production from leisure time, and, indeed, the withering of the entire public sphere effected by suburbanization and the spread of TV, transform the hitherto socially backed authority of the Father into an increasingly diminished and abstract principle. It is symptomatic, not coincidental, that at no time in its ten-year-plus run on TV did Ozzie and Harriet ever disclose where, or even if, the affable, bemused Ozzie worked. At the same time, however, Mother was implicitly invested with a new if always dubious authority, by being saddled with the exclusive responsibility for the primary socialization of the child. Such transformations, together with the entrance of increasing numbers of women into the paid workforce, serve to erode (but not, as yet, wholly dissolve) the socially constructed polarities around which gendered identities had formerly been constructed: for example, male = authority/autonomy/ freedom/power/public sphere, female = nurturance/identification/

connectedness/love/private sphere. And the result of these partial dissolutions is in turn a partial dissolution, decentering and devaluation of the autonomous ego (together, of course, with its fully inflatable, completely internalized super-ego)—which in turn is variously deplored as the road to a narcissistic, spectacularized hell and cautiously celebrated and encouraged as a first step toward a "true differentiation" in which "mutuality and autonomy, nurturance and freedom, identification and separation" would be united in "creative tension" with one another within the single self.[16]

The public sphere

I see the states
　　across this big nation
I see the laws
　　made in Washington DC
I think of the ones
　　I consider my favorites
I think of the people who are
　　working for me

　　(Talking Heads, "Don't Worry
　　About the Government,"
　　Talking Heads 1977 [1977])

When TV signals are sent out, they don't stop. They keep going. They pick up speed as they leave the solar system. By now, the first TV programs ever made have been traveling for over thirty years. They are well beyond our solar system now. All those characters from cowboy serials, variety hours and quiz shows are sailing out. They are the first true voyagers into deep space. And they sail farther and farther out, intact, still talking.

　　(Laurie Anderson,
　　United States, Parts I–IV [1979–83])

Rather than linger over these substantive debates about the decline of oedipality, however, let us move on to consider the configurations of the public world which confronts the post World War II PMC-bound subject. In this archetypal story of the socialization of our typical baby-boom PMCer, be he/she working- or middle-class in background, acquaintance with the actual world of production comes last. (Indeed, for at least some of those from middle-class backgrounds, it is an hour that hardly strikes at all.) Here a personal anecdote may serve in lieu of fuller explanation and development to come. I come from a small factory town and vividly remember, from somewhere in the late 1950s in the middle of my elementary school years, a day when the teacher asked us what our fathers (just fathers, of course) actually did for a living. Most of us, middle-class and working-class alike, realized—with some trepidation and anxiety, I seem to remember—that we had no idea, not a clue; and my guess is that our ignorance was typical of the times.

If the realm of production appeared to us only as an absent or misty shape, it was no more veiled than the shape of the state, no more obscure than the notion of political struggle. Politics for most of us found no place in the privatized household; while at school, from primary to college, American politics and history were at best delivered up to us in a narrative as a series of "social problems" addressed and eventually resolved by a happily coincident series of great men, who thus rose to the top.[17] These were, of course, until late in the 1960s, the golden years of the "American Century," in which our country happily and profitably served as the "policeman of the world," and of the joyously proclaimed "end of ideology," years when organized labor was largely bought off and incorporated, thanks to the induced consumerist hunger of its rank and file from below and state coercion from above, and when U.S. foreign investment and military might lived on a seemingly perpetual round-the-world honeymoon with one another, virtually undisturbed by any rivals. The formative notion of our politics, which still remains alive behind subsequent shocks and revaluations, was a bizarre combination of meritocratic-professionalist and consumerist ideologies whose most perfect expression is probably still the image of JFK (unless and until replaced with that of Reagan), as the ultimate in snappy looks (a good image, an attractive commodity) and problem-solving pragmatism (from "The Freeze" to any number of "new ideas" candidacies).

The inculcation of meritocratic-professionalist ideology is, of course, the special mission of our educational system, with all its up-to-date methods of testing, tracking, and evaluation.[18] Most notable for our purposes, however, at least in state-supported post-secondary education, is the profound diversification and specialization during this period of what we may accurately describe as the "knowledge industry," now rationalized into a new set of class-divided and dividing "layers" or "tiers"—vo-tech schools and community colleges, public and private universities— each of which is itself further fragmented from within by new subdisciplines and specialized areas with their own jargons or idiolects.[19] We need to understand this development dialectically: it is not merely the result of state-industrial imperatives, or some *zeitgeist* of specialization, but of pressure from below as well, not least from the desire of corporatized working-class parents both to send their children to college and to secure for them a specific, marketable set of techniques and skills. The consequence of such rationalization and fragmentation, however, as Terry Eagleton has recently noted, has been the virtual dissolution of the university as an autonomous public sphere and its reconstitution as meritocratically legitimated sorting mechanism for the market in labor power.[20] The baby-boom PMCers witnessed and embodied (and, occasionally, rebelled against) this transition, briefly standing to speak at campus rallies and demonstrations for "free speech" on behalf of an ephemeral public sphere of which their own presence signalled the demise.

Nothing, finally, epitomizes the utter subsumption and fragmentation of the public sphere at the hands of the market more succinctly, or conveys the ideology of consumerism more effectively, than the television we grew up watching. For most of us, in fact, television was all the public sphere we had: it brought us the world in the comfort, safety, and privacy of our living rooms; it told us what was happening, what the new looks, the new products were, what was news; it kept us in touch, it came from a space or realm beyond discussion, not only in the sense that we had (and have) no control over what's on, but in its overwhelming physical-visual credibility; and it landed in a space which at the time at least was beneath discussion—the realm of hearth and home, where, as Todd Gitlin says, "our guard is down when we watch."[21] Such a trajectory gave television enormous power—power to scoop up our attention and sell it to advertisers, to socialize us into uniformly depoliticized citizens, to negotiate and promote on a national level the very definitions of what is legitimate and desirable. Television is thus, as we shall see, on even the deepest levels of aesthetic-dramatic rhythm and form, the *lingua franca* of this generation and class; at the same time, its deployment constitutes the *sine qua non* of what John Brenkman has called the "mass-mediated public sphere" at work, a sphere, or pseudo-sphere (in the sense in which it is finally only an uninhabitable mirage), which "is formed only as it continually appropriates, dismantles, and reassembles the signifying practices of social groups."[22]

Production and the PMC

So think about this little scene
Apply it to your life
If your work isn't what you love
Then something isn't right

Just think of Bob and Judy
They're happy as can be
Inventing situations
Putting them on TV

(Talking Heads, "Found a Job,"
*More Songs About Buildings and
Food* [1978])

They grow it in those farmlands
Then they bring it to the store
They put it in their car trunks
Then they bring it back home

And I say
I wouldn't live there
    if you paid me

(Talking Heads, "The Big Country,"
*More Songs About Buildings and
Food* [1978])

The classic definition of the PMC's place in the relations of production of contemporary capitalism is, of course, the Ehrenreichs': situated "between labor and capital," the PMC consists of "salaried mental workers who do not own the means of production and whose major function in the social division of labor may be described broadly as the reproduction of capitalist culture and capitalist class relations."[23]

Such a site has no clear borderlines on either side. Those placed in the top income brackets of what the U.S. Bureau of the Census calls "managerial and professional specialty occupations," for example, may be politically as fully recuperated by capital as nurses or elementary and secondary teachers, at the bottom of this salariat, are recuperable by labor. Yet it includes all those responsible for administrating, rehabilitating, ameliorating, mediating—in short, of reproducing the capital–labor relation, from the point of production, where the industrial engineer is deployed, to the dizzy, whirling realms of distribution and realization, where the admen and marketing people live with all their retinues, from the provinces of social service workers, those colorless halls in which the "safety nets" are spread out for those qualified to be caught up in them, to those most apparently abstracted and autonomous realms of "cultural production" from MGM in L.A. to Mary Boone in Soho to New Haven's Yale.

What binds these obviously gelatinous and heterogeneous "middle strata" together as a class, though, is more than this external, functional description; it is also constituted by a class ethos which includes as one of its leading elements an internal set of norms, values, and attitudes towards work—both the work we do, and the work of our parents and peers in the old middle and working class. This "mind-set" towards work is overdetermined and accentuated by generational difference, but is nonetheless fundamentally enabled by the peculiar nature of PMC work processes themselves, dependent as they are for their proper functioning on some combination of the internalization of bureaucratized norms (academic and/or legal regulations, company policy, etc.), specialized discourses and behaviors ("being a professional"), and, not least, an almost guildlike sense of individual autonomy and ability within the more-or-less horizontally perceived company of one's peers, with whom one not only works but "networks" for the final satisfaction of each and all.[24] Such requirements and values (for which the way is laid, as we have seen, by education) differ markedly both from those of traditional middle-class and/or petit-bourgeois sectors (that is, from both the "organization man" and the small-scale entrepreneur), and from traditional working-class notions of solidarity and cohesion in the face of direct pressures and controls applied from above. For the PMC, by contrast, Foucault's otherwise rather dubious ontology of power is experientially true. His view that power, "permanent, repetitious, inert, and self-reproducing," has no definable or limitable sources, "comes from everywhere,"[25] has been met with such acclaim by PMC intellectuals here precisely because the mixture of canniness and befuddlement it contains and effects expresses the perspective of an entire class, an entire way of life.

On the one hand the particular durée of PMC working life, with its historically strange concatenations of contingent work assignment or project, bureaucratized procedure, and internalized norms of professional conduct; on the other hand, the sense of self as a member of a profession, with all that entails, from possession of specialized skills and training to vocational pride and identification. If, looking up from this vantage point and with these values, up through the layers they themselves compose, the PMC finds it hard to fix on the ruling class, it can likewise only look back and down at the working class across an enormous gulf of differing meanings, values and experiences constituted first and foremost by differences in work. Yet we should not forget that this gulf is often enough a literal, physical fact as well: much PMC working life is utterly different and separate from any large-scale organized industrial produc-tion of material things; such production, in any case, is truly disappearing from our national landscape. As Mike Davis notes in "The Political Economy of Late-Imperial America," an article whose argument we shall have occasion to examine in more detail below, during the 1980–82 recessionary period alone, while blue-collar employment fell by 12 per-cent, the number of managers and administrators grew by 9 per cent.[26] Similar transformations characterize the entire post-war period; their sharper pace and greater visibility at present are merely one more symptom that the benefits of the post-war accords between organized labor, big business and the federal government have been derived and used up by all—those in the upper brackets of labor who gave up control over the shop floor and investment policy in exchange for wage increases for themselves and social mobility for their children; those corporations who poured the profits from post-war consumerism and productivity gains to U.S. military-backed investment in new plant and production abroad with low slave-labor wage inputs, or into purely speculative enterprise: and the government which, in this new situation, now finds it necessary to switch the focus of its already truncated Keynesianism from consumerism and the social wage to military spending (the military remaining as vanguard of what is left of the domestic economy and as guarantor of U.S. capital's newly expanded, multinationalized accords).[27] In their childhood and adolescence, they were major benefi-ciaries, unwitting dupes and target audiences of and for the old post-war capital–labor–government accords, but today's baby-boom PMC finds itself a critical stake in the formation of this new regime—though, so far at least, hardly a fully knowing or mobilized agent in its construction.

II
POSTMODERNISM, CULTURE OF THE PMC

Having thus limned the overall constituent features of PMC construction in the postwar period, I am now finally in a position to analyze postmodernism—or at least a sector of it, a postmodernism within the Postmodernism Jameson has described—specifically as the culture of this same PMC, a reworking into aesthetic form of its central experiences, preoccupations, and themes. Such constitutive elements, of course, do not neatly sort themselves out in any one-to-one way as delimitable causes, sources or origins of postmodernist work, but rather appear within the works we shall examine as the more or less mediated social aspects of an overdetermined aesthetic-cultural field. As Brecht once said, our problem lies not with the concept of determination itself, but with the fact that there are always so many of them—and this fact holds no less true for culture than for any other kind of human endeavour. Inevitably, in the analysis that follows, we will be dividing up the terrain of postmodernism into categorial aspects whose separateness is provisional and heuristic at best, and mapping the same ground on a number of overlapping grids. Searching out the level of the concrete through such tracings and retracings is, finally, the only way to do justice to the social object under study—by which here I mean both the PMC and its cultural universe—and avoid the pernicious temptation of first fixing on, then projecting, totalizing, and judging, that object's single origin or end.

a common thesis (among both Marxists and non-Marxists) about the nature of contemporary culture which I myself once embraced: that there has been, in contemporary American society and culture as a whole, "a decisive breakdown in the hitherto antagonistic yet mutually dependent categories of high culture on the one hand, mass or 'popular' culture on the other."[28] To such a statement, it is quite easy to staple any number of equally global assertions concerning, say, the collapse of culture as a zone of relative autonomy, the infiltration of the Symbolic through all other categories, the divorce and free-floating release of the Signifier from the Signified—assertions which I object to now not on the grounds that they are false, but rather that they are incompletely and unevenly true. To return to our opening example, we may ask: for whom is the "breakdown" of the mass/high culture distinction more real, the American working class or the PMC? The answer is as salutary as it is obvious, insofar as it brings us back to the concrete question of what constellation of specific social practices and experiences enables such a breakdown to take place, and is affected in its turn by it—back to, among other factors, the concatenated effects of a long and deep acquaintance with consumer culture on and off the tube and the acquired taste for high culture which it is the business of the liberal arts "component" of a college education to transmit.

Thanks to these and other class-specific experiences, then, our PMC subject typically finds him/herself an extraordinarily well-rounded, complete cultural consumer and connoisseur, eminently capable of taking pleasure in a spectrum of choices (all within postmodernist territory, as we shall see) ranging from just a step ahead of mass culture (the low, stoned funkiness of *Saturday Night Live*) to just a foot short of high (the Glass/Wilson "opera" *Einstein on the Beach*). We can, in fact, quite easily construct the array of postmodernist works from which we shall be drawing our examples in what follows along just such a spectrum, from general accessibility and relatively low mediation to limited access and its associated formalist highs:

Saturday Night Live	*Ghost-busters*	*Repo Man*	Talking Heads	Laurie Anderson	*Einstein on the Beach*
mass culture					high culture

What common aspects of these works—a popular television show, a blockbuster film and an independent feature, an art-rock band, a performance artist, and an avant-garde spectacle of new music, dramaturgy and dance—reproduce the social experience and constitution of the present-day PMC and, in doing so, enable us to describe them as postmodernist? We are now prepared to provide some partial descriptions and tentative reconstructions in answer to this question.

I *Deindividualization and the déjà lu*

Bud: Hey, Look at that. Look
    at those assholes . . .
Ordinary fuckin' people
I hate 'em.

    (*Repo Man* [Alex Cox, 1984])

You're walking. And you don't
    always realize it,
But you're always falling.
With each step, you fall forward
    slightly.

Home . . . is where I want to be
But I guess I'm already there

> (Talking Heads, "This Must
> Be the Place (Naive Melody),"
> *Speaking in Tongues* [1982])

This is the time.
And this is the record of the
    time.

> Laurie Anderson, "From the Air,"
> *Big Science* [1982])

And then catch yourself from
    falling.
Over and over you're falling
And then catching yourself
    from falling
And this is how you can be walking
    and falling at the same time.

> (Laurie Anderson,
> "Walking and Falling,"
> *Big Science* [1982])

Like all the constitutive features of postmodernism I will be discussing
here, deindividualization emerges through both form and content. In
works near the mass culture "pole" of our spectrum, of course, its
presence is so obvious as to be virtually beneath comment: all the
characters in the quick sketches that compose a *Saturday Night Live*
program are obviously, deliberately two-dimensional piles of mass media
stereotypes and PMC "lifestyle" clichés (for example, two PMC
"singles" out on a date). Similarly, on the high culture end of our scale,
in *Einstein on the Beach* there is no question of identifying (with) any
speaker or *actant* on the stage as an individualized character, given both
the assemblages of discontinuous slogans, pop culture quotations, and
stray verbal junk that comprise the opera's spoken utterances—for
example:

I feel the earth move under my feet, I feel tumbling down tumbling down. I
feel it. Some ostriches are like into a satchel. Some like them . . .

One of the most beautiful streets of Paris is called 'Les Champs Elysée,' which
means: The Elysian Fields. 'It is very broad, bordered with trees, and very
pleasant to look at.

SWEARING TO GOD   WHO LOVES YOU
FRANKIE VALLI   THE FOUR SEASONS[29]

—and the utterly depersonalized (hieratically intoned or recited deadpan; drawn out or repeated *ad nauseam*) mode of their utterance. So,
too, David Byrne, the singer/composer of the art-rock band Talking
Heads, "sings" the tag-end, often slightly askew common language
clichés and phrases which make up the lyrics of his songs in rigid

enunciations punctuated by atonal swoops and squawks; in live concert
he alternately stands tensely at the mike, eyes staring straight forward,
bugging and glazed, and twitches spastically and/or mechanically about
the stage. Laurie Anderson blocks what we might call the "expressivity
effect" that simultaneously renders the performer a distinct, unique
individual and, enfolding us within that expressivity, confirms our own
sense of unique "personhood" as well. By alternately recycling her voice
through a variety of distorting electrical filters (through which it may
emerge, for example, as either that of an electrified child or a playback of
a white businessman's voice at a slightly dragging speed) and assuming a
breathy affectlessness inflected only by a tinge of boredom and a *soupçon*
of religious awe—like the tone of the recorded operator on the phone as
it tells you just what time it is about to become—she gives her voice a
"duplicity" which, as Janet Kardon has said, "re-peoples an absent self,
or more accurately, a self that is turned down almost to zero."[30]

We may thus view this thematic of deindividualization along our
mass–high culture spectrum as running from the utterly stereotypical and
clichéd (*Saturday Night Live*), through meretricious or merely shallow
emptiness (*Ghostbusters'* Bill Murray character, Dr. Peter Venkman, or
Repo Man's Otto) to nearly total effacement and dispersal (Talking
Heads, Laurie Anderson, *Einstein on the Beach*). And such a continuum
in turn supplies us with an important clue to the whole thematic's
rootedness in that dialectic of colonization and privatization we have
already described in our discussion of the "private sphere" above, insofar
as it mimes the ceaseless process of the consumerized self's construction,
fragmentation, and dissolution at the hands of a relentless invasive world
of products. As William Leiss has it, within what he overly tactfully
refers to as the "high-intensity market setting," the privatized subject
learns "to identify states of feeling systematically with appropriate types
of commodities":

> The vast number and variety of material objects enjoins the person to break
> down states of feeling into progressively smaller components and instructs
> him in the delicate art of recombining the pieces fittingly. The "wholeness,"
> the integration of the components, tends to become a property of the
> commodities themselves . . . [The] fragmentation of needs requires on the
> individual's part a steadily more intensive effort to hold together his identity
> and personal integrity. In concrete terms this amounts to spending more and
> more time in consumption activities.[31]

Postmodernist work may recode this perpetual vicious cycle of constructing oneself and dispersing into heaps of *de trop* rubble—of "walking and
falling" as Laurie Anderson has it—in a variety of ways, and strike a

variety of attitudes towards it. One attitude might be the instantly self-cancelling nostalgia for the authenticity of the non-coded, non-commodified "real" expressed in the Talking Heads line quoted at the beginning of this section. Something like the same reluctance to part with the concept of the non-commodified self may play its part in *Repo Man*'s depiction of its main character. Otto (Emilio Estevez) is at first pointedly distinguished from all those who, like his friend Kevin (shown singing a 7-Up jingle in a mindless trance as he stocks the supermarket shelves) or his zonked-out parents (in late-hippie costume, slack eyes glued to the born-again evangelist shilling on the screen), live only under the sign of the commodity; yet, lacking any other means of characterization outside of or beyond just such signifying systems, the film can only recode him as a numbly reactive vacuity throughout most of the rest of its length. Similarly, the central guarantee of Bill Murray's Peter Venkman in *Ghostbusters* as "our hero" is a level of crass self-interest so low as to be resistant to any of the stereotypical roles that ensnare, delude and trivialize the film's secondary characters, from the EPA zealot to Riek Morani's techno-twit PMCer, Venkman's dialectical Other, whom the film systematically lampoons and derides.

One attitude, then, towards the commodification and fragmentation of the self is horror and disgust towards those trapped in and defined by the endlessly proliferating codes, clichés and slogans of everyday life: a horror whose underlying anxiety that even the subject him/herself feeling it is not "free" emerges in the mumbled choruses of Talking Heads' "Once in a Lifetime" ("Same as it ever was ... same as it ever was ..."), and which, in both this and other Talking Heads' songs, as well as in Bud's casually savage, off-the-cuff remark to Otto ("Ordinary fucking people, I hate 'em") is tied in turn to a specific *class* anxiety. For the life with car and home and wife threateningly conjured up in "Once in a Lifetime," the lives of the kids playing in the streets of L.A. out beyond Bud's windshield, are images which conjoin unselfconscious immersion with middle- and (urbanized, ghettoized) working-class life. The flip side for the baby-boom PMC of the attentuated, contradictory desire for "home" will be the bliss of escaping from codification and definition altogether, by dispersing and scattering oneself through the codes and clichés—what I would call, borrowing yet another line from Talking Heads, the pleasure of "Burning Down the House." And this pleasure will be a featured attraction of performances and works on the high culture end of our spectrum: the Heads themselves, Laurie Anderson, *Einstein on the Beach*.

To these already quite complex readings and ramifications of the deindividualization "thematic" we must then introduce another, more directly psychoanalytic level of complication as well. However much the decline of oedipality and the erosion of the autonomous male ego as both actuality and cultural ideal may be results of the deep structural workings, struggles, and necessities of the post-war system, they retain an important specificity and dynamic of their own. In that light, we can return to read Anderson's "Walking and Falling" not only as a description of the individual self stumbling from one commodified, fragmented signification to another, but as a cunning metaphorical exposé, from a point on the other side of oedipality—a backward glance, as it were, on the autonomous, unified, and efficacious ego as a half-truth at best. Similarly, through and beyond all the motifs of shallowness, vacuity, and dispersal we have already described, especially in their problematizing effects of narrativity itself, we may discern the problems and possibilities inscribed within the concept of the post- or non-oedipal self—just as we may usefully (mis)read "Deconstruction" in the Eagleton quotation that follows as equally a narrative/dramatic and a social process, whose problematic implications for both the aesthetic activity of plotting and the political activity of strategizing and organizing he well (if not entirely intentionally) describes:

> In a curious historical irony, the death of the free subject is now an essential condition for the preservation of that freedom in transformed style. Deconstruction rescues the heterogeneity of the subject from its hypostatiz-ation, but only at the cost of liquidating the subjective agency which might engage, politically rather than textually, with the very ideological systems which necessitated this strategy in the first place. It is for this reason that it reproduces a blending of bleakness and euphoria, affirmation and resign-ation, characteristic of the liberal humanist position.[32]

We will return to the question of the political valence of the PMC, including and especially the problem of political agency written into both its internal "character" and its pivotal position within the structure of the U.S.-dominated world capitalist system, in the closing pages of this chapter. Here, let us instead linger for one final moment over the obverse of deindividualization—the déjà lu or "always-already-read"[33] on the other side of its coin, as it were, whose constitutive omnipresence in these postmodern works we have not yet attempted to read as typically multivalent and overdetermined responses to and reworkings of the experiences of the baby-boom PMC in both the public sphere and the realm of production. One way of recovering those experiences is to analyze the pleasures offered us by and through the presence of the déjà lu in these works. Who gets the joke of Don Pardo's (resurrected seemingly unaltered from the days of that infamous game show of the 1950s, The Price is Right) announcing "Live from New York—it's Saturday Night!"? What potential delights spring from the foregrounded *bricolage* of past films and film genres in *Repo Man* and *Ghostbusters* (in the former, just for starters, *Rebel Without a Cause*, sci-fi B-films of the Cold War 1950s, and *Close Encounters of the Third Kind*; in the latter, those same 50s B-films with their small teams of heroic scientists, occult films of the 1960s and 70s, and old Andy Hardy re-runs)? In whose cultural universe are both the Einstein and the Patty Hearst figures of *Einstein on the Beach* fully resonant? Who smiles with the hippest satisfaction at the simultaneously slightly wrenched and *recherché* character of Laurie Anderson's and/or David Byrne's lines? The answer is, of course, the baby-boom PMC, but not only or simply because of its uniquely thorough and comfortable familiarity with both the mass and high branches of the culture industry. What Janet Kardon admits of Anderson's performances is generally true of all postmodernist work, even *Saturday Night Live*: "the most ingenious and educated 'get the most out of it.'"[34] Nor is there anything particularly new (or innocent) within class society about this pleasure of simple cultural recognition, of identifying oneself as a member of a small, broadly literate elect. For the PMC these simple pleasures are compounded and problematized by the lived experience, in both the public sphere and the realm of production, of what Anderson herself (following William Burroughs) describes as the "virus" of language: language devolved, that is, from medium of communication to fragmented materiality which in turn is consumed and internalized as so many fragmented discourses, political, professional, consumerist, etc., etc. The PMC pleasure of recognition is thus nicely complicated and extended by the gnawing, teasing sense that the sign or convention, even when correctly read, recognized, and comprehended, makes no real or necessary sense, supplies no true social significance. As Sigourney Weaver says to the smirking Bill Murray in *Ghostbusters*, "You don't look like a scientist, You look like a game show host." His Dr. Peter Venkman thus stands for us as an icon both of the sleaze and absence which are the end of the line for the old, unitary, unassimilated self, and of the fallen materiality of language within the fragmented ruins of the public sphere and the mystified, bureaucratized, abstracted work-world of the PMC.

II *Kenosis and apocalypse*

Miller: A lot of people don't really realize what's going on. They view life as a bunch of unconnected incidences and things. Suppose you're thinking about a plate of shrimp. Suddenly somebody'll say something like 'plate' or 'plate of shrimp,' out

It's hard to imagine
How nothing at all
Could be so exciting
Could be so much fun.

(Talking Heads, "Heaven,"
Fear of Music [1979])

of the blue, no explanation. No
point in looking for one either. It's
all part of the cosmic unconsciousness.

    (*Repo Man* [Alex Cox, 1984])

We have already established that acts of cultural recognition are
especially characteristic of the baby-boom PMC, given its unique
familiarity with the whole terrain of cultural production from mass to
high; now we need to ask more specifically what such actions feel like to
us, how and how much experientially, existentially, they mean. Bear in
mind that what is recognized, especially if it comes from or through the
pseudo-discourse of mass media, is apt to be already estranged, pried
loose from its point of origin in any genuinely social discourse or personal
experience, distorted and crystallized into an infinitely manipulable,
reproduceable fragment which, in this new stereotypical form, may be
rubbed up and recombined with any other and then returned, as
intrusively and insidiously as possible, to the consciousness of the
privatized viewer/consumer to be recognized and chosen as "my
program," "my perfume," "my song." Thus the serialized logic of the
"lifestyle" and the "taste-group" simultaneously feeds on and undermines any genuinely social discourse or collectivity; it substitutes the
always-shifting pseudo-collectivity of "lifestyle" and "taste-group" for
the public realm lost. Recall, too, the obvious fact that for years now the
baby-boom PMC has been the primary target of many, if not most, of the
commodified messages, from M&M ads to *Masterpiece Theatre*, beamed
out by the U.S. culture industry to the world, due to the unique
combination of our numbers and our overall share of disposable income.
These facts then translate, in terms of the experience of cultural
recognition or "tagging" on the part of the baby-boom PMC, into an
extraordinarily steep and foreshortened "half-life" or abrupt decay from
the pleasure traditionally attendant on cultural recognition as a confirmation of one's membership in a genuine collectivity (class-based or
otherwise) sharply downward to weariness, indifference, or even disgust.

    Postmodernist form takes its distracted bearings and stumbling pulse
from such constant manic swings from exhilaration to contempt. The
quick fade—in pleasure, in confirmation, in the possibility of meaning
itself—is built into the nature of *Saturday Night Live*, whose sketches and
bits are almost entirely about other TV shows, films, and ads and their
standard formats. There is, of course, sound business reasoning behind
the marked brevity of most of these discontinuous comic sketches, which
seem to become both briefer and more discontinuous as the evening
wears on and the number of real commercials per comic sketch begins to

climb. But I would suggest also that behind the brevity and discontinuity also lies the problematic dynamic we have just described: once each sketch has received its share of initial laughs from its own playfully distorted reference to mass culture (for example, a dull Sunday afternoon or late-night interview format, a ridiculous ad for a useless or bizarre product), there is nowhere to go comically or dramatically but down—or on to the next bit.

Much the same aesthetic-dramatic impulse informs Laurie Anderson's work: the basic unit of her massive six-hour-plus *United States*, Parts I–IV, for example, is a verbal/visual/musical "bit" less than two minutes long. Potentially dramatic material is sketched out but never developed; instead, it is typically interrupted and/or brought to a halt by abrupt *non sequitur*. The sound and feel of the work as a whole bears a more than accidental resemblance to the experience of moving your radio dial across the bands, pausing to listen a few seconds to what's on each station, or to flipping through the channels on the tube in the typically yearning, loathing project of "seeing what's on." Shorten each bit still more, to a single scrap of common language, slightly wrenched or verbatim, and we are once again near the territory of the Talking Heads song, and a new understanding of lead singer David Byrne's behavior—alternatively enthusiastic, even vehement, and estranged—towards lyrics that in obvious ways both are and are not "his own":

NO VISIBLE MEANS OF
SUPPORT
   EVERYTHING'S STUCK
   TOGETHER
I DON'T KNOW WHAT YOU
EXPECT

FIGHTING FIRE WITH FIRE
AND YOU HAVE NOT SEEN
NUTHIN' YET

STARING INTO THE TV SET

("Burning Down the House," *Speaking in Tongues* [1982])

Imagine these lyrics sung in such a way atop a thick, intricate musical texture of minimalist rock'n'roll chops, synthesizer tracings and doodlings, and heavy African polyrhythms, and you have captured the Talking Heads sound itself as a distilled expression of the privatized, channel-flipping self riding the waves of a serialized collectivity he/she can finally neither take nor leave.

Similarly, of what is now one of her best-known single "bits" or pieces, "Let $X = X$," Anderson says that it "was saying let this code alone, this code is self-reflexive."[35] Yet the message that all signs, including those of language, are codes, and should not (and/or cannot—for this is both warning and prohibition) be broken, derives not only from PMC immersion in the pseudo-universe of round-the-clock

entertainment and consumption, but from the PMC's relations of and
to production as well. Divorced from both the site and the experience
of material production, separated by virtue of the mystified opacity of
our own professional codes from the real systemic function of the
reproductive functions we serve, what appears around us in our lives
as administrators, social service workers, teachers, etc., is apt to look like
a welter of random codes to be administrated and observed. Insofar as
the code succeeds in passing itself off to us as "self-reflexive," the
resultant view taken towards one's work will inevitably be at once
frustrating, depressing, self-contemptuous and blissfully self-exonerating.

The result of these impulses and experiences on the level of aesthetic
or dramatic form are those larger structurations of repetition and
discontinuity which promote the quite distinctive effect of *kenosis*—
evacuation of content, numbing-out of feeling and sense—associated
with so much postmodernist work. If in the public world signification is
always a ruse or a shuck, in the world of the professions an auto-
referential result at best, on the cultural terrain the PMC prepares for its
own delectation, the draining-off of sense and referentiality will become
an aesthetic principle. Think, for example, of how the figures of Albert
Einstein and Patty Hearst are processed in *Einstein on the Beach*, how
virtually all sense of their former significance (Einstein as socialist-
pacifist, author of relativity theory, "father" of the atom bomb; Patty
Hearst as wealthy young heiress turned bank-robbing terrorist) is worn
away and used up through literal replication of the figures, repetition of
non sequiturs and inexpressive, unreadable actions—and, not least, by
the immersion of their mystified and multiplied presences within a music
whose hypnotically rapturous, obsessional, claustrophobic and/or infinitely expansive repetitiousness is from time to time without warning
starkly cut off, only to be replaced by another seemingly endless block of
sound. Or, moving back down our spectrum, think of the extent to
which *Repo Man* reproduces in its own tone and tempo that very relation
between the bone-numbing vacuity and circularity of daily life and work
(driving around those blank, uncharacterizable, rundown spaces of L.A.)
and sudden jolts of sensationalized, idiotic violence and spectacularity
(flight from government agents; mad scientist with dead aliens in the
trunk) which it is thematically about.

My principal claim concerning the form of postmodern works is
identical to a speculation of Todd Gitlin's on the formal dynamics of
commercial TV: in both, "regularity and discontinuity, superficially
discrepant, may be linked at a deep level of [social] meaning."[36] By way
of conclusion to this section, let me concede that all these peculiar
amalgams of disjunct successions without transition and long *durées* also
derive some of their power and possibility from the dynamics of

"deoedipalization" in the private sphere of PMC life. The collapse of the public/private distinction, the erosion of the division of labor, psyche, and affirmed value on which the construction of both the reality and the ideal of the oedipalized ego depend, also help the PMC subject to construct and enjoy works proferring ambiguous pleasures of immersion and circulation quite different from the more traditional (and even more ambivalent) narrativized dramas of oedipal desire and its always frustrated or ironized fulfillment. I have already suggested that there are indeed some distinct political difficulties as well as opportunities posed by this dynamic of deoedipalization, both of which might be drawn out here from considering the full implications of supplanting dramatic forms pitting the heroic, oedipalized self-versus-the-world alongside postmodern work where selfhood is portrayed as at best the most liminal possibility on the veriest edge of dispersion in a maelstrom of fragmented, ceaselessly circulating codes. Here, though, we may rather content ourselves with some brief consideration of the more restricted question of the nature and possibility of climaxes and conclusions within postmodern work. Given the combinations of senselessness, dispersion and *durée* it effects, given its aesthetics of numbness and *kenosis*, how can such works end? How may they themselves take up the question of ending in any meaningful way?

Let us start with what is obvious from even the most casual acquaintance with *Saturday Night Live*, the music of Talking Heads, Laurie Anderson's performance work, and/or *Einstein on the Beach*: neither climaxes nor significant endings are strictly necessary; winding down, dribbling away, or simply coming to an arbitrary halt are perfectly okay. Yet the impulse towards dramatic shape and conclusive ending often stages its own return of the repressed within these works in explicitly apocalyptic figurations and motifs. Of course there are also other and more external reasons in the Reagan 1980s why such motifs are popping up; but the bomb that drops with such, at first agonizing, then finally numbing slowness in *Einstein*, the Statue of Liberty that turns into a missile taking off in *United States*, Part IV, *Repo Man*'s alien visitations, and *Ghostbusters'* Armageddon also suggest the simultaneous desire for and dread of some ultimate, externally imposed moment of truth which might once and for all put an end to the endless, senseless repetitions and switching operations of which these works and our lives seem to be made. This possibility is simultaneously called up and mockingly cancelled: the take-off of the Statue of Liberty is just another bit in the middle of a pointedly shapeless show; *Einstein*'s bomb, like Einstein or Patty Hearst, finally doesn't mean or matter all that much; Otto's final ascension with the aliens is merely one more brief occasion for him to feel "intense." But the most extraordinary, laceratingly hilarious and terrifying spectre of this doom—one whose appearance and psychic function both sum up and depend on all the social processes we have described here, from privatized consumption to deoedipalization—is surely that of the monstrous Sta-Puff marshmallow man helplessly conjured up by Dan Ackroyd in *Ghostbusters*, in response to the devil's offer and command for Ackroyd and his pals to choose the image in which their doom will be sealed. Under the shadow of this image-spectre and its scandalous, delicious fusion of endless circularity, uninterrupted maternal nurturance (Ackroyd explains to his shocked friends that the marshmallow man was the one being he knew would never hurt him, who would always be there), and threat/promise of a final end, we must now try to draw from this discussion of the PMC and its culture some conclusions concerning the valence, and indeed the very possibility, of a PMC politics.

CONCLUSION: FROM IMPASSE TO OPENING

Duke: I know a life of crime led me to this sorry fate. And yet I blame society. Society made me what I am.

Otto: That's bullshit. You're a white suburban punk, just like me

Duke: But it still hurts. (*Dies*.)

(*Repo Man* [Alex Cox, 1984])

I'm tired of travelling
I want to be somewhere

(Talking Heads, "The Big Country," *More Songs About Buildings and Food* [1978])

Where you're going, you've always known it
Where you're going, it's Michelob.

(Jingle from beer commercial broadcast during program hours for *Saturday Night Live*, January 1985)

Recall this essay's opening premise: that the value of a conjunctural analysis of postmodernism must lie in the usefulness and specificity of the strategic questions that analysis puts before us and the projects it suggests. I will now try to sketch out, very briefly, what some of those questions and projects are; but first let me say something about what they will not be. It seems to me useless to make any recommendations, predictions or suggestions concerning the aesthetico-political future of postmodernist cultural works. If a good deal of postmodernism is a cultural expression and crystallization of the life-experience of the baby-boom PMC, that future obviously turns on the political future of the PMC— on what it ends up doing, and who it does it with, from here on.

To see this point more clearly still, and to begin to strategize that future, it will help to touch on a point we have not yet mentioned concerning the internal lineage of postmodernist cultural work: to look, that is, to its historical position as successor to and supplanter of the "counter-culture" of the 1960s. The social-historical origins of this latter, officially dubbed "counter-culture," with its often quite addled mixture of consumerist, alternative, and oppositional themes, have been recovered by John Clarke and others in *Resistance Through Rituals* as a result and expression of a wide-ranging mutation within the dominant culture attendant on the formation of the new class position of the PMC. In this new, strange social space, Clarke and his coauthors argue, and in some measure against it, the baby-boom PMC constructed a "'negating' of a dominant culture" which yet emerged "from within that culture."[37] This contradiction, they maintain, "may account for the continual oscillation" or "'negative dialectic'" of 1960s counter-culture "between two extremes: total critique and—its reverse—substantial incorporation." Thus,

> by extending and developing their "practical critique" of the dominant culture from a privileged position inside it, they have come to inhabit, embody and express many of the contradictions of the system itself. Naturally, society cannot be "imaginarily" reconstructed from that point. But that does not exhaust their emergent potential. For they also prefigure, anticipate, foreshadow—though in truncated, diagrammatic and "Utopian" forms— emergent social forms. These new forms are rooted in the productive base of the system itself, though when they arise at the level of the "counterculture" only, we are correct to estimate that their maturing within the womb of society is as yet incomplete . . . These larger meanings of the rise of the counter-culture cannot be settled here—if only because, historically, their trajectory is unfinished. What they did was to put these questions on the political agenda. Answers lie elsewhere.[38]

We should not overlook the more than temporal distance that lies between (for example) the old *East Village Other* and the present-day *Village Voice*; and yet the applicability of these words to contemporary postmodernist work still seems to me significant. Postmodernism—or at least those aspects and examples of it we have here examined—remains a counter-culture in the terms set and described by Clarke as a "diffuse . . . milieu" which is "divergent with respect to both traditional middle-class and working-class values and strategies."[39] Indeed, as we have seen, that diffuseness is foregrounded as an obvious and enabling feature of postmodernist work; that disaffiliation its most basic formal principle. And what seems most worth noting here by way of an update to Clarke, circa the early 1980s, is the extent to which what is left of the older,

traditional working and middle classes has formed into a culturally and
politically reactive and reactionary core that has proved highly suscept-
ible to the material and ideological blandishments offered by Reagan and
the New Right.

   This latter point is, it seems to me, obvious; but it requires further
elaboration here, if only because it directly contradicts the widely held
notion on the left that it is the PMC, not the working class, which
together with the traditional middle class has supplied the indispensable
support the ruling class needs to complete its replacement of the post-war
"Fordist" consensus by the new Raw Deal of the "Reaganist" regime.
This is the view taken, for example, by Mike Davis in the article cited
earlier. Davis sees and explores, often with great insight and intelligence,
the same political-economic dynamics we have described here: the
erosion of the post-war consensus; the emergence of the PMC, described
by him as a "sub-bourgeois mass layer of managers, professionals, new
entrepreneurs and rentiers";[40] the development of Reaganism as both a
new politics and a new economic regime. Yet for all his local and specific
criticism of big labor's collusive partnership in the corporatist-consumer-
ist consensus of the post-war years and subsequent refusal in the heat of
the 1960s to join with the civil rights, anti-poverty, and anti-war movements in what might then have been "a genuinely hegemonic reform
force,"[41] Davis turns away from any larger acknowledgement of either
the effects of the always uneven and contradictory working-class struggle
in the 1950s and 60s to liquidate itself by launching its sons and
daughters through college and into the PMC, or of its subsequent equally
corporatist and deeply racist reaction against those classes and class
fractions immediately above and below it in the 1970s and 80s.[42]

   The point here is not to demonize the U.S. working class as a whole,
not even its most corporatized, reactionary, and racist sectors. Indeed, it
seems to me not at all hard to understand why a white workforce stung
by both inflation and unemployment, socked by a grossly disproportion-
ate share of the cost of all social welfare programs, both proud and
resentful of the degree of its children's access to education, white-collar
jobs, "alternative" politics and lifestyles, should turn ugly and join that
petit-bourgeois-ruling-class coven which conjures up Reagan. Here, the
argument Stuart Hall has made with reference to wide sectors of the
British working class is equally applicable: "it has to be acknowledged
that sexist and racist and jingoist ideas have deeply penetrated and
naturalised themselves . . . drawing exactly on 'immediate experience,'
and simply mirroring it."[43] Similarly we must give suburbanization and
the TV their due credit in accounting for the debasement and destruction of any potentially counter-hegemonic working-class public sphere.
But the argument that it is the "new *haute bourgeoisie*," that is, the baby-

boom PMC, whose relentless "overconsumptionism" fueled the overall "strategy of cost-displacement towards the working and unwaged poor" from the tax revolts of the mid-70s to the present is simply and seriously wrong. It was not primarily PMC "overconsumptionism" which, together with ruling-class interests, gave rise to the right-wing populism that brought us Reagan; it was also white working- and middle-class *ressentiment*.

Having made this point, however, I hasten to make equally clear what I am not claiming of the baby-boom PMC. It is not untouched by Reaganism and the "overconsumptionist" demiurge; it is not, in and of itself, a potentially revolutionary class. Rather, as the culture it makes for itself implies, and despite fractional consolidations and tendencies both left and right,[44] it is still to date most accurately characterized by its resistance to incorporation—a resistance which, as I have argued, coexists uneasily and inevitably with a concomitant desire for home. Today, every attempt is being made to recuperate the baby-boom PMC *in toto* under the very sign of "overconsumptionism" under which Davis seeks to pillory it. To see such an attempt in full swing, one has only to read the Michelob jingle quoted at the beginning of this section; or, better still, to see the full commercial itself, with its sleek young professionals networking and laughing away as they unwind; or to slide through the slick, dishonest prose of the recent cover story on "The Year of the Yuppie" in *Newsweek*[45]—an issue which, fortuitously, also triumphantly predicts of *Einstein on the Beach* that, on the basis of recent revival performances, "With its status as a masterpiece assured, '*Einstein*' will endure."[46]

The flip side of such attempted consolidations is the possibility that sections of the baby-boom PMC may still be assimilable to a new counter-hegemonic bloc. This hope—admittedly, a slim one at best—is based on experiences and aspects of PMC existence which do not so much belie "overconsumptionist" preoccupations with "lifestyle" as walk paradoxically along with them. From the PMC's ambiguous coign of vantage, for example—though probably not above lower and middle managerial and professional levels at best—may come a relatively full awareness of the international division of labor in multinational capitalism, which in turn may breed an informed, global anti-imperialist solidarity with struggling peasants and workers from the Philippines to South Africa and El Salvador. From its numbers in the health and social services sectors comes a vivid and immediate knowledge of what the abandonment of traditional manufacturing industries, the slashing of social welfare budgets, and the new "top-down" race war against blacks and all other minorities have meant in human terms. And out of the dynamic of its own still incomplete "deoedipalization" comes new sensitivities to and critiques of militarism, the wholesale destruction of nature, and the full panoply of depredations wrought by authorized, masculinist Power, as well as struggles to develop new forms of non-hierarchical, non-vanguardist social organization on both the micro- and macro-level in and through which a sense of unity in difference, and a differentiation through mutual recognition, may be extended and evolved.

It would be sheer fantasy to suggest that such tendencies and possibilities can be much further developed or extended over many factions of the PMC in the absence of inter-class, multi-racial, and multi-national alliances with large sectors of the international working class, including and probably beginning with those members of that giant "reserve army" who live within our boundaries without having yet been incorporated into any "Fordist" or "Reaganist" deal; it would be worse than fantasy to suggest that these necessary alliances will be quick or easy to construct. But the possibility that much of what we now call postmodernism might be turned and engaged in more progressive political directions is finally a function of the extent to which such alliances are constructed, such a political bloc, with its concomitant new public sphere, evolved.

Let us conclude, then, by noting that in addition to all the other elements, themes and subthemes we have attempted to read in the postmodernist works examined here, we may also find traces and occasional figurations of just such an alliance—or, if you will, of the "Utopian" desire which pre-figures and projects its possibility—in the inter-racial, cross-class relationships lamely and lately portrayed in *Ghostbusters*, offered as pure sensationalist adventure in the climactic chase scenes of *Repo Man*, served up as a complexly layered sound and group performance dynamics by Talking Heads, and coolly sublimated into something like a design motif in the selectively black-and-white choreography of *Einstein on the Beach*. In each case, we can easily see ways in which the portrayal is vaingloriously delusory, even downright politically offensive; what has to be emphasized again, moreover, is that all such figurations are at present no more than trace elements of a dream whose concrete realization would require on all sides enormous amounts of hard work and painful struggle. Yet the dream of such an unprecedented collectivity, *qua* dream, does exist, and is as much a product of the routines and rhythms of life for many within the baby-boom PMC as that far more widely vaunted privatized, consumerized cynicism attributed to it as its single essence and ethos.

One final word concerning the relationship between these dreams and desires in postmodernist culture, and the possibility of their realization during our actual social and political lives. I yield the floor to Gramsci, still our foremost expert and best guide to such difficult projects as the one whose liminal possibility I have suggested: "But this reduction to economics and to politics means precisely a reduction of the highest superstructures to the level of those which adhere more closely to the structure itself—in other words, the possibility and necessity of creating a new culture."[47] The future of postmodernist cultural production—and, of course, of a good deal more than that—rides precisely on whether, when, and how this "reduction" will be made.

(1985)

NOTES

1. *New Left Review* (July–August 1984), pp. 53–92. This essay is also in effect a "totalization" of several earlier addresses and essays on the same subject, specifically: "Theories of Postmodernism," delivered at the Conference on Marxism and the Interpretation of Culture, University of Illinois at Champaign-Urbana, July 1983; and "Postmodernism and Consumer Society," in *The Anti-Aesthetic*, ed. Hal Foster (Port Townsend, WA: Bay Press, 1983), pp. 119–34.

2. Jameson explicitly theorizes the correlations he makes between modes of production and cultural dominants in "Science versus Ideology," *Humanities in Society* 6, 2–3 (Spring–Summer 1983), pp. 283–302.

3. See "The Modern Prince," in Antonio Gramsci, *Selections from the Prison Notebooks*, ed. Quintin Hoare and Geoffrey Nowell-Smith (London: Lawrence and Wishart, 1971), especially pp. 177–8.

4. The specific quotations are from John Clarke, Stuart Hall, et al., "Subcultures, Cultures and Class," in Hall et al., *Resistance through Rituals* (London: Hutchinson 1976), p. 10. I acknowledge my indebtedness throughout this essay to the groundbreaking theoretical work of Stuart Hall and his former colleagues and students at the Birmingham Centre for Contemporary Cultural Studies.

5. Barbara Ehrenreich and John Ehrenreich, "The Professional-Managerial Class," in Pat Walker, ed., *Between Labor and Capital* (Boston: South End Press, 1979), pp. 5–45.

6. Aronowitz's term appears in "Cracks in the Historical Bloc: American Labor's Historic Compromise and the Present Crisis," *Social Text* 5 (Spring 1982, pp. 22–52; Albert and Hahnel's in "A Ticket to Ride: More Locations on the Class Map," in *Between Labor and Capital*, pp. 243–78.

7. U.S. Bureau of the Census, *1980 Census of Population* (Washington DC: U.S. Government Printing Office, 1984), vol. I, part I, table 280, pp. 232–7.

8. Figures for all 25–35 year-olds in the population are taken from U.S. Bureau of the Census *Statistical Abstract of the United States 1984*, 104th edition (Washington DC: U.S. Government Printing Office, 1984), p. 34.

9. "The Professional-Managerial Class," p. 31.

10. The conception of the "public sphere" from which the "private sphere" is derived, both by implication and through the actual historical development of bourgeois society, comes originally from Jürgen Habermas, *Strukturwandel der Öffentlichkeit* (Neuwied: Luchterhand 1962).

11. For an incisive account of a post-war suburbanization, see Gwendolyn Wright, *Building the Dream: A Social History of Housing in America* (New York: Pantheon Books, 1981), pp. 240–61.

12. Barbara Ehrenreich and Deirdre English, *For Her Own Good: 150 Years of Experts' Advice to Women* (Garden City NY: Doubleday, 1978), pp. 283 ff.

13. Ibid., pp. 211–65.

14. Ehrenreich and Ehrenreich, p. 29.

15. Ehrenreich and English, pp. 269–324.

16. The literature on the erosion of oedipality, both feminist and anti-feminist, is extensive. For an example of the anti-feminist depiction and analysis of this "problem," see Jon R. Schiller's "The new 'family romance'," *Triquarterly* 52 (Fall 1981), pp. 67–84; and for a dismantling of Schiller's (and Christopher Lasch's) position, see Jessica Benjamin, "The Oedipal Riddle: Authority, Autonomy, and the New Narcissism," in Mark Kamm, et al., *The Problem of Authority in America* (Philadelphia: Temple University Press 1981), pp. 195–224.

17. The "great man" ideology of history as progress and its depoliticizing effects are vividly described in Jonathan Kozol, *The Night Is Dark and I Am Far from Home* (New York: Bantam Books, 1976), pp. 43–7.

18. See Samuel Bowles and Herbert Gintis, *Schooling in Capitalist America* (New York: Basic Books, 1976), pp. 18–49, 102–48.

19. Bowles and Gintis, pp. 201–23.

20. Terry Eagleton, *The Function of Criticism* (London: Verso, 1984), p. 87.

21. Todd Gitlin, *Inside Prime Time* (New York: Pantheon Books 1983), p. 333. My discussion of the cultural and political effects of television here and throughout owes much to Gitlin's work.

22. John Brenkman, "Mass Media: From Collective Experience to the Culture of Privatization," *Social Text* 1 (Winter 1979), p. 108.

23. Ehrenreich and Ehrenreich, p. 12.

24. This description of the work ethos of the PMC both draws on and differs from that of the Ehrenreichs; cf. "The Professional-Managerial Class," p. 26.

25. Michel Foucault, *The History of Sexuality*, vol. I, trans. Robert Hurley (New York: Pantheon Books, 1978), p. 93.

26. *New Left Review* 143 (January–February 1984), p. 23.

27. For four distinct but overlapping accounts of this shift in the political economy of U.S. capitalism, see the article by Mike Davis cited in note 26 above, pp. 6–38; Aronowitz, "Cracks in the Bloc", Samuel Bowles, David Gordon, and Thomas Weisskopf, *Beyond the Waste Land* (Garden City NY: Doubleday 1983), pp. 62–94; and Alan Wolfe, *America's Impasse* (New York: Pantheon Books, 1981), pp. 13–48.

28. The phrase is quoted from my own "Postmodernism as a 'Structure of Feeling'," in *Marxism and the Interpretation of Culture: Limits, Frontiers, Boundaries*, ed. Cary Nelson and Larry Grossberg (Urbana: University of Illinois Press, 1988). It now seems to me that this earlier essay is seriously flawed by an urge to subsume and explain all features of postmodernist cultural work under the concept of the deoedipalization of the American middle-class home, and project a revised radical project exclusively from it.

29. Texts quoted from the booklet accompanying the original recording of Robert Wilson and Philip Glass's *Einstein on the Beach* (Tomato Records, TOM-4-2901, 1979). First and third excerpt by Christopher Knowles, second by Samuel Johnson.

30. Janet Kardon, "Laurie Anderson: A Synesthetic Journey," in Kardon, ed., *Laurie Anderson: Works from 1969 to 1983* (Philadelphia: Institute of Contemporary Art, 1983), p. 29.

31. William Leiss, *The Limits of Satisfaction* (Toronto: University of Toronto Press, 1976), p. 19.

32. Eagleton, p. 99.

33. The term is Roland Barthes' in *S/Z*, trans. Richard Howard (New York: Hill and Wang, 1974); see especially pp. 18–21.

34. Kardon, p. 30.

35. Laurie Anderson, "*United States*: A Talk with John Howell," *Live Art* 5 (1981), p. 7.

36. Todd Gitlin, "Prime-Time Ideology: The Hegemonic Process in Television Entertainment," *Social Problems* 26, 3 (February 1979), p. 255.

37. Clarke, et al., "Subcultures, Cultures and Class," p. 63.

38. Ibid., pp. 70–1.

39. Ibid., p. 60.

40. Davis, "Political Economy of Late-Imperial America," p. 21.

41. Ibid.

42. Though both processes are noted: the first on p. 12; the second on p. 34.

43. Stuart Hall, "The Battle for Socialist Ideas in the 1980s," in *The Socialist Register 1982*, ed. M. Eve and D. Musson (London: Merlin Press, 1982), p. 5.

44. While Davis is correct to label and condemn the "overconsumptionism" of those sectors of the PMC (located, be it noted, towards its upper reaches) which call for "accelerated depreciation allowances, unfettered speculative real-estate markets and rampant condominiumization, sub-contracting of public services," etc., is it not equally obvious that other PMC sectors, chiefly "professionals and licenced technicians," supply the core of both the feminist movement and the white American left?

45. See the 31 December 1984 issue, pp. 14–31, in which *Newsweek*'s staff writers make the same move as Davis, only far more crudely and blatantly: having conceded that, of the voting bloc of 20 million it finds among the baby-boom PMC, only 4 million make $40,000 or above per year, *Newsweek* proceeds to construct its "Yuppie" image (the equivalent of Davis's "overconsumptionist") entirely from examples of the lives and values of this latter elite of the PMC.

46. Alan Rich, "Once More onto the Beach," *Newsweek* (31 December 1984), p. 67.

47. "State and Civil Society," in *Prison Notebooks*, p. 276.

Marxism, Feminism, and

Postmodern Culture

The general rubric under which I speak today is "Marxism and Culture";[1] so I want to begin by considering for a moment some of the implications such a label throws off. Chief among them, I think, is the sense that "Marxism and Culture" is something like a broader version of, say, "Marxism and Imperialism" or "Marxism and the Media"—that is, a critical survey of the way Marxism as a theoretical perspective is put to work to analyze or interrogate or expose x, y, or z. It would, of course, be of no small value to attempt just such a survey, concluding with a set of suitable recommendations for future work in the area. The only problem with such an approach is the extent to which it tacitly places Marxism somehow magically *outside* culture, as if Marxism itself were not precisely a specific, if evolving, determinate cultural product of a given historical moment in the life of the developed industrial world.

So, if only to avoid such privileging, let us look instead at the culture *of* Marxism within late capitalism, and especially at the following antinomy within that culture, as it is so well summed up in Tom Nairn's sardonic description of the newest twist in its own internal dialectic between thoughtlessness and formalism, the big sky and the monastic cell:

> Though a permanent dilemma of any democratic or mass politics [the problem of accessibility] has become impossibly aggravated for the left by the consolidation of academic Marxism since the later 1960s. That is, by the existence of a distinct social stratum now numerous and established enough to possess its own idiolect. This speech-mode is regulated around the key concept of *rigour*, a notion suitably combining professional strictness and quasi-Leninist disciplinarianism. Rigour in the new tribal sense is counterposed for its justification to what one might call numbskull populism, an item never in short supply on the left.

Rigourists believe that Marxism is a science, in an exciting new sense, demanding new terminology and conceptual technicians for its development. Populists stick to the conviction that anything *worth* saying must be accessible to the humblest IQ in the land, and translatable into *Daily Mirror* [or, in the U.S., *New York Post*] rhetoric. Typically fixated by methodology and language, rigourism perceives departure from its own discourse-categories as mere slobbering humanism or (in the political version) "reformism" and "revisionism." Populism answers, naturally enough, with impatient dismissal of the new priesthood. Ever suspicious of elites, socialists could hardly avoid paranoia over such a blatantly hermetic we-group.[2]

To this wincingly tart formulation I would want to add only two further specifications. First, that what I take to be an equally stern yet quite different emphasis on rigor, dogma and discipline from the theoreticism Nairn describes characterizes the cultural/political styles of those Marxist-Leninist groups and organizations whose membership—not accidentally—includes significant numbers of people of color and/or of the traditional blue-collar industrial working class; and secondly, that now, thanks to Althusserian notions of "ideology" as a *necessarily* imaginary construction of the subject's relation to the Real, it is possible for some Marxist intellectuals to inhabit both terms of the contradiction Nairn describes—to work at the inevitably necessary populist reductions and crude myths necessary to gather up the masses, and at the same time with one's colleagues to insist on the strictest standards for the "scientific" purity and theoretical rigor of all concepts produced and deployed in the struggle for knowledge in its most perfectly uncontaminated form.

Nonetheless, the basic reality within the contemporary Marxist subculture of the developed world is encompassed by this contradiction between brahmin and unwashed, purity and urgency, hermetic difficulty and sloganistic ease. And as I think about this contradiction within the late capitalist subculture of Marxism, three non-exclusive readings of it occur to me. First of all, it is possible to read this apparently insoluble contradiction between "rigorism" and "populism" in something like class terms, as a function of the overwhelmingly intermediate, professionalist class status of many of Marxism's leading adherents. In that case, the contradiction is a symptom of this class or class fraction's objectively limited possibilities for mass revolutionary action, at least as traditionally conceived, or for any transcendence of the split between theory and praxis.[3]

But if the clue for this first reading of the contradiction between rigorism and populism is the class status of most members of the Marxist subculture, at least in white America, the clue for the second lies in the startling similarity of this contradiction to another more widespread and familiar set of dialectical oppositions: that which we have learned to identify as the contradiction between high culture and mass culture in general. This similarity is not simply a clever analogy, either; rather, the first is a synecdoche of the second, as any number of examples would make clear. Take, as one small example, the fact that the two most sustained and brilliant readings produced by our foremost literary critic, Fredric Jameson, are of the modernist high culture texts of Conrad and Wyndham Lewis,[4] while in the editorial offices of South End Press, the one full-scale national leftist press committed to publishing politically engaged fiction alongside its other titles, a fairly traditional sort of romantic social realism is receiving a tawdry second life.[5]

Finally, though, it is possible to understand the contradiction within contemporary Marxism between an ever more hermetic theoreticism on the one hand and an ever more desperate polyglot populism on the other, by way of yet a third reading. For this reading, though, we have to pursue the cultural reflexes that produce the high/mass split into their lair, not only within institutions but within subjectivity itself. We must ask, in other words, what psychic habits and proclivities produce the high/mass split within industrial society, and, even more significantly, what the historical and material determinants of these psychic behaviors are. For such an investigation we are, first of all, indebted to Jameson's groundbreaking extension of Frankfurt School theory in an essay called "Reification and Utopia in Mass Culture."[6] In that essay, he proposes that the constitutive action involved in the production/consumption of high culture is characterizable as *sublimation*, a reactive defense against both the raw hungers and fears of contemporary social life and the cheap blandishments of commodity culture; whereas the production and consumption of mass culture are characterized by the more direct mechanism of *projection* of those same desires and fears, in a form whose predictable conventions of firm, and generally happy, resolution guarantee a safe confinement to their expression. What Jameson's essay does not really tell us, however, is which underlying material conditions determine that these two reflexes, sublimation and projection, should become the paradigmatic defense and gratification mechanisms of industrial culture as a whole. For the answer to this question, I believe, requires us to move outside (if not beyond) Marxism altogether, to the increasing historical reach and explanatory power of that branch of feminist and gay theory which argues that the history of human societies is materially grounded in the construction of gendered human subjectivities, sex-coded selfhoods engendered out of the patterns of identity, difference and authority which first surround each of us.

This is hardly the place to attempt a full-scale feminist-historical reading of the emergence of the dialectically related strategies of projection and sublimation as privileged ways of expressing and handling needs and fears within developed capitalist society; and in any case, I am not the right person to attempt it. Yet even so, it is possible to suggest that such a third reading would find those dual strategies and the culture to which they give rise to be deeply bound up with the historic development of oedipal patterns of domination within the nuclearized family units of, first, the bourgeoisie and, ultimately, the working class, including the rise to hegemonic power of the discrete, individualized, empowered male ego against woman, nature, collectivity, and the libidinal self.[7] We know from Freud, after all, that sublimation and projection are preeminently strategies of the ego; and we know too that he considered them, like the oedipal scenario itself, normal, inevitable, and within bounds, even healthy stratagems.

Yet we can now see that the culture of oedipality, of developed industrial capitalism in full flower, is not a universal fact of life; nor are the more-or-less compulsive regulatory operations of the individual ego necessarily normal and inevitable. In fact, I would want to suggest that the very possibility of a feminism capable of reconceptualizing the cultural productions of industrial society, including that of Marxism itself, as emanations of an oedipal field, a given, site-specific moment in the long history of patriarchy, stems from the waning power and authority of the Father within the contemporary American middle-class family. The old pathologies of power, those Freud treated, were typically pathologies of the overactive, hyper-repressive ego, whose contortions of control showed up in the cryptic form of the hysterical symptom, the displaced compulsions of neurosis; but the new middle-class pathologies, we are told, increasingly take the form of weak egos, and manifest themselves overtly in the form of borderline psychoses and other behaviors which *act out*, as if to make Authority appear.[8] The forces behind the deauthorization of the Father (or, if you like, Father-position) in the sex-gender system of the middle class are many, their interactions complex; but finally, on the basis of such leading forces as the bureau-cratization of work, the proliferation of commodified signs, the rise of consumer society, the dispersion of state apparatuses, and, not least, the irreversible entry of women into the workforce, accompanied by their intractable demands for their rights, I think we could argue that this process of deauthorization is in large part a perverse dialectical outcome of the earlier triumph of oedipal, acquisitive, dominating bourgeois man.

More to the point, I want to conclude this sketchy and schematic treatment by suggesting that it is not merely feminism as a new materialist theory which grows out of our present moment, but feminism as a new set of cultural and political practices as well—a set which, varied as it is, is itself only part of a far larger range of cultural practices which reach beyond the old antitheses of high and low, theory and practice, to a new level and moment we might still without too much confusion call the *postmodern*. This evolving moment is not just the moment of psychotic breakdown, paranoia, and Reagan, that great horrible televised Father figure of Authority whose office is nonetheless more and more often forced to take up the untenable, scandalous position of neither-confirm-nor-deny. It is also just possibly the moment of a whole new conception of cultural and political struggle, a conception which refuses to separate the two or to privilege into hierarchy any one modality or production over another. I am thinking here, for example, of the exemplary ways in which feminist artists and writers have over the last ten years produced work and contested norms in *every* male-dominated arena, at every site from science fiction to high modernist art; and also of feminist criticism's use of all registers and methods from sociology to semiotics to remake the shape of critical theory head to toe. I am thinking of the ways in which first feminists and gays, and now increasingly anti-nuclear, environmentalist, anti-militarists and even DSA socialists have begun to learn to choose and move between and among the full array of organizational forms and strategies, from small-scale consensus task forces to national clearing-house organizations, and from micro-politics to electoral lobbying to mass action. And I am thinking of the models for such movements towards a radically demo-cratic society which have begun to emerge, however tenuously, in such books as *Beyond the Fragments* by Sheila Rowbotham, et al., or Andre Gorz's *Farewell to the Working Class*; models which, for all their flaws, insist on the identity between culture and politics at every step, like the *praxes* from which they grow.[9] These examples, movements, forces, models, preliminary and tentative though they may be, speak of the possibility of a postmodern cultural politics, and political culture, which move away from the potentially pathogenic and literally reactionary culture of deoedipalized man towards a non-authoritarian world dedi-cated to the shrinking of the realm of both psychic and material necessity.

To make this move fully and successfully, of course, this middle-class postmodern culture will have to come to terms with class and race, and articulate its political vision and strategy with the far more unitary, ordered currents of radical will within other, more directly threatened groups and races, whose differential sex-gender systems and cultural dynamics give rise to far different needs and strategies. To say the least, though, it remains to be seen whether Marxism is capable of regenerating its concepts and renewing its perspectives sufficiently in the light of postmodern culture and the rise of the feminist critique to be able to assist in this or any other task in the formation of this new culture; or whether it will remain obstructively moored to its own originating, authorized moment in historical time.

(1983)

NOTES

1. This chapter was presented at the first Socialist Scholars Conference, Cooper Union, New York City, April 1–3, 1983.

2. Tom Nairn, "Antonu Su Gobbu," in Anne Showstack Sassoon, ed., *Approaches to Gramsci* (London: Writers and Readers, 1982), pp. 162–3.

3. My reading of this contradiction as a symptom of intermediate class position follows closely on the conclusions of Barbara Ehrenreich and John Ehrenreich's "The Professional-Managerial Class," in Pat Walker, ed., *Between Labor and Capital* (Boston: South End Press, 1979).

4. Jameson's reading of Conrad's *Lord Jim* constitutes the climax of *The Political Unconscious: Narrative as a Socially Symbolic Act* (Ithaca NY: Cornell University Press, 1981), while the work of Wyndham Lewis is the object of the book-length study, *Fables of Aggression: Wyndham Lewis, the Modernist as Fascist* (Berkeley: University of California Press, 1979).

5. A short one, as it turned out. At this point—late 1989, as this volume goes to press—South End has not printed any new fiction titles for years, given the poor critical reception and weak sales of the fiction they put out in their early days. On the other hand, Curbstone Press and Thunder's Mouth Press, with less national visibility but far greater political and aesthetic acumen, have slowly but steadily been publishing contemporary fiction of the greatest interest to anyone interested in the problems and possibilities of politically committed narrative today. For catalogs, write to Curbstone Press at 321 Jackson St., Willimantic, CT 06226, and Thunder's Mouth Press c/o Persea Books, 225 Lafayette St., New York, NY 10012.

6. *Social Text* 1 (Spring 1979).

7. The literature on this claim, and on its relevance to cultural studies, is as vast as the claim is large, but here are a few recommended texts: Andreas Huyssen, "Mass Culture as Woman: Modernism's Other," in Tania Modleski, ed., *Studies in Entertainment* (Bloomington: Indiana University Press, 1986); Carolyn Merchant, *The Death of Nature: Women, Ecology, and the Scientific Revolution* (San Francisco: Harper and Row, 1983); Tania Modleski, "Mass Culture as (Mass)querade," in Colin MacCabe, ed., *High Theory/ Low Culture; Analysing popular television and film* (New York: St Martin's Press, 1986); Klaus Theweleit, *Male Fantasies*, vol. I, trans. Stephan Conway, Erika Carter, Chris Turner (Minneapolis: University of Minnesota Press, 1987)—though one might well want to stop reading at the close of the first section of the latter, before Theweleit's analysis collapses into a rapturous babble. Janice Radway's forthcoming study of the history of the Book-of-the-Month Club, with its brilliant analysis of the national debate over the nature and definition of the "middlebrow," promises to be a groundbreaking work.

8. For some clinical evidence of these trends, see Jon Schiller, "The New 'Family Romance'," *Triquarterly* 52 (Fall 1981), and David Michael Levin, ed., *Pathologies of the Modern Self: Postmodern Studies on Narcissism, Schizophrenia, and Depression* (New York: New York University Press, 1988).

9. Since this essay was written, other works of equal importance have appeared, among them Stanley Aronowitz, *The Crisis in Historical Materialism* (South Hadley MA: J.F. Bergin, 1983); Stuart Hall, *The Hard Road to Renewal* (London: Verso, 1989); Donna Haraway, "A Manifesto for Cyborgs: Science, Technology and Socialist Feminism in the 1980s," *Socialist Review* 80 (1985); and, for all its hypertheoretical vaporousness, Ernesto Laclau and Chantal Mouffe, *Hegemony and Socialist Strategy* (London: Verso, 1985).

Postmodernism and Our Discontent

"In political, ideological, and philosophical struggle," Althusser tells us, "words are also weapons, explosives or tranquilizers and poisons. Occasionally, the whole class struggle may be summed up in the struggle for one word against another. Certain words struggle amongst themselves as enemies. Other words are the site of an ambiguity; the stake in a decisive but undecided battle."[1] I'd like to begin with the modest, and I hope uncontroversial, assertion that the word "postmodernism," and the arguments over that concept's definition and political valence, are to be read in just this way. There are, as we know, other words and arguments whose importance as a site of the struggle towards socialism is far greater—words like "democracy," "freedom," and "justice," most notably. Yet, if you will allow me to develop the classically martial metaphor a little farther, it may be the case in this instance that a report from one of the less hotly or centrally contested flanks of the long campaign, if properly decoded, may tell us something crucial about how things are up at the front.

For the special virtue of the debates over "postmodernism"—over what it is, where it came from, how it works, what it does—is that in a very broad sense left cultural theorists, artists, and reviewers have been uniquely able to wrest this concept away from its circumscribed definitional boundaries within the traditionally high-culture, formalist narrative of art movements and moments. In this safe formalist framework (now somewhat tattered but still far from defunct), postmodernism is what politely follows modernism, offering those of us who are sufficiently hip and respectful a new set of gurus and avatars—John Ashbery to replace Wallace Stevens, Thomas Pynchon for James Joyce, Rauschenberg for Picasso, Cage for Stravinsky, and so on.[2] You may rightly suspect that one important source of objection to such a pantheonic succession of white males has been feminism, with its trenchant and still

132

evolving critique of masculinist representation and fetishization at the core of our received notions of transcendental value and beauty, and with its tonic vested interest in opening up new space for otherness and difference. Such oppositional emphases, embodied in a wide array of artistic and critical practices, are responsible for the construction of a quite different and far more politicized notion of postmodernism. Under its banner, on a field of fine art production extended to include such newcomers as photography, video, and performance art, a new gener-ation of artists and critics now practice and valorize the same moves their elitist, bourgeois, patriarchal counterparts had sought to wrap with aura—techniques of "seriality and repetition, appropriation, intertext-uality, simulation or pastiche." Yet in the cunningly allusive photographs of Cindy Sherman, the photo-assemblages of Barbara Kruger, and even, it was claimed, the deconstructive moebius-strip cameos of a Laurie Anderson performance, as well as in reviews of such work by Abigail Solomon-Godeau, Craig Owens, Kate Linker and others, such practices were employed and affirmed only when they were (or at least appeared to be) "employed as a refusal or subversion of the putative autonomy of the work as conceived within modern aesthetics," towards the goal of "a socially grounded, critical, and potentially radical art practice that focused on representation itself."[3]

The warrant for the claim implicit here, that the process of represent-ation *as such* in our culture is perniciously ideological ("the imperialism of representation," as the editors of *wedge* put it in the title of one of their most interesting issues), is derived in its turn from what one might by now describe as a "counter-canon" of critical texts drawn largely from Paris in its poststructuralist heyday of the early seventies, when a variety of formidable critical and theoretical "apparatuses"—each, it was claimed, necessarily difficult to master, albeit fun to employ—were constructed with the aim of destroying once and for all the myth of the autonomous, centered, unified bourgeois (male) subject, as well as his trusty sidekick the autonomous and immanent work of art. But what then happens if we focus on the theoretical systems or anti-systems of Althusser, Lacan, Foucault and Barthes not as the newest touchstones—or, more accurately, pudding-stones—of revealed, progressive truth, but rather as historically bound symptoms, together with the art practices and projects they inspire, of the newest mutation of cultural life within the constantly moving, metastasizing box of late capitalism in the developed world? This magisterial view of postmodernism as "the cultural logic of late capitalism," however hedged round it may be with nuance and demurral, has been most powerfully put forward by our foremost Marxist cultural and literary theorist, Fredric Jameson, whose fundamentally bleak assessment has been seconded and extended in recent work by the English Marxists Terry Eagleton and Perry Anderson.[4] In their view, as is implicit in the Jameson subtitle just quoted above, "postmodernism" is something both more and less than a new banner under which a host of oppositional critical and aesthetic practices can march. Such practices, and those who employ them, are swept up in the newest bitter ruse of History into the grinning rictus of Late Capital bathing down on the inhabitants of consumer society a spectacularized grin quite sufficient to extinguish in them any retrograde bourgeois tendencies to behave or believe in themselves as centered, unified subjects. The postmodern consumer-subject does not need postmodern artists or art critics to explode the myth of her/his autonomy or the illusion of authenticity or aura in art; we are already quite happily splintered by the fragmentation of older work and family codes and rhythms, already washed over in the flood of shiny commodities and glossy images that runs past and through us each day in this "society of the spectacle." So we react to the "film stills" of Cindy Sherman, or the radio-dial anti-self of Laurie Anderson, not with the shock of subversive enlightenment but with a guffaw; we are already, in the deepest darkest sense, in on the joke.

These then are the two concepts of "postmodernism," each radical at least in intent, which have both separately and together overtaken and superseded its original formalist-elitist definition, by putting forward a descriptive analysis and evaluative framework whose adequacy and explanatory reach far outstrip those pale efforts of the official wardens of the Museum of Culture. Yet you will also have noticed by now that these two radical theories of postmodernism also radically oppose each other: that, to put it crudely, what the first theory valorizes as breakthrough, the second stigmatizes as pathology (albeit without any overt nostalgia for older bourgeois notions of selfhood or art). The stage of left cultural politics is thus set for a fresh round of arguments around questions of cultural-aesthetic strategy and aesthetico-political value like those engaged in by Bloch and Brecht against Lukács a half-century ago, as the first two sought to defend the practices of Expressionism and modernism, respectively, against Lukács' denunciations of both as symptomatic deformations of a properly dialectical and historical Realism, mutilations of consciousness inflicted by degenerate and degenerating Capital.[5] Yet as one looks or listens across the terrain of the postmodernist debate today, within a political moment whose darkness and urgency is scarcely less great than that of Nazi Germany in the mid-thirties, what is most striking is precisely the absence of polemical debate on all sides, the curious hollow silence in the air—or, more precisely, the Pinteresque sight of two parties sitting at the same breakfast table talking straight past each other, each happily at home in a different monologue.

Such a collusive schizophrenia—or is it autism?—can be glimpsed quite readily through even a casual perusal of either of the two best anthologies of postmodern art theory and criticism extant in the United States, Brian Wallis's *Art After Modernism* and Hal Foster's *The Anti-Aesthetic.*[6] The question I would like to pose here is: what factors enable the feminist affirmations of postmodernist practice uttered by, say, a Kate Linker, Constance Penley, or Abigail Solomon-Godeau to stand along-side the pessimistic intonements of a Jameson or the black-hole cacklings of a Baudrillard within the same volume, as if the two postmodernisms they describe form part of the same progressive consensus of What We All Know Now?[7] What enables the editors of these anthologies, both quite able and intelligent beings, largely to pass off the dilemma of this contradiction as a new solution, an uneven but distinct breakthrough? Or, to put the matter still more sharply: what factors present in the situation lived by progressive artists and cultural theorists in the Germany of the 1930s *necessitated* those earlier debates, but are not present or available to us now?

To ask the question this way is, I believe, to begin to answer it. We can speak with some justice of the extent to which critical discourses from the hothouse contemporary artworld do float in a quite different atmosphere and milieu from that which enfolds the heavier gases of cultural theory billowing forth from academe. More cogently still, we might read the absence of joined debate over these two positions on postmodernism as a measure of the real gulf that still lies between feminism and Marxism, a gap on this issue, as elsewhere, still too summarizable in terms of the old weary deadlock in which the men don't see there's a problem, and the women are too fed up even to bring it up. Yet when placed in the context of the comparative historical question I have just framed, both the distance between artworld and academe and the division of feminists from Marxists appear as aspects of what I would consider to be an even larger and more debilitating problem for the left in this country: *the absence of a left oppositional public sphere, or (but it is the same thing) of any real strategy for revolutionary political organization and practice.*

Let us return to the German case for a moment by way of comparison to our own. There, in the early 1930s, as John Willett tells us,

> the German Communists lived in a world of their own, where the party catered for every interest. Once committed to the movement you not only read the *AIZ* and the political party press: your literary tastes were catered for by the Büchergilde Gutenberg and the Malik-Verlag and corrected by *Die Linkskurve*; your entertainment was provided by Piscator's and other

collectives, by the agitprop groups, the Soviet cinema, the Lehrstuck and the music of Eisler and Weill; your ideology was formed in Radványi's . . . Marxist Workers School . . .; your visual standards by Grosz and Kollwitz and the CIAM; your view of Russia by the IAH. If you were a photographer, you joined a Worker-Photographers' group; if a sportsman, some kind of Workers' Sports Association; whatever your special interest Muenzenberg had a journal for them. You followed the same issues, you lobbied for the same causes. And so all records and recollections of the German left in this period move the reader at once into a quasi-autonomous sphere, where the notion of a successful battle to take over the vacant political, economic and cultural establishment seems entirely natural.[8]

Whatever we might want to criticize today about the overall strategy of the KPD—this is a party, after all, which by any account committed a number of disastrous tactical errors, and which in a few years from the moment just conjured up will be all but obliterated by the Nazis—we are nonetheless forced to admit that it is only within the context of a strategically developed oppositional public sphere that a serious debate over what constitutes a radical art can and must take place. And not merely because only within the space of that shared project can artists and reviewers and cultural theorists speak meaningfully to each other; also because only within that space, the space of "party" in a Gramscian sense, with a lower-case "p," can these intellectuals teach and learn from and within a larger collectivity, conduct their own work in organic relation to an audience which is truly their own.

You might suspect that at this point in my argument I will make one of two moves: either issue a ringing call for the construction of such a public sphere to begin forthwith, or demonstrate with Hegelian agility and Jamesonian pessimism the utter futility in the present historical moment of making any such attempt. Instead, I would rather direct your attention to what, following Stuart Hall, I see as the central *strategic* dilemma we are faced with when we bracket off for the moment all that depresses and blocks us concerning the hegemony of the spectacularized image in consumer society, or the entrenched heterosexism of the male left, or the deep hold of racism, sexism, individualism, and anti-communism on the working class and nearly everyone else. All these are real obstacles to any mass radical politics, to be sure: yet more troubling still is the impasse we face the moment we begin to acknowledge the fact that both Leninism and grass-roots populism, the two essential strategies we on the left have imagined and applied for organizing intellectuals and non-intellectuals (or "vanguard" and "mass," to use the old Leninist buzzwords) into a mobilized and radicalized collectivity capable of making a democratic revolution, have failed to produce the desired result anywhere in the developed world.[9] Nor, however much we may hope for one (and however much I am aware of my necessary distance from the field), do we see any new strategic model arising from feminism yet.[10]

My contention that we on the left need and lack a new strategic vision is bound to be a controversial one; and I welcome the opportunity to question and discuss it. But for now, by way of moving toward a conclusion, I want to return to the less contestable proposition that we lack a left public sphere, and reverse it a moment towards utopia. Suppose we did inhabit one: what possibilities might then be opened up for what is presently the postmodernist non-debate? I have already suggested that within such a public sphere and, by implication, in relation to a feminist-socialist revolutionary project, a genuine debate over just what constitutes a radical art practice would necessarily take place; but I would like to think a good deal more might be possible besides, especially if some way could be found beyond either Leninism, with its tendency towards rule of the *apparatchiks* in matters of culture, or grass-roots populism, with its mindless rote celebrations of any and all perceived instances of "people's" culture (often concealing a larger indifference toward cultural production in general) and its bewildered hostility in the face of more formally complex or experimental work. For then, in the space created by an ongoing, collective project, it might be possible for the category and practice of postmodernism to be widened to include other quite markedly similar cultural practices beyond the galleries and museums of an elite white world—say, for example, hip-hop, the indigenous amalgam of rapping, scratching, breaking and tagging which, arising from the urban ghettoes of the late seventies and early eighties, nonetheless does not bow to artworld postmodernism in its employment of techniques of "seriality and repetition, appropriation, intertextuality, simulation or pastiche" towards ends and effects which are quite commonly political with a vengeance.[11] Under present conditions, hip-hop more-or-less inevitably has been greeted by that tiny section of the white left which deals with culture at all with a typically bland and covertly dismissive acceptance ("That's nice, dear"); while in the work of those few erstwhile radical white postmodernists who have bothered to notice it at all, it functions largely, regardless of intent, as piquant quotation, a fresh exotic scent wafting through the performance space, an "interesting" new seme in the newest video installations. Is it not possible, instead, to imagine a public sphere in which a far more fruitful dialectic, both theoretical-critical and practical, between white postmodernism and hip-hop might take place? And is it utterly off the charts to imagine, or at least long for, some either altogether new or radically revised public spaces—meaning "spaces" here in its most literal sense—where such convergences and exchanges, along with others, could be staged, without the molestation, repression and containment now inherent in any new work's insertion into a gallery/museum/art-mag setting (or for that matter, in corporate trade publishing or the music industry)?

At this moment, yes, it is probably off the charts. But I have brought such questions up nonetheless because I think it essential for all of us who do what we hope is progressive cultural work to bear in mind what the absence of a left public sphere costs us, the degree to which that absence stunts our work and its effects, and deforms our analysis of both. Nowhere is that cost more clear today than in the non-debate within what I have broadly labeled the white left over the radical definition of postmodernism, where, for all their success in dislodging the old classically bourgeois notion from its throne, and for all the undoubted brilliance of many of the artists, critics, and theorists involved, the adherents on both sides of the question of postmodernism continue their monologues in a vacuum uncontaminated by any serious attention to the central question of audience, of whom postmodernist cultural production either is or could be *for*, of how it might reach out and be received.[12] The almost total lack of interest in the question of postmodernism as a *sociological* issue is of course yet another, and hardly the least costly, of the damages inflicted by the absence of a collective political culture and project: a lack of interest that results in a creeping idealist-formalism within both sets of arguments I have outlined here.[13] For those who champion an erstwhile radical postmodernism, the meaning and valence of even the most recondite work is simply read out of the text, as if each audience member or spectator came fully equipped nowadays with a mastery of Lacanian psychoanalysis, a principled distaste for auratic art, and an unlimited puritanical zeal for the anti-sensual pleasures of rigorous theoretical work. For the cultural theorists, on the other hand, postmodernism is less a set of practices than a sign to be read out of the culture and unscrambled, using the Marxist master code.[14] Yet I hope it is clear by now that we ourselves ought to take our discontent with such formalisms, together with the limits and lacunae that attend them within the postmodernist non-debate, not as charges to be laid at the door of this or that artist, critic, or theorist, but as the woeful result of quite specific inertial tendencies secreted by our larger failure so far to conceive of any strategy through which a new political movement and culture might be built.

What Stuart Hall says of events in general is, after all, true of aesthetic production as well:

Events and their consequences can always be interpreted in more than one ideological framework. That is why there is always a struggle over ideology: a struggle as to which definition of the situation will prevail. This is a struggle over a particular kind of power—cultural power: the power to define, to "make things mean." The politics of signification. What matters is, which definitions fill out and articulate the "common sense" of a conjuncture, which have become so naturalised and consensual that they become identical with common-sense, with the taken-for-granted, and represent the point from which all political calculation begins.[15]

And what those of us who do cultural work need above all is for the question of postmodernism to be opened up in just that way, to be linked up with and become part of a politics of signification and desire in precisely this larger strategic and collective sense. Until that happens, though, and we become able to assist in the construction of such a political culture, the best we can do is to remember—and remember to *use*—our discontent.

(1986)

NOTES

1. Louis Althusser, "The Politics of Philosophy," quoted in Stuart Hall, "The Battle for Socialist Ideas in the 1980s," in Ralph Miliband and John Saville, eds., *The Socialist Register 1982* (London: Merlin Press, 1982), p. 12.

2. For two examples of such sightings of postmodernism as the newest blessing of high culture, taken more or less at random, see Christopher Butler, *After the Wake: An Essay on the Contemporary Avant-Garde* (New York: Oxford University Press, 1980), and Ihab Hassan, *The Dismemberment of Orpheus: Towards a Postmodern Literature* (Madison: University of Wisconsin Press, 1982).

3. Abigail Solomon-Godeau, "Photography after Art Photography," in Brian Wallis, ed., *Art After Modernism: Rethinking Representation* (Boston: David R. Godine, 1985), p. 80.

4. Jameson's fullest treatment of the subject may be found in "Postmodernism, or the Cultural Logic of Late Capitalism," *New Left Review* 146 (July–August 1984), pp. 53–92. Perry Anderson's trenchant internal critique of poststructuralism should be read in its entirety in *In the Tracks of Historical Materialism* (London: Verso, 1984), while his brusque dismissal of postmodernism may be glimpsed at the end of his "Modernity and Revolution," *New Left Review* 144 (March–April 1984), pp. 96–113. Terry Eagleton's thoughts on the matter, certainly the least coherent or univocal of the three mentioned here, yet in my view quite the most usefully and justly ambivalent are recorded in his "Capitalism, Modernism, and Postmodernism," *New Left Review* 152 (July–August 1985), pp. 60–73.

5. For a partial record of these important debates, see *Aesthetics and Politics* (London: Verso, 1977), pp. 9–85.

6. Hal Foster, ed., *The Anti-Aesthetic* (Port Townsend WA: Bay Press, 1983); for *Art After Modernism*, see note 3 above.

7. A signal exception to the absence of joined debate here is the challenge issued to Jameson by Craig Owens in "The Discourse of Others" (in *The Anti-Aesthetic*, pp. 65–90; see especially pp. 74–5)—a challenge that so far as I know has gone unanswered to date.

8. John Willett, *Art and Politics in the Weimar Period* (New York: Pantheon Books, 1978), p. 204.

9. For a good measure of my clarity and conviction on this point (and many others), I

am indebted to the work of Stuart Hall. See especially pp. 12–13 of the article cited in note 1 above.

10. This is by no means to disparage the value of consciousness-raising, affinity group structures, or non-hierarchical facilitation-rotation techniques, all innovations we owe to second-wave feminists; it is merely to insist that these do not in themselves add up to a strategic vision. However, see Sheila Rowbotham, et al., *Beyond the Fragments* (Boston: Alyson Publications, 1981), whose arguments and descriptions constitute an indispensable step toward the construction of such a vision, as well as Stanley Aronowitz, *The Crisis in Historical Materialism* (New York: Praeger, 1981), whose attempts to map out such a vision are informed by a rare degree of concern for the construction of a left public sphere.

11. Any analysis of the cultural politics of hip-hop would of course have to situate its practices also within the specifically black and Latino cultural histories from which it has emerged. For a brief summary of these antecedents, see the introduction to Nancy Guevara's "Women Writin' Rappin' Breakin'" in Mike Davis, et al., *The Year Left*, vol. 2 (London: Verso, 1986).

12. See above, " 'Makin' Flippy-Floppy.' "

13. A rare exception to this rule, Martha Rosler's "Lookers, Buyers, Dealers and Makers: Thoughts on Audience," *Art After Modernism* (see note 3 above), pp. 311–39 suggests one reason why radical artists and their critics don't analyze the social and institutional parameters that surround their work more often—because the results of their investigations would be so brutally dispiriting.

14. At least the latter half of the Eagleton essay cited in note 4 above should be partially exempted from this charge.

15. "Battle for Socialist Ideas," p. 12 (see note 1 above).

From Firesign Theatre to Frank's

Place: On Postmodernism's Career

A long time ago now, back when it really was still the sixties (give or take a few years) and the only people who used the word *postmodern* were high-cult theorists like Ihab Hassan and Harold Rosenberg, a bunch of brilliant borderline psychotics calling themselves The Firesign Theatre cut a prophetic LP called *Don't Touch That Dwarf, Hand Me the Pliers*. *Dwarf* purports to be the audio portion of a long evening in the life of one George Tirebiter, simultaneously couch potato and protagonist/ guest star/political candidate in the sitcoms, ads, quiz shows and old movies he switches through and across to help make it through another night up in the hills in Sector R. And one of the shows he watches and stars in is a kind of hallucinated World War II movie, complete with weary multi-ethnic scouts, Pico and Alvarado, and the grizzled, growling officer who listens to their scouting report of the enemy's strength and position ("There are gooks all around here—Yeah, they *live* here, Lieutenant!") and issues the appropriate command to the company: load up, move out and surround the enemy. "Ooh," coos the stoned Alvarado when he hears the order, "that'll be *easy*, Leftenant. There's *meel*-yuns of 'em, on all three sides of us!"

The big joke being, back then, Vietnam—or, more broadly, any imperialist "peacekeeping" mission in which the native citizenry is the noxious element to be pacified to death. Yet these days the same lines play as a joke about what we think we're surrounding when we use the word *postmodernism* as well. By "we" here, I mean specifically my generation of the white academic–intellectual left here in the U.S., which for the past six or seven years now has embraced, interrogated, argued over and celebrated the term as a period concept of the present. Yet if the notion of postmodernism as a break with and conclusion to the whole long cultural project of modernity from the Enlightenment on, and as a new, distinctive space–time all its own, is particularly ours, and if the progressive wing of the white American intelligentsia can justly claim credit for constructing this concept and filling out the arguments around its meanings and directions, it is also true—suspiciously true—that doing so was *easy*, man. The concept, or what the concept points out, was everywhere for us; it had us surrounded the whole time.

It was Fredric Jameson's "Postmodernism, or the Cultural Logic of Late Capitalism"—published, in its most complete version, in *New Left Review* in 1984—which kicked off the postmodernist debate in America, and became that debate's foremost canonical text. Jameson's work incorporated earlier definitions of postmodernism—by Irving Howe and Harold Rosenberg, Ihab Hassan and Daniel Bell—yet stretched off beyond them in at least three ways. First, he moved the term out of its formalist corral, insisting that postmodernism is not simply a name for the high art that follows in modernism's wake (for example, John Cage in music, Rauschenberg in visual arts, Thomas Pynchon in fiction) but refers to a whole cultural condition in which the old constitutive opposition between high and mass culture has collapsed. Secondly, he used his readings of such cultural artifacts as L.A.'s Westin Bonaventure Hotel and Michael Herr's *Dispatches* to build up a phenomenological image or *gestalt* of postmodernism as a historically distinct and unprecedented experience of profound spatial dislocation and temporal blur, coincident with the related erosion of our collective sense-memory of duration and development under the ceaseless shocking impact of a spectacularized, immobilizing present. And thirdly, as his title suggests, Jameson went on to read the *gestalt* he had so brilliantly evoked as *the* cultural dominant of late capitalism. This postmodern "structure of feeling" (to borrow a term from another great socialist intellectual, the late Raymond Williams) is, for Jameson, compelling evidence of the fact that everything French poststructuralist and post-Marxist theory has been ecstatically deploring over the last twenty years or so—Guy Debord's "society of the spectacle," Baudrillard's implosion of self, agency, and history into the void of the simulacra, even the Lacanian/Derridean deconstruction of the sign—has in some sense already come true, both in the landscape of the First World and in your very own head, thanks to your old friend the Fetishized Commodity, together with his new pals the Information Technologies and the Multinationals, whose reign of darkness Jameson counsels we must learn to read "dialectically"—i.e., stoically, I guess—but who nonetheless look on this account like the most monolithic and unstoppable Masters of the Universe a body could (not) want.

Now, from that subset of a subset of the professional-managerial class on the academic left I belong to, from barely greying baby-boomers down to the newest crop of graduate school kids, Jameson's magisterial piece has provoked a tumultuously mixed response. On the one hand, it was well-nigh impossible to read his near-novelistic conjurations of what he sometimes calls the "postmodern sublime" without a thrill of recognition; here, a major left theorist was not only discussing the stuff we actually acquire, inhabit, view, and consume, but describing the existential "feel" of doing so as well—and then theorizing that "feel" as no less than the new cultural dominant of late capitalism. Yet such narcissistic pleasures of the text had their down side as well. If we—or, more precisely, our postmodern "sublime"—played the lead in a new, spectacular epic, it was one more like *Pee-Wee's Big Adventure* than *The Ten Commandments*, full of vertigo and simulacra, signifying nothing and going nowhere.

Here, for example, is Jameson at his most optimistic and sybilline, near the famous essay's close: "the new political art—*if it is indeed possible at all*—will have to hold to the truth of postmodernism, that is to say, to its fundamental object—the world space of multinational capital—at the same time at which it achieves a breakthrough to some *as yet unimaginable* new mode of representing this last, in which we may again begin to grasp our positioning as individual and collective subjects and *regain a capacity to act and struggle which is at present neutralized by our spatial as well as our social confusion*"[1] (italics mine). This, obviously, is more like What Is To Be Prayed For than What Is To Be Done, and consistently so; for within the iridescent narcotic bubble of postmodernism as defined by Jameson, the possibility of substantive or effective action is ruled out in advance. So it is hardly surprising that since the publication of the *NLR* postmodernism piece in 1984, Jameson has concentrated on constructing a complementary myth of Third World cultural production which, while as reductive and homogenizing as his description of cultural life on the Death Star, comes out as high on the former as he was down on the latter: if under the android plastic of even so well-intentioned a project as Doctorow's *Ragtime*, say, there is only a roaring red-hot vacuum, beneath the authentic skin of the post-colonial text a progressive "national allegory" can, and will, always be "found."

Yet, though Jameson has moved away from the subject, his work on postmodernism continues to throw off enough energy and fission products to fuel at least one academically based conference on Post-modernism and Something or Other—Feminism, Theory, Politics, History, you name it—every month at least for the last two or three years. Today, roughly speaking, you might say that there are within my crowd of white progressive intellectuals two ways of thinking about the P-word—ways I'll describe as ideal types, though they often enough show up in some fairly contradictory blends. The first resembles Jameson's in its penchant for describing the postmodern condition as a one-size-fits-all essence or aura which comes with Death of the Referent, End of History, and/or any number of equally enormous negative slogans from the nihilistic night-side of contemporary French theory stamped on the side. The current ultimate along these lines, so far as I know, is one Arthur Kroker, a Canadian who makes his dates arrestingly attired in gold-rims and black leathers, and half-mumbles, half-rants his current delirious *mélange* of post-Baudrillardian gummed meta-phrases: "excremental culture" and "panic-states of the *fin de millennium*" are two of my personal favorites, though it may be that you have to be actually out there in the audience, floating on the flow, to appreciate their full mind-stunning effect. But Kroker's voice is merely the shrillest and silliest of a host of hyper-theoretic, heavy-hitting others I've heard and read over the past few years from various imported and domestic stars—such as J.-F. Lyotard, Perry Anderson, Edward Said—whose discourse seems to glide over specific examples, especially from mass culture (Said has even gone so far as to declare, in the age of punk, post-punk, hip-hop and Talking Heads, that there seems to be no identifiably postmodern music!) to arrive at the shared conclusion that whatever postmodern culture might be, it is one in which the possibility of effective radical politics is lost in funhouse space.

One way of dealing with such claims, of course, is to return to the sentence quoted above from the Jameson piece, and ask a few rude questions of it: such as exactly when was that fine lost moment when "we" did "grasp our positioning as individual and collective subjects" with "a capacity to act and struggle"—and, as Tonto says to the Lone Ranger when the Indians close in, "What you mean *we*, White Man?" Surely, after all, there is something dangerously misguided in the notion that in a mythical former age "we" corresponded in some unmediated, transparent way to or with the "real"—that, Amazing Grace working in reverse, we once were found but now are lost. Moreover, many of us who have grown up in the contemporary mediascape have come to feel some suspicion of the hyper-theorists' preference for high-cult examples over contemporary mass culture—for postmodern architecture rather than MTV, Andy Warhol rather than Phil Donahue—and for the blithe ease with which the latter is either summed up, denounced, and dismissed, or simply ignored. Indeed, for many younger theorists of postmodernist American culture, the heavy-hitting hyper-theorists' definition of postmodernism as a spectacularized, depoliticized ether in which we all now move appears to be at least in part a desperate sandbagging operation against the flood of heterogeneous, promiscuously intermingled discourses— including and perhaps especially those issuing from women and non-white others—that wash through and over us every time we switch on the radio or turn on the tube.

Take, for example, *Frank's Place*, the CBS series which premiered this past season, a program so generically weird that together with a few others like ABC's *Moonlighting* it has given rise to a new hybrid coinage within the TV industry—the "dramedie." The show, which features a virtually all-black cast, is set in New Orleans, to which the title character, a black former professor of romance languages, has returned following the death of his restaurateur father. Clearly, then, the series derives in part from the successful, long-running *Cheers*, a relatively standard ensemble sit-com set in a Boston bar. But *Frank's Place* is not consistently funny—and even when it is, its punchlines are uncued by a live audience or laughtrack. Moreover, typically its plots involve a struggle over just where and what Frank's place really is in a complex network of caste, class, and color—a struggle which from week to week is only minimally and provisionally resolved. In one episode, for instance, Frank lurches out of a terrifying yet comic encounter with an impoverished voodoo woman he is trying to turn out of the decaying apartment building he has inherited along with the restaurant from his father. We are told the woman has to go because she's become a nuisance to the other tenants, but this is a hard point to remember, since Frank is the landlord and she is visibly poor; at any rate, in his terror, anxiety, and guilt, Frank resorts to a lightskinned professional member of the local creole aristocracy whose academic specialty is voodoo. Our professional—another woman, by the way—responding to Frank's frightened helplessness with cool contempt, prepares a powder for him to administer to his demonically obstreperous tenant (and coolly charges him a whopping professional's fee for the service). Frank returns to the apartment building and manages to dust the lowly voodoo woman's face with the powder as required; she screams, Frank runs out the door, across the building's front porch and down the steps with her shriek in his ears—and the show is over 'til same time, same station, next week.

Now I don't believe this episode of *Frank's Place* is a paradigm of revolutionary cultural practice. But I would argue that in the irresolution of its episodic plot, its construction of its protagonist as the unstable intersection point of a host of contradictory images and discourses of class, race, and gender, and in its weird, unapologetic generic miscegenation, it serves as a good example of a kind of ground-zero multivalent complexity which the heavy-hitting theorists of postmodernism often fly too high to see. Down on the ground—on street-level, as it were, instead of up in the towers of the Westin Bonaventure Hotel—postmodernism seems less a single cultural dominant than an ongoing situation in which no one aesthetic, narrative, or cognitive strategy of cultural production or consumption holds sway. Accordingly, for the authors of much of the best work from within this second way of conceiving postmodern culture—Post-M 2, let's call it for short—there's hardly any need to invoke the concept in general at all. Postmodernism as the dispersed variety of coding and decoding practices, a multiply determined cultural sprawl, operates merely as deep background for more specific readings and investigations of the ways things attract, give pleasure, and make sense. I'm thinking here, for example, of some of the best essays in a recent collection edited by Tania Modleski and published by Indiana University Press under the title *Studies in Entertainment*; of Kaja Silverman's notes on the collapse of the authority of the fashion industry for women in the wake of second wave feminism, and of the return of sartorial narcissism for men; of Jean Franco's dialectical analysis of the attractions of the Mexican Corin Tellado novels for women workers as against the blandishments of Harlequin paperback romances for middle-class North American women, and her call for us to "consider the position of different mass culture narratives within the international division of labor;"[2] and of Modleski's own meditation on the similarity between the feminization and demonization of mass cultural pleasure one sees and senses in the work of Post-M 1 theorists like Baudrillard, and the delirious, ritualistic violence meted out to women in the contemporary horror film.

Such approaches to contemporary postmodern culture derive largely from Anglo-American feminism and from the new strain of cultural studies emanating from Britain's Birmingham Centre for Contemporary Cultural Studies since the mid-seventies—arguably the two most unabashed, concretely political and anti-elitist bodies of theory progressive humanists have to work and think with now, in terms of both their methods and objects of study. But that doesn't mean Post-M 2 is without problems and blind spots of its own. There are times when all our new, productive ways of ferreting out the subversive "tensions" of, say, the prime-time soap opera, come close to validating such programs and pleasures as, if not outright progressive, at least the best we are likely to get, imagine, or make. Similarly, resistant cultural practice in and of itself may be valorized as an acceptable substitute for more explicit and contestatory forms of politics—as when, at the end of her very smart piece on the disruption of fashion, Silverman concludes by plumping for "retro dressing" as "a sartorial strategy which works to denaturalize its wearer's specular identity, and one which is fundamentally irreconcilable with fashion."[3] It is equally possible for the activity of constructing ever more sly, complexly undecidable readings to become an end in itself. There is, after all, only a thin, albeit crucial, line between Angela McRobbie's "it is no longer possible, living within postmodernism, to talk about unambiguously negative or positive images,"[4] and *Crocodile Dundee* star Paul Hogan's response to questions about his politics: "I can't say anything without losing my credibility."[5] So, for some of the hippest young commentators on contemporary culture I am herding under the umbrella of Post-M 2, the goal is no longer even to imagine political change and social transformation, much less work toward it, but to write towards the goal recently set forth by the editors of the newly launched, trendy left journal *New Formations*: that of "keeping theory moving."[6]

Such depoliticizing short circuits are not wired into the very premises of Post-M 2—as others are, I would say, into those of Post-M 1. But the fact that they're not only brings us more sharply up against the question of why they so frequently occur—and from there, I think, to our own privileged and contradictory position within both contemporary cultural production and, more generally, within the relations of production of what I still want to call late capitalism. By "we," once again, I mean that section of the progressive white intelligentsia which, as it has submerged itself in these debates over postmodernism, has also tended to project its class-based experience on to other classes, and across the whole spectrum of cultural production and consumption. It is we, for example, as members of a college-educated, TV-trained professional-managerial class, for whom the opposition between mass and high or elite culture has largely disappeared; for my working-class pals from high school, I guarantee you, the level of resentful alienation from art museums and Masterpiece Theatre is as high as ever, as, I would guess, is ruling-class antipathy to bowling leagues.

Accordingly, we need to be able to distinguish more clearly between the overall flood of discourses and cultural practices which washes over virtually all First World consumers regardless of class within the hyper-mediated universe of late capitalism, and our own quite distinctly privileged and ambiguous position in the thick of that flow: that is, as its best and most ardently wooed target audience, given our flexible expertise in appreciating high and low; our unresolved collective identity problem, situated as we are with built-in ambiguity between labor and capital; and our historically high levels of disposable consumer cash. This, you might say, is the partial truth embedded in Jameson's original article, and the basis of its appeal: his postmodernist *gestalt* as the cultural dominant of life as a late capitalist *professional*. And these are the reasons why it is so hard for us to find a passage through the layers of text and discourse surrounding us towards any coherent or effective sense of political identity, agency, and will. You might even imagine it as the premise of our own collective "dramedie," in which the ongoing postmodernism debate constitutes merely a *leitmotif* or subplot: to be, like Frank (himself a displaced professional, you'll recall) an empty signifier, simultaneously comic and pathetic in its free-floating anxiety, struggled over ceaselessly by the Others above and below, with only the weakest of resolutions available from episode to episode, and with no clear end in sight.

(1988)

NOTES

1. "Postmodernism, or the Cultural Logic of Late Capitalism," *New Left Review* 146 (July–August 1984), p. 92.
2. Jean Franco, "The Incorporation of Women," in Tania Modleski, ed., *Studies in Entertainment* (Bloomington: Indiana University Press, 1986), p. 120.
3. Kaja Silverman, "Fragments of a Fashionable Discourse," in Modleski, p. 150.
4. Angela McRobbie, "Postmodernism and Popular Culture," *Journal of Communication Inquiry* 10, 2 (Summer 1986), p. 145.
5. Cited by Meaghan Morris in "Tooth and Claw: Tales of Survival, and *Crocodile Dundee*," *Art and Text* 25 (July–August 1987), p. 60; the quotation appeared originally in *The Daily Telegraph* (Australia) on October 21, 1986.
6. Editorial statement, *New Formations* 3 (Winter 1987), p. 4.

PART III

Montage Dynasty: A Market Study in

American Historical Fiction*

What happens when we interrupt and reverse the kind of reading which begins—or, more accurately, imagines it begins—with the internal contents and formal relations of works and then moves outward to their evaluation and slotting as bestseller on the one hand, literature on the other? What do we get if we read as much *from* the publicity that precodes these texts *into* their internal forms and substances as the other way around? In pursuit of some answers to these questions, I have chosen two works from the mid-1930s, Edna Ferber's *Come and Get It* and John Dos Passos's *U.S.A.*: the first published in 1935 as a bestseller, the other in its full, final form in 1937 as a work of modernist literature, an aesthetically and politically radical masterpiece of high art.[1] The strategy of this chapter is to look at these novels within the context of the publicity that surrounds them as paradigmatic *events* within an ongoing turf fight for space on an always already codified and commodified terrain of capitalist cultural production. It is my hope that by doing so—by moving back and forth, that is, from the internal processings of these texts to and from the value-laden claims and descriptions which are affixed to them, and through that labelling, to the audience towards which these texts were targeted—we can flush out and interrogate a few of our own received notions about both the dynamics of mass and high culture and the related pleasures of melodrama and modernism. By doing so we might then be able to open up some new understandings of the

*This chapter, in somewhat altered form, was originally presented at the Center for the Humanities at Wesleyan University in March 1988. For advice on how to do the research on which it rests, I owe thanks to Jan Cohn, and a heavy debt of gratitude to Trinity College librarian Pat Bunker. For helpful comments on and criticisms of the original version, I am indebted to Michael Denning, Richard Ohmann, and, especially, Kachig Tölölyan. Finally, thanks to my dear friend Judith Branzburg for the conversation on Ferber and middlebrow women's fiction that first set me off along this path.

politics of cultural production in which we are still enmeshed today.

Pierre Bourdieu, in his pathbreaking *Distinction: A Social Critique of the Judgement of Taste*, urges us "to remove the magic barrier which makes legitimate culture into a separate universe," and thereby "see intelligible relationships between choices as seemingly incommensurable as preferences in music or cooking, sport or politics, literature or hairstyle"[2]—relationships which, as we shall see, are bound up with determinations of class and gender which those choices also help to negotiate and reproduce. But before entering the specific spaces colonized by these two texts and their publicity, let us take a brief look at the cultural spectrum along which spaces had to be made or cleared for them, and from which they could then be found and chosen by their respective readerships.

The sociological literature on reading choices and habits in Depression America is sketchy. But from what little there is we can construct a rough sociological outline of options and tastes. In general, we know that within the urban, industrial population—the only one studied, unfortunately, so far as I know—almost everyone read newspapers, 50 percent of the population read magazines, and between 15 and 20 percent of the population read books. But that 15 to 20 percent must have read a good many of them: in the 1920s, according to Hart, "the fictitious average American bought two books a year, withdrew two from public libraries, rented two from circulating libraries, and borrowed one from a friend, a total of seven volumes annually read by each mature individual."[3] These figures dropped off, of course, during the Depression—the figures, that is, for book publication and purchases in general, including fiction—yet it is telling that these declines were nowhere near as steep as those during the same period for paid admissions to movie theaters. In fact, aside from a certain measurable shift away from fiction reading towards "books on economics and sociology," whose sales "almost doubled," for obvious reasons, and an equally predictable shift within fiction readers towards historical novels[4]—no doubt for both escape from and instruction in the social and economic crisis in which the nation was caught—the data we have suggests that overall reading patterns and preferences remained basically unchanged from the decade before.

This is still too general for our present purposes, though; what we need more than total sales figures for average readers is a class- and gender-specific sense of who read what. Let me try, then, to summarize what relevant information we have regarding consumption of both books and magazines in this period. In 1934, Douglas Waples and his research associates conducted surveys of magazine reading in South Chicago, "a steel mill community in which relatively few books of any sort are read," and in a "normal [sic] middle class residential population" in St. Louis, and came up with some surprising, as well as some unsurprising, results.[5] Unsurprising ones first: the working-class reading community consumed a relatively high number of "sensational" magazines compared to the middle-class readers of St. Louis, who instead demonstrated a marked preference for "parents', women's, and home magazines"—like the *Woman's Home Companion* we'll be looking at shortly. This readership for sensational literature is in turn subdivided—along gender lines, I suspect—into two subcategories: detective/adventure for men, and true story/love for women (although the available evidence regarding *True Story*, the most spectacularly popular example of the latter, suggests that its formula story of a heroine "buffetted by events she cannot understand" which put her into "headlong flight down the line of least resistance" to "her inevitable sin" and "punishment, physical or moral,"which "was immediate and sure," had a strong appeal for many male working-class readers as well).[6] But the most surprising and significant finding is that although the percentage of middle-class readers consuming "parents', women's, and home magazines" is slightly less than double that of working-class readers, the latter figure is by no means a negligible one—indeed, at 17.9 percent, it is distinctly *higher* than that for either the detective and adventure stories (12.4 percent), or the story-magazines featuring tales of love, sin, and romance (13.2 percent). Similarly, from the chart of Waples's findings combining both the book and magazine reading habits of that same South Chicago population—a chart which breaks down the largely working-class population into socio-economic categories which include a distinction between professional and middle-class readers, and subdivides those categories by gender—we can see that while working-class women generally read less in absolute terms than middle-class or professional women, a sizable proportion of what reading time they had was devoted to "parents', women's and home magazines" *and* what the surveyors designated as "good fiction," as *well* as to "movie, love, and radio" magazines.

The defining oppositions, however, within Waples's categories between "good fiction" on the one hand, and both "other fiction" and "literature" on the other, bring up the snarly little questions of just where in his schema the works of two writers like Edna Ferber and John Dos Passos would be slotted in. But even here we have a few clues to go on, thanks to a 1935 doctoral dissertation by one Jeannette Howard Foster, whose topic was the relationship between rural reading and socio-economic status, and whose categories Waples sets out in his summary of research on reading groups and habits during the Depression. Unfortunately, Waples tells us nothing of Foster's actual findings in terms of who read what; but the qualitative schema that she used to categorize and valorize the novels her reading population consumed, and that Waples reproduces for us, is valuable for our purposes even so.

For one thing, it turns out Ferber herself is listed there—under the topic category "Love," oddly enough (there is no category labelled "family saga" or "social melodrama," in which her work would more fittingly belong), and in column number 3, mid-way between the lowest and highest class reading materials, numbered from 1–6, (though, significantly enough, under "Love" only Emily Brontë makes column 5, and column 6 has been left blank; apparently the subject matter itself militated against the highest quality as far as Foster was concerned). Moreover, though Dos Passos is not listed in Foster's chart, Sinclair Lewis, Willa Cather, Hemingway, Joyce, Conrad, and Woolf are: the latter three securely lodged in the upper reaches of the pantheon in column 6, where of all American writers, only Melville gets to stay; Hemingway and Cather, along with Hawthorne, Twain and Wharton are in column 5—home, I suppose of the medium-greats; and Sinclair Lewis, the crossover writer of his day, critically praised for books that also sold steadily and well, remains down with Ferber in column 3. On the basis of these listings and slottings, and of the publicity framings we'll be looking at shortly, it can be said that Foster's column 3 corresponds to Waples's category of "good fiction," or, if you like, middle-class, middlebrow bestsellers; and that Dos Passos's work, which, as we shall see, appeared in many of the same places as Hemingway in this period, and received much the same sort of praise, would have been lodged by Foster together with him in column 5, and considered by Waples as "literature."

In any case, the big point to make about the books in Waples's "literature" category and the authors in Foster's honorific columns 5 and 6 is quite simply that no one, middle-class or otherwise, much read them. Of all the gender-divided socio-economic groups Waples lists in his South Chicago survey, more professional women read "literature" than any other group; but even here, a mere 2.4 percent of them did. By contrast, 8.4 percent of these presumably well-educated career women constituted a readership for "good fiction," while 24.2 percent of them constituted a readership for "parents', women's, and home magazines." Likewise, in his history of American literary taste, Hart tells us that in 1933, "there were 472 copies of [Sinclair Lewis's] books in the St. Louis Public Library, 310 in the Newark Public Library, and 290 in the Boston Public Library, while ... the same libraries had respectively only 30, 101, and 3 copies of the works of Hemingway."[7]

In one sense, then, the fragmentary data I've been summarizing sketch a picture of small-l literary production and consumption as familiar to us as the parallel to the classical Freudian model of the psyche it inevitably calls up in its wake: you've got your sensational, immediately gratifying fictions for the lower orders; ego-enhancing pleasures of meat-and-potatoes realism, cultural/historical instruction, and character identification for the middlebrow, middle-class and professional readers; and finally, up on the sublimated peaks, the rarefied *frissons* of high art for those happy few—drawn mainly from the ranks of the middle class and intermediate professional strata—with the good sense and good training to appreciate what the critics know best. But the same data, I think, also suggest a certain blurring of the edges of these same categories, a permeability which seems at least as real and important as the pat tripartite model I have just laid out. Choosing another, by-now stale, analogy, we might say that these three modes of literary production and consumption—modes which, as we shall see, are themselves regulated, revised, and reproduced through a web of specific material and institutional practices, from advertisements to serial publication and through laudatory or negative reviews—take on their definitions through their distinctions from one another in the same way signifiers do in Saussure's proto-structuralist conception of *la langue*, depending on each other for their significance in the same way that the signifier *cat* depends on its differentiation from the signifiers *mat* and *cap*.

But the interrelated dependence of these modes arguably goes beyond that of linguistic signifiers insofar as each mode of literary production and consumption not only defines itself against those that lie next to it, but, in effect, "poaches" readers from it as well, by incorporating within itself—that is, not only within the text but within the ad- and review-hype in which the text comes wrapped—themes and buzzwords lifted and shipped in from those other modes. We have already seen some evidence of such overlapping and poaching, in the relatively high percentages of working-class women who consumed *Woman's Home Companion* and, presumably, Edna Ferber, as well as *True Stories*: and we shall soon gather more evidence of this phenomenon as we look at our two texts together with their wrappings and framings. What I'm proposing, then, is that we see these instances of cultural production and consumption not within any simple binary opposition of mass versus high, nor within the watertight compartments of low-, middle-, and highbrow taste, but on an always shifting cultural terrain—one whose width, as it were, is defined by a spectrum line running more-or-less continuously from low to high (though, as we shall see, the high side bends around towards low in peculiar ways), and whose depth is constituted by the whole range of other, equivalently coded, regulated and ranged cultural choices, as, to quote Bourdieu again, "seemingly incommensurable as preferences in music or cooking, sports or politics ... or hairstyle." This, then, is the complex field on which the commodified cultural products of capitalist society jostle, shove, and steal from one another for attention and space;

this jockeying for position, audience, and prestige is what, from the standpoint of everyday capitalist production, the struggle for cultural hegemony is about.

With this landscape provisionally sketched in, let us look at these two texts and their respective promotions as specific events on that terrain of ongoing skirmishes. Let's say we're in America, and it's somewhere around 1935–37. A new Ferber novel comes out in 1935, Dos Passos's *The Big Money* in 1936, the *U.S.A.* trilogy as a whole in 1937. Both novelists are praised in significantly different ways, and for different reasons, for their depiction of America's near historical past, from the last decade of the nineteenth century through the first few decades of the twentieth on into the 1930s. But before we compare those depictions themselves, we need to ask what kinds of positions are prepared for these books on the terrain we have described. By what means, in other words, and towards what target audiences are these products pitched?

One place to begin is with the already-established position and reputation of our two writers, the ground on which they were already situated prior to any prepublication publicity for these two specific titles. Given his subsequent canonization, it is not hard to guess what kind of praise Dos Passos's work had already received, or from what quarters that praise had come. By the time *The Big Money* and the *U.S.A.* trilogy that volume completed came out in 1936 and 37, he was a well-nigh iconic figure, not only of but for an aggressive and insecure New York-based intelligentsia for whom the aesthetic path of intransigent modernist experimentation and the Marxist road to socialist revolution were unproblematically, if momentarily, convergent, if not identical. Given such a perspective, it is hardly surprising that his earlier work from *Manhattan Transfer* (1926), the first novel in which Dos Passos's aesthetic of modernist montage appeared fullblown, to *The 42nd Parallel* (1930) and *1919* (1932), the first two volumes of *U.S.A.*, should have received strong praise (mixed in with some politico-aesthetic reservations) from Mike Gold in *New Masses* and Malcolm Cowley in *The New Republic*[8]—left publications which, by the way, Waples's surveys suggest attracted a minuscule readership confined almost completely within the ranks of the emerging professional–managerial class.[9]

Instead of examining the critical hype put out by this left-modernist intelligentsia, though, I would like to focus on the very important front-page review *Manhattan Transfer* received in the *New York Times Book Review* in 1926, from none other than that crossover phenomenon, the bestselling author who was also America's first Nobel laureate, Sinclair Lewis. Lewis was, of course, the ideal reviewer for *Manhattan Transfer*, given his own switch-hitting ability to win high-culture acclaim while chalking up bestseller sales; and the praise he showered on Dos Passos's montage-novel is significant for the way it also shuttles back and forth across the middlebrow/modernist divide. On the one hand, Lewis extolls the novel's "breathless reality," its use of "the technique of the movie, in its flashes, its cutbacks, its speed"; yet even as he reels off the names of a slew of pantheonic authors, he offers the review's readers the middlebrow bait. "Dos Passos *may* be," he writes, "more than Dreiser, Cather, Hergesheimer, Cabell or Anderson the father of humanized and living fiction."[10]

"Humanized," "living"—the invitation implicit in these buzzwords is for the middle-class reader to come enjoy the connoisseur's self-delight at knowing he or she is in the company of the contemporary great, inside bona fide literature-land, while deriving at the same time the more comfortable, robe-and-slippers pleasures of what are still called "well-rounded" or "three-dimensional" characters in realistic yet dramatic situations—the very pleasures of spurious identification, simultaneously self-approving and self-dissolving, which Lennard Davis has recently analyzed and critiqued in his *Resisting Novels*, and which Elizabeth Long's recent studies of middle-class reading groups reveal unmistakably to be still the primary motivation behind middle-class (and especially middle-class *women's*) reading choices and tastes.[11] And even when, in other reviews, the weight of the rhetoric is more decisively skewed towards valorizing the modernist difficulty and originality of Dos Passos's novels, and thereby inviting an elite audience, I believe we can hear through the challenge thrown down the distinct though subordinated accents of an appeal to middle-class, middlebrow readers—as when, reviewing *1919* in the *Atlantic Bookshelf* in 1932, Mary Ross writes, "It is not a book for the mere beguiling of an idle hour: it asks and deserves concentration. It will offend some readers by its directness of word and unconventional point of view [aesthetic *and* political point of view, one presumes]. *But I cannot believe that any who will grant the author his outlook . . . can fail to be stirred by its richness, honesty, and power*" (my emphasis).[12]

Let us compare this rhetoric, which through the appeal to stern, heroic reading attempts to suture a valorization of Dos Passos's modernist-elite originality and difficulty to the middlebrow pleasures of "humanizing" and "stirring," with that which constructs Edna Ferber as a figure to be read and reckoned with within her own margin-blurred literary space. I'll start with two quotations from William Allan White, the widely read and respected midwest editorialist whose name had long since become the Good Housekeeping seal of a thoroughly domesticated middle-class populism, and whose promotional efforts on behalf of Ferber's work, from the 1910s, when her fiction first appeared, well into the 1930s, were tireless. First, from an introduction to an early volume of short stories, *Cheerful by Request*, a swatch of hype which reappears in the ad copy and end paper advertising of Ferber's subsequently published books throughout the 1920s:

> In its social boundaries [Ferber's] field is ... compact; chiefly lying in the middle class, sometimes taking in those who are just climbing out of poverty, and often considering those who are happily wriggling into our plutocracy. But one thread will string every character she ever conceived; all her people do something for a living. She is the goddess of the worker. And from her typewriter keys spring hard-working bankers, merchants, burglars, garage-helpers, stenographers, actors, traveling salesmen, hotel clerks, porters, wholesalers, pushcart men, wine touts, welfare workers, farmers, writers— always doers of things: money makers, men and women who pull their weight in the boat ... In the great American Short Story ... Edna Ferber's section will be among the workers. Mrs Wharton and Henry Fuller and Sherwood Anderson can have the loafers, in high and low life. But Miss Ferber's people will come from the stores and offices and workshops. They will, as the Gospel Hymn has it, come rejoicing, bringing home the bacon.[13]

Clearly enough, White's conjuration is intended not merely as a characterization of Ferber's creations, but as a construction and interpellation of a particular reading formation as well. His "middle-class" is probably derived from that politically charged and contested opposition between the "middle" and "producing" classes, two terms which, as Michael Denning has recently argued, were mobilized as competing modes of incorporation into, and myths about, the American Republic.[14] In White's rhetoric, however, the subsuming hegemony of "middle" over "producing classes" seems to be taken as assured; the integrity of the capitalist Republic, the democracy of "money making," is an unproblematic, cheerful given. Here, the opposing term evoked by the references to Wharton, Hergesheimer (Hergesheimer?!) and Anderson is cultural capital: that is, those purveyors and consumers of elite literary culture whose depraved tastes incline them—unproductive loafers that *they* no doubt are—to wallow around in a decadent, slothful, morose literature.[15]

This basic construction of Ferber and her "middle-class" mass readership is then given a new twist in the wake of Ferber's turn in the 1920s and 1930s to a set of historical novels, beginning with *The Girls* (1921), running through *Come and Get It* in the mid-30s, and stretching off, ultimately, to *Giant* (1954) and *Ice Palace* (1958), Ferber's last two bestsellers—all three-generation family sagas, each of which stages its own dynastic drama against the parallel historical tale of a regional history. Here are the indefatigible White's words of praise for these latter productions, which I quote from the back of the first-edition dustcovers for *Come and Get It*:

"A course in the novels of Edna Ferber," once wrote that eminent American editor and statesman William White, "would be for a European or a South American or a New Zealander a highly developed course in American geography—told socially, historically, industrially, racially, indeed from every interesting angle of life. All her books are good, there is no best or worst. They make her readers happy, make them wise ..."[16]

There's an element of pleasure here, obviously, in the promise of happiness; but notice, first, how that pleasure is literally surrounded by and submerged within the wider appeal to a middlebrow readership's ostensibly continuous desire for a "highly developed course in American geography"—pleasure alone cannot be acknowledged, cannot be enough—and secondly, how that evaluation is not directly or even primarily offered to the native middlebrow reader, but rather to a hypothetical foreign reader—with Europeans proposed first on the list.

The full resonance of this invocation of the foreign, and especially European, reader comes out more strongly in an appreciation of Ferber's work written by friend and fellow middlebrow novelist Louis Bromfield for *Saturday Review* in 1935, the year of *Come and Get It*'s publication. For in this article Bromfield locates the value of Ferber's work precisely in its opposition to the aesthetic and political doctrines of the diseased, high-falutin civilization on the other side of the Atlantic. "She knows profoundly the difference between what is American and what is imitation European," Bromfield writes. "She will never be one of those American writers who espouse the cause of the Left Wing or one of those who are influenced by the decadence of Europe. About everything she writes there is an atmosphere, a treatment, a penetration which is profoundly American."[17] Again, the intended effect of this nativist-populist discourse is precisely to constitute the largest possible "middle-class" readership and to assuage any anxiety or sense of inferiority regarding its preferred reading habits and tastes.

This hype for Ferber, in short, executes a double motion: it reaches down through the social formation to gather up as many readers from the lower orders as are willing to perceive themselves as hard-working money makers and knowledge seekers, full card-carrying, pleasure-subordinating members of a bourgeois culture; and it defines and valorizes that audience by adamantly refusing any alliance with the cultural aesthetic equivalent of the ruling class. Such operations, then and now, simultaneously constitute a kind of struggle—even a political struggle—constructed on the terrain of culture itself, and a displacement of properly political resentments on to commodified cultural terrain where they can be safely defused and resolved. (After all, shifting the target of our hostility from the holders of economic capital to the holders of cultural capital remains a favored move of proven effectiveness for American opinion-makers from politicians to editorialists and right-wing journalists down to this day.) In any case, what I want to emphasize here is the antagonistic relation between such rhetoric for Ferber and the rhetoric pumped out for Dos Passos: antagonistic, precisely insofar as both attempt to prepare contiguous and partially overlapping spaces for the products they extoll in their respective attempts to construct what we might call a "coalition readership" whose ranks include a sizable number of readers from the old—properly speaking, petit bourgeois—and new— that is, professional-managerial—"middle class."

Yet these class distinctions are not the only distinctions worked through by the hype for Ferber and Dos Passos in its attempt to hail and direct specific coalitions of readers towards each author's new work. The collective subjects they respectively address and constitute—indeed, constitute *by* addressing—for the products they promote is typically a *gendered* subject as well. The existence of this gender-specific address becomes starkly obvious when we look at where and how prepublication serializations of and excerpts from these two writers' forthcoming work appeared in the years 1934–36. Partly, of course, the contrast here *is* a simple high/low, elite/mass one: Dos Passos excerpts show up in the stern, crisp, virtually adless pages of the newborn *Partisan Review and Anvil*, *The New Republic*, and (in Roman-numeraled series with other "Work in Progress" by William Faulkner and Thomas Wolfe) in *The American Mercury*; Edna Ferber's new novel is serialized in a mass-market magazine. But other excerpts from *The Big Money* do show up in one mass magazine, whose target audience was as gender specific as was the one for the magazine that ran *Come and Get It*.

But take a look at the covers of two issues of these magazines carrying our authors' work, and let them speak for themselves (figures 1 and 2). You'll notice two things right away about these covers: first, the not-so-subtle invitations they both issue to their prospective readerships to imagine themselves as affiliated, if not outright identified with the well heeled; secondly, the obvious gendered difference in their imagery and mode of address, a difference which carries through their respective framings of the fiction and articles within. The *Esquire* cover, deploying an oedipally rivalrous irony, simultaneously invites the male buyer to sneer at the goofy, lecherous *Esquire* codger in his tux and, under the cover of that sneer, to get off on the nearly bare-breasted showgirl; whereas the *Woman's Home Companion* does its positioning quite straightforwardly and with the same elegant seriousness evidenced by the visibility of the brushstrokes in the realistic cover illustration—the flattering and reassuring *imprimatur*, as it were, of high-minded, classy artistry. We may sense the latter note being struck again in the plush, stiff dignity of format and graphic on the first page of the serialization inside (figure 3), with the magazine's "classical" logo alongside another four-color illustration—executed, we are told in stately yet subordinated capital letters, by John Alan Maxwell. The designers of *Esquire*, by contrast, see no percentage in naming the artist for the Dos Passos excerpt they title "None But the Brave" (figure 4); but the creator of the culturally hip "photomontage" for "Personal Appearance" in a sub-sequent issue does receive acknowledgement by name (figure 5). *Esquire* assuages its male readers' cultural anxieties indirectly, through a some-what complex jeering humor rather than by straightforward elevation: through the openly snobbish and aggressive humor of the *New Yorker*-ish cartoon on the page facing "Personal Appearance" (figure 6), and through the subheadings under the titles, which—as in *Esquire* today—issue an invitation to come cruising through the salacious world of babes, booze, and tacky mass culture, with the implicit double assurance that you're too male to stick up your nose at this kind of slumming in the name of some stuffy bourgeois-woman's standards and ideals, and too cool—like the rest of us, editors and authors alike—to be besmirched by whatever muck we decide to wallow in.

Let me try to sum up a few things about the framings we've moved through so far on our way into these two novels themselves (though not, as should by now be abundantly clear, *in* or *of* themselves). In both the pre-existing critical hype and the densely coded sites in which excerpts or serializations of these works first appear, we can detect two gender and class-specific processes of cultural siting and readership interpellation in operation: one that attempts to articulate middlebrow and highbrow audiences, and beams its signal primarily to males; another that tries to construct a mass audience of culturally anxious and defensive lower- and middle-class readers under the hegemony of a bourgeois cultural aesthetic rectitude, and issues its call primarily to women. These sitings and strategies, moreover, are also distinguishable by their respective incorporations and employments of lowbrow culture—as we can see, for starters, if we read the Ivory Soap ad on the page facing the opening of the Ferber serialization in *Woman's Home Companion* (figure 7) against the *Esquire* subheadings just analyzed. The soap ad's format of dramatic "stills" and pseudo-sensational headings, the mini-narratives with their instant pseudo-dramatic plot hooks—all this explicitly evokes the lurid lowbrow universe of tabloid newspapers, confession magazines, and Hollywood film, even as that world is simultaneously cleaned up and tamed, just as each dramatic situation, however sensational-sounding its headline and its opening hook, rapidly turns out to pose no problem whatsoever for the happy middle-class Gibson family. Such lulling, cleansing action, though not unlike that claimed

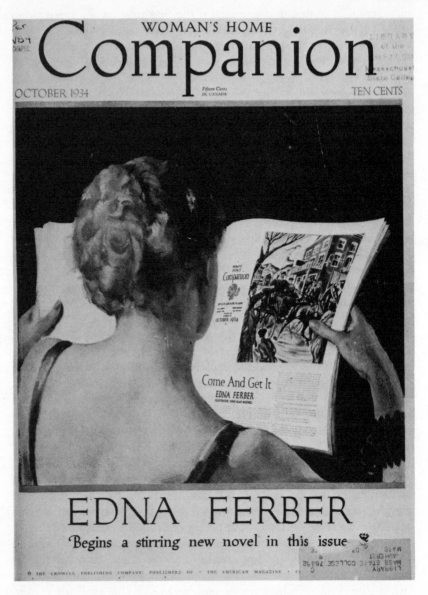

Figure 1

Figure 2

Swift as was his progress, Barney saw everything

★
WOMAN'S
HOME
Companion

EDITED BY GERTRUDE B·LANE

WILLA ROBERTS   HENRY P·QUINAN
MANAGING EDITOR   ·ART DIRECTOR·
VOLUME·LXI
NUMBER··10
OCTOBER 1934
★

Come And Get It

EDNA FERBER
ILLUSTRATOR: JOHN ALAN MAXWELL

DOWN THE stairway of his house came Barney Glasgow on his way to breakfast. A fine stairway, black walnut and white walnut. A fine house. A fine figure of a man, Barney Glasgow himself, at fifty-three. And so he thought as he descended with his light quick step. He was aware of these things this morning. He savored them as for the first time. He always was deeply conscious of the richness about him, yet certainly he should have been used to luxury by now, after a quarter of a century of it. His feet sank into the thick pile of the stairway carpet as soundlessly as an Indian's moccasin on woodland moss, and his gratified senses etched a tiny invisible record on his consciousness. His fingertips just touched the banister. His eyes followed the flow of it. He thought it looked, with the morning light on it, like duck gravy, the patina of polish overlaying the dark wood like gleaming golden fat over meat stock. But then, you had only to glance at his eyes, long-lashed for a man's, and a trifle protuberant, or at his mouth, full-lipped and a shade too red beneath the fine wings of his black mustache, to know that he always would be thus responsive to material delights. This morning his senses must have been even more than ordinarily acute for they recorded a dozen little shocks of pleasure or amusement as he made the brief journey from bedroom to dining-room. He was, as a matter of fact, stimulated by the excitement of secret revolt planned against the women of his household, against Emma Louise, that iron woman, his wife, and against his daughter Evelyn, the curl-shaker. Emma Louise's iron will was corroded now with the acid of years, and Evelyn's curls were restrained by the mold of her modish pompadour. But then, time and soft living had taken their toll of Barney too, so that the impending fray had the exhilarating quality of uncertainty.

He came the length of the broad upper hall from either side of which the bedroom doors gave, in massive walnut dignity. In the exact center of the hall, which had the proportions of a large room, was a black walnut tête-à-tête chair, upholstered in crimson plush. Absurdly placed there, it represented the taste of Emma Louise's departed parents and the thrift of Emma Louise herself. Superb walnut wood, indestructible plush, she

Copyright, 1934, by Edna Ferber

Figure 3

42   ESQUIRE

None But the Brave

**The band was playing Dardanella
and homing heroes got a gulp
of American beauty and of gin**

by JOHN DOS PASSOS
· FICTION ·

THE ratfaced bellboy put down the bags, tried the faucets of the washbowl, opened the window a little, put the key on the inside of the door and then stood at something like attention and said "Anything else, Lootenant?" This is the life, thought Charley and fished a quarter out of his breeches pocket. "Thank you, sir, Lootenant." The bellboy shuffled his feet and cleared his throat. "It must have been terrible overseas, Lootenant." Charley laughed: "Oh, it was all right." "I wish I coulda gone, Lootenant." The boy showed a couple of ratteeth in a chinless grin. "It must be wonderful to be a hero," he said and backed out the door.

Charley stood looking out the window as he unbuttoned his tunic. He was high up. Through a street of grimy square buildings he could see some columns and the roofs of the new Penn Station and, beyond, a blurred sun setting behind high ground the other side of the Hudson across the trainyards. Overhead was purple and pink. An L train clattered raspingly through the empty Sunday evening streets. The wind that streamed through the bottom of the window had a gritty smell of coal ashes. Charley put the window down and went to wash his face and hands. The hotel towel felt soft and thick with a little whiff of chlorides. He went to the lookingglass and combed his hair. Now what?

He was walking up and down the room fidgetting with a cigarette, watching the sky go dark outside the window, when the jangle of the phone startled him. It was Ollie Taylor's polite fuddled voice. "I thought maybe you wouldn't know where to get a drink. Do you want to come around to the club?" "Check . . . that's nice of you Ollie, I was just wonderin' what a feller could do with himself in this man's town." "You know it's quite dreadful here," Ollie's voice went on. "Prohibition and all that, it's worse than the wildest imagination could conceive. I'll come and pick you up with a cab."

Charley put on his tunic, remembered to leave off his Sam Brown belt, straightened his scrubby sandy hair again, and went down into the lobby. He sat down in a deep chair facing the revolving doors. There was music coming from somewhere in back. The lobby

was crowded. He sat there listening to the dancetunes, looking at the silk stockings and the high heels and the furcoats and the pretty girls' faces pinched a little by the wind as they came in off the street. There was an expensive jingle and crinkle to everything. Gosh it was great. The girls left little trails of perfume and the warm smell of furs as they passed him. Need *beaucoup* jack in this man's town. He started counting up how much he had. He had a draft for three hundred bucks he'd saved out of his pay, four yellowbacked twenties in the wallet in his inside pocket he'd won at poker on the boat, a couple of tens in his back pocket, and let's see how much change. The coins clinked in his pocket as he fingered them over.

Ollie Taylor's red face was nodding to him above a big camelshair coat. "My dear boy, New York's a wreck . . . They are pouring icecream sodas in the Knickerbocker Bar . . ." When they got into the cab and he turned towards Charley a reek of highgrade rye whiskey came from him. "Charley, I've promised to take you along to dinner with me . . . just up to ole Nat Benton's you won't mind . . . he's a good scout. The ladies want to see a real flying aviator with palms."

At the club everybody seemed to know Ollie Taylor. They stood a long time drinking Manhattans at a dark panelled bar in a group of whitehaired old gents with a barroom tan on their faces. It was Major this and Major that and Lieutenant every time anybody spoke to Charley. Charley was getting to be afraid Ollie would get too much of a load on to go to dinner at anybody's house. At last it turned out to be seventhirty, and leaving the final round of cocktails, they got into a cab again, each of them munching a clove, and started uptown.

There was a terrible lot of marble and doormen in green at the apartmenthouse where they went out to dinner and the elevator was all panelled in different kinds of woods. Nat Benton, Ollie whispered while they were waiting for the mahogany door to open, was a Wall Street broker. Everybody was in eveningdress waiting for them

for dinner in a pinkishcolored drawingroom. They were evidently old friends of Ollie's because they made a great fuss over him and they were very cordial to Charley and brought out cocktails right away, and Charley felt like the cock of the walk.

There was a girl named Miss Humphries who was as pretty as a picture. The minute Charley set eyes on her Charley decided that was who he was going to talk to. Her eyes and her fluffy pale green dress and the powder in the little hollow between her shoulderblades made him feel a little dizzy so that he didn't dare stand too close to her. Ollie saw the two of them together and came up and pinched her ear. "Doris you've grown up to be a raving beauty." He stood beaming, teetering a little on his short legs. "Check on that," said Charley.

"Isn't he a darling?" she said when Ollie turned away. "We used to be great sweethearts when I was about six and he was a collegeboy."

When they were all ready to go into dinner, Ollie who'd had a couple more cocktails, spread out his arms and made a speech. "Look at them, lovely, intelligent, lively American women . . . There was nothing like that on the other side, was there Charley? Three things you can't get anywhere else in the world, a good cocktail, a decent breakfast and an American Girl, God bless 'em."

"Oh, he's such a darling," whispered Miss Humphries in Charley's ear.

There was silverware in rows and rows on the table and a Chinese bowl with roses in the middle of it, and a group of gilt-stemmed wineglasses at each place. Charley was relieved when he found he was sitting next to Miss Humphries. She was smiling up at him. "Gosh," he said grinning into her face, "I hardly know how to act."

"It must be a change . . . from over there. But just act natural. That's what I do."

"Oh no a feller always gets into trouble when he acts natural."

She laughed. "Maybe you're right . . . Oh 'do tell me what it was really like over there . . . Nobody'll ever tell me everything." She pointed to the palms on his Croix de Guerre. "Oh Lieutenant Anderson you must tell me about those."

They had white wine with the fish and red wine with the roast beef and a dessert all full of whipped cream. Charley kept telling himself he mustn't drink too much so that he'd be sure to behave right. Miss Humphries' first name was Doris. Mrs. Benton called her that. She'd spent a year in a convent in Paris before the war and asked him about places she'd known, the church of the Madeleine and Rumpelmeyers and the pastryshop opposite the Comédie

Figure 4

32   ESQUIRE

Personal Appearance

Newsreel of the U. S. A. in 1926
featuring the funeral of the
Sheik known as Pink Powderpuff

by JOHN DOS PASSOS
• ARTICLE •

COOLIDGE PICTURES NATION
PROSPEROUS UNDER HIS POLICIES
there was nothing significant about the
morning's trading. The first hour consisted of
general buying and selling to even up accounts,
but soon after eleven o'clock prices did less fluctu-
ating and gradually firmed

TIMES SQUARE PATRONS LEFT
HALF SHAVED
Will let crop rot in producers' hands unless
prices drop

RUSSIAN BARONESS SUICIDE
AT MIAMI
The gain in listings on the New York Stock
Exchange over the last decade measures the coun-
try's great expansion in wealth

HUNT JERSEY WOODS FOR
ROVING LEOPARD

PIGWOMAN SAW SLAYING
Saw a Woman Resembling Mrs. Hall
Berating Couple Near Murder Scene,
New Witness Says
Several hundred tents and other light
shelters put up by campers on a hill south of
Front street which overlooks Hempstead
Harbor were laid in rows before the tornado
as grass falls before a scythe

3000 AMERICANS FOUND
PENNILESS IN PARIS

NINE DROWNED IN UPSTATE
FLOODS
Rudolph Valentino, noted screen star,
collapsed suddenly yesterday in his apartment at the Hotel Ambassador. Several hours
later he underwent

SHEIK SINKING
The seventeen year old son of a
veterinary in Castellaneta in the south
of Italy was shipped off to this country
like a lot of other unmanageable young
Italians at the time to sink or swim and
maybe send a few lire home by international postal money order. The family
was through with him. But Rodolfo
Guglielmi wanted to make good.

He got a job as assistant gardener in
Central Park but that kind of work was the
last thing he wanted to do. Money burned
his pockets and how could he make a living
when he couldn't keep away from the bright
lights?

He hung around cabarets doing odd
jobs, sweeping out for the waiters, washing
cars; he was lazy, handsome, good-tempered
and vain; he was wellbuilt, slender, elastic
of step with sidetabs and a smooth olive-
shaped face; he knew the tango; he was a
born adagio-dancer.

Lovehungry women thought he was
a darling. He began to get engagements
dancing the tango in ballrooms and cabarets; he teamed up with a girl named Jean
Acker on a vaudeville tour, and took the
name of Rudolph Valentino.

Stranded on the Coast he headed for
Hollywood, worked for a long time as an
extra for five dollars a day; directors began
to notice he photographed well.

He got his chance in *The Four Horsemen*
and became the gigolo of every woman's dreams.

The automotive boom was on; the
men were away all day making money,
over their sweeping, over the dishes stacked
in the sink, after the shuffle of shopping in
the crowded stores, when the housework or
typing was done, in Chinese restaurants,
dance palaces, beautyparlors, tearooms
women dreamed of Valentino.

They crowded into the ten cent
theaters and the new cathedrals of the
screen;
(the great age of the matinee idols
had gone with the war; the men had had
plenty of girls in the whirring mechanical
revery offered for sale so cheap in the close
quiet of the movie theaters); now it was
the women's turn to dream
of their adagio dancer:

Valentino spent his life in the colorless glare of Kleig lights, in stucco villas
obstructed with bricabrac, oriental rugs,
tigerskins, slicking down his hair in the
bridal suites of hotels, lounging in silk
bathrobes in private cars, staring at his
own face silvery grey in rushes and previews,
oliveskinned in mirrors.

He was always getting into limousines
or getting out of limousines
or patting the necks of fine horses.
in front of the cameras.

Wherever he went the sirens of the
motorcyclecops screeched ahead of him
flashlights flared,
the streets were jumbled with hysterical faces, waving hands, crazy eyes;
they stuck out their autograph books,
yanked his buttons off, cut the tails off his
admirably tailored dresssuit; they stole
his hat and yanked at his necktie; valets
removed young women from under his
bed, in the smoky pinkish gloom and
the low moaning swaying boom of jazz
orchestras in nightclubs and cabarets
actresses letching for stardom made
sheepseyes at him under their mas-
caraed lashes; hat check girls went
hot all over when his hand touched
their hands when they reached for his
hat that smelt of the new leather band
and the pomade on his sleek hair.

What could the poor devil do?
He wanted to make good under the
glare of the milliondollar spotlights
of Eldorado.

The Sheik, the Son of The Sheik
Personal appearances.

He wanted to make good
Maybe it was from so wanting
to make good that he married his old
vaudeville partner, divorced her, married the adopted daughter of a million-
aire, went into lawsuits with the producers who were debasing the art of
the screen, spent a million dollars on
one European trip,
he wanted to make good.

When the *Chicago Tribune* called him
a pink powderpuff
(which was as near as they got in the
presidency of Calvin Coolidge to calling a
punk a faggot) and everybody started wag-
ging their heads over a slave bracelet he
wore that he said his wife had given him
and his taste for mushy verse of which he
published a small volume called *Daydreams*
and the whispers grew about the testimony
in his divorce case to the effect that he and
his first wife had never slept together
it broke his heart.

Wasn't he an amateur of boxing?
Didn't he have a stable of Arabian
horses?

He tried to challenge the *Chicago*

Continued in center of page 181

PHOTOMONTAGE BY KENNETH HEILBRON

Figure 5

February, 1936 33

"He says he kept his hat on so he wouldn't have to watch it, and still somebody swiped it!"

Figure 6

Figure 7

for Ivory Soap itself, is the very action the male *Esquire* reader *doesn't* want; for him, access to the unredeemed realm of lowbrow sensation is the guarantee of his freedom from the gender- and class-specific family ties that bind the separate panels of the Ivory ad together (albeit a guarantee which carries its own gendered and sexualized threat, as we shall see), at one and the same time inviting the lower- or working-class reading consumer into a sutured reading and consumption formation, and domesticating the lurid, low-class element of its format into bland, bourgeois conformity.

What I want to do now is look for these same cultural strategies within the novels themselves, in the kinds of material each takes up and in their ways of working that material out. But first I'm going to have to give you some basic sense of what these novels are like. I'll begin with Dos Passos's trilogy-novel *U.S.A.* since despite its sprawling length it is the easier of the two to describe. The novel opens with a brief sketch of a young man hungry for work and experience, walking eagerly through the streets of America, and ends some 1600 pages later with "Vag," who may or may not be a destitute later version of the same young man, now broke, hungry, and out of work, hitchhiking wearily down the road, "wants crawl[ing] over his skin like ants," as, on a plane overhead, an unnamed "transcontinental passenger," loaded with food and money, vomits up "the steak and mushrooms he ate in New York."[18] In between these two framing passages, through *U.S.A.*'s three novel-length sections, *The 42nd Parallel*, *1919*, and *The Big Money*, four kinds of writing are constantly juxtaposed: 51 Camera Eyes, which comprise an impressionistic and largely unpunctuated autobiography of Dos Passos's life to date; 68 Newsreels, montages of song lyrics, headlines and enjambed bits of news stories from the years covered in the novel as a whole: 27 prose-poem biographies of various leading figures in this period of American history, from Big Bill Haywood, William Jennings Bryan, and Woodrow Wilson to Isadora Duncan (the only woman so profiled in all of *U.S.A.*), Frank Lloyd Wright, and Thorstein Veblen; and 12 occasionally intersecting lines of fictional narrative, each titled for the particular character it features: adman J. Ward Moorehouse, coopted inventor and engineer Charley Anderson, culturally ambitious Eleanor Stoddard, *et cetera*.

The most notable aspect of these narrative lines, as many Dos Passos critics have noted, is the peculiar deadpan with which each story is "told," a flatness which forestalls all but the most diehard impulses towards empathic identification, even with those characters whose actions and commitment we are meant to admire. Here, for example, is a passage from one of the narratives concerned with radical activist Mary French and a problem she is having with her fellow militant and lover, Ben Compton:

Of course she could have the baby if she wanted to but it would spoil her usefulness in the struggle for several months and he didn't think this was the time for it. It was the first time they'd quarreled. She said he was heartless. He said they had to sacrifice their present feelings for the working class, and stormed out of the house in a temper. In the end she had an abortion but she had to write her mother again for money to pay for it. (*The Big Money*, p. 447)

All the characters' subjectivities in *U.S.A.* are rendered in this ruthlessly publicized and exteriorized way—as Sartre observed in his famous homage to Dos Passos's work, "in the deadpan style of a statement to the Press."[19] "Dos Passos's characters," says Claude Edmond Magny, "do not have their own inner rhythm; its place is taken by the objective, mechanical rhythm of social facts, which replace at every moment the personal time, the 'lived time,' that Charley, Margo, and Mary French are incapable of possessing."[20] Nor does the lyrical impressionism of the autobiographical Camera Eye sections supply us with the sense of rich and developing interiority which these fictional passages so pointedly lack; on the contrary, as the name of these sections suggests, the raw photographic immediacy of perception rendered within them in telegraphically spaced fragments and chunks precludes our construction of any single, knowable character. The Camera Eye sections thus serve as a kind of paradoxical internal reminder of the author's impersonal Joycean existence out somewhere behind his handiwork, paring his fingernails—or, in this case perhaps, up in the office pushing the buttons and activating the switches that mash together headlines and doggerel in the equally flattened Newsreel sections, and crosscut Camera Eyes, great-man prose-poem bios, and eviscerated, exteriorized narratives on the speeded up beltlines of the *U.S.A.* machine, his "four way conveyor system," as Dos Passos once called it himself.[21]

In these ways, then, *U.S.A.* is justly considered a paradigmatically modernist work whose exemplary purpose is precisely to deconstruct historical time as what Althusser (that consummate modernist of Marxist theory) called "expressive causality," and narrative sequence as melodrama, that is, as a mode of writing which first plants and then "discovers" an apparently naturalized, immanent allegory within the supposedly secular objects, persons, and processes it pretends merely to re-present.[22] Within *U.S.A.*, as Joseph Frank once said of modernist literature in general, "history becomes ahistorical, for the dimension of historical depth has vanished ... past and present are apprehended spatially, locked in a timeless unity that, while it may accentuate differences, eliminates any feeling of sequence by the very act of juxtaposition."[23] Yet, as in so many other modernist masterworks, the melodrama or expressive causality that is so explicitly flayed, mocked, and condemned in the foreground or on the surface of the text nonetheless hangs around its horizon—and occasionally steals in through the back door.

There *are* stories in *U.S.A.* in which individual characters simultaneously have power *over* history and stand as allegorical figures or types for underlying historical forces and processes: for example, the prose-poem biographies, which not coincidentally are with one exception devoted to white males. Moreover, and still more significantly, *U.S.A.* does rest on its own narrative myth—albeit one whose enabling existence Dos Passos's modernist machine simultaneously works to repress and deny. This myth is a lapsarian one, a contradictory oedipal story of the fall. Its presence is suggested, first of all, by an implicit though unrendered narrative of the decline of the hopeful "young man" of *U.S.A.*'s prologue into the bedraggled, impoverished "Vag" of the trilogy's close, and, concomitantly, of the decline of American language first celebrated and affirmed in Whitmanesque terms and rhythms as the unifying, authentic, organic "speech of the people" ("linking tendrils of speech twined through the city blocks, spread over pavements grow out along broad parked avenues, speed with the trucks leaving on their long night runs over roaring highways, whisper down sandy byroads past wornout farms, joining up cities and filling stations, roadhouses, steamboats, planes groping along airways; words call out on mountain pastures, drift slow-down rivers widening to the sea and the hushed beaches" [*U.S.A.*, preface, pp. vi, v]), only to be overwhelmed and replaced by a debased, inauthentic language of power and commercial hype, of buy and sell ("went to school, book said opportunity, ads promised speed, own your home, shine bigger than your neighbor, the radiocrooner whispered girls, ghosts of platinum girls coaxed from the screen" [*The Big Money*, p. 561]).

More explicitly, this myth makes its appearance in that section of *U.S.A.* which most resembles a melodramatic climax. I mean those pages of *The Big Money* in which the Sacco-Vanzetti trial briefly gathers Newsreel, fictional narrative, and Camera Eye around itself, towards this extraordinary moment of climactic illumination:

America our nation has been beaten by strangers who have turned our language inside out who have taken the clean words our fathers spoke and made them slimy and foul....

But do they know the old words of the immigrants are being renewed in blood and agony tonight do they know that the old American speech of the haters of oppression is new tonight in the mouth of an old woman from Pittsburgh of a husky boilermaker from Frisco ... in the mouth of a Back Bay

social worker in the mouth of an Italian printer of a hobo from Arkansas the language of the beaten nation is not forgotten in our ears tonight. . . .
we stand defeated America (*The Big Money*, pp. 462–4)

The Camera Eye section from which these excerpts come is surely the most amazing and scandalous passage in all of *U.S.A.* Amazing, first of all and most obviously, for the brutal swiftness with which it squelches its own moment of left-populist rapture; but also insofar as within *U.S.A.* as a whole the narrator–author suddenly converges with the shadowy figure towards which the raw sensory impressions of earlier Camera Eye sections have gestured (following more than three hundred pages, by the way, from which the Camera Eye has been absent) and emerged center-stage to deliver a sermon. And scandalous, finally, insofar as the unified moral position from which this jeremiad issues, and the historical myth it proposes, are alike characterized by exactly the kind of depth, immanence, and integrity which it is the business of the rest of the text to deride and efface through flat narration and levelling montage. Indeed, the prolonged absence of the Camera Eye from the montage mix leading up to this moment is itself one sign of the internal transgressiveness of such explicitly mythic thinking and moral speech: as if the *U.S.A.* machine were simply unable to narrate any story of how the fragmented, passively percipient, detached subject of the Camera Eye became a historically informed, politically engaged moral center speaking out in a unified prophetic voice.

I want to come back later to this contradictory blend of modernism and melodrama, and try to read it off in terms of the gender- and class-specific reading formation which, as we have seen, was already there waiting for Dos Passos's new work. But before I do that, let me lay out a brief summary of Ferber's novel by way of contrast—a contrast that begins precisely with the difference between description and summary, space and time. For *Come and Get It* cannot be described as a montage or set of juxtapositions; it can only be summarized as a plot, albeit one which divides fairly neatly into seven more-or-less distinct sections. In the first (pp. 1–68),[24] we are introduced to Wisconsin timber baron Barney Glasgow (nicknamed "Gusto" since his childhood) in 1907, as he stands in the prime of middle age and at the height of his power and achievement; to dried-up, unattractive Emma Louise, whom Barney married years ago to gain a pathway to his present fortune; and to Barney's grown children, the energetic yet cold-hearted Bernie, whose efforts to modernize and streamline the family operation are derided by his father, and the equally strong-willed yet warm-hearted Evvy, who on the eve of her marriage to the lackluster scion of another one of Butte des Morts's leading families, has fallen in love with a virile young workman, Tony Schwerke, employed at Barney's paper mill. This opening section ends as Barney flees his business responsibilities and stale domestic life to enjoy a brief vacation back up in his hunting camp near the rough-and-tumble town of Iron Ridge, where his old friend and fellow lumberjack, Swan Bostrum, still lives with his daughter and grand-daughter. While on the upstate train, Barney falls asleep thinking of his life so far. So we get a summary (pp. 68–107) of his early life as a child of hardworking Scots–Irish immigrants in lumber camps from Maine to Wisconsin. During the course of this westward progress Barney's heroic-ally strong and skilled father met his death saving the life of another logger, leaving Barney's mother to become a lumbercamp cook, with young Barney as her "shanty boy," until her own death from sheer overwork. Barney, though, grows up to be a hearty and courageous logger himself, differing from lumbercamp mentors like Swan Bostrum only in his hunger to rise up and get ahead in the world—thanks to which ambition he soon finds himself working as a covert partner to Jed Hewitt, and courting his old-maid daughter Emma Louise.

Barney's plans are then shaken by the entrance of the disreputable saloon performer Lotta Morgan into his and Swan's life (pp. 108–48); having come down from the lumbercamps with the other jacks to whoop it up in Iron Ridge, the two men find themselves rescuing the notorious Lotta from an unruly mob audience at a seedy vaudeville house, and, it is suggested, both falling in love with her, despite her lurid past. Yet only Swan acts on his desire; he and Lotta are married, as are Barney and Emma Louise, although Barney and Lotta carry on an intensely charged friendship that lasts through the birth of her child Karie, and up to her violent death at the hands of a demon-lover from her former criminal low-life. At this point the extended analepsis of the past eighty pages comes abruptly to an end, and we return to the novel's 1907 present (pp. 149–271). Barney arrives at Iron Ridge, where thanks to a minor mishap that has befallen his hunting camp, he is forced to stay in town; and there he meets Lotta's now-grown daughter Karie Lindbeck and *her* lovely sixteen-year-old daughter Lottie, with whom he falls immediately in love. Driven by his new, illicit desire, which in its turn is further whet-ted by his sense of homeful ease within the Bostrum family as a whole, he lingers on with Swan and the two women in Iron Ridge, barely making it back to Butte des Morts in time to participate in the empty spectacle of his daughter Evvy's marriage to her well-born blob of a fiancé, in spite of the love she bears for the millhand Tony Schwerke, a love she confesses to a horrified, stricken Barney just before the wedding begins. Soon after the wedding, Barney returns to Iron Ridge, and scoops up the Bostrum family on a dazzling private-car railway trip to Chicago, an excursion whose high point is a dress fitting for the beautiful, ambitious Lottie under "Gusto's" lustful, discriminating eye at Marshall Field's.

Ultimately—in fact, by the beginning of the next sequence (pp. 272–321)—Barney has his Bostrum family moved down to Butte des Morts and set up in the little bungalow he has built for them, with cushy millwork jobs for Karie and Swan, and classes for Lottie at the local business school. His visits and attentions to the Bostrum family become the talk of the town—all the more so since Lottie Lindbeck has also been spotted out on a summer evening's ride with young Bernie Glasgow every now and then. Having declared his love for Lottie, and received an evasive response from her, Barney is thrown into torments of jealousy when he learns of these meetings. One night, when he drops in on the Bostrums, he finds his son Bernie already there, discoursing with smug pedantry on the history of paper. The next day Barney forbids Bernie to visit the "mill-hand's daughter" again, and when Bernie scoffs at the prohibition, orders him transferred to a new Chicago office of the family's dynastic operation. This oedipal rivalry then reaches its height at the family's annual lawn party, when Barney discovers Lottie and Bernie locked in an embrace in Bernie's study, upstairs in the Glasgow manorial home; Barney throws himself wildly at his son, who subdues him fairly handily; afterwards, in the shock of his double defeat, Barney submits numbly to the ministrations of his wife Emma Louise, who believes Barney is merely upset because his son wants to marry a "common girl."

Here, handled differently, is where the novel might have ended—and where the Wyler/Hawks film "based on" the novel does come to a close: in the latter case, with Barney's (Edward Arnold's) hysterical laughter booming out over the soundtrack, as somewhere off-camera Bernie (Joel McCrea) walks off with Lottie (Frances Farmer, whose casting as both Lotta *and* Lottie bares the incest theme that drives the main plot). But surprisingly, the book goes off instead in a very different direction at this point—and keeps on going, for almost two hundred pages more. In the next and briefest section, (pp. 322–41), Barney, Emma Louise, the pregnant Evvy, and her blimpy husband Orville are all in their various miseries blown to bits when a lighted match tossed away by Barney catches in a clogged vent of his antiquated yacht. So Bernie and Lottie are free to marry and become inheritors of the Glasgow kingdom. But in the long and notably undramatic concluding sequence of the book (pp. 342–516), which brings the Glasgow family through the Great War and the roaring twenties to the Depression of the present day, the focus of the narrative is uncertain. For some time it rests on Lottie as, snubbed by the elites of Butte des Morts, she establishes herself (with her indomitable, good-hearted mother Karie always by her side) in Europe and New York as a woman of culture and sophistication. Meanwhile, under Bernie's streamlined management, the Glasgow enterprises undergo an exponential expansion; yet the old bonds between employer and workman that existed in Barney's time are gone, and now, despite the health, safety, and nutrition experts who come trooping and lecturing through the plant, workers like old Tony Schwerke stand on the edge of revolt against the new Fordist regime—and are duly, impersonally punished for their resistance.

Towards both these developments—Lottie's rise to international social prominence, the Glasgow enterprise's emergence as an industrial giant—we are invited to take up an attitude that might be described as ambivalent at best. Yet this same ambivalence is as much diluted as it is illustrated by the steady decline of narrative pace, dramatic energy, and characterological interest as Ferber's plot approaches her own present. Bernie and Lottie's twin children Brad and Dina, for example, grow up into two singularly unconvincing characters, "beautiful mechanisms" as Ferber's narrator herself calls them, functioning mainly as exemplars of the New Age and as mouthpieces of thematic reiterations (for example, Brad: "Old Barney sounds like the real stuff, doesn't he. One of those two-fisted sons of guns you read about in the American novels." [p. 471]), which in preceding sections set in earlier times would have received dramatic incarnation. The twins' favorite person, in turn, is Tom Melendy, son of an old lumberjack pal of Barney's and Swan's, now a left-progressive college teacher and writer whose energetic, incoherent populist orations come in long block paragraphs and delight the children, horrify the by now snobbish Lottie, and so enervate the already exhausted right-progressive Bernie that at the end of one particularly prolonged string of them he gets up from his chair and falls over dead.

Therefore—therefore?—the novel ends with a strangely phatic, strained ceremonial event. Photographers, reporters, and motion-picture cameras are on hand to record the felling of a hundred-year-old tree by Swan Bostrum, at eighty-five the oldest lumberjack still in the woods, and great grandson Brad Glasgow, who so resembles his grandfather physically that Swan mistakes him for the long-dead Barney-Gusto. The cameras roll; the great tree falls. Good-hearted Karie appears at the kitchen door of the old Bostrum house. "Come and get it," she yells to call them in to dinner—and the novel is done.

The foregoing summary has necessarily taken some time. But I hope it conveys a sufficiently accurate sense of the novel's length and ambition to suggest how well *Come and Get It* delivers the middlebrow satisfactions its dustflaps promised prospective buyers, when it offered them an author who could "deal as brilliantly with period background as with character" and a novel "[r]ich with the exciting quality of life itself," one "which binds the present to both the remembrance of the past and the imperatives of the future." The bulk of the narrative makes good on these claims by providing the reader with a social melodrama in which psychological and dramatic conflicts, though individualized, are also endowed with a typical or representative aspect which renders them also legible as elements in an allegory of class, sex and history. We can see these processes at work, for example, in *Come and Get It*'s long first section, which sets Barney and his family inside their meaningful behaviors and milieux just as Balzac in 1834 placed his lodgers in the hierarchy of Madame Vauquer's boarding house in the opening section of *Père Goriot*—that is, by "hiding" what Auerbach so wonderfully calls "allegorical witches"[25] under or within each action and detail, then "discovering" them there and "reading them out":

> Down the stairway of his house came Barney Glasgow on his way to breakfast. A fine stairway, black walnut and white walnut. A fine house. A fine figure of a man, Barney Glasgow himself, at fifty-three. And so he thought as he descended with his light quick step.... He always was deeply conscious of the richness about him, yet certainly he should have been used to luxury, after a quarter of a century of it. His feet sank into the thick pile of the stairway carpet as soundlessly as an Indian's moccasin on woodland moss, and his gratified senses etched a tiny invisible record on his consciousness. His fingertips just touched the banister. His eyes followed the flow of it. He thought it looked, with the morning light on it, like duck gravy, the patina of polish overlaying the dark wood like gleaming golden fat over meat stock. But then, you had only to glance at his eyes, long-lashed for a man's, and a trifle protuberant, or at his mouth, full-lipped and a shade too red beneath the fine wings of his black mustache, to know that he always would be thus responsive to material delights. (p. 1)

There is hardly any need to interpret such writing—though we might want to take note of the emphatic, albeit partial feminization of this strapping emblem of robber-baron capitalism, especially given Ferber's largely female mass audience, and in affiliation with Barney's highly developed, finely tuned appetite for connoisseurship and consumption. The meanings intended by the prose appear, as it were, fully cooked and ready to eat. And to these neat hermeneutical servings of singular reference and cultural-historical significance, the Ferber formula adds the tight, dependable bindings of what Barthes calls the proairetic, the forward-leading ligatures of plot.[26] A symbolically loaded lack, that is, the failure of Barney to connect up with Lotta Morgan, generates his belated desire for her grand-daughter Lottie Lindbeck, whose combination of ambition, intelligence, and sensuality both mirrors and complements his own; while Lottie's alliance with Barney's son Bernie works at one and the same time as a credible function of her individual ambition and desire and as a moment in a smoothly unfolding allegory of American political and economic history—one in which the woman, typically enough, is handed over from one male-defined epoch to the next.

In these ways, *Come and Get It* does just what the original bookjacket promises Edna Ferber's novels set about doing: "BOXING THE COMPASS OF AMERICA." Oddly enough, that slogan finds its echo in the Camera Eye narrator's statement of the task Dos Passos sets for him in *U.S.A.*—but with a telling difference: "box *dizzyingly* the compass," that narrator says (*The Big Money*, p. 126—my emphasis). Within *U.S.A.*, and perhaps within modernism—and now high-art postmodernism—in general, that dizziness is rendered through montage or multiple irony, spatialization of time or A-effect; decoded as the destruction of bourgeois or oedipal narrative, as critique and dispersal of male and/or bourgeois and/or western subjectivity, or, in the case of much Dos Passos criticism, from Sartre and Alfred Kazin to Barbara Foley, as the positing of History itself as protagonist and/or moving force;[27] and, finally, consumed as the authenticating mark of the real. With *Come and Get It*, by contrast, and for the middlebrow social melodrama in general, the trademark and guarantee are that the "boxing" will, above all, *not* be dizzying, that we can know where we are and what each action or description signifies at every point.

Yet just as in *U.S.A.* melodramatic story elements and satisfactions are smuggled in through the back door, *Come and Get It* also fails on occasion to deliver on its promise of fully dramatized and accessible significance. I'm thinking here especially of the two most obvious "flaws" in the architecture of the novel: first, the severe compression into forty obliquely rendered pages of the subplot concerning Barney and the dance-hall girl Lotta Morgan, which is so crucial a motivation for Barney's subsequent desire for Lottie (and which, by the way, the Wyler/Hawks film fully acts out); and second, even more prominently, the astonishingly arbitrary explosion that blows Barney out of the book and produces the nearly two hundred pages of dilatory narration and undramatic speechifying that follow. I need to say a little more about what specifically goes on in those forty pages devoted to the Lotta Morgan subplot, for their internal relations and proportions are themselves out of whack as well. The 22-page chapter in which Lotta appears, lives and dies begins with a considerably extended description of the Alcazar Theater in Iron Ridge in which Lotta is to appear. There's Sid LeMaire, owner and manager, who "[i]n his fawn-color topcoat and his high glossy silk hat, his diamond shirt stud and shiny boots ... resembled the pictures [the jacks] had seen of the notorious James Fisk—Jubilee Jim—the most famous of New York's gay dogs—he who had been shot and killed a few years back by Stokes in a quarrel over the actress Josie Mansfield." (p. 126) We also get a prolonged look at the posters pitching the fun inside to the flush lumberjacks: "At one side of the entrance in crude orange and green and scarlet like a circus poster was a picture of the can-can dancer herself, a substantial damsel in a long voluminous skirt lifted to show a stout calf. On the other side, in curious contrast, was a blood-curdling poster of a girl standing poised for a death-defying leap from the top of a high wall. Her face was distorted with fear. Behind her, fangs bared, eyes rolling, leaped a pack of slavering bloodhounds." (p. 127) And then we are given Sid's barker's rap for Lotta and the show—a rap that combines the two posters' promises and appeals: "Come in and see the can-can, the wicked dance of Pa-ris! . . . See Miss Lotta Morgan, the famous beauty of the old Stockade! She escaped from durance vile. She was pursued by howling buh-*lud*hounds! She leaped a forty-foot wall!" (p. 127)

This evocation of the world of lurid lower-class entertainments and the connection of that world to Lotta Morgan are developed still further in the pages that follow, in which the narrator takes up a panoramic standpoint that occasionally turns collective, as in the following passage giving us still more dirt on Lotta from the point of view of the jacks themselves:

> Well, there was still this Lotta Morgan. That promised to be good. Some of them boasted of knowing her. Before she came down to the Stockades she had been the girl of one of the big iron miners. . . . After the escape from the Stockades, followed by the fire, she had disappeared. The north country had lost track of her. They said she had died, they said she had married and turned respectable, they said she had been mixed up with some bank robbery or other and been sentenced to a prison term, though nothing had actually been proved against her. (p. 131)

Finally, after all this preparation, Lotta Morgan appears onstage and begins her act; it goes badly, the rowdy crowd of jacks and miners starts to riot, Barney and Swan together rescue her, and at last we have what we've been built up to expect—a fateful scene between Barney and Lotta, a star-crossed meeting. But this scene lasts for less than one page, in which the two of them exchange only three lines of thin dialogue. (Barney gets two—"It's all right. Come with us. We'll take care of you," and "Don't cry"; Lotta one—"What a pretty boy!" [pp. 136, 137]) The first sentence of the next paragraph reads: "Before Swan went back to the woods for the river drive that spring he and Lotta Morgan were married" (p. 137); and from here on to the end of the chapter, things move very swiftly indeed. The next eleven pages cover nearly ten years, through a distanced, oblique summary which retreats again to telling us what the community of Iron Ridge knows and thinks of Lotta, Swan, and Barney and their goings-on. That is how we hear of Barney's marriage to Emma Louise and his ongoing, apparently intense, gossip-provoking relationship with Lotta; of the birth of a daughter to Lotta and Swan; of Lotta's brutal death at the hands of the convict and former lover who once had her "tattooed between the breasts with a picture of Christ on the Cross" (p. 138), and who leaves her with her scalped skull "crushed with a woodsmen's axe" in a "sort of gulley" out behind her house; and finally, of the funeral, after which "there was a furious rush to the saloons on Silver Street. They did the best business in years." (p. 148)

What sense can be made of such a curiously lurid, off-pace performance? We can answer this question, I think—or get a good piece of it, anyway—by returning to the problems of audience and siting we worked through on our way to this novel, and thinking of the Lotta Morgan subplot as continuous with them—that is, as an *intratextual* equivalent of the reviews and advertising hype in which the text and Ferber's work in general came wrapped. Specifically, you'll recall, one of the main effects that rhetoric sought to conjure up was an imagined reading formation in which low-class readers could find their own satisfactions under the hegemony of the middlebrow. In this sense, the Lotta Morgan subplot, compressed as it is, takes on further importance in addition to its motivating significance for the unfolding of the rest of the Barney Glasgow plot. Or perhaps we could say that its significance for *and* subordination to the rest of that plot are symptomatic of the kind of incorporation it is trying to bring off, through its elaborate and only slightly historically displaced evocation of the sensational world of the five-cent newspaper (the reference to Jim Fisk's seamy affair and seamier murder), of the sado-sexual pulp novel or stage melodrama (girl on cliff, slavering bloodhounds), and, not least, through Lotta's own story, the story of a woman whose past sins catch up with and kill her, of *True Story* itself, the most popular magazine of its day. This crucial, and crucially compressed and distanced subplot, in other words, has the same effect in *Come and Get It* as the pseudo-sensational headlines and graphic format do within the Ivory Soap ad that faced the first page of the novel's serialization in *Woman's Home Companion*: to get the lowbrow reader-consumer on board, then let the rest of the text keep her in line.

But in this sense all of *Come and Get It* enacts a dramatic allegory of its own relations to other positions on the cultural terrain we have described. In the narrative sequence I've just been summarizing, for example, it's significant that Barney himself is not very interested in the low-class offerings of Iron Ridge, the dance-halls and saloons. Though he may be drawn to Lotta, to "her neat little ways ... the lurid melodrama of her past life, the rumor of the strange sadistic mark on her body,"

(p. 139) the very order of the listed items given here tells us which cultural tastes are still regnant within them. His disinclination for low enjoyments becomes, in fact, the sign of his virtue, just as his subsequently healthy but discerning (and, as we have seen, female-coded) epicureanism in clothes and furnishings is proof enough that he deserves what he gets.

Yet this allegory is a three-sided one: down the spectrum lies someone like Swan, who lacks all ambition, is content to guzzle down whatever Iron Ridge has to offer, and towards whom the novel invites us to direct a condescending, humorous affection; and up the scale we have Lottie Glasgow née Lindbeck. Following Barney's abrupt removal, Lottie is still treated sympathetically so long as her tastes and education remain within middle-class bounds—as, for example, in books:

> Faithfully she toiled through [the young but wise] Tom Melendy's list: History of France; History of England; H.G. Wells; Ida Tarbell; John Galsworthy; Jack London. She understood parts of these. Finished, she borrowed books from the public library ... *The Rich Mrs Burgoyne*, by Kathleen Norris; *Marriage*, by H.G. Wells; *V.V.'s Byes*, by Henry Sidnor Harrison; *Daddy Long-Legs*, by Jean Webster; *The Danger Mark*, by Robert Chambers [also author of *Love and the Lieutenant*, by the way, the novel whose serialization is closing out in *Woman's Home Companion* just as *Come and Get It* starts up] ... [I]n the pages of their books she met people, was introduced to situations toward which she had been groping these past five years. She seemed at once strangely content yet excited. (pp. 403–4)

Later on, though, the text makes it equally clear that her long stay in the society circles of New York and London has twisted her healthy appetite into a snobbery that even makes her rail back at her old mentor Tom Melendy when he spouts off, and leads her own incorrigibly perky American children to say of her, "Poor darling Mother; she dates like a 1918 Rolls." (p. 503)

The point is clear: middle-class being, middlebrow taste, the satisfaction of being "strangely content but excited" are best, even if these norms can only be figured in the novel's plot and character scheme by the passage up towards and on past such a blissful yet solid state (as in many of Ferber's other middlebrow novels, there is not a single middle-class person in the book). But as we saw while making our way through the hype surrounding Ferber and this novel, this middlebrow cultural position is defined not only by its attempted assimilation of lowbrow taste and lower-class audiences, but by its anxious and defensive hostility towards elite cultural formations as well. Could it then be this defensiveness which drives Ferber to devote so many dull pages of circumstantial summary to Lottie and Karie's high-society life in New York and Europe, just as it seems to require her every so often to throw in a lame swatch of stream of consciousness (Barney on Lottie at the fateful lawn party: "I could cover her with diamonds and emeralds and a string of pearls big as a tow rope I been a fool for a year what the hell are you afraid of Barney," etc. [p. 309]) or a ham-handed Freudian analysis ("he never knew that his marriage to the energetic Emma Louise Hewitt, older than himself and terribly managing, could be traced to the influence of this powerful woman on her child. He had married, in short, his mother" [p. 72]). Indeed, I almost want to say that such high-class references and devices are *supposed* to arrive stillborn: that their very ineffectuality gives the middlebrow reader the assurance that she too can handle the high-falutin stuff, and reassures her that it's hardly worthwhile to do so; the real richness, the most dramatic, resonant satisfactions lie, like the "bird with feathers of blue" in the old Tin Pan Alley song, "Back in Your Own Back Yard."

Yet this admittedly perverse line of argument only begins to explain the wearying length and dramatic weakness of that long hortatory section which follows Barney's death and maps World War I, the 1920s and the onset of the Depression against the rise and fall of the Glasgow-Hewitt empire under Bernie's coldly brilliant management, Lottie's self-elevation to near-nobility, and their twin children's flowering, under Tom Melendy's wise and watchful eye, into two savvy, dynamic young Americans. To explain such a gross malfunction of the novel's melo-dramatic machinery, we have to search for some other overdetermining factors and dynamics as well. One of these may be the very absence of a secure position for middle-class identity just remarked on; or, to put it another way, it may have to do with Ferber's sense of the decline of the old middle-class of small-scale merchants, bankers, tradespeople and farmers from which she herself came, and of its once-hegemonic culture. In 1935, that culture is of course still suffering the ravages of economic depression; but it is also increasingly disarticulated by and subordinated to both an increasingly powerful class formation of professionals and managers on the one hand, and an ever more extensive mass culture of movies, radio, and mass advertising on the other. In this context the endless, incoherent yet desperately positive speeches by narrator and character alike with which the book nears its end[28] and the weirdly meaningless media event with which it finally closes do make some sense after all: they are Ferber's strained attempts to console, reassure, and reconsolidate all the sectors of her audience, to resolve a set of social contradictions she cannot, even aesthetically, get to come out right.

Yet a third and arguably more powerful level of determination is equally visible in *Come and Get It*. To see it, we have to reconsider this long last section together with the arbitrary explosion which, by blowing up Barney and most of his family, also detonates all the gathered momentum of the plot, leaving the few remaining characters, chiefly Bernie and Lottie, to drift through the remainder of the book like so many subatomic particles in the wake of a nuclear blast—to reconsider, that is, both explosion and aftermath in relation to gender, the one register we have left largely uninterrogated up until now. It will be recalled, first of all, that we are talking about a middle-class white woman writing primarily for other middle-class white women in a pre-feminist age;[29] and then that in Lottie and Barney, the two principals of Come and Get It, Ferber gives us, beyond all the baffles of generational difference and quasi-incestuous desire, two equally—indeed, almost identically— ambitious, dynamic, sensuous, and sensitive characters, and incites our desire to see them get together. Ultimately, of course, the text veers away from any such resolution. Lottie allies herself with Bernie, the man who is generationally right but dead wrong in terms of any allegory of gender. She becomes a rather tedious snob; Barney blows himself up; and by the end all that is left of the androgynous dialectic which charged the first two-thirds of the novel is the watered-down complementarity of the vapid twins, the boy who looks just like Barney and the girl who is just like him (or so we are told, again and again), every inch as strong willed, sensitive and passionate. Could it not be, then, that the aesthetic and dramatic weakness of this final third of Come and Get It is also the sign of a desire on the part of Ferber herself and her female audience for a *feminist* heterosexuality—one founded, that is, on the free flow of reciprocating, ungendered needs and capacities rather than on rigid, gendered antinomies[30]—and, simultaneously, of that desire's impossibility in this period; of a feminist hope for a "Lotta-Gusto" union cancelled by its own despair?

If this be so—and I guess I think it is—it suddenly becomes a little harder to see which is the more radical work of the mid-1930s, the melodramatic Come and Get It or the modernist U.S.A.—especially if, as we turn now to the latter one last time, we reverse our direction by starting with gender and working out towards class. For insofar as U.S.A. refuses melodrama's linkage of external datum with interior and immanent meaning (as in both fiction narratives and Camera Eyes), opting instead, through the montage of the Newsreels and the structure of the work as a whole, for the project of "robbing things of their meanings,"[31] it distances itself from a reading formation which we have seen is defined by gender as much as by class. In this sense, U.S.A., despite its putatively radical politics, is perfectly right for Esquire magazine. Certainly it is true to Dos Passos's own gender-loaded comments on the kind of middlebrow writing and reading he despised most; in a 1916 article entitled, significantly enough, "Against American Literature," Dos Passos wrote:

"The tone of the higher sort of writing in this country is undoubtedly that of a well brought up and intelligent woman, tolerant, versed in the things of this world, quietly humorous, but bound, tightly, in the fetters of 'niceness', of the middle-class outlook."[32]

The binding ties from which Dos Passos needs to escape to make his own authentic Art are, I want to say, the very ones which, as the Ferber dustjacket proudly claimed for her work, tie "period background" together with character, and bind "the present to both the remembrance of the pasts and the imperatives of the future." The woman from whom he needs to escape is someone very like the Ferber author and/or reader herself. Yet U.S.A.'s flight from this melodramatic mode into the insignificant and untotalizable flows of a mass culture's demotic vernacular is also a leap from the kettle to the pot. For, beginning in the mid-nineteenth century and continuing well into the mid-twentieth, as Andreas Huyssen and Gilbert and Gubar have argued, the sphere of vernacular, mundane or mass culture has been coded as a "no-man's land" of feminine blackness, vacuity, and babble against which the male artist must defend himself, or, horror of oedipal horrors, be overwhelmed and washed away by its senseless rush.[33] Such fear is evident throughout Dos Passos's text, not least in the number of his male characters from Joe and Mac to Charley Anderson, whose virtually inevitable falls from commitment and possibility into squalor and/or death are almost obsessively enacted through their sexual liaisons with and entrapments by women, and by the often-noted inadequacy of U.S.A.'s female characters, a flaw Dos Passos himself acknowledged in a letter to Hemingway in terms which explicitly equate the middlebrow writer/reader/character with the spectre of slippage off the heterosexist map: "Whole trouble with the opus," he wrote, "is too many drawing-room bitches—never again—it's like fairies getting into a bar—ruin it in no time."[34]

How, then, does Dos Passos defend himself against this slippery flux which threatens to overwhelm secure gendered identity and "ruin the bar"? What kind of protection does he wear and offer to his male-coded reader when he dips into it and invites us to do the same? One way, I would argue, is precisely through the construction of that gender-coded lapsarian myth we looked at above as the deep background of U.S.A.—a mythic narrative, you'll recall, whose central event is the appropriation of the "clean words our fathers spoke" by "strangers" who turn them into something "slimy and foul." Feminist criticism invites us to note and name the patriarchal and misogynist horror that underlies such language and such tales; from its perspective U.S.A. appears as at least in part hard-wired with a deep, and deeply misogynist, sexual fear.[35] U.S.A.'s mythic background narrative of historical process, far from inviting in any

members of the female middlebrow audience, or functioning as a radical
call to arms, serves as reaction-formation against a female-coded contem-
poraneity towards which Dos Passos and his male-coded readers can feel
only terror and disgust: one whose retrospective positing of an originary,
"clean" *sermo patrius* works an oedipal exorcism rite to keep the witches'
babbling, befouled *lingua materna* at bay.[36]

But this oedipal myth has, after all, only a liminal presence in the text;
nor is it Dos Passos's only line of defense against the wash of language he
has himself invited into his text to distinguish it from the equally female/
bourgeois realm of melodrama. If the position of "the fathers" and the
"purity" of their own language practices are no longer available to us
men, another kind of integrity and clarity is, as Dos Passos made clear in
his remarks to the American Writers' Congress in 1935, remarks entitled
"The Writer as Technician": "The professional writer," he said, "discovers some aspect of the world and invents out of the speech of his time
some particularly apt and original way of putting it down on paper. If the
product is compelling and important enough, it molds and influences the
ways of thinking to the point of changing and rebuilding the language . . .
In his relation to society a professional writer is a technician just as much
as an engineer is."[37] The other thing you can do with the senseless flow
of contemporary history and the demotic vernacular is to rationalize it
into separate beltlines—to become a modernist engineer yourself.
Accordingly, as Bruce Robbins notes, the *U.S.A.* machine features a
"high proportion of scientists, engineers, and inventors among the
figures accorded the privilege of continuous biographical treatment and
[an] overwhelming admiration for their technical ingenuity—despite
political reservations and in a novel where there is little admiration to
spare."[38] It offers us Thorstein Veblen as the most heroic figure of the
biographies, and Veblen's "hope that the engineers, the technicians, the
non-profiteers whose hands were on the switchboard might take up
where the workingclass has failed" (*The Big Money*, pp. 103–4) as the
novel's only fully affirmed (albeit defeated) hope. And, as many critics
have noticed, it treats the story of engineer-mechanic Charley Anderson's catastrophic fall from clarity and competence, thanks to his unholy
alliances and liaisons with both women and unscrupulous business types,
with a sympathy and pathos denied to every other character in the trilogy
(with the possible exception of radical activist Mary French).[39]

There is nothing particularly original about noticing the discrepancy
between the claims made for—and within—*U.S.A.* as a radical novel on
the one hand, and Dos Passos's allegiance to, and self-definition within,
the ideals and perspectives of the professional-managerial class on the
other. But I am suggesting that this contradiction may disappear if we
think of *U.S.A.* as an attempt, within a gender- and class-coded literary

culture, to displace and resolve along *class* lines a problem—or, more accurately, a terror—arising from the threat to oedipal masculinity in an age when the older, patriarchal authority of the bourgeois father in social and familial life was clearly and rapidly eroding; and if we see the continuity of Dos Passos's defensive actions as correlative with those executed in the texts surrounding and framing his work, from the high austerity of *The American Mercury* to the winking and scoffing of *Esquire*, to protect the anxious, threatened white male oedipal ego from being constrained by the female bindings of middlebrow culture, or swamped and washed out to sea by the flood of the mass.

At this point, by contrast, we may wish to recall Ferber's quite different and far more critical construction of professionalism in *Come and Get It*'s increasingly cold-hearted, passionless Bernie, a depiction which runs counter to Dos Passos's, not only in its negativity but in the ways it codes its critique in sexual-vitalistic terms (both the Ferber narrator and Lottie herself note how slight, compared to Barney's, are Bernie's capacities for sensual enjoyment—or excitement). Yet Ferber's portraiture, while largely negative, is muted, even murky; in this and in her other novels of the 1920s and 30s, nothing much is finally made of it (perhaps for fear of alienating some part of her audience). Nor can Dos Passos univocally celebrate the professionalist-scientific ethic to which he and his male-identified audience nonetheless cling for dear life. For both authors, then, and both class- and gender-based reading audiences, the meaning and valence of professionalism are still undecidable; the professional-managerial class's emergence as a major force on the American scene, and the work of placing this new class within a gender- and class-specific coalition of cultural consumption—both processes and projects were clearly underway back in the mid-1930s, and just as clearly unresolved, as they are still today.[40]

In any case—in *every* case, that is, within commodity culture—the work of cultural siting and interpellation hardly ends with the appearance of the product in the marketplace; indeed, until the product's shelf life is exhausted, that work is never done. So *Come and Get It* and *U.S.A.* come out, and the hoopla goes on. A New York newspaper columnist prattles "Had I a million I would bet it / On Edna Ferber's *Come and Get It*,"[41] while Bernard DeVoto in *Saturday Review*, praising the "[e]xperimentation, technical versatility," and "imaginistic brilliance" of *The Big Money*, nonetheless complains "that the thing lacks something in warmth."[42] Likewise, *Time* magazine, itself engaged in a major back-page bid for cultural status, contemptuously labels *Come and Get It* a "smoothly machined product," "Grade B entertainment, an honest product at an honest price,"[43] while waxing eloquent and longwinded on

Dos Passos's attempt in *U.S.A.* to take "as his subject the whole U.S. and ... organize its chaotic, high-pressure life into an understandable artistic pattern. To find the equivalent of his nationalism," purrs *Time* full-throatedly beneath three photos depicting Dos Passos the male artist-writer drinking a beer, "one must look abroad, to Tolstoy's *War and Peace*, to Balzac's *Comédie Humaine*, to James Joyce's *Ulysses*."[44]

The invocation of high-class Europe versus the plea for warmth, the derogatory slotting of one product as mass-produced, machine-made, and the canonization of another as a masterwork of high art—all sound familiar, don't they? We have tracked the path of such loaded claims, curses, and blandishments not only up to but into these two texts themselves, taking the texts as only one condensed and critical skirmish within a larger and longer battle to plant the flag with the product logo on it precisely *here* on the cultural terrain, on this rise or that one, where the right audience—right, that is, in both class- and gender-based terms—will be able to see the flag, flock to the site, buy the product and confirm themselves by eating it up. As indeed the texts canonized as Literature, the novels peddled as "good fiction," and the formula fiction ground out to satisfy lowbrow sensational tastes truly are—commodities all, each one wrapped up in the packaging appropriate to it. That is how I have tried to read these texts: as positioned and positioning commodities for sale to class- and gender-specific audiences, which they not only assemble but help to construct. If such a reading by no means exhausts the meanings of either work, it does, I hope, at least suggest the kind of sense we might make of the cultural commodities that get called "art" or "junk" or "pulp" in our time as well, and lead us away from the temptation to valorize *any* one technique or pleasure as being somehow in and of itself politically or aesthetically superior to any or all others. Is *U.S.A.* a better, that is, truer or more artful or more politically right-on, work than Edna Ferber's *Come and Get It*? Which is better, melodrama or modernist montage? I will be happy if I've made such unsituated, context-free questions unanswerable—and happier still if I have made them less likely even to be asked.[45] For in a culture still as riven by class, gender, and racial divides as our own, it seems to me they are both the wrong place to start thinking about the cultural commodities we have to choose from and the wrong place to stop.

Back in 1936, between the publication of *Come and Get It* and *U.S.A.*, Theodore Adorno wrote his friend Walter Benjamin a characteristically brilliant and patronizing letter in which he described mass culture and high culture as the "torn halves of an integral freedom, to which however they do not add up."[46] From the two test cases in audience construction and interpellation we have looked at here, in relation to each other and to other "higher" and "lower," masculine- and feminine-based appeals, I think we can respond to Adorno that there are more than two pieces of the integral freedom he describes lying around; and from our own existence in a world that contains *Pee-Wee's Playhouse* and *Miami Vice*, among other things, we can say that some of the pieces get put together in some pretty strange ways nowadays. But I still want to hold on to the notion of the fallen totality here, if only as my own frankly mythic Marxist-feminist version of the old lapsarian tale—a broken totality of damaged desires and partial truths which we ought not to think of homogenizing into unity, but whose present variety—in culture and politics alike—it would be our task to liberate and extend, out beyond the enforced soul-breaking coercions of class and race and gender, and out from under the domination of the marketplace, to form part of a socialist and feminist world in which all our life-choices, including the ones we mean when we use the word *culture*, would be greater and freer than ever before. That is how I want to conclude—not by making a choice between two competing commodities from the past, but by urging us beyond them in the present, towards some model of expanded yet egalitarian cultural production and choice we have yet to think up and construct.

(1988)

NOTES

1. For other work along these same lines, see Tony Bennett, *Bond and Beyond* (New York: Methuen, 1988); Richard Ohmann's essays on canon formation and contemporary fiction in his *Politics and Letters* (Middletown CT: Wesleyan University Press, 1987); and Janice Radway's forthcoming work on cultural politics of and around the Book-of-the Month Club.

2. Pierre Bourdieu, *Distinction: A Social Critique of the Judgement of Taste*, trans. Richard Nice (Cambridge MA: Harvard University Press, 1984), p. 100.

3. James D. Hart, *The Popular Book: A History of America's Literary Taste* (New York: Oxford University Press, 1950), p. 229.

4. Ibid., pp. 248, 261.

5. Douglas Waples, *Research Memorandum on Social Aspects of Reading in the Depression* (New York: Arno Press, 1972; reprint of 1937 edition published by the Social Science Research Council), p. 150. The categories and data cited in this and the following two paragraphs are drawn from chapter 5 of this text, pp. 145–82, except where specifically noted.

6. Roland Marchand, *Advertising the American Dream: Making Way for Modernity, 1920–1940* (Berkeley: University of California Press, 1985), p. 54; however, in all but the final quoted phrases within this sentence, I am citing Marchand's quotation from George Gerbner's analysis of the *True Story* formula in "The Social Role of the Confession Magazine," *Social Problems* 6 (1958), pp. 29 and 40.

7. Hart, p. 237.

8. See "A Barbaric Poem of New York," Mike Gold's review of *Manhattan Transfer*, in *New Masses* 1 (August 1926). Gold praises Dos Passos's achievement but concludes by

declaring that he "must read history, psychology and economics and plunge himself into the labor movement." (p. 25) Likewise, in his *New Republic* reviews of *The 42nd Parallel* and *1919*—collected together under the title, "John Dos Passos: The Poet and the World," and reprinted in *Dos Passos: A Collection of Critical Essays*, ed. Andrew Hook (Englewood Cliffs NJ: Prentice-Hall, 1974), pp. 76–86—Malcolm Cowley complains about the decadent lyricism of the Camera Eye sections of *The 42nd Parallel*, but subsequently declares that in *1919* Dos Passos has escaped from the bourgeois subjectivism which tainted the earlier novel.

9. In his South Chicago survey, Waples reports that "literature" accounted for a mere 1.3% of professionals' reading: a tiny percentage, obviously, yet the highest by far of those recorded for all the socioeconomic groups surveyed. It may also be relevant to my overall argument here, moreover, that within the professionals category, women mixed far more "literature" with the rest of their reading (2.4%) than men did (0.9%). See table XXXI in Waples, pp. 152–3.

10. Lewis's review is quoted in Linda Wagner, *Dos Passos: Artist as American* (Austin: University of Texas Press, 1979), p. 47.

11. See Lennard J. Davis, *Resisting Novels: Ideology and Fiction* (New York: Methuen, 1987); and Elizabeth Long, "Reading Groups and the Postmodern Crisis of Cultural Authority," *Cultural Studies* 1, 3 (October 1987), pp. 305–25.

12. *Atlanta Bookshelf* (April 1932); quoted in *Book Review Digest 1932* (New York: The H.W. Wilson Co., 1933), p. 167.

13. Quoted in Rogers Dickinson, "Edna Ferber," his afterward to the original edition of Ferber's *So Big* (New York: Grosset and Dunlap, 1924), p. 367.

14. Michael Denning, *Mechanic Accents: Dime Novels and Working-Class Culture in America* (London: Verso, 1987), p. 45.

15. Note here the curious overlap between White's rhetoric and the otherwise opposed hype of Mary Ross's *Atlantic Bookshelf* review of Dos Passos just quoted, in which it is precisely the middlebrow pleasure of slack "beguiling of an idle hour" that is stigmatized. The readerly villains of one puff-piece may be the heroes of the other, but in both cases the mark of Satan is slothfulness, the signs of Fordist virtue "concentration" and "work."

16. Back dustcover, *Come and Get It* (New York: Doubleday, Doran and Co., Inc., 1935).

17. Quoted in Julie Goldsmith Gilbert, *Ferber: A Biography* (Garden City NY: Doubleday, 1978), pp. 226–7.

18. *The Big Money*, pp. 560, 561, in John Dos Passos, *U.S.A.* (New York: Random House, 1937). Subsequent quotations from the trilogy by volume and page number are from this edition and are incorporated in the text.

19. Jean-Paul Sartre, "John Dos Passos and *1919*," in Hook, *Dos Passos*, p. 66.

20. Claude-Edmond Magny, "Time in Dos Passos," in ibid., p. 130.

21. Quoted in George J. Becker, *John Dos Passos* (New York: Ungar, 1974), p. 58.

22. Althusser's definition and critique of "expressive causality" may be found in Louis Althusser and Etienne Balibar, *Reading Capital*, trans. Ben Brewster (London: New Left Books, 1977). For my definition of melodrama I am chiefly indebted to Peter Brooks, *The Melodramatic Imagination: Balzac, Henry James, Melodrama and the Mode of Excess* (New Haven: Yale University Press, 1976). But see also "The Flâneur at *River's Edge*," in this volume.

23. *The Widening Gyre* (Bloomington: Indiana University Press, 1963), p. 59.

24. Page numbers given here and subsequently in the main text of the essay are from the first edition of *Come and Get It*; for full citation, see note 16 above.

25. Erich Auerbach, *Mimesis: The Representation of Reality in Western Literature*, trans. Willard R. Trask (Garden City NY: Doubleday, 1957), p. 416.

26. Roland Barthes, *S/Z*, trans. Richard Howard (New York: Hill and Wang, 1974).

27. See Alfred Kazin, "Dos Passos, Society, and the Individual," in Hook, *Dos Passos*, pp. 101–19, and Barbara Foley, "From *U.S.A.* to *Ragtime*: Notes on the Forms of Historical Consciousness in Modern Fiction," *American Literature* 50, 1 (March 1978), pp. 85–105. These critics are, of course, only two of the most notable of a wide number of

commentators who have made the same claim for Dos Passos's work.

28. Here, for example, is the long block paragraph of speechifying that delights the children, affronts the snobbish Lottie, and fells the exhausted Bernie—a climactic speech, indeed, which nonetheless typifies the weird, windy rhetoric that dominates the last hundred pages of the book in its desperate, thrashing attempt to construct a space in which the contradictions between the left-populist discourse of the 1930s, the new jazzy blandishments of mass culture, and the old capitalist-populist "producer" rhetoric of her earlier work might be resolved or effaced:

"Tom Melendy strode over to Karie, and kissed her first on one cheek, then the other, just where the circle of rouge lay high and naive, deceiving no one. "Karie, you're priceless, you're perfect, you're my Dream Girl. Lotta darling, listen. Bernie, it isn't what they'll learn there [up at the Midwest public university where Tom teaches]. It's what they'll see and feel and hear. Kids, forgive me for talking about you as if you weren't in the room. But look. It's up to you, and kids like you, to decide what kind of world this is going to be in the next twenty years. Don't you see!" He turned squarely to Bernie. "We'll be through. We're through now, nearly. Physically these kids and all the kids of their generation are the most beautiful human specimens since early Greece. Spiritually they've been hit over the head with a meat-axe by the last ten years. They're beginning to come to. Give 'em a chance.... Democracy! We know that the world can't be made safe for Democracy. It can't be made safe for anything. There's nothing less safe than the world. You take a chance the minute you come into it.... The only lasting thing in life is the spirit you bring to it.... Somebody else said that.... Tell you what I want to do. Next summer let me take the twins and drive right slap-bang across the continent. There's what I call education. The East, the Middle West, the Rockies, the desert. Not just scenery. People. Detroit, Chicago, Kansas City. The factories, the farm lands. Look, my generation got all steamed up about war and death. They sent millions and millions of kids to live in mud and lice and wet and cold in order to kill a lot of other kids they'd never seen and everybody got wildly excited about the whole idea. Can you believe it now! Women gave up food and clothes and luxuries. And the speeches! Say, if we could hear some of those speeches now we'd probably die laughing—or crying. But you've got to say this: right or wrong, foolish or wise, the spirit of the people was something to thrill you. They cared, by God! They cared. Where is it now! It's in all those kids who are going around like beautiful sleep-walkers. We—you and I and the rest of us—have been so damned hurt and fooled and scared that we've brought them up to pretend nothing matters. Don't show emotion. Be hard-boiled. Crack wise. What the hell. Applesauce. Boloney. Nerts. Sometimes I get sick and fed up with it, and then along comes the Sacco-Vanzetti thing, or those Scottsboro boys, and I see thousands of men and women willing to give time and energy and money and their very lives—for what! To try to get justice for a couple of Wops and a bunch of nigger boys. They're fighting to keep alive something much more valuable than the men themselves. It's justice, and the spirit of America they're—" (p. 500)

At which point, Ferber has capitalist technocrat Bernie rise, declare the whole babble "Communist"—and fall over dead.

29. Pre-second-wave feminism, that is. Throughout the 1930s feminist currents from the decade before continued to affect women's actions, thoughts, and writings; even more obviously, women were an active, distinct force within a variety of reformist and radical groups and causes of the time.

30. Here I am drawing chiefly on my reading of Jessica Benjamin's important work. See, for example, her "A Desire of One's Own: Psychoanalytic Feminism and Intersubjective Space," in Teresa de Lauretis, ed., Feminist Studies/Critical Studies (Bloomington: Indiana University Press, 1986), pp. 78–101.

31. William Stott, Documentary Expression and Thirties America (New York: Oxford University Press, 1973), p. 120.

32. New Republic 8 (October 14, 1916); quoted in Wagner, Dos Passos, pp. xiv–xv.

33. See Andreas Huyssen, "Mass Culture as Woman: Modernism's Other," in Tania Modleski, ed., *Studies in Entertainment* (Bloomington: Indiana University Press, 1986), and Sandra M. Gilbert and Susan Gubar, *No Man's Land: The Place of the Woman Writer in the Twentieth Century*, vol. I, *The War of the Words* (New Haven: Yale University Press, 1988).

34. Quoted in Wagner, *Dos Passos*, note 21, p. 190.

35. Richard Ohmann has drawn my attention to the ways in which the sections immediately abutting this climactic Camera Eye implicitly specify the heroes and villains, the "we" who compose "America our nation" and the treasonous "strangers" who oppose "us." The Mary French narrative which precedes Camera Eye 50 concludes by arriving precisely at the same desperate final moment of the Sacco-Vanzetti affair which is the reference point of the latter section. As the last demonstration is assaulted by the police, Mary links arms with "a little man with eyeglasses who said he was a music teacher," and "a Jewish girl, a member of the Ladies' Fullfashioned Hosiery Workers" (shades of the underdog immigrant crowd heroically evoked in Camera Eye 50), and forgets "everything as her voice join[s] . . . all their voices, the voices of the crowds being driven back across the bridge in singing: *Arise, ye prisoners of starvation . . .*" (*The Big Money*, pp. 460, 461).

In the brief Newsreel that follows, moreover, Dos Passos continues to unfurl the lyrics of the *Internationale*, crosscutting them against headlines announcing Justice Holmes's denial of a stay of execution and the inevitability of Sacco and Vanzetti's death; while on the other side of the climactic Camera Eye, the next Newsreel begins its demotic babble of headlines and Tin Pan Alley songs with a swatch of anti-communist rhetoric from Henry Ford, followed by an appropriately savage prose-poem biography of William Randolph Hearst. I have no desire to deny the existence of such pointing and naming, or to downplay the intended significance of its valorizations and condemnations here. But I do mean to suggest that the moment of Camera Eye 50, and the lapsarian myth enacted there, are complex and crucially *overdetermined* by a gender-loaded, patriarchal-misogynist language whose shaping power here and throughout *U.S.A.* has hitherto, to my knowledge, been overlooked.

36. My terms here are borrowed from Gilbert and Gubar's discussion of Joyce's verbal strategies in *Ulysses*; see pp. 252–60.

37. John Dos Passos, "The Writer as Technician," in *American Writers Congress*, ed. Henry Hart (New York: International Publishers, 1935), p. 170.

38. Bruce Robbins, "Working Knowledge: Dos Passos and Professionalism" (unpublished manuscript).

39. In fact, the intersecting plotlines of Charley Anderson's fall to squalid death and Margo Dowling's serendipitous rise to Hollywood stardom so dominate the crowded stage of *The Big Money* that a thoroughly habituated middlebrow reader may easily read the book as a more-or-less straightforwardly Dreiserian melodrama of gender and class. Such a possibility may in part account for the widespread critical acclaim *The Big Money* received when it came out, and for the degree to which it remains the preferred volume chosen over *The 42nd Parallel* and *1919* in college courses "covering" Dos Passos today. Indeed, Richard Ohmann, who teaches such a course, tells me that his students often take in *The Big Money* in just this "airbrushed" way.

40. See " 'Makin' Flippy-Floppy': Postmodernism and the Baby-Boom PMC," in this volume.

41. Quoted in Gilbert, p. 329.

42. *Saturday Review* 14, 3 (Aug. 8, 1936); quoted in *Book Review Digest 1936* (New York: The H.W. Wilson Co., 1937), p. 277.

43. *Time* 25, 9 (March 4, 1935), p. 67.

44. *Time* 28, 6 (Aug. 10, 1936), p. 53. Dos Passos and *U.S.A.* are, in fact, the cover story for this issue of *Time*.

45. "Unsituated" and "context-free" are the key words here, as I hope the rest of this essay has already made clear. Certainly I do not mean to deride those readers whose radicalization has been helped along by their encounter with *U.S.A.*—including that friend of mine who insists that his unself-conscious bourgeois faith in a benign, meritocratic destiny was shattered when he read the trilogy in high school. Nor, of course,

has it been my intention to canonize *Come and Get It* as a socialist-feminist masterpiece. Rather, my aim has been to point to the already situated specificity of any reading— including my own here—and to open up theoretical and critical space for the full, and fully situated, variety and determinate complexity of reading experiences that we construct from our own places within the social world.

46. Bloch et al., *Aesthetics and Politics*, (London: Verso, 1977), p. 123.

The Flâneur at *River's Edge*; or,

A Cruise of the Strip

In the torpid summer of 1987, during the dog days of a corrupt and reactionary pseudo-populist regime, a film called *River's Edge* was released, to a critical reception which, while generally favorable to the film itself, struck an interestingly symptomatic note of hostility towards its teenage protagonists. Directed by Tim Hunter, a veteran of other, rather more amiable "brat-pack" films, and based on a real murder and its aftermath in Milpitas, California in 1981, *River's Edge* depicts the lack of response—or lack of "proper", conventional response—by a group of teens to the murder of one of their crowd by another. The latter freely admits his crime, and even takes his friends to the river's edge to see the slowly discoloring nude corpse of his former girlfriend sprawled on the bank. Yet for hours thereafter, most of them remain at a loss for a reaction, radically unsure both of what they feel and of what they ought to do. Only Layne the budding speed-freak has an idea and a plan: that John the murderer is still their friend and still alive, and so must be protected, hidden from the authorities, and allowed to escape. Yet Layne's hysterial heroics and proposed rescue project receive little support from the rest of the group, who largely beg off and slip away, back into a pot- and booze-fueled drift through school classes in which they are harangued by their teacher, a sour and self-righteous baby-boomer, on the contrast between their fallen times and morals and the glorious days and movements of the 1960s, and through various glancing encounters with their distracted, anomic baby-boom parents in their disintegrating suburban ranch-style homes.

Beyond these characters, the collective protagonist of the film's queasily slack plot, there are two other complicating presences: Feck, a burned-out, reclusive ex-biker who supplies the kids with weed and is gradually drawn in to Layne's frantic project, despite his own increasing horror at John's sociopathic affectlessness; and Tim, an 8-year-old depicted throughout the film as a nearly demiurgic force of vengeful wrath and amoral, debased need, whose appetitive fury is only disarmed by an implausible last-minute reconciliation with his older brother Matt. Each of these actants injects the action's otherwise languid course with an occasional burst of dramatic or expressive momentum (as when Dennis Hopper's Feck twitches and bugs his startled eyes at John's blank indifference, or as Tim, packing a stolen pistol, cruises in a stolen car through the early morning to find and kill his brother). Moreover, each appears radiating his own specific generic nimbus, the figure of Feck inevitably referencing Dennis Hopper's long career as countercultural deviant, from the dissident sixties hippie of *Easy Rider* to psychopathic gonzo in the mid-eighties *Blue Velvet*, just as Tim calls up an equally long, if somewhat more generically stable, list of horror films built around the figure of the demonically possessed, insatiable child, from *Rosemary's Baby* and *The Exorcist* to *Firestarter*.

But *River's Edge* is, even without Feck and Tim, already resonant with other generic allusions and the expectations they provoke: most obviously, those of the early-eighties "brat-pack" film itself, in which typically a group of affluent yet troubled white teens (as in John Hughes's *The Breakfast Club*, a paradigm of the species) draw out and resolve their individual problems through a kind of rough-and-tumble group therapy *cum* assorted hi-jinx; and, of course, the cheerfully scrubbed Spielbergian suburbs of *Close Encounters of a Third Kind* and *E.T.*, in which broken homes and troubled families are magically reconstructed or restored with a single wave of a suitably high-tech, Disneyesque wand. Indeed, a full analysis of this film and its claim on our attention would necessarily involve an appreciation of the peculiar genius of its reprocessings of these generic raw materials, which are all subjected in *River's Edge* to a demythologizing acid-bath via the raw and grainy naturalism of its camera eye, in which the suburbs go dingy, the chipper, struggling families turn into a harried and snarling congeries of impotence, anger and need, the kids' clothes are torn and dirty, while the kids themselves, zonked and ripped, compose a collectivity as slack as the plot. To their credit, several of the film's original reviewers were sensitive to such genealogical echoes and resonances, which, unfortunately, I will have to scant here, in favor of the rather more sweeping historical context and broad-brush approach I am interested in. For over and above the indubitable social significance of the blending and debasement of these separate generic ideologemes, it is the project of demythologization itself in *River's Edge* which it will be the business of this chapter to place as one contemporary end-point in a long series of attempts to deal with the vexations of secularity as a problem—indeed, in some sense, as *the* problem—of bourgeois perception and bourgeois narrative form: the difficulty, as *Hill Street Blues'* Mick Belker used to put it, of "reading the street."

Beyond detectives and criminals, the crime novel and the cop show, western culture offers us one other major figure or trope for the street-reader: the flâneur, from its first incarnation as strolling Baudelairean dandy to its male and female descendants, teenagers and adults, now killing time in the nearest mall. This chapter, it must be confessed, will share the flâneur's chief shortcomings: we will slide from one display window to the next, pausing to handle and taste each professed sample, in all too perfect ignorance of the specific historical conditions of its production, and of its very ingredients. Yet, if we can avoid the "drowsy numbness" of connoisseurship here, and keep in mind the looming existence of all the marks of production that have been occulted, even effaced, by the dilettantish sampling method of this piece, we might be able to salvage from this walking tour some lesson to be gained from the admittedly "grand récit" I want to sketch out, not only about the scandal of capitalist secularity for bourgeois perception and politics, but for the construction of a socialist consensus as well.

For what is finally the problem, and the stake, in bourgeois narrative, is consensual value itself, in a social order in which there are, as it were by definition, no longer any binding codes for reading the street. This much is well known on both the left and right, and we already have no dearth of intelligent and provocative scholarship (for example, Richard Sennett's *The Fall of Public Man*; or, in a different vein, much of Fredric Jameson's work on the passages from Balzacian realism through modernism and post-modernism)[1] exploring the subject and teasing out its political effects. Why then tackle it again here, in a single chapter which already announces the shortcomings of its own impressionistic non-method? Because, I think, it is a problem that we on the left, given our historic commitment to secularity, have a hard time facing squarely, that is, without either swerving away into an insular, dismissive rationalism in the face of the perpetual return of the "irrational" repressed (the sight of "kooks" and "fascists" beating people up over the flag, or "screaming mobs of Muslim militants" in the squares of Teheran), or, worse, devolving Lasch-like into some species of regressive nostalgia for some earlier *Gemeinschaft* of class, region, or race. Because, in short, as the good doctor said, we must repeat what we cannot master.

And because there are always others on our right who will offer to master this dilemma themselves; and particularly in the present moment, we have no reason to discount their powers and effects. Indeed, we can hear the latter's presence with ominous clarity in the mainstream critical response to *River's Edge*; for example, in this excerpt from David Ansen's *Newsweek* review.

This is the scariest vision of youth since the alarming Brazilian movie "Pixote," but there one could point a finger at the appalling poverty that drove the kids into crime. Hunter ... isn't a finger pointer.... "River's Edge" pitches the audience inside this nightmare world of affectless middle-class kids and lets us watch them wallow their way through moral dilemmas they can only half articulate. The 60s-generation adults don't have answers; they helped create the mess.... [T]he values on display are so upside down the movie reaches moments of near surreal comedy.[2]

We may pass over the standard bourgeois repudiation of didactic or *Tendenz* art, and the endorsement of the proper division of labor between artist and critic (the good artist doesn't point fingers; the good reviewer does), and move straight to the proferred moral. What screwed these kids up, what rendered them incapable of articulating their "moral dilemmas"? Why the sixties themselves, of course, and the generation which came of age within the sixties—or rather, which refused to do so, and in the process of its anarchistic, narcissistic refusal tore apart the cultural fabric of the country, shredded its moral vocabulary, and evacuated its (white, western, canonical) values.

Had Ansen been poring over the pronouncements of Education Secretary Bennett when he wrote this review? Is he a pal of Hirsch or Bloom, or simply a kindred spirit, a presaging voice? It hardly matters by this time, I think. As even the most infrequent reader-viewer of mainstream magazines and TV over the past decade and a half can attest, the hegemonic project of demonizing and ridiculing the social activism and alternative cultural politics of the 1960s has been gathering steam for quite some time. There are two ways of responding to such negative reframings, both of them necessary. The first, which I will not develop here, is to insist that those same sixties were in fact the last time in our nation's history when large numbers of its people had, and acted on, a sense of conscience, around and towards a vision of social justice, and to argue the extent to which the relative moral poverty of the country today is precisely the *result* of the extirpation and repression, through various combinations of coercion and hegemony, of that collective moral will. The second, however, is to reject the parochial framing of the argument altogether, to historicize not only differently, but *more*, so that same destitution appears as the end of a much longer drama built around value and significance within capitalist society, one staged in no small part within canonical Western narrative itself. It is in the service of this project, towards the construction of this latter counter-narrative, then, that I invite you on the following stroll.

DISPLAY WINDOW 1

All fixed, fast-frozen relations, with their train of ancient and venerable prejudices and opinions, are swept away, all new-formed ones become antiquated before they can ossify. All that is solid melts into air, all that is holy is profaned, and man is at last compelled to face with sober senses his real conditions of life, and his relations with his kind.

(Marx and Engels, *The Communist Manifesto* [1848])[3]

... the history of the human heart, traced thread by thread, social history set down in all its parts—there is the foundation. It will not be imaginary facts; it will be what happens everywhere.

(Balzac to Countess Hanska, on *La Comédie Humaine* [1834])[4]

We might as well have begun our walking tour with a look at a page or two of Defoe, prose-poet of the first days after the first bourgeois revolution, perhaps focusing on those passages in *Robinson Crusoe* in which the drab prose of sheer instrumentality, of supplies salvaged and precisely counted, survival stratagems drearily described and applied, is abruptly interrupted by one of those swatches of pious, moralizing rhetoric which supply the novel with whatever slight and arhythmic dramatic punctuations it possesses. The circle that the Balzac letter tries to square and Marx and Engels's exuberant prophecy dismisses, is already present in a singularly raw and obvious form: the problem of how social action may have or be given significance—including dramatic significance—within a social order in which transcendent systems of meaning and value have been banished with the rule of kings and priests, leaving only their ruins behind. But let us skip ahead instead to Balzac, Marx and Engels' favorite poet of realism, the first author at whose hands, as Franco Moretti observes, "the 'prose of the world' ceases to be boring."[5]

How, specifically, is such a feat accomplished in the Balzac novel? The very antinomies so offhandedly juxtaposed in the quotation above begin to supply us with our answer, as would even the most casually symptomatic reading of Balzac's Preface to *La Comédie Humaine*: through a constant shuttling between the sociologically specific—a *quartier*, a suit of clothes, a *feuilleton*, and their respective social standings and economic worth in the utterly secular system that is Paris—and the allegorized universal, between "social history" and "what happens everywhere." The new, internalized space of the *immanent*, of "the human heart, traced thread by thread," is in Balzac the effect of this constant dialectic without synthesis, whose workings may be discerned at both the "molecular"

level of the interplay of sentences within a given scene or descriptive
paragraph and on the "molar" level, that is, in the plot-logic of the
Balzac melodrama, including its distinctive reluctance to end.[6] Peter
Brooks's *The Melodramatic Imagination*, a work to which this entire
chapter, and especially this section, is indebted, proposes to us both that
melodrama is the quintessential generic form of post-revolutionary,
bourgeois narrative, and that Balzac's work is a particularly striking
instance of the attempt to "re-sacralize" the secular, to fuse the "world of
representation and a world of signification that do not coincide and do
not necessarily offer access from one to another."[7] So, on the molar
level, the project strains through a welter of sociologically specific
descriptions and scenes of sordid plotting and scheming, towards a few
climactic moments of ineffable synthesis, when language becomes
transparent, and signification is at once purified and naturalized into a
single "mute gesture," as Brooks puts it, in which all the clotted, humid
energies of the plot up to that point are cataclysmically discharged[8]—as,
for example, at the instantaneous moment in *Père Goriot* when Vautrin
drops his mask upon being apprehended at Madame Vauquer's boarding
house, "the convict's terrifying head was revealed without disguise," and
"everyone present instantly understood the manner of man Vautrin
was." Yet such moments of incandescent immanence, however arduously
prepared, are doomed to fail as soon and as much as they succeed, and
not only because within a few pages the boarders will be back to their
sordid speculations and vacuous word-games, but because the Balzacian
narrator himself, at the very instant of naturalized transcendence, will
always have to code/decode what is supposed to speak for itself. Thus,
the climactic mute gesture must be surrounded by a frenzy of reading
which it was supposed to have rendered superfluous:

> ... the convict's terrifying head was revealed without disguise. *The short,
> brick-red hair lent a shocking suggestion of strength combined with cunning to the
> face; the whole head gave an impression of power in harmony with the powerful
> chest and shoulders, and at that moment the soul and spirit of the man were
> apparent in his face as if he stood in a lurid glare thrown by the flames of hell.*
> Everyone present instantly understood the manner of man Vautrin was, *his
> past, present and future, his pitiless doctrines, his religion of his own good pleasure,
> the royal power given him by his contemptuous appraisal of other men and his
> cynical treatment of them, and by the strength of an organization that was prepared
> for anything, and stopped at nothing.*[9] (italics mine)

Red hair as code for strength and cunning, a physique as a sign of satanic
power: here is no transparency, but rather precisely the opposite, a shard
of allegory, in all its flaunted arbitrariness. Yet this moment of allegory
(whose codings here, as often in Balzac, are drawn from the master code

of Christianity) is itself inherently vertiginous.[10] Suddenly, and as it were in the same breath in which we "instantly understand" Vautrin as a transcendentally satanic creature, we are returned to the level of the merely historical and social, in the appositions of the final quoted sentence, which comprise a list of the behaviors and attitudes of a given individual scheming in time. Thus, the Balzac novel is condemned forever to behave as Eugène de Rastignac does at the conclusion of *Père Goriot*, when he stands at the highest point of Père-Lachaise, on the threshold of this world, and the next, to issue his defiance—and then, "by way of throwing down the gauntlet to Society," goes "to dine with Madame de Nucingen." (p. 304)

But this same movement from transcendence to secularity, or, rhetorically speaking, from allegory to metonymy, is also active on the molecular level in Balzac, where it most often occurs in reverse. In a given scene or description, that is, placed somewhere on the long run-up to some shattering climax, we will also find the language of social typology, of easy metonymic legibility ("one of those smart cabs which flaunt the luxury of a spendthrift existence, and imply the possession of all that is desirable in Parisian life" [p. 79]; "he said abruptly, with the passionate insistence that women find so flattering" [p. 58]) sliding fleetingly toward and into other, higher and more arbitrary realms of signification, as in the description of the neighborhood within which the Vauquer boarding-house will be set:

> A Parisian straying here [the lower end of the Rue Neuve-Sainte-Geneviève] would see nothing around him but lodging-houses or institutions, misery or lassitude, the old sinking into the grave or the cheerful young doomed to the treadmill. It is the grimmest quarter of Paris and, it may be said, the least known. The Rue Neuve-Sainte-Geneviève especially is like a bronze frame, the only one suited to this story, for which the mind must be prepared by gloomy colours and heavy thoughts, as a traveller descending to the Catacombs sees the light of day grow dim and hears the sing-song of his guide grow hollow as he goes down step by step. It is a true comparison, for who can decide which is more horrifying, the sight of empty skulls or of withered hearts? (pp. 28–9)

The mechanisms of the passage from "representation" to "signification," as Brook describes it, are foregrounded and depicted with a rare explicitness. The voice of the sociologically knowledgeable guide grows insubstantial, inadequate, "hollow," as the landscape rendered ceases to be a socio-historical datum, and turns instead into a Dantesque moral and spiritual realm. Thus we are prepared for the sight of the boarding-house itself, the quintessential Balzacian "milieu," whose contradictory ontological and epistemological status Auerbach's famous analysis has disclosed to us as a site in which "organic and demonic unities" are forged, and "allegorical witches lie hidden."[11]

But not quite forged, and not quite hidden, as this brief analysis has attempted to show. The witches are all too easily seen, the moment of transparent revelation an unstable compound which breaks down into its scandalously irreconcilable component elements as soon as it is formed, forcing the Balzacian project ever onward towards the next swatch of description, up towards the next shattering, yet finally unsuccessful climax, in its doomed trajectory towards an asymptotic synthesis of allegory and metonymy, signification and representation, it will never be able to reach.

DISPLAY WINDOW 2

Yet in a later moment, however briefly and unevenly, it would seem that just such a fusion is achieved, in the works of a scant handful of bourgeois novelists of the third quarter of the nineteenth century, to whose writing practices the term "organic form" will be retrospectively applied to designate the seemingly natural embedding of significance within and through representation itself:

> Mr. and Mrs. Casaubon, returning from their wedding journey, arrived at Lowick Manor in the middle of January. A light snow was falling as they descended at the door, and in the morning, when Dorothea passed from her dressing room into the blue-green boudoir that we know of, she saw the long avenue of limes lifting their trunks from a white earth, and spreading white branches against the dun and motionless sky. The distant flat shrank in uniform whiteness and low-hanging uniformity of cloud. The very furniture in the room seemed to have shrunk since she saw it before: the stag in the tapestry looked more like a ghost in his ghostly blue-green world; the volumes of polite literature in the bookcase looked more like immovable imitations of books. The bright fire of dry oak-boughs burning on the dogs seemed an incongruous renewal of life and glow—like the figure of Dorothea herself as she entered carrying the red-leather cases containing the cameos for Celia.[12]

We will not linger over this zenith of bourgeois narrativity, if only because it has been sufficiently explored and celebrated by a generation whose "New Criticism" posits its practices and effects as the norms against which all previous and subsequent literary productions were to be judged. In passing, however, let us grant the successes these critics have so often and triumphantly described. Everything here, from the weather to the books on their shelves, speaks of the deflation of Dorothea's hopes for her marriage with Casaubon—and, as it were, "naturally" so. The signs of production, of the *labor* of signification, have been smoothed out of the text, as have the boundaries between narrator, character, and reader, so that the significance of "white branches against the dun and motionless sky" is, we feel, the same for all, and Dorothea herself, through a slight, smooth shift in focus, may become another figure in the carpet, testifying mutely yet transparently to the general truth of the perception which is also her own private state of mind.

Aesthetic conventions, as Stephen Greenblatt has recently reminded us, are themselves social agreements as to what can be rendered in what ways: agreements which both rest on and enable other, more obviously social and political consensuses.[13] So, while it will not do to explain "organicism" merely by dissolving its achievements into some totalizing, reductionist narrative of the consolidation in western Europe of the rule of the bourgeoisie, I would still insist on the degree to which "organic form" is indissociable from such hegemonic consolidation, by which such practices were at least in part enabled, and to which project it contributed in turn. This said, however, I also want to echo Terry Eagleton's point in his magisterial essay on the subject of "organicism," "Ideology and Literary Form," by pointing both to the transitory and scattered nature of this aesthetic achievement (what, for example, could be the French equivalent of *Middlemarch* or *Anna Karenina*, the two greatest examples of bourgeois organic form?), and to the necessarily peripheral location of its operations.[14] Tolstoy's Russia, still on the nether, feudal edge of liberal democracy and western capitalism, Eliot's idyllically rural, largely pre-industrial townships, and the signifying practices that render and emplot them, thus need to be placed alongside the urban landscapes and aesthetically unharmonized, *inorganic* practices of their contemporary counterparts, *L'Education Sentimentale*, *Bleak House*, and, for that matter, even *Crime and Punishment*, and the lesson drawn: even at the zenith of what Hobsbawm calls "The Age of Capital," it is still apparently not possible to produce an organic melodrama that is able to read the urban street.

The importance of Conrad, then, our principal display in this second window, lies in his attempt to construct an organicist social and aesthetic vision against the grain of a signifying practice which persistently, even derisively, pulls such syntheses apart into *abymes de texte* that expose their epistemological and social impossibility—as in Mr. Verloc's famous morning walk through the London streets:

Such was the house, the household, and the business Mr. Verloc left behind him on his way westward at the hour of half-past ten in the morning. It was unusually early for him; his whole person exhaled the charm of almost dewy freshness; he wore his blue cloth overcoat unbuttoned; his boots were shiny;

his cheeks, freshly shaven, had a sort of gloss; and even his heavy-lidded eyes, refreshed by a night of peaceful slumber, sent out glances of comparative alertness. Through the park railings these glances beheld men and women riding in the Row, couples cantering past harmoniously, others advancing sedately at a walk, loitering groups of three or four, solitary horsemen looking unsociable, and solitary women followed at a long distance by a groom with a cockade to his hat and a leather belt over his tight-fitting coat. Carriages went bowling by, mostly two-horse broughams, with here and there a victoria with the skin of some wild beast inside and a woman's face and hat emerging above the folded hood. And a peculiarly London sun—against which nothing could be said except that it looked bloodshot—glorified all this by its stare. It hung at a moderate elevation above Hyde Park Corner with an air of punctual and benign vigilance. The very pavement under Mr. Verloc's feet had an old-gold tinge in that diffused light, in which neither wall, nor tree, nor beast, nor man cast a shadow. Mr. Verloc was going westward through a town without shadows in an atmosphere of powdered old gold. There were red, coppery gleams on the roofs of houses, on the corners of walls, on the panels of carriages, on the very coats of the horses, and on the broad back of Mr. Verloc's overcoat, where they produced a dull effect of rustiness. But Mr. Verloc was not the least conscious of having got rusty. He surveyed through the park railings the evidences of the town's opulence and luxury with an approving eye....[15]

Our passage opens with a vision of aesthetic and social harmony which, but for the occasional hint of irony ("comparative alertness"), at first appears to be a prime example of organic synthesis, of the happy equivalency of subjective perception with external objects as registered and guaranteed by an untroubled narrative frame. Yet this same synthesis is constructed only to be disturbed (first by the swift, illegible glimpse of the "skin of a wild beast" and "woman's face and hat" in the victoria), ironized (by the sardonic disengagement from the narrator from this pleasant unity, with the demur of the "bloodshot" sun), and further disarticulated by the dissociation of the natural from the social sign, and of the subjective perceptions of Mr. Verloc from the objective facts. The "red, coppery" light is, in effect, peeled away from both social landscape and individual subjectivity, becoming an atmosphere in which both bathe without awareness; so that the easy traffic the passage describes between serene *haut bourgeois* order, and Verloc's complacent approval, now appear mocked and diminished by a light quite literally other than the one in which the two see themselves.

And this same process of disarticulation proceeds as well and as often in the opposite direction, splitting private sensibility apart from public convention, rendering each major character a "person unknown," even the stolid yet shady personage of Verloc itself. The passage just cited continues:

Mr. Verloc, without either rubbing his hands with satisfaction or winking sceptically at his thoughts, proceeded on his way. He trod the pavement heavily with his shiny boots, and his general get-up was that of a well-to-do mechanic in business for himself. He might have been anything from a picture-frame maker to locksmith; an employer of labour in a small way. But there was also about him an indescribable air which no mechanic could have acquired in the practice of his handicraft however dishonestly exercised: the air common to men who live on the vices, the follies, or the baser fears of mankind; the air of moral nihilism common to keepers of gambling hells and disorderly houses; to private detectives and inquiry agents; to drink sellers and, I should say, to the sellers of invigorating electric belts and to the inventors of patent medicines. But of that last I am not sure, not having carried my investigations so far into the depths. For all I know, the expression of these last may be perfectly diabolic. I shouldn't be surprised. What I want to affirm is that Mr. Verloc's expression was by no means diabolic. (pp. 8–9)

The metonymic reading of Verloc as externally legible social type here gradually runs into a set of slippages and qualifications so intricately hemophiliac as to require an act of sheer narratorial assertion to stem the hemorrhage of significance that ensues. Verloc appears to be an artisanal workman or petty bourgeois—except for that "indescribable air," which is, in fact, never described, but through which our attention is shunted both to another, and shadier, "class of people," and, through them, to another and quite opposite moral signification. At this moment the implicit allegory which sustains the movement from metonymy to metaphor, representation to signification, is itself problematized, with the narrator's admission of his own ignorance as to whether the "indescrib-able air" which ought to connect the social type (gambling den owners, detectives, quacks) to its allegorical meaning (as "moral nihilism") even exists—leaving us, at the paragraph's end, with a figure whose description and value are alike problematic, whose meaning is so lost in a haze of assertion, qualification, and retraction that he is finally only described, and at the last moment, by what he is not.

Small wonder, then, that this long description of Verloc's walk through London concludes by describing and half-humorously railing against the lack of sensible order in the addresses of the buildings in the *haut bourgeois* neighborhood at which he arrives; or that the plot of *The Secret Agent* will be built around the attempt to blow up the Greenwich Observatory from which all bourgeois time and space are literally measured; or that the two climactic moments of that plot—the acciden-tal detonation of the bomb, which blows up its bearer, innocent Stevie, the idiot boy, and Winnie Verloc's murder of her husband—remain "indescribable" moments of ultimate significance which the text cannot render except as what Eagleton, speaking of Conrad's work as a whole, calls "central absences."[16] For all Conrad's explicit contempt for the opponents of British bourgeois democracy, his novel can only proceed by the most elaborately sidereal circumlocutions in space, time, and perspective around such absences (he wrote despairingly to Cunning-hame Graham, "I am one of those who are condemned to run in a circle"[17]), and, on the molecular level, through a tortuously contradic-tory interplay of incommensurate modes of registration and signification, in which the social is increasingly evacuated of significance, and ultimate, transcendent meaning is only liminally possible along a horizon in which the most private and the most inhuman levels of cognition mystically coalesce, a site depicted as simultaneously beneath and beyond mere words:

> The veiled sound [of Mr. Verloc's last remark to Winnie] filled the small room with its moderate volume, well adapted to the modest nature of the wish. The waves of air of the proper length, propagated in accordance with correct mathematical formulas, flowed around all the inanimate things in the room, lapped against Mrs. Verloc's head as if it had been a head of stone. And incredible as it may appear, the eyes of Mrs. Verloc seemed to grow still larger. The audible wish of Mrs. Verloc's overflowing heart flowed into an empty place in his wife's memory. Greenwich Park. A park! That's where the boy was killed. A park—smashed branches, torn leaves, gravel, bits of brotherly flesh and bone, all spouting together in the manner of a firework. She remembered now what she had heard, and she remembered it pictorially. They had to gather him up with the shovel. Trembling all over with irrepressible shudders, she saw before her the very implement with its ghastly load scraped up from the ground. Mrs. Verloc closed her eyes desperately, throwing upon that vision the night of her eyelids, where after a rainlike fall of mangled limbs the decapitated head of Stevie lingered suspended alone, and fading out slowly like the last star of a pyrotechnic display. (p. 189)

We are a good distance here from both Balzac's labored histrionics and the naturalized significations of Tolstoy and Eliot. Vautrin's revealed essence and Dorothea's transparently legible character yield to a new sense of psychological *interiority*, an utterly private and virtually non-verbal realm of hidden perceptions and cognitions that is as inaccessible to public visibility and externalised, conventional signification as the implacably inhuman and mechanistic laws of the universe with which its representation here is mingled in the ironically transcendent, grisly image of Stevie's head, itself simultaneously a hypercharged fragment of subjectivity and a mere dead thing. Thus, for all the conservative organicism of Conrad's declared political perspective,[18] the ironic and skeptical fusions of representation and signification effected by his writing practice itself are preeminently emblems of the *asocial*, of that for which virtually by definition there can be no consensually legible signs out on the street. Accordingly, *The Secret Agent*, one of his most viciously reactionary novels, will end with a final sight of its most officially despised character, the nihilistic terrorist known as The Professor walking along with his bomb strapped to his body and his hand on the triggering device, a figure of perfect inscrutability "wired up for instant self-consignment to eternity,"[19] moving emblem of the impossibility of any organicist synthesis:

> He walked frail, insignificant, shabby, miserable—and terrible in the simplicity of his idea calling madness and despair to the regeneration of the world. Nobody looked at him. He passed on unsuspected and deadly, like a pest in the street full of men. (p. 227)

DISPLAY WINDOW 3

> Suppose I could run all the scenes together more?—by rhythms chiefly. So as to avoid those cuts; so as to make the blood run like a torrent from end to end.
>
> (Virginia Woolf, *A Writer's Diary*[20])

A dead world of objects and contingent events and an intense but private realm of interiorized subjectivity, whose opposition is scantly mediated through a thin and largely misleading, even useless tissue of social order and public "common sense"—this scandalous and at least in part involuntary vision created by Conrad's writing practice is perhaps most dramatically summed up within *The Secret Agent* in the image of a new "blood-time," simultaneously inert datum and intensely lived subjective experience, which succeeds Winnie's murder of her husband.

> Mrs. Verloc cared nothing for time, and the ticking went on. She concluded it could not be the clock, and her sullen gaze moved along the walls, wavered, and became vague, while she strained her hearing to locate the sound.... Her fine, sleepy eyes, traveling downward on the track of the sound, became contemplative on meeting a flat object of bone which protruded a little beyond the edge of the sofa. It was the handle of the domestic carving knife with nothing strange about it but its position at right angles to Mr. Verloc's waistcoat and the fact that something dripped from it. Dark drops fell on the floorcloth one after another, with a sound of ticking growing fast and furious like the pulse of an insane clock.... It was a trickle, dark, swift, thin.... Blood! (p. 192)

Yet as both the likenesses and differences between this passage and the above quotation from Virginia Woolf's diaries suggest, one of the chief characteristics of the moment of high literary modernism that follows Conrad will be the refiguration of this alienation into a new revelation, via a valorization of the very syntheses Conrad's prose constructed yet deplored.

In the English and Anglo-Irish modernism of T.S. Eliot, Joyce, and Woolf above all, public discourse and conventional signification appear most often as demotic scraps of debased language whose montaged scatterings impede more than they assist understanding or knowledge. Consensual codes of meaning and value lie in ruins for these modernist writers all across the "immense panorama of waste and futility" which T.S. Eliot, praising Joyce's Ulysses in his famous review, defined as contemporary history.[21] Yet this panorama of bankrupt or exploded allegory, not perhaps so far from the "allegorical ruins" Walter Benjamin recovered or constructed in his contemporary essay on the German Trauerspiel,[22] is typically joined and redeemed by modernist practices at the extremes of its horizons, out there where intense, and intensely private, subjectivity begins to fade ineluctably into a transcendentally mythic or religious realm altogether beyond time and history.

Fredric Jameson, following Adorno, has frequently described the impulse underlying modernism as the desire to resist commodification, to construct and defend a sphere of production and value lying beyond both traditional bourgeois society and the newly emergent and aggressive terrain of mass-produced, mass-consumed culture.[23] But I want to transliterate his description, at least for the purposes of our stroll here, into a more idealistic and epistemological dialect. The altered formulation would then go something like this: within a situation characterized by the erosion of bourgeois hegemony, both by the "decoding" secularizing energies set loose by capitalism itself, and by the rising power and pressure of other classes and cultures pressing up from below, the modernist project, especially as it is taken up in the English-speaking world, consists of a desperate attempt (or, in Joyce, a derisive one) to discover or construct a place in which significance is still possible, where events and experiences may still somehow naturally mean. Yet, to the extent that this zone is of necessity walled off from any realm of public sign-production, now seen as both inherently debased and irreversibly balkanized, the narratives that result from such an impulse must necessarily be rather literally uneventful, and the temporal successions of linked, exterior scenes and transformations around which earlier novels were built are demoted in favor of the new architecture that Joseph Frank's classic formalist essay denominated as "spatial form."[24]

The famous phrase refers, in effect, to the molar functioning of modernism, to the construction of a sense of unity and coherence through the whetting and satisfaction of "a new type of interest," as Jameson describes it, "in which our reading minds are asked to tie bundles of cross-references together, to begin to lose sight of the character for the motif."[25] Yet here again I want to quibble with Jameson's formulation, while agreeing with its basic sense: it does not seem to be character we "lose sight of" so much as plot. In these texts worldly events are, strictly speaking, meaningless except insofar as they serve, on the molecular level of the text, as random and contingent catalysts for secretions of subjective resonance, or, on the molar level, as unwitting signposts towards "some ultimate zone of reality in which everything turns out to be related to everything else."[26] The external world, the social world, merely so many phatic, evacuated data in itself, has meaning only as the meaningless hinge between the ineluctably private and the ultimately mythic; as an intrinsically phatic way of getting from one internal and/or transcendental moment or motif to the next.

The immediate experience of this new narrative system, as worked by one of its most famous authors, is described by James Naremore as follows:

> a smooth, liquid stream of sensibility [is] abruptly interrupted by the violent contact of life outside in the form of a sound like a backfire or a doorbell. In a larger sense, this watery world, where identity is muted and the self seems to blend with the outside, where in solitude the individual feels at peace and harmony with an elemental form of life—this world *is* Virginia Woolf's style.[27]

The description, once again, seems to fit Winnie Verloc nearly as well as Clarissa Dalloway, with the signal difference that what is depicted as pathology in Conrad's work is now, in Woolf, largely a valid epistemology, if not an occasion for outright joy. So, in *Mrs. Dalloway*, the waves of sensation from external stimuli ripple out, the "leaden circles dissolve in air," and are received into the private Sargasso of each individual subjectivity, without pausing for rest or mediation in the stabilizing conventions of public signification. Clarissa herself "would never say of any one in the world now that they were this or were that,"[28] and the novel endorses her refusal to do so, in its depictions of the unhappy-to-vicious inadequacies of those like Doctors Bradshaw and Holmes or Doris Kilman, who show themselves willing to apply the socially given labels and evaluations to what they see and do, and in the novel's digressively explicit linkage of such behaviors to the giant allegorical figures of "Proportion" and "Conversion," social order without and ideological submission within, twin pillars of a stagnant bourgeois culture at the center of an unjust Empire. Against such wholly inadequate, indeed even vicious, signifying practices, then, stands that ceaseless, promiscuous mingling of inner and outer which is the genuine democracy of perception, that ever-dispersed, uncontainable interaction which in and of itself signifies "real life":

> For having lived in Westminster—how many years now? over twenty—one feels even in the midst of the traffic, or waking at night, Clarissa was positive, a particular hush, or solemnity; an indescribable pause; a suspense (but that might be her heart, affected, they said, by influenza) before Big Ben strikes. There! Out it boomed. First a warning, musical; then the hour, irrevocable. The leaden circles dissolved in the air. Such fools we are, she thought, crossing Victoria Street. For Heaven only knows why one loves it so, how one sees it so, making it up, building it round one, tumbling it, creating it every moment afresh; but the veriest frumps, the most dejected of miseries sitting on doorsteps (drink their downfall) do the same; can't be dealt with, she felt positive, by Acts of Parliament for that very reason: they love life. In people's eyes, in the swing, tramp, and trudge; in the bellow and the uproar; the carriages, motor cars, omnibuses, vans, sandwich men shuffling and swinging; brass bands; barrel organs; in the triumph and the jingle and the strange high singing of some aeroplane overhead was what she loved; life; London; this moment of June. (pp. 4–5)

What we have here, however, is something more complex than mere "stream of consciousness," the "attempt," as Auerbach puts it, "to render the flow and play of consciousness adrift in the current of changing impressions."[29] That play of consciousness and impressions, of localized subjectivity, is in Mrs. Dalloway always in danger of slipping away, dangerously and/or deliciously, into some very much more watery and indistinct realm. On the structural level, as we have already noted, that realm is indicated by the ever more portentous recurrences of the various motifs—the leaden circles dissolving, a scrap of Shakespeare floating over and through the text—through the particular subjectivities and moments portrayed, while on the stylistic level its presence is everywhere suggested by the presidence of what Dorrit Cohn speaks of as a "disincarnated narrator-consciousness" speaking in a "gnomic present."[30] This narrator's existence is fleetingly apparent within the passage just quoted above, in the suspended uncertainty as to the precise location of the point of view in the paragraph's first sentence, in which the borders between Clarissa's own internal monologue and another, equally lyric yet more unplaceable narration are impossible to specify. But throughout Mrs. Dalloway it is just as likely to float up explicitly out of either private subjectivity or public event, quite often as a metaphoric comparison or conceit which ultimately overwhelms and evaporates its referent:

Quiet descended on her, calm, content, as her needle, drawing the silks smoothly to its gentle pause, collected the green folds together and attached them, very lightly, to the belt. So on a summer's day waves collect, overbalance, and fall; collect and fall; and the whole world seems to be saying "that is all" more and more ponderously, until even the heart in the body which lies in the sun on the beach says too, That is all. Fear no more, says the heart. Fear no more [here, an echo of the Shakespearean motif, a line from *Cymbeline*], says the heart, committing its burden to some sea, which sighs collectively for all sorrows, and renews, begins, collects, lets fall. And the body alone listens to the passing bee; the wave breaking; the dog barking, far away barking and barking. (p. 59)

Such dispersals of centered subjectivity and objectively specifiable space-time are not always rendered as transcendence and triumph in *Mrs. Dalloway*, to be sure; the example of war veteran Septimus Smith and the motif of the Shakespeare quotation itself remind us of the "downside" of such dissolutions, loss of boundaries as psychosis and/or death. Nonetheless, such a mysticized "blood-time," depicted as the living antithesis of now-demoted bourgeois notions of centered subjectivity and fixed space-time, and stretched between an intensely private "lived experience" and a transindividual, asymptotic unity, is consistently affirmed throughout the novel, and many if not most other modernist texts, on both the molar and molecular, the stylistic and the structural levels or registers.

The debate still rages, of course, and perhaps especially within feminism and the left, over the extent to which such narrative and aesthetic strategies ever constituted a successful or meaningful assault on dominant (that is, bourgeois/patriarchal/capitalist—though the precise terms chosen clearly exert a considerable influence over the respective judgements reached) culture.[31] More important to our purposes than such arguments and judgements, however, is a clear sense of such strategies as a new moment along our walking tour, and within the admittedly crude history we have been sketching of the dialectical relations constructed between representation and signification within a ruthlessly developing and secularizing capitalist culture. Then, whatever else modernism might be (for example, in Woolf, a radical critique and deconstruction of the patriarchal Symbolic, and representation/enactment of a fluid, permeable feminist perspective; or, in Woolf, and modernism in general, a premonitory aestheticization of precisely the serialized alienation and dispersion that, in the era of Fordism and mass culture, was coming up next), it should be understood as a kind of end run around the wreckage of the organic synthesis of representation and signification which we glimpsed briefly in Eliot's work, and then saw collapse in Conrad. Representation now appears as sheer, contingent facticity; publicly significant representation, officially or consensually designated meaning, as banality or scam. What remains is private significance, personal resonance alone, at an irrevocable remove from the social: the inevitable result, perhaps paradoxically, of the general experience of a new age of mass culture and monopoly capitalism, as Eli Zaretsky describes it, of "the sense of an isolated individual ranged against a society he or she cannot affect."[32] And the resort to myth, or mysticism, within modernism, the consistent gestures towards "some ultimate point-of-view-less experience that we approach only as an outside limit,"[33] then become comprehensible as both an indication of the *impossibility of social significance*, and a necessary substitute for the community, and communicative possibilities, which now seem degraded or lost.

DISPLAY WINDOW 4

What happens next, within at least a certain sector of the cultural field we now call "postmodernist," is that such hermetic syntheses themselves are invaded and contaminated by the demotically public "environmental waste" they were constructed to hold at a distance or keep out. Thomas Pynchon's *The Crying of Lot 49*, for example, can be read in just this way, as precisely a subversive assault on the methods and meanings of the modernist aesthetic it follows, beginning on its first page, with the train of associations and/or memories which the news-datum of her former lover's death touches off in Pynchon's protagonist, Oedipa Maas:

> Oedipa stood in the living room, stared at by the greenish dead eye of the TV tube, spoke the name of God, tried to feel as drunk as possible. But this did not work. She thought of a hotel room in Mazatlan whose door had just been slammed, it seemed forever, waking up two hundred birds down in the lobby; a sunrise over the library slope at Cornell University that nobody out on it had seen because the slope faces west; a dry, disconsolate tune from the fourth movement of the Bartok Concerto for Orchestra; a whitewashed bust of Jay Gould that Pierce [the now-dead lover] kept over the bed on a shelf so narrow for it she'd always had the hovering fear it would someday topple on them.[34]

The reader conversant in high modernism enters such a moment expecting both to be able to read out from this list some sense of the character's "inner," psycho-emotional life, and to spot and tag a motif or two from that same list for further tracking, towards the ultimate end of comprehending the text through mapping out its own distinctive "spatial form." But Pynchon's text invites such a reading, and such expectations, only to mock and frustrate them. The separate images, most of them quite chunky, even contradictory, in and of themselves, cannot be taken in as a coherent, totalizable series adding up to any single or articulable emotional complex. As "objective correlatives," to invoke T.S. Eliot's famous phrase, they are abject failures, mere white noise; nor, for that matter, will either the reference to Bartok or the robber baron Jay Gould ever show up again, or link unequivocally up to the other, equally disparate references to various cultural icons high and low to bound the text and make it mappable.

Yet, as every Pynchon groupie knows, "unequivocally" is the key word here; for somewhere on or within the enormous heap of cultural references thrown off in this text there may well be, in fact probably are, a tempting scatter of allusions which, if followed out, just might begin to compose what could seem to be a meaningful motivic structure around, say, Hungarian composers or famous American capitalists. Such, at any rate, is the thematic equivalent of and complement to the text's mockery of the intensely authentic asocial subjectivist self posed by modernism—as here, in Oedipa Maas's pseudo- (or quasi-pseudo?) mythic epiphany on the slopes of Southern California's San Narciso:

> She drove into San Narciso on a Sunday, in a rented Impala. Nothing was happening. She looked down a slope, needing to squint for the sunlight, onto a vast sprawl of houses which had grown up all together, like a well-tended crop, from the dull brown earth; and she thought of the time she'd opened a transistor radio to replace a battery and seen her first printed circuit. The ordered swirl of houses and streets, from this high angle, sprang at her now with the same unexpected, astonishing clarity as the circuit card had. Though she knew even less about radios than about Southern Californians, there were to both outward patterns a hieroglyphic sense of concealed meaning, of an intent to communicate. There'd seemed no limit to what the printed circuit could have told her (if she had tried to find out); so in her first minute of San Narciso, a revelation also trembled just past the threshold of her understanding. Smog hung all around the horizon, the sun on the bright beige countryside was painful; she and the Chevy seemed parked at the centre of an odd, religious instant. As if, on some other frequency, or out of the eye of some whirlwind rotating too slow for her heated skin even to feel the centrifugal coolness of, words were being spoken. She suspected that much. She thought of Mucho, her husband, trying to believe in his job [as a deejay]. Was it something like this he felt, looking through the soundproof glass at one of his colleagues with a headset clamped on and cueing the next record with movements stylized as the handling of chrism, censer, chalice might be for a holy man, yet really tuned in to the voice, voices, the music, its message, surrounded by it, digging it, as were all the faithful it went out to; did Mucho stand outside Studio A looking in, knowing that even if he could hear it he couldn't believe in it? (p. 13)

The distinctive brilliance of such a passage, and of the best of what we might call "high postmodernism" in general, from Pynchon and Barthelme to DeLillo and Acker, lies precisely in its ability to have its cake and eat it too: to evoke and deride the couplet of subjectivist immanence/mythic transcendence which modernist textual practice constructs as its own particular machine for the production of significance, and to do so, in effect, in the same breath. We seem to be, with Oedipa and the Pynchonian narrator, hovering very near the same liminal edge of pure, totalized Being that grips Woolf's Clarissa Dalloway, connects her up and disperses her out to, and beyond, all the rest of London and the world. Yet the names themselves here—San Narciso, Oedipa and Mucho Maas—simultaneously suggest both a non- or post-individualist sense of character, and the larger possibility that all Oedipa almost senses as the Real could just as easily be in someone's (Oedipa's? her dead lover's? the author's? the reader's?) head. Moreover, if the possibility of pure narcissistic projection nibbles away at this vision of ultimate meaning from one side, the presence of brand-name commodities and high-tech cultural artifacts and practices—the Chevvy Impala, the printed circuit, and deejaying Top 40 as an extended metaphysical conceit—crowds it on the other. Indeed, in this same light we might compare Clarissa's own stated attitude towards Death-and-Beyond (one fully backed, as we have seen, by Woolf's textual practice)

> that somehow in the streets of London, on the ebb and flow of things, here, there, she survived, Peter survived, lived in each other, she being part, she was positive, of the trees at home; of the house there, ugly, rambling all to bits and pieces as it was; part of people she had never met; being laid out like a mist between the people she knew best, who lifted her on their branches as she had seen the trees lift the mist, but it spread ever so far, her life, herself (Woolf, p. 12)

to Oedipa Maas's rather more anxious, not to say paranoid, suspicion that

> someday she might replace whatever of her had gone away by some prosthetic device, a dress of a certain color, a phrase in a letter, another lover. (Pynchon, p. 121)

If modernism's task was to redeem the brute secularity, the sheer dumb facticity of the world through a mix of intensely private and unknowingly transpersonal signification, high postmodernism tends to run the same film in reverse: to "reveal" in what were heretofore the most sacred, subjective, and/or authentic moments imaginable the scandalously constitutive yet soiling presence of the commodity and the cliché, the stupid, empty, inescapable word-as-thing/thing-as-word.

Thus, to choose only a few related examples, the typical anecdote of a Laurie Anderson performance, in which the information on mythic rites and customs given to the anthropologist by the native informant turns out to have been roughly translated from an American sitcom rerun on TV; the David Salle canvas, on which the abstract-expressionist brush-stroke vies inconclusively with the drawing-class sketch and a few Disney characters for presence and authority; or, for that matter, much contemporary theory itself, with its implacable critique of any and all claims to objective knowledge or truth, its aesthetic preference for the "free play of signifiers" and the practice of pastiche, and its socio-political preference for the new language of "difference" and "subject-position" over older perspectives based on concepts of structural opposition, centered subject and absolute Other. In all such cases, including that of the Pynchon novel, what is most notable for our purposes is that the project of signification, of the construction and maintenance of some collective system of consensual meaning and meaning-production, some universalistic "politics of representation," has been abandoned, and the project of that older project's *problematization* taken up. Yet as I and several other commentators have been arguing for some time now, though the old distinction between "high" and "low" or "mass" culture no longer holds water (if, indeed, it ever did), we can nonetheless discern even within contemporary postmodernist culture something like a hierarchically ordered spectrum of practices.[35] At the top, for those with the cultural and literal capital to take it in, at private liberal-arts schools or at BAM or in the pages of *representations*, we can find, and situate, the postmodernism of problematization I have just been describing; at the bottom, or, more precisely, for practically everyone in our society, there is the unproblematic spectacle of apparently endless, and endlessly mutating (albeit commodified) choice, in the genial, incessant intertextuality and free play of TV, and the hundreds of advertisements every one of us is now supposed to see and take in on some level of consciousness every day.

At the moment, though, I am less interested in sketching the positions along this spectrum than in returning, finally, to the text with which we began, to see what it looks like now, from the other side of this admittedly extended yet still all-too-superficial stroll past a few exemplary displays of various moments in the dialectic between representation and signification in western capitalist society. For *River's Edge* seems to me to take up a well-nigh unique position along the spectrum I have just evoked, and to take on a distinctive project from that position: accessibly pitched, and marketed for a "crossover" audience, playing a mixed art-house/movieplex circuit for its first run, the film can be read as taking signification as its subject matter, yet, paradoxically, doing so within a naturalistic aesthetic framework, as a "real-life" dilemma engaged by a sociologically and culturally specific group of disarticulated, white, downwardly mobile West Coast teens. Yet, if the window-shopping ramble I have just been hauling us along has any value, it would be in the long historical light it throws on this dilemma, and the long, unsettled tradition of partial resolutions and fresh dissolutions in which it is imbricated and with which it enriches the specificities of this text.

For this purpose, in fact, we might return briefly to that moment of exuberant prophecy near the beginning of full-scale capitalism and bourgeois reign, when Marx and Engels announce that at this moment, in the wake of all feudal regimes, "man is at last compelled to face with sober senses, his real conditions of life, and his relations with his kind." The famous phrases summon up a dream of transparent, natural significance, of social meaning without any social code, an ideal rationalist reality whose figurations may be found across a wide historical and ideological spectrum, stretching (at least) from the Enlightenment *philosophes* to John Stuart Mill. Yet what we have seen in our stroll is that while such a dream has been formally constitutive of novelistic narrative for centuries, its realization within narrative has proven—to say the least—relentlessly difficult. So much, I suppose, is obvious—was obvious, indeed, before we started on our tour; it will have come as no surprise to most readers that the time of bourgeois realism and "organic form" is long gone (and was inherently shortlived and vertiginous when it was around). But the dream that fueled such narrative experiments is still far from dead, and not least on the left itself, where "ideology," while now admitted in at least some circles as a semi-autonomous force of its own, with its own institutions and material effects, nonetheless remains a separable object of study from the point of view of a secularized materialist science which stands outside and/or above the field on which it works. Critics writing from such an epistemological perspective will then tend to explain the failure of bourgeois realism, its mutation into modernism and postmodernism, by reference to one or several concomitant social processes, from the "bad guys" of commodification, patriarchy and imperialism to the feminist, non-white, anticolonialist return of the repressed, the "good guys" now, on some views, seen to be pressing modernism into postmodernism from below.[36] While such causal linkages seem indubitably real and important to me, I must confess they do not seem fully *adequate* as explanations for the shifts in narrative (and, as I see it, epistemological) practice they concern. Rather, at the clear risk of being labelled and dismissed as a retrograde idealist myself, I want to argue that above and beyond such contextual determinations, the realism–modernism–postmodernism story may also be read as a fable about the impossibility of either man or woman ever facing the "real conditions of life" and their "relations to their kind" in any non-ideological way; and about the strange dialectical contortions and devolutions that result when that impossibility itself is not faced.

Along these lines, indeed, a great deal more might be said, albeit crudely and riskily, about the rough coincidences and similarities between the various stages of left theory and strategy—from natural, unassisted working-class consciousness and the scenario of inevitable, indeed organic transformation, to the vanguard Party and the necessity of revolution, and from there to the "new social movements," now defined and constructed from "discursive formations" and brought together (in the theory, that is) by a politics of "articulation"—and the three modes of narrative practice which we have just flâneured past.[37] But such a project lies beyond the scope of the present chapter, in which I have conjured up this little narrative on narrative mainly to set both one specific filmic narrative, River's Edge, and the dilemma of meaning and value which is its more-or-less explicit theme, within a longer view and a richer context than have previously been granted them. Rather than conclude with a burst of grand theoretical pronouncement, let us return to the place, and text, we started with and see what its operations and thematics look like when viewed in this altered and enlarged context, as our final and most recent exhibit in this series of narrative attempts to "read"—i.e., to construct a readable version of—the bourgeois-capitalist street.

For River's Edge is about, explicitly, a reading problem, after all: the problem of how to take in and react to the dead body of Jamie, the teenage woman who has been strangled by her boyfriend John early in the morning on which the film's action opens. But that action begins, interestingly enough, not with the murder itself, whose enactment will be reserved, as we shall see, for retrospective display as part of the film's dramatic-thematic climax, but with an eerie parallel to it, in the boy Tim's "murder" of his little sister's doll, which he drops into the river from the bridge on which he has also caught sight of John the murderer sitting howling on the river's edge next to the nude corpse of his girlfriend. For some time thereafter, as the film introduces us to its primary actants and narrative lines, it will continue to tie those lines around other women's bodies and (and in some sense as) their representations: around Clarissa, whom Layne, the teenagers' ringleader, claims as his in his first scene with Matt—the film's hero, and the one who finally calls the police—who is himself ultimately chosen by Clarissa in the course of the film as her at least temporary boyfriend; around the doll, "drowned" by Tim, Matt's rather strikingly androgynous younger brother, and symbolically buried by Matt and his sister in the back yard of their dingy tract home; around ex-biker Feck's sex doll Ellie, with whom he dances and talks as if it were a live lover, even as he obsessively confesses to shooting a former lover years ago; and around Jamie's body itself, abandoned to the river, like the little sister's doll and like Ellie, eventually, as well.

Around such a brutally violent and denigrating "traffic in women," we might well be tempted to construct a feminist reading of the relations of meaning and authority which circulate in the text, and which, using the familiar device of the Greimas square, we could diagram in the following way:

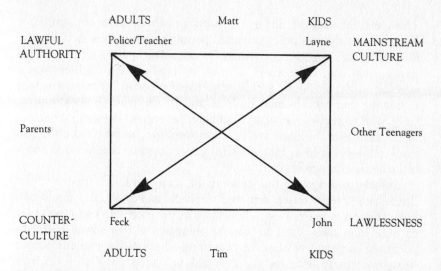

Here the teenagers' leader Layne functions as the contrary of the hectoring policeman and hip, sixties-haunted teacher who bully Matt and Clarissa, respectively, as to whether they "felt anything" at all in response to their friend's death, insofar as he too has, and presses, his own culturally sanctioned reading of what Jamie's murder means and what the group therefore ought to do. As he says to Matt and John on the way back from his first viewing of the corpse:

> It's like some fuckin' movie, you know? Friends, since second grade, fuckin' like this, and then one of us gets himself in potentially big trouble. And now we've got to deal with it. We've got to test our loyalty against all odds. It's kind of—exciting. I feel like . . . Chuck Norris, you know?

For Layne, whose imagination is a storehouse of references from movies and TV, Jamie's murder has a clear and unambiguous meaning: friends help friends, no matter what, so the body must be disposed of and John helped to escape, even if and when Layne's reading of the situation must be urged against John himself. "How do you expect other people to care about you?" he protests against the blank wall of John's apparent affectlessness:

> It's people like you who are sending this country down the tubes. No sense of pride, no sense of loyalty, no sense of *nothing*, man. Why do you think there's so many fuckin' welfare cases in this country? Why do you think that Russia's gearing up to kick our asses, man? . . . These things are important to me. And believe it or not—you're important to me.

This speed-freaking riff, and its reactionary overtones, plays in significant contrast with the one other extended political monologue enacted in the film: Clarissa's high-school teacher's narcissistic paean to the radical sixties, in which, as he says, "as crazy as it all seemed . . . there was a *meaning* in the madness, a clear and a real purpose." Yet both sets of claims are immediately met, by John and by the teenage class respectively, with scornful disbelief and indifference, and subsequently depicted, in the course of the narrative's further workings, as little more than so much self-serving cover for the bullying megalomania that lies at the root of such officious posturing.

Outside and against the pressure of such officially sanctioned yet threadbare interpretative activity, are Feck and John, the film's two linked figures of lawlessness, who will be thrown together by Layne's plot to hide John away until he can be smuggled out of town. Both are portrayed as outsiders from the beginning—Feck as the pathetic hermit living shut away with his sex doll and unloaded pistol in a decrepit bungalow from which he emerges only to hand out dope to his "friends," the kids who come by; John, as he tells the convenience store clerk from whom he tries to buy some beer, as one who doesn't "give a fuck about you and [doesn't] give a fuck about your laws." And both have killed women, their lovers. But, throughout the long night they spend together in the film's middle section, the differences between them are painstakingly drawn. Feck's bid for culture-hero status as tough-guy king of affectlessness in his story of how he lost his leg is impressive enough:

> My leg was right out in the middle of the street. I remember lying in the gutter, all bleeding and shaking, staring at my leg right next to a beer can. And I remember thinking, "That's my leg. Wonder if there's any beer in that can."

But it pales, and Feck shrinks, in the face of John's elegant summary of his own "philosophy": "You do shit; and then it's done; and then you die." Likewise with the exchange between them—Feck full of intensity, John simply declarative—on the subject of their respective murders and their victims:

> Feck: I killed a girl once, and it was no accident. Got her right in the back of the head, blew her brains out the front. I was in love.
> John: I strangled mine.
> Feck: Did you love her?
> John: (shrugging) She was okay . . .

Such contrasts between Feck's angst- and guilt-ridden consciousness and John's pathological indifference will then reach their crescendo in their long vigil back at the river's edge, as Feck first looks on horrified while John shouts gleefully back at his own calls out through the echoing void of the night ("Don't give me no shit! You eat me! No, you eat me!"), and then, at John's insistence, returns to the vexed subject of their brotherhood in crime.

> John: You wanted to show her who was boss.
> Feck: I don't know if you can understand: I *loved* her.
> John: So why'd you kill her? She tell you to eat shit?
> Feck: No. No.
> John: Feck, I'm with you. I mean, I killed a girl too. I wanted to show the world who's boss.

Our thematic square may then be neatly filled in with those actants who occupy intermediate or resolving positions between these basic poles of contrasting meaning. Between Feck and the stern officialdom of the detective and the teacher go all those parental figures, particularly Matt and Tim's mother and her loutish live-in lover, who are uniformly depicted as distracted, feeble presences, most ineffectual precisely in their pathetic attempts to exert some shred of authority over their children's whereabouts and behavior; and, across the square, the other teenagers themselves, adrift in a vacuum of response somewhere in between Layne's histrionics and John's affectlessness. Likewise, as the false, or negative resolution of the film's dynamics, Tim serves as a figure of seemingly boundless malignant rage; while his older brother Matt, the teen who notifies the police and is then taken up by Clarissa, obviously functions as the positive resolution, or utopian figure, of the text.

And the way then lies clear for a feminist interpretation of the text's circulation of figures and meanings. For what else does the landscape we have sketched out describe but a social field characterized by the decline of the oedipal/patriarchal authority once squarely lodged as the center and generative principle of the bourgeois nuclear family, and linked symbolically and psychologically with the structures of official authority and morality present in the public world? The decline, that is, without replacement by any other psychic and social principles for meaning, individuation, and order: for, as feminist psychoanalyst Jessica Benjamin has observed, though the sex/gender system of the middle-class nuclear family may be disintegrating under a myriad of social and economic pressures, in the present conjuncture no other yet appears to be emerging to take its place.[38] In such a morbid situation, marked by the devaluing of both private and public figurations of significance and signifying power, pathologies run rampant, especially insofar as, for men, the dissolution of the oedipal "solution" to the task of separation and individuation from the female mother opens the way to a vast outpouring of fearful misogynist rage, and a desperate, protofascist attempt to restore patriarchal authority in the private and public realms at all costs.

Benjamin's analysis, which she uses both as an explanation of the psycho-social forces channeled by the New Right and as an argument for the construction of a new theoretical model of feminist subjectivity in the name of which a new, and more fully humane sex/gender system might be forged,[39] seems in many ways to illuminate the text of River's Edge so well that she might have written its script. In a world where the answer to "Are your mommy and daddy at home?" is, in Matt's little sister's offhand words, "Mommy's at work, Jim's at a bar, I don't have a daddy," the old power relations and gendered division of public and private have clearly eroded almost beyond recognition; accordingly, the cop and the teacher, traditionally emblematic of the classic division of the ideological state apparatus into its coercive and hegemonic modes, are in this text seen to be, for all their blustering, bankrupt as well. And so, in the absence of such formerly structuring institutions and powers, the terror-driven male desire to deny connection with the female, the need to establish dominance over women through objectification and violence, runs riot; the master–slave dialectic Benjamin borrows from Hegel to describe the operations of male-dominant heterosexual desire[40] takes on its most extreme forms, in Layne's jeering and bullying relationship with Clarissa (alternating, as she tells Matt, with his trembling fear of sex with her), in Tim's "drowning" of his little sister's doll, in Feck's otherwise inexplicable murder of his lover and replacement of her with a sex doll he treats as alive, and, of course, most notably in John's self-described and simultaneously reenacted murder of Jamie.

John's monologue at this point, following his obscene shouting through the night and his interchanges with the ever-more-horrified Feck, is clearly delivered to us as half the climax of the film, and recapitulates the terms of the master–slave dialectic almost schematically in their most severe, and finally self-defeating working-out. Beginning, as we have seen, with the clear suggestion that Jamie was "telling him to eat shit" as far as he was concerned, and with the desire to "show the world who's boss," John's monologue climaxes with the ecstatically rendered and reiterated phrase, "I had total control of her," and then comes down via the following interchange with Feck:

John: It felt so real. It felt so real. She was dead there in front of me, and I I felt so *fucking alive*. . . . Is that how you felt, Feck?
Feck: Not quite.
John: Funny thing is, I'm dead now.

The master's ability to wrest acknowledgement of his dominance, his being-as-dominance, from the slave; the male need to wrest such acknowledgement from the woman, simultaneously reaches its highest point and collapses, taking the entire dialectic of power down with it, leaving the subject itself a mere dead object as well, shouting impotent, vicious obscenities into the void he has made out of the world. And this thematic emerges all the more clearly in the film for being crosscut against the representation of its utopian-feminist opposite; for precisely as John's speech reaches its height in the fantasy of reality as total control, the camera crosscuts between the enactment of the murder and Matt and Clarissa's lovemaking, previously initiated by Clarissa.

Our feminist reading of this film would then crystallize around this literally and dramatically climactic dialectical figuration: Jamie's head shot from above with John's hands around her neck, John's head shot from below as he kills her/Matt's head shot from above, as he writhes into orgasm, Clarissa's head shot from below as she rides him, in the park where they have camped for the night—the constellated opposition of these two orgasmic moments standing as the negative and utopian points in between which the rest of the film's actions and actants might be mapped. And, in Matt's softness and sensitivity, his willingness both to call the police and to yield power to Clarissa, we might claim, lies the film's own resolution—its feminist moral, even—of and to the post-oedipal dilemmas it has represented to us. Yet, for all the explanatory power and reach of the reading I have just sketched out, for all its clear warrant in the text itself, I must now confess I do not find it fully satisfying or complete. For one thing, there is the extent to which the film both manifestly invites and derides such a socio-psychological reading, by issuing the invitation to its explanatory register through the mouths of some of its least sympathetic characters: for example, when Layne attempts to explain away Jamie's death to Clarissa with the argument that she must have been taunting him about his deceased mother, and is echoed by another member of their group, who slurs out

"Yeah, he's got a couple loose springs when it comes to dealing with his dead mother"; or when Tim jeeringly explains to Matt that the malignant delinquency he and his buddy visit on the world happens "Because of our fucked-up childhood." For another, there is the curiously prolonged denouement of the film which, far from following swiftly or neatly from the climax we have just analyzed, continues to meander its way through a variety of scenes, episodes, and partial conclusions for another twenty-five minutes or so (Layne's apprehension; Feck's shooting John; the scenes at school the next day; the discovery of John's body, and Tim's reconciliation with Matt; Feck's monologue in the hospital) before it finally, feebly concludes at the funeral service for Jamie. Similarly, there is what I can only call the weakness of Matt, or of the Matt/Clarissa couplet if you like, as a figure in which the dilemmas posed by the film are positively resolved, a weakness which shows most explicitly in their brief precoital dialogue on the film's central subject of what and how it is possible to feel:

> Matt: I kept seeing her face, Clarissa. Didn't you keep seeing her face? I mean, it affected me. Didn't it affect you?
> Clarissa: It did.
> Matt: And even that close, we don't even feel like we've lost anything.
> Clarissa: I cried when that guy in *Brian's Song* died. You'd at least figure I'd be able to cry for someone I hung around with.
> Matt: It'll hit us. I know it will. Probably sometime around the funeral.
> Clarissa: Sometimes I think it'd be a lot easier to be dead.
> Matt: That's bullshit. You couldn't get stoned any more. (They laugh.)

Clearly, the gap between affect and effect, between feeling and its meaningful, significant, effectual articulation, is massive, even in the thoughts and utterances of the film's most sympathetic, "utopian" characters, just as their union, and the film's apparent climax, fail to solve, or even effect, the drive towards violence of the androgynous devil-imp Tim. He, and the utterly nihilistic energies for which he stands, are only defused by a last-ditch resort to a familial system of values and ethics the rest of the film has taken considerable pains to deride and subvert: Matt persuades Tim to drop the gun Tim has aimed at him by insistently repeating "You're my brother." I read the very contradictoriness, inconsistency, and forced sentimentality of such a dramatic "solution" to this subplot as a sign of desperation, of the film's inability to answer or resolve the questions it has raised. Correlatively, the sociopsychological register we used to construct our feminist reading of the text appears itself to be, while not wholly invalid, eroded by the same unstaunchable, deauthorizing semic drift to which all other constructions of meaning and value are subject in the film: yet another pallid cover story, in effect, to place alongside the teenagers' equally casual references to the Bomb and its apocalyptic presence as the explanation for why they can't seem to care.

The film's depiction, then, of the relationship between authority, culture and narrative as a gendered relationship, while forceful, is not itself able to serve as the "master code" of the text, which I want to say is finally about a rather larger crisis than even the breakdown of bourgeois-oedipal patriarchy. It seems to me, even in its very inadequacies and dramatic flaws, to be about precisely the absence of such "master codes," "*grands recits*," or totalizing strategies not only for narrative in its narrow sense—aesthetic forms and conventions for the production of imaginative texts—but for what I might here call *life-narratives*, ways of constructing meaningful understandings of and (re)actions towards perceptions and events. If much contemporary postmodern theory and aesthetic practice has been bent to the task of deconstructing all the essentialisms, to exposing them all, from "authenticity" to "Otherness," as untenable shards of long-broken codes once disguised as immanence, *River's Edge* might be said to have a plot and array of characters precisely designed to "try on" just what it is like to inhabit a position on the other side of all such essentialistic thinking and practice—and not as a theoretical position, either, but as the unselfconscious *a priori* paradoxically "behind" any genuine experience whatsoever: to try on such a position and to posit the result, deliberately or not, as an apparently intractable social, moral, *and* narrative dilemma, a vicious circle which cannot be squared.

That is why I have felt justified in placing this text, even though a film rather than a novel, at the end of our stroll through the history of bourgeois narrative; why its desolately vacuous suburbs constitute a terminus to our series of variously legible cityscapes, of all those diverse, vertiginous, and finally doomed attempts to "read the street" as in some way, however mystically or ironically, a secular immanence. This text's very existence seems to me in the widest sense to mark the end of the project of confronting the "real conditions of life" face to face; to represent not just what comes after the Father, but what little remains after the demythologization/problematization process leaves us only that smorgasbord of subject positions, identities and narratives we now designate as contemporary postmodern culture, high and low. And, perhaps, in so doing, to pose, if only by implication, the difficulties confronting any "post-Marxist" project of left politics founded on the tonically non-essentialist concept of "discursive formations" and a consequent strategy of "articulations," such as the one Laclau and Mouffe have recently proposed.[41] For what are *River's Edge*'s teens if not paradigmatically decentered subjects, individually and collectively slipping and sliding around on an ever more loose and gelatinous field of "discursive positions," none of which is strong enough to secure the subject, or to be articulated with any other discourse to form a general framework and guide for action? To the extent that such characters and their situation are recognizable and credible for us—insofar as they constitute, as Blake once said, an "Anything that is possible to believe" which is therefore "an image of the Truth"—they and their rigorously deauthorized fields of discursive play might quite rightly raise or strengthen our doubts *vis-à-vis* the new strategic project of attaining socialism through discursive articulation *sans* any ordering principle or *a priori* category of the Real (such as "working-class"—or, for that matter, either "woman" or "Black"); not so much whether it is the way to go (for what other way could there be, given the exhaustion of all the strategies for immanence we have seen, the collapse of all contenders for the transparently meaningful Real?) as how, in the world we share with the kids in *River's Edge*, it could ever work.

Yet if *River's Edge* stands with *Hegemony and Socialist Strategy* at the end of a long, doomed search for authenticity and immanent meaning whose left variants Laclau and Mouffe have vigorously critiqued, I want to close this already quite loosely speculative, flâneuristic inquiry on a blatantly idiosyncratic note, with an even more obscure, hastily sketched, and "personal" reading of the film than any I have trotted out so far. For it seems to me that although *River's Edge* hardly offers a resolution of the socio-epistemological dilemma it renders, it nonetheless manages to gesture toward a Real that lies outside it, one whose liminal presence is suggested by the film's title itself. As Stanley Aronowitz has put it, in his trenchant review of Laclau/Mouffe:

> Whether the external world obeys laws independent of human intervention may be debated. But incontestible is its moment of autonomy, that it is a "subject" the ignorance of whose regularities portend dire consequences for humanity.... It may be that the floating signifier, discourse without object and related doctrines of cultural primacy are by no means simple literary flourishes. Semiotic *philosophy* ... is merely the cultural expression of the doctrine of the domination of nature which has become a destructive material force in contemporary history.[42]

Here I have neither the space nor the competence to do more than suggest what I hope might be the obvious: that however designated, for example, as "the environment" or "Nature," there is an outside within which human society is located, whether our social or signifying practices take account of the fact or not. An outside, which, as we are now learning in the age of acid rain and tropical deforestation, ozone depletion and the greenhouse effect, may be so permanently despoiled, thanks to our characterization of it as pure inertia, the *tabula rasa* on which we perpetually write ourselves and project our wills, as to make the future of both human and other forms of life increasingly problematic. It would, of course, be absurd to claim that *River's Edge* contains any conscious or explicit critique of the western project of the domination of nature, or issues any call for a radical politics based on the combined authority and fragility of the realm of the non-human Real.[43] Yet the film seems to me nonetheless to make a space for that Real beyond and at least to some extent against the enervated and imploded realm of the "floating signifier" within which its teenager characters fidget and drift. I am thinking here, first of all, of the initial sequence of the film, whose opening image is, for a long moment, literally illegible: an apparently "raw" and unpatterned gestalt of rough black patches on white, into which first natural sounds, then color, are gradually bled in, until we are, at last, able to read the image as river, just before the human action (Tim's "drowning" of his sister's doll, John's howling by the nude corpse of his girlfriend) begins; then, of the stark and terrible scene in which John shouts his vicious obscenities, solipsistic and self-hating, across the river and into the night, as if both were merely empty space in which, narcissistically and endlessly, to project the self; and, finally, of that long static moment just after the film's dramatic climax and just before Feck's shooting of John, in which nothing human or dramatic whatsoever appears to be happening, and we see, first the river again, then the park in which Matt and Clarissa are now asleep, both in medium-long shot and with natural sound. In these moments, the film gestures towards a place which strictly speaking cannot be used up or gutted out by our significations of it, however much it may now be vulnerable to our physical abuse.

It is now more than fifty years since Karl Polanyi wrote, "It is an illusion to assume a society shaped by man's [sic] will alone. Yet this was the result of a market-view of society which equated economics with contractual relationships, and contractual relationships with freedom."[44] Might it not be right, then, for the whole long tour of the urban strip we have taken here to end with the challenge and possibility such moments on the other side of that decrepit and disabling illusion provide us, out here past the cities of elaborate yet unsuccessful signification past which we have strolled, and past the postmodern suburban space that sprawls out from their ruins until it finally gives out, too, and something else happens or goes on happening, alongside yet without us here at, and beyond, the river's edge?

(1989)

NOTES

1. Richard Sennett, *The Fall of Public Man* (New York: Knopf, 1976); Fredric Jameson, *The Political Unconscious: Narrative as a Socially Symbolic Act* (Ithaca NY: Cornell University Press, 1981), and "Postmodernism and Consumer Society," in E. Ann Kaplan, ed., *Postmodernism and Its Discontents: Theories, Practices* (London: Verso, 1988), pp. 13–29.

2. *Newsweek* (June 1, 1987), p. 89.

3. Karl Marx and Friedrich Engels, *The Communist Manifesto* (New York: Pathfinder Press, 1970), p. 19.

4. Quoted in Erich Auerbach, *Mimesis: The Representation of Reality in Western Literature*, trans. Willard R. Trask (Princeton NJ: Princeton University Press, 1968), p. 480.

5. Franco Moretti, *Signs Taken for Wonders: Essays in the Sociology of Literary Forms*, trans. Susan Fischer, David Forgacs, and David Miller (London: Verso, 1983), p. 115.

6. The constitutive distinction between "molar" and "molecular" derives originally from Gilles Deleuze and Felix Guattari, *Anti-Oedipus: Capitalism and Schizophrenia*, trans. Robert Hurley, Mark Seem, and Helen R. Lane (New York: Viking Press, 1977), but comes to this paper via Fredric Jameson's *Fables of Aggression: Wyndham Lewis, the Modernist as Fascist* (Berkeley: University of California Press, 1979) where it is pressed into the comparatively narrow literary-critical service to which I have put it here as well.

7. Peter Brooks, *The Melodramatic Imagination: Balzac, Henry James, Melodrama, and the Mode of Excess* (New Haven: Yale University Press, 1976), p. 148.

8. Ibid., p. 79.

9. Honoré de Balzac, *Old Goriot*, trans. Marion Crawford (New York: Penguin Books, 1951), p. 219. All subsequent quotations from this novel will be from this edition; page numbers will be given in the text.

10. Pierre Macherey also notes this inherent vertiginousness in his chapter on Balzac in *A Theory of Literary Production*, trans. Geoffrey Wall (Boston: Routledge and Kegan Paul, 1978): "This extremely simple narrative organization depends on a systematic representation of a plot: the plot is derived from the impact of a 'moral force' on a real situation, which produces displacements and readjustments. The moral world is always confronted with the real world, but is always autonomously determined. The situation and the individual 'force' are reciprocal but never mingled." (p. 291)

11. Auerbach, pp. 473, 472.

12. George Eliot, *Middlemarch: A Study of Provincial Life* (London: Oxford University Press, 1947), p. 291.

13. Stephen Greenblatt, "Murdering Peasants: Status, Genre, and the Representation of Rebellion," *representations* 1 (February 1983), p. 16.

14. Terry Eagleton, *Criticism and Ideology* (London: Verso, 1976), pp. 102–61.

15. Joseph Conrad, *The Secret Agent* (New York: Bantam Books, 1984), p. 7. All subsequent quotations from the novel will be taken from this edition; page numbers will be given in the text.

16. Eagleton, *Criticism and Ideology*, p. 137; but see also his "Form, Ideology, and *The Secret Agent*," in *Against the Grain* (London: Verso, 1986), pp. 23–32.

17. C.T. Watts, ed., *Joseph Conrad's Letters to R.V. Cunninghame Graham* (Cambridge: Cambridge University Press, 1969), p. 131.

18. England, and English liberal democracy, he wrote, are "the only barrier to the pressure of infernal doctrines born in continental back slums." J.-G. Aubry, ed., *Joseph Conrad: Life and Letters*, vol. I (Garden City NY: Doubleday, 1927), p. 84.

19. Eagleton, *Against the Grain*, p. 28, also cites this figure as a "graphic image of the text."

20. Virginia Woolf, *A Writer's Diary* (New York: Harcourt, Brace and Co., 1953), p. 160.

21. "Ulysses, Order, and Myth" (1923), quoted in Richard Ellmann and Charles Feidelson, eds., *The Modern Tradition* (New York: Oxford University Press, 1965), p. 321.

THE FLÂNEUR AT RIVER'S EDGE   225

22. Walter Benjamin, *The Origin of German Tragic Drama*, trans. John Osborne (London: Verso, 1977).

23. See, for example, his "Reification and Utopia in Mass Culture," in *Social Text* 1 (Spring 1979), pp. 130–48.

24. "Spatial Form in Modern Literature," in *The Widening Gyre* (New Brunswick NJ: Rutgers University Press, 1963), pp. 3–62.

25. Fredric Jameson, "Seriality in Modern Literature," *The Bucknell Review* 18, 1 (1970), p. 66.

26. Ibid., p. 67.

27. James Naremore, *The World Without a Self: Virginia Woolf and the Novel* (New Haven: Yale University Press, 1973), pp. 110–11.

28. Virginia Woolf, *Mrs. Dalloway* (New York: Harcourt, Brace and World, 1953), p. 11. All subsequent quotations are from this edition of the novel; page numbers will be given in the text.

29. Auerbach, p. 535.

30. Dorrit Cohn, *Transparent Minds: Narrative Modes for Presenting Consciousness in Fiction* (Princeton NJ: Princeton University Press, 1977), p. 75.

31. For a reading of modernist literary practice that places it at the junction between monopoly and consumer capitalism, and reads it as a symptom of the tensions between the two, see the chapters on *Ulysses* and *The Waste Land* in Moretti, *Signs Taken for Wonders*; and for a reading of Woolf's modernism as quintessentially radical—albeit radically feminist—see the chapter on Woolf in Patricia Waugh's *Feminine Fictions: Revisiting the Postmodern* (New York: Routledge, 1989). I cite these texts here, however, merely as good examples of this apparently irreconcilable debate over the tendency of modernism in its most current moment and terms.

32. Eli Zaretsky, *Capitalism, The Family and Personal Life* (New York: Harper and Row, 1976), p. 58.

33. "Seriality in Modern Literature," p. 73.

34. Thomas Pynchon, *The Crying of Lot 49* (New York: Bantam Books, 1967), pp. 1–2. All subsequent quotations will be taken from this edition; page numbers will be given directly in the text.

35. See, for example, Jim Collins, "Postmodernism and Cultural Practice," in *Screen* 28, 2 (Spring 1987), pp. 11–26; Michael Denning's "The End of Mass Culture" (unpublished lecture); and my own "'Makin' Flippy-Floppy': Postmodernism and the Baby-Boom PMC," in this volume.

36. For postmodernism as capitalist secretion, see Fredric Jameson, "Postmodernism; the Cultural Logic of Late Capitalism," *New Left Review* 146 (July–August 1984), pp. 53–92; for postmodernism as a product of liberation struggles "from below," see Andreas Huyssen, "Mass Culture as Woman: Modernism's Other," in Tania Modleski, ed., *Studies in Entertainment: Critical Approaches to Mass Culture* (Bloomington: Indiana University Press, 1986), pp. 188–207.

37. Ernesto Laclau and Chantal Mouffe's *Hegemony and Socialist Strategy* (London: Verso, 1985) is, of course, the most trenchant current critique of the first two strategic moments, as well as our foremost example of the third.

38. Jessica Benjamin, "The Oedipal Riddle: Authority, Autonomy, and the New Narcissism," in John Diggins and Mark Kann, eds., *The Problem of Authority in America* (Philadelphia: Temple University Press, 1981), pp. 195–224.

39. Ibid.; but see also her *The Bonds of Love: Psychoanalysis, Feminism, and the Problem of Domination* (New York: Pantheon Books, 1988).

40. *The Bonds of Love*, pp. 51–84.

41. See note 37 above.

42. Stanley Aronowitz, "Theory and Socialist Strategy," in *Social Text* 16 (Winter 1986/87), p. 13.

43. For such critiques, and some indications of the politics that follow from them, see William Leiss, *The Domination of Nature* (Boston: Beacon Press, 1974), a classic historical critique; Murray Bookchin, *The Ecology of Freedom* (Palo Alto CA: Cheshire Books, 1982); and the important new journal *Capitalism/Nature/Socialism: A Journal of Socialist*

Ecology (P.O. Box 8467, Santa Cruz, CA 95061).

44. Karl Polanyi, *The Great Transformation* (New York: Rinehart and Co., 1944), pp. 257–8.

Plot and Patriarchy in the

Age of Reagan: Reading

Back to the Future and *Brazil*

"Now it's time for 'Back to the Future'."

(President Ronald Reagan,
on the United States)

"It's about the impossibility of escaping from reality."

(Terry Gilliam, on *Brazil*)

In this chapter, I want to propose a Marxist-feminist reading of two recent and, to me at least, peculiarly related films, a reading that concentrates mainly on their plots and plottings, their *histoires* and *récits*. Robert Zemeckis's *Back to the Future* was the box-office smash of 1985, a hugely popular "pure-entertainment" film which managed in its first six months to roll up one of the highest domestic grosses ever recorded, upwards of $200 million in ticket sales alone. *Brazil*, directed by Terry Gilliam of Monty Python fame, barely managed to get released in the United States at all in its present form, despite its director's reputation as a proven money-getter, and the film's considerable economic and critical success in Britain and Western Europe. *Back to the Future*, of course, was shaped and aimed to be a "blockbuster" film, following a familiar pattern of heavy advance advertising and simultaneous openings at major downtown theaters and shopping-mall cinderblocks around the country. *Brazil*'s American distributor, Universal, directed it mainly at an art-house crowd, for whom the story of the film's narrowly won release served as attractive publicity, offering the lure of the nearly repressed. Yet despite these differences in origin and venue, the two films share some common features: chiefly that although both fall most readily into the category of science-fiction film, the imaginary futures of both are composed mainly of pieces of the white American and/or·western past—

or, perhaps more precisely, of the historical Imaginary of white western culture; moreover, the plots of both lead up to a climax in which the male protagonist willfully alters or erases some portion of the past. By reading the plot dynamics of these two films against each other, then, I want to get at the pleasures offered us in the play these films enact with our received notions of historical moments and period styles; to get at that pleasure and then underneath it, to the historically symptomatic desires and fears in which those pleasures originate, and which may then themselves be read out or recoded in a more directly political way as a sign of the times in which we struggle to imagine and construct a different—non-exploitative, non-patriarchal—form of life.

The analysis I offer here also proceeds from, and is ultimately intended to illuminate, two other rather large assumptions. The first, an openly social and political one, I hope I can merely state here without supporting argument. It is that within the First World metropole as a whole, and perhaps especially in the United States, there has throughout the post-war period been a gradual erosion in the traditional structures of authority—familial, economic, and political—which, reaching a critical level in the late 1960s and 1970s, has been answered throughout western industrial society by an authoritarian backlash, broad based (if well orchestrated by ruling elites), nostalgic and vociferous, manifesting itself at all levels of society.

The other assumption, whatever its political implications may be, is first of all a literary-theoretical one, and will take rather more unpacking than the first. It concerns the nature and function of plots, especially in what we now call the "classical realist" modes of nineteenth-century prose fiction and twentieth-century Hollywood film. From Roland Barthes's influential S/Z through a good deal of subsequent left-feminist poststructuralist theory, it has been argued that what characterizes such classical realism is the hegemony of what Barthes called the "proairetic" and "hermeneutic" codes of the narrative—or, in more ordinary language, the predominance within the narrative of the chain of consequential causality (the proairetic), which leads us on from some initial state S to a transformed state S_1, and in so doing both develops and ultimately resolves some enigma (the hermeneutic)—from "What kind of a character is she really?" to "How are things going to come out?"[1]

It should be clear that to speak about the dominant place of the proairetic and hermeneutic registers within classical realist narrative is, in effect, to speak of the importance within such narratives of what we usually simply call *plot*, a term which Yale critic Peter Brooks—neither leftist nor feminist, as far as I can tell—has recently defined as a way of "channeling and tying up the mobile energies of life," of "binding those energies into shapely structures of narrative form."[2] Brooks goes on to describe that "binding" process and the risks it undertakes to negotiate in terms we will find almost uncannily appropriate to our discussion of the plots of our two films. "As the word 'binding' itself suggests, these formalizations and the recognitions [the proairetic and hermeneutic] provoke may in some sense be painful," he writes; "they create a delay, a postponement in the discharge of energy, a turning back from immediate pleasure, to ensure that the ultimate pleasurable discharge will be more complete."[3] Or, even more tellingly:

> It is characteristic of textual energy in narrative that it should always be on the verge of premature discharge, of short circuit. The reader experiences the fear—and excitation— of the improper end, which is symmetrical to—but far more immediate and present than—the fear of endlessness. The possibility of short circuit ... most often takes the form of temptation to the mistaken erotic object choice, who may be of the "Belle Dame sans merci" variety, or may be the too perfect and hence annihilatory bride. Throughout the Romantic tradition, it is perhaps most notably the image of incest ... because its fulfillment would be too perfect, a discharge indistinguishable from death, the very cessation of narrative movement.[4]

Such loaded terminology already suggests the way in which this essentially formalist analysis can be psychoanalytically decoded and revealed as a distinctly oedipal politics of the text: an argument *for* plot, in effect, as that feature of narrative which, like the Lacanian Phallus, operates on a dividing line between the dangerous dissolute flux of the preoedipal Imaginary and the frozen, empty signifiers and categories of the oedipal/patriarchal Symbolic, a line whose destiny it is both to construct and subvert. Indeed, Brooks himself speaks of plot as "the organizing line, demarcating and diagramming that which was previously undifferentiated"; yet, he adds, "the organizing plot is more often than not some scheme or machination, a concerted plan for the accomplishment of some purpose which goes against the ostensible and dominant legalities of the fictional world, the realization of a blocked and resisted desire."[5]

If this account of what plot is and how it works to satisfy us is accepted, we will have to admit that the oedipal story constructed by classical psychoanalysis is itself a paradigmatically plotted narrative: a story line which moves from a preoedipal mother-love and attachment (S) to an oedipalized love of woman-as-object (S_1), through a painful process of "binding" and "channeling" desire into acceptable forms and towards an acceptable object choice. Indeed, the similarities between the oedipal story and the terms in which Brooks and others have described plot are so strong and charged that some at least putatively radical poststructuralists have been led to suggest that plot—that is, the encoding and demarcating action of the proairetic and hermeneutic codes—is inherently, irremediably, perniciously oedipal, a tainted emanation of the dominant, and dominating, white male bourgeois Self.[6] But I would rather bring this long preamble to a close by proposing a less sweeping and slightly more historically nuanced hypothesis about plot: that in a patriarchal-capitalist society like our own, plot will ordinarily be driven by oedipal energies and bound by oedipal restraints; yet it may also be self-reflexively, even critically, *about* those same energies and restraints, or may even, in certain exceptional cases, be directed *against* them instead.

But it is time now to fill out these terms and propositions by applying them to our two films. What, we might begin by asking, is overtly oedipal about the story lines of Back to the Future and Brazil? The question is most easily answered for Back to the Future, which begins by placing its protagonist, young Marty McFly, in relation to two paternal figures, neither of whom is fully authorized or capable. There is Marty's friend Doc Brown, the brilliant but daffy scientist and inventor of the automotive time-travel machine, a Rube Goldberg genius who at the end of the film's first section, when Marty catapults into the past, seems to have just been gunned down and killed by Libyan terrorists. And there is Marty's biological father George, a pathetic aging nerd, crudely bullied and exploited by his loutish boss Biff, and cowed by his blowsy semi-alcoholic wife, with whom he has engendered—in addition to the anomalously cool and handsome Marty—two other equally unattractive and ill-equipped children. Doc Brown, with his comically wild white hair and rolling eyes, is daffy enough to have stolen some plutonium from the U.S. government and cheated the Libyans to whom he had promised it in order to complete his time-travel machine; George McFly titters dutifully at Biff's insults, eats breakfast cereal at the dinner table, and brays helplessly at *Honeymooners* re-runs on TV. Both, moreover, bear some responsibility for the cloud under which Marty lives: Doc Brown because his experiments with time inadvertently make Marty late for school; George because of his reputation for inadequacy, which Marty has now inherited.

In classical terms—and the narrative of Back to the Future is, as we shall see, for the most part a very classical one—the burden of the plot and the task of the primary actant will be to find or construct from such unpromising paternal source materials some version of legitimate authority through which the self can pass. So Strickland, Marty's high school principal (and George's before him) says to Marty: "No McFly ever amounted to anything in the history of Mill Valley"; to which Marty answers, "Well, history's gonna change." That vow becomes, in effect, a double promise in the rest of the film: Marty will be able to move into the past in a DeLorean refitted as a time machine and alter it; and through that alteration he will rewrite the paternal signifier, the family name, in an authorized and authorizing way. But these two projects, once Marty has traveled back to 1955, in turn become entangled with two others: forewarning Doc Brown of his impending death at the hands of the Libyan terrorists he will double-cross, back in the mid-1980s present; and (to the delight of the audiences I sat with, who found more and greater laughs in this subplot than any other in the film) resisting the desire of Lorraine, his mother-to-be, whose libidinous teenage self belies her subsequent account—which we've already heard in the film's opening section, set in 1985—of her impeccable chastity and propriety in the "good old days" of her youth.

Thus, in *Back to the Future* the movement from S to S_1 is a double project: through enabling both father figures—Doc Brown to escape death, George to find and assert his authority and power—and resisting and deflecting the unknowingly incestuous desire of the Mother, Marty works his way past both endlessness (here, the danger of being permanently stuck in 1955) and short circuit (of vanishing along with his brother and sister if he yields to Lorraine's desire, or otherwise fails to bring his parents-to-be together), as Brooks has described them the Scylla and Charybdis of classical plot. In this final stasis of S_1 back in the Mill Valley of 1985, Marty finds himself a member of a successful, happy, affluent Yuppie family—a family which, unlike the family of the film's first section, is capable of producing someone like himself. He has, in effect, returned to the beginning of the film as he has come back home in space and time, and found it the right place at last.

In *Reading for the Plot*'s discussion of the plot of *The Red and the Black*, Brooks suddenly throws out a perceptive historical aside that fits well here, when he speaks of how in order to succeed any political restoration or reactionary coup must project the illusion "that the way things came to be as they are ... does not belong to history, that the place of each thing, and person, in the structure of things is immutable."[7] So, too, at the end of *Back to the Future*, for Marty and for us in the audience: having seen history changed, we are now invited not only to enjoy and approve of the results in the altered present, but to savor our privileged knowledge that that present is in no way a natural or immutable one, as the rest of Marty's transformed and redeemed family must find it. This pleasure, of simultaneously seeing-with-approval/seeing-through, corresponds to an analogously contradictory position to which the film's plot also invites us: we both endorse the constitution of the legal, rightful family unit, headed by a suitably empowered father and a mother whose desire has been suitably channeled and tamed, and wink at that family as a put-up job. Indeed, at the apex of the Reagan eighties, a time marked, as Robert Ray has said, by constant oscillations between cynicism and nostalgia,[8] we might well suspect that the film's construction of such a contradictory position, along with its attendant double pleasure of seeing-with-approval/seeing-through, is a key component of its enormous success.

Moving from these preliminary considerations of *Back to the Future*'s plot to *Brazil*, we notice first of all a considerable difference between the *place* of plot in the two movies, a difference which shows up as soon as one attempts to draw up a plot segmentation of both. For *Back to the Future*, the ease with which we can slot each scene into its rightful numbered or lettered place on a list is a clear indication of the clarity of the chain of narrative causality, the ordered hierarchical structure of events. Conversely, the difficulty of separating out the flow of *Brazil* into discrete narrative moments, and of ordering them into any structured list of primary and secondary events, suggests that this film manages to effect an at least partial escape from the domination of the proairetic and hermeneutic codes, a semic or semiotic surplus unmastered by the textual economy of classical narrative.

Take, as a specific example of this overall contrast, the very first moments of the two films, beginning with that extended horizontal pan of Doc Brown's workshop which opens *Back to the Future*, an apparently off-handedly obligatory establishing shot which draws our attention to a digital clock whose time is off (meaning, we'll soon come to realize, both that Marty's late for school and that Doc Brown's time-travel machine works), and a TV set displaying a newsman announcing the theft of some plutonium (stolen, we will learn, by Doc Brown to power his machine). The trick, in other words, is to get us ready for the plot that is about to begin in earnest, by focusing our unself-conscious attention in an apparently unforced way to details and events each of which has its own distinctly assigned place and function in the narrative chain. By contrast, from its opening title and sequence, *Brazil* seems to slide across such conventional, and conventionally naturalized, tasks of spatio-temporal placement and proairetic assignment. *Brazil*'s opening title, projected over clouds, reads "8:49 a.m. Somewhere in the twentieth century": the first datum meaninglessly specific, the second unhelpfully vague. Then we cut to a TV commercial that the camera pulls back to disclose playing on one of a number of sets in a window which explodes as an anonymous shopper walks past with his cart. Through the flames we return to the canted screen of a shattered yet still functioning TV, now broadcasting an interview with Helpman, head of the counter-terrorist apparatus; and through this interview we cut to an answering counter-shot set in a lab-coated bureaucrat's office, in which the bureaucrat kills a fly whose corpse falls into a printer which then misprints Tuttle as Buttle, a quite literally metonymic shift that will be characteristically mistaken by the counter-terrorist state apparatus for a piece of a plot. So the hapless Buttle is seen as a terrorist, is seized and killed, and the plot of the film, such as it is, is under way.

These differences in the opening gestures and actions of each film are typical of their respective *récits*, that is, the way plot happens, in both. Throughout the rest of *Back to the Future*, each scene and shot sequence positions us stably and specifically not merely in space, but within the film's chain of causality and consequence, its story line. But *Brazil*'s project seems just the opposite: to use not only the associative flow of its narration but also the deliberately jumbled iconography of its *mise-en-scène*—the blur of references made by its sets, costumes and lighting to various period styles as well as to genres and conventions from *noir* to sci-fi, from Dickens to *1984* and *The Road Warrior*—as strategems and devices to disturb and disrupt our sense of secure placement inside a distinct story line, to keep the film's semic flow and allusive slides from ever being fully recuperated by the Symbolic overcoding of plot.

In this sense, we might begin to speak of *Back to the Future* as a classically *oedipal* text, that is, one whose every move is arranged in accordance with the dictates of an overarching proairetic-hermeneutic destiny, and of *Brazil* as a work whose texture constantly resists and cuts across the Symbolic's structuring and coding operations of plot. Yet the contrast between these two films is by no means as simple or clear-cut as that. For one thing, *Brazil* does have a plot—one which is, moreover, shot through with oedipal elements and implications. Note, first of all, that the action which ends the opening sequence just described is the abduction-erasure of the *paterfamilias* of the Buttle family, first seen grouped about the Christmas hearth in a parodically perfect 1930s-British vision of domestic bliss, up to and including Mrs. Buttle's reading of *A Christmas Carol* to the Buttle children. And the wrongful seizure of Buttle—our first example, by the way, of mistaken plotting by the state and/or the characters in the film, of plot *as* mistake—moves us into a series of relays and ramifications that will eventually collide so catastrophically with the oedipal fantasies of a minor servant of the state apparatus, Sam Lowry, as to make Sam a protagonist propelled along his own mistaken narrative path, in what will become the film's main story line.

When first introduced to us shortly after the Buttle abduction, Sam is living a deliberately plotless life as a minor functionary in Information Storage, where he is content to act as supporting son to his comically ineffectual, authority-less superior, Mr. Kurtzmann. Over lunch, Sam tells his ruling-class mother, who is pushing him to accept the promotion to Information Retrieval she has finagled for him, "I don't want dessert. I don't want promotion. I don't want anything, not even dreams." Yet at the moment Sam utters these words, we already know he is lying, or else repressing his erotic dream-fantasy of a literally higher calling in which as a winged silver knight he enjoys the love of a diaphanously-robed, long-haired maiden in the clouds. In the first and only dream sequence we have seen at this point in the film, this dream-woman calls his name, then looks on rapturously as he approaches, kisses her, spreads his wings and does a loop-the-loop. It is all as openly, self-mockingly campy as the vision of the cozy Buttle family at Christmas—and so it may seem campy of me in turn to suggest that its flaunted shoddiness lends all the more weight to a reading of it as a figure for the fantasy of the Imaginary moment when one is both recognized by and in loving union with the Mother.

In any case, as this fantasy develops in Sam's dreams and daydreams over the next few days, the bliss of such merger and recognition is blocked, its satisfaction of desire impeded, as the sky is violated by massive thrusting buildings, the distraught Dream-Love is dragged down to the earth and caged, and Sam's knightly dream-hero self must rescue her by destroying with his flaming silver sword the massive god-figure named (by the movie's end credits) Ninja Warrior. It is this unabashedly corny fantasy of oedipal desire overcoming the resistances and obstructions of the giant threatening patriarch which at last sets the plot into motion; Sam goes to the Buttles to give Mrs. Buttle her check (since Information Retrieval, in its own mistaken plotting, has processed the wrong man, she is owed a refund of the costs incurred in his torture) and mis-recognizes Jill Layton, the Buttles' upstairs neighbor, as the woman of his dreams. Henceforth, as his dreams are literally cut ever faster and closer to his waking life, until the two modalities begin to interpenetrate one another, Sam has a project, a quest: first to find Jill, then to defend her from the authority of the state. And it is precisely in order to attain these classically oedipal ends, to fulfill the terms of the dream he has now projected onto her and his waking life, that he will make use of classically oedipal means: will shift allegiance from the powerless Kurtzmann to the powerful Helpman, friend of his dead (absent) Father; will enter the chilling empty chamber of Patriarchal/State power (with its photograph of Sam's mother on the desk); will, in Lacanian terms, take on the Phallus in order to erase its legal fiction of Jill Layton as a terrorist who must be found and destroyed, to counter its legal fiction with his own, newly authorized one, after which he can go home and claim his rightful love.

Oddly enough, then, both Brazil and Back to the Future feature as the climax of their plots the alteration of official history, the legal fictions in which their protagonists have been caught. Yet the intentions and effects of such alterations in these two cases could hardly be more opposed. Marty changes history in 1955, as we have seen, precisely to *restore* both it and the Father in an even more authorized and powerful form; the climactic shot of the entire film, in fact, is the close-up in which we see his father-to-be George's hand clench itself into a fist, with which he'll punch out Biff. Along the way, we may note in passing, Marty enacts twice a classic fantasy of liberal colonialism and/or racism: first, by placing the dream of becoming mayor someday in the head of Goldie Wilson, the buck-and-shuffle black man who sweeps up in the soda shop, and who we already know will be mayor of Mill Valley in 1985; and second, when he jams with Marvin Berry (who, in a movie in which hands, you might say, *really* count, has injured his too badly to play) and launches into a "Johnny B. Goode" whose r-and-b sound so excites Marvin that he calls up his brother Chuck on the spot so Chuck can hear over the phone the exact sound he's been looking for.

What all this suggests, together with the disciplining and direction of his mother's sexual desire, is that if *Back to the Future* enacts an oedipal plot, and a particularly reactionary one at that, it is also one with a perverse new wrinkle in it: throughout the entire developmental section set in 1955, Marty the teenager must himself be the enabler, the magic constructor of power, capacity, authority; must operate himself as the Name of the Father and be Father to the Man. Tempted as he may be by the prelapsarian world of 1955, in which public time as registered on the courthouse clock moves steadily ahead, progress is promised (and, we may assume, delivered) by the white mayor Red Thomas, and the enemy horde is only a bunch of easily outwitted small-town bullies, he must renounce this Beulah land and the desire of the Mother-lover to which it is linked in favor of a return to the present in which time (on the clock tower, anyway) is stuck in Goldie Wilson's city, a porno house stands on the littered town square, and the enemy horde has become a pack of snarling Libyans with an enormous red-tipped phallus-rocket mounted atop their Volkswagon van.

Yet for all that, the rewards for Marty's self-actuated renunciation (whose certainty is never in doubt, no more than our secure knowledge of what's going on or where we are in the plot) are great, both for Marty and, we might guess, for the teenagers who constituted the majority of the film's mass audience: not only an enabled father (or two) and a tamed and rehabilitated mother, but a set of parents who, when they reappear at the end of the film, having just come in from tennis, are themselves just a couple of aging but fun-loving consumerist kids, albeit newly enabled and safely positioned ones. If, as I have already suggested,

one of the symptomatic or habituative pleasures offered by the plot of
Back to the Future in the age of Reagan is that of altering history so it
comes out the way you want it to, and naturalizing that alteration (a
pleasure-project in which our President himself was particularly expert,
as we know), then another pleasure specifically offered the (white) youth
of Reagan's America must be that of having the power to author your
own parents while at the same time enjoying and seeing through them as
just kids—like you, except maybe not so smart. To such perverse,
reactionary ends, such renunciations and satisfactions, have the energies
set loose in the youth and student movements of the late 1960s now
been reconstructed and canalized.

From the plot summary I have given so far of *Brazil*, it might seem that
it is not all that different from *Back to the Future*. It appears as if, however
much the semic escapes the proairetic and hermeneutic codes from shot
to shot or scene to scene, on the level of those codes themselves the film
is staunchly oedipal—boy wants girl, invokes the Name of the Father to
get her, boy gets girl. Yet considered in more detail, the workings of the
plot expose and subvert the conventional meanings and emphases of this
basic story line. First, and most obviously, there is the resistance of Jill
herself to the double plot-projection Sam maps on her: both the official
state fiction that she is a terrorist, and his dream-vision of her as his true
love, a double fiction of Woman as enemy other and Woman as maternal
imago. Thanks to this paradigmatically oedipal projection of Mother/
Other on to her, from the time Sam first apprehends her in the ominous
halls of state in which he works, he can only enact and re-enact a
comically hysterical shuttling between recriminations and confessions of
love, one which remains completely oblivious to her own truck-hauling
performance as a kind of female Mad Max. This shuttling, however, has
its own horrifying consequences; it only begins to abate once he has quite
literally *made* Jill an enemy of the state by forcing her to drive her truck
straight through a security checkpoint, only to discover at the end of the
chase, after a real bomb explodes in the shopping mall to which they
have fled, that the package she has been carrying the whole time
contains only the same dumb Christmas-gift commodity nearly everyone
in the movie at one point or another receives from someone else.

Moreover, such corrections or subversions of Sam's plotting are
themselves matched by the film's own intra- and extra-diegetic subversions, its deliberate mis-emphases and mis-articulations, which both
bare the devices of the Hollywood code and subvert their effects. From a
descending glass elevator, Sam sees his dream-woman Jill in the lobby of
the Ministry building; a gush of romantic strings builds towards a
throbbing climax as the elevator descends—and sinks past the main
floor, past Jill, and into the basement. Or we cut from Sam's receipt of an

invitation to a party at his mother's to a long film-noir shadow falling at the base of a spiral stairwell—which turns out not to be Sam, who is halfway up the stairs; or cut from Sam humming along in his little car on his way to give the refund check to Mrs. Buttle, to a wide-angle shot of what seems to be the landscape of clean pastel towers opening steadily before him—which, as the camera lifts, we realize is an abandoned scale model set out in the middle of the actual blighted landscape in which the Buttles live, a toytown version over which a grizzled drunk now shakes his bottle and leers back out at us. In *Back to the Future*, Marty's perky virtue combines with the classically emphatic articulations of the film's conventional style to guarantee the integrity of plot and of our own centered subjectivity; in *Brazil*, the delusory plots Sam makes true for himself and Jill are undercut, and the fiction of our safely grounded, knowing subjectivity eroded, in the playful treachery of the cinematic enunciation itself.

Finally, though, the oedipal plot of *Brazil* is critiqued and undone within its plot by the hallucinatory chain of events which follows the climactic moment when Sam erases the authoritarian-patriarchal fiction of Jill, and replaces it with his own—a moment whose parallel in Sam's dream-narrative, we ought to note, is Knight Sam's defeat of the Ninja Warrior, and the ensuing discovery that behind his mask the giant warrior has Sam's own face. After Sam has deleted Jill's file, he returns from Helpman's office to his mother's apartment, where presumably he is awaited by Jill. But the woman he finds in his mother's bedroom has long hair, not Jill's short punky cut; she whirls around in a diaphanous gown, just as in his dreams; and the dialogue runs this way:

> She: Well, what do you think? Is it me?
> He: You don't exist any more. I've killed you. Jill Layton is dead.
> She: (leaning across the mother's bed) Care for a little necrophilia?

He leaps for her; they fall together on the bed as the camera shoots down on them through a circular canopy that swirls in to close out the scene.

Two more details from the film, one coming from this moment and one after, are necessary before our analysis of what we might call this nodal point can begin. First, throughout the film up to this time, Sam's mother has been glimpsed at various stages of full-body plastic surgery, each time appearing younger and more erotically charged; when, earlier, Sam and Jill first enter the mother's apartment, shortly before he leaves to "save" her, he tells her that his mother is away, going through the last stages of the process. Secondly, in one segment of the hallucinatory chain through which Sam will subsequently flee in the film's conclusion, his mother appears as a promiscuous red-haired Jill surrounded by attentive young male lovers, and shoos him away. Put these details together, and two points about *Brazil*'s climactic scene in turn become almost excessively obvious: that the registers of dream-fantasy and waking life which the film's narration has been bringing closer and closer up have now fused (and will henceforth remain so); and that it is similarly impossible to adjudicate whether the woman won is Jill or the Mother herself, whether the crime the final shot of this scene absorbs into a swirling *omphalos* is fictional necrophilia or real incest.

How are we to read this moment and the nightmarish chain of apprehension, punishment, escape and pursuit which it seems to initiate? The reading I propose is constructed by bringing together one tenet from the family romance narrative of classical psychoanalysis with another from the poststructuralist critique of classical narrative. The first has it that the story of oedipalization is complete only insofar as the Imaginary (mis)recognition of the Mother is masked and repressed by the accession which possession of the Phallus allows and requires to the over-codings of the Symbolic; the second is that those proairetic and hermeneutic codes whose workings constitute plot are themselves instances of the oedipal (or Symbolic) overcoding of a pre-oedipal (or Imaginary) semic flow. To answer the question we began with, then, I propose that we ask another plot question—Why doesn't Sam's oedipal project succeed?—and answer that with the point I have been arguing all along about the narration or enunciation of this film: because the Symbolic, oedipal overcodings of the plot have been derided, undercut, subverted by the film's semic (and, if you will, preoedipal or Imaginary) flow throughout, a flow whose escape from the binding operations of plot in turn provokes a hysterical retribution from the Symbolic in the form of images of maternal betrayal, false escape, torture, and death.

It is on the basis of such a decoding that I would begin to recode *Brazil* as a *political* text or allegory in ways that bear upon our present situation. First, though, we should note the extent to which the semic/proairetic-hermeneutic and Imaginary/Symbolic relationships the film offers us correlate with another far more obvious oppositional tension within *Brazil*'s futurific landscape: that is, between the commodified, consumerist society of the spectacle *par excellence* and the hierarchical, paranoiac, authoritarian police state. This opposition may of course be flagrantly ideological in the old, bad sense of the term; the example of Argentina under the rule of the generals, for instance, certainly suggests that consumer society and the police state may be far less antithetical than we elsewhere in the developed west are likely to think. Yet the opposition *is* real insofar as it is lived and believed, as precisely the consumerist definition of free choice—of commodities, of course—people have in mind when they think or say of western democracies "It can't happen here." Perhaps, then, it is no accident that all three "terrorist" explosions in the film—one which blows up a storefront of TVs, one in a posh restaurant, one in a department store—take place in consumer-land; nor is it inconsequential that no real culprits or terrorists are ever discovered behind any of them. In *Brazil* the irrepressibility of the semiotic, its slippage out from under the workings of plot is echoed within that plot in the inability of the authoritarian state to master, order, and police those zones of spectacular consumption where the dumb or disgusting, endlessly replicating and mutating commodities of consumer capitalism—the yes/no Christmas gift, the pablum on the elegant dinner plate—circulate.

With this reading in mind, we can at last move back to the first assumption with which we began, concerning the crisis of political and patriarchal authority in western bourgeois society, a crisis to which both *Brazil* and *Back to the Future* might now be understood to respond. I would like to think that by now on the left we have some shared perception of this crisis as an overdetermined effect of deep and dialectically related shifts within political culture, the mode of production, and the sex-gender system: of challenges to America's imperialist hegemony, and white America's racist oppression; of the supersession of the individual father's authority by "increasingly bureaucratic ... and depersonalized forces,"[9] and of the very principle of repression itself in the carnivalized world of mass consumption; of women's demands for equality, autonomy, and freedom of desire, and of the equally historic if less often noted evolution of less authoritarian modes and models of child-rearing. The reign of Reagan himself, our national Father-Knows-Best, offers us at one and the same time a symptom of this crisis, insofar as he exists only as an abstract and spectacularized *paterfamilias*, and an imaginary resolution of it; the same might also be said of Marty's rewriting of history in *Back to the Future*, his fathering of himself and his whole family. And in comparison to both these reactionary responses, insofar as both its oedipal plot and plotting are systematically subverted and critiqued, *Brazil* must be recognized as a distinctly progressive film.

But this is one of those binary bad/good judgments which a fully dialectical Marxism urges us to suspect. Besides, to rest here would leave behind a troubling question: if it is appropriate to correlate *Back to the Future* with the political practices and ideologies of Reaganism, to what kind of politics might we link *Brazil*? One possible answer might be with the feminist politics of a Kristeva, whose position exalts and is devoted to the release of an essentially female Imaginary from the domination of Oedipal man and the Symbolic. Another related one might be that of someone like Baudrillard, whose "post-political" program—insofar as he has one—for accelerating and superheating the circulation of signifiers to

the point of brown-out, the moment when all the switching centers blow
a fuse, is suggested in *Brazil* not only by the terrorist explosions but by
Sam's two moments of triumph in the pre-climactic portion of the film:
first, by connecting together the In and Out pneumatic message tubes in
the Information Retrieval office; second, by coupling an air duct and
sewage duct together, so that the Central Services workers wrecking his
apartment fill up with shit and then explode.[10]

Yet for reasons both specific to *Brazil* and more generally political, I
am reluctant to endorse any such swooning into the plenitude of the
woman-mother's body, or any cackling celebration of what Baudrillard
speaks of as the breakdown of borders into continuum. Such a move or
valorization, first of all, represses what we might call the "down-side" of
semiotic excess and energy: both the horror of what Baudrillard himself
calls the "unclean presence of everything,"[11] which in *Brazil* is suggested
most powerfully by the pulsing mass of *Alien*-like quasi-organic, tentacu-
lar ducts and tubes which spill out into Sam Lowry's apartment, and by
the equally repugnant stale nausea produced by this nominally sci-fi
film's flaunted failure to show us any future which is not a pastiche of
other films and film genres (*Battleship Potemkin*, *Blade Runner*, film noir,
etc.), a self-mocking composite simulacrum of the new.

And there is a political argument to be made here, too, against *any*
binary opposition, such as plot and seme; or oedipal–Symbolic–male
over preoedipal–Imaginary–female, or vice versa. It is just such oppositions which, I would think, we ought to deconstruct and move beyond,
by transforming our own political practices, along with their accompanying narratives. Here is what Jessica Benjamin has said, for example, about
the inherent perniciousness of the polarities some feminist poststructuralists have accepted, albeit with their conventional valences reversed:

> The argument in favor of parental authority is that without the father's
> rational authority the mother would permit endless fusion, blur all differ-
> ences, keep us in a swamp of undifferentiated narcissistic bliss. Such a view of
> the other can clearly be seen as a *result* of the gender polarity. This is how
> women-mothers appear once domination is institutionalized.[12]

With variations, this is how *any* Other is viewed—working-class, non-
white, non-heterosexual—"once domination is institutionalized" over
themselves as well: as a group whose threat thenceforward is said to
consist precisely in its "mindless," "irrational" capacity to break down
distinctions, to overrun or overwhelm. Nor is even the strategic narrative
of classical Marxism itself—or, more accurately, Marxist-Leninism—
wholly free from the bad habit of such privileging and polarizing
projections, which show up in its constitutive distinction between "van-

guard" (the party as rational authority, as "brain" of the proletariat) and "masses." The way past such power-riven oppositions, wherever they appear, lies neither in accepting their terms nor reversing their valuations; it lies in refusing and deconstructing the terms of the oppositions themselves, and doing so not merely or even primarily through theoretical deconstruction, but by myriad forms of political intervention and struggle from the level of the state to that which we call "everyday life."

Such a radical project calls for a new utopian and strategic narrative of how a just society might be constructed by a self-constituted community of different groups and interests without priorities and without repression of difference (not, for example, "under the leadership of the working class"). And the strengths and weakness of those several contemporary attempts to sketch out such a narrative—by, for example, Nancy Hartsock, Stanley Aronowitz, Ernesto Laclau and Chantal Mouffe[13]— inevitably tell us much about the practical successes and failures so far of attempts to link together a host of liberatory groups and struggles without subsuming them under the sign of any "primary contradiction," any new domineering set of priorities. As such linkages emerge and evolve, accompanied and assisted by that new utopian and strategic narrative, we will begin at last to find our way past not only classical or bourgeois realist narrative, but beyond the constraining opposition of plot/seme and all its allies as well. For now, though, we may take Brazil as a marker measuring out where the limits of narrative still stand for us— or perhaps we should say the limits of male-based narrative, anyway. Beyond them we must still struggle to reach, bearing in mind the hopeful words of Bertolt Brecht. "There are many ways of telling a story," that astringent comedian of history once said: "some already known, and some still waiting to be discovered."

(1986)

NOTES

1. Aside from Barthes's S/Z itself (English translation, New York: Hill and Wang, 1974), see "Realism and the Cinema: Notes on Some Brechtian Theses" and "Principles of Realism and Pleasure," in Colin McCabe, Tracking the Signifier (Minneapolis: University of Minnesota Press, 1985), pp. 33–57 and 58–81; "Constructing the Subject: Deconstructing the Text," by Catherine Belsey, in Judith Newton and Deborah Rosenfelt, eds., Feminist Criticism and Social Change (New York: Methuen, 1985), pp. 46–63; and "Rewriting the Classic Text," the final chapter of Kaja Silverman's The Subject of Semiotics (New York: Oxford University Press, 1983), pp. 237–83.

2. Reading for the Plot: Design and Intention in Narrative (New York: Knopf, 1984), p. 121.

3. Ibid., pp. 101–2.

4. Ibid., p. 109.

5. Ibid., p. 12.

6. Such a position seems implicit to one degree or another in all the writings listed in note 1 above; but for an explicit articulation of it, see Robert Burgoyne, "Narrative and Sexual Excess," *October* 21 (Summer 1982), pp. 51–61.

7. Brooks, p. 80.

8. Robert B. Ray, *A Certain Tendency in the Hollywood Cinema, 1930–1980* (Princeton: Princeton University Press, 1985), pp. 366–7.

9. Jessica Benjamin, "The Oedipal Riddle: Authority, Autonomy, and the New Narcissism," in John Diggins and Mark Kann, eds., *The Problem of Authority in America* (Philadelphia: Temple University Press, 1981), p. 195.

10. Though the reading of *Brazil* I've been constructing here focuses more or less exclusively on what we might call the psycho-politics of the text, some mention must be made of the crude labor-bashing implicit in the cartoon portraits of the two spiteful, form-ridden and form-mongering Central Services workers Sam blows up with the help of that distinctly American freelancer, Harry Tuttle—and of the fact that the stupider of the two mumbles his few lines with a distinctly Irish accent. This portrait of swinish socialized workers, and of the moronic Irish—*Brazil*'s equivalent to the offhandedly racist-chauvinist portrait of the gibbering, subhuman Libyan terrorists in *Back to the Future*—greeted its first British audiences, moreover, not long after the agonized collapse of organized labor's most serious challenge to Thatcher's rule, the miners' strike of 1984–85.

11. I have taken Baudrillard's phrase from Pam Falkenberg, who quoted it in a paper she gave on "national cinemas" at the Institute for Culture and Society in Pittsburgh, Pennsylvania, on June 25, 1986; given Baudrillard's own theories, it seems only right that I cannot get any closer to the quotation's original source than that.

12. Benjamin, p. 212.

13. See Ernesto Laclau and Chantal Mouffe, *Hegemony and Socialist Strategy* (London: Verso, 1985); Stanley Aronowitz, *The Crisis in Historical Materialism* (New York: Praeger, 1981); and Nancy Hartsock, "Reconstituting Marxism for the 1980s" *New Politics* 1, 2 (Winter 1987), pp. 83–96. Part of my reason for singling out these particular authors and works is that although they are all working on the same problem—the problem of constructing a new strategic and utopian narrative—their disagreements with each other, at least as I read them, are large. These differences in turn make the fact that each follows up a strong and valuable critique of the left's outmoded strategy and vision with a weakly general, abstract, or, in the case of Laclau and Mouffe, hopelessly theoreticist set of strategic conclusions, that much more telling; their shared weakness seems broadly symptomatic of how far our practice as activists still has to go before a new strategy can be more concretely laid out, a new utopian landscape more vividly seen.

Potholders and Subincisions:

On *The Businessman, Fiskadoro,*

and Postmodern Paradise

There is a well-known drawing—it often shows up in books on visual perception in the fine arts or in cinema—which, depending on how it strikes you, looks either like a properly fitted-out young Gibson girl, the ideal type of young womanhood in early twentieth-century America, or like an ugly old street hag: the point, of course, is simply that it is impossible to see the drawing simultaneously as both. Yet that point, so quickly noted and passed over in the textbooks, hardly exhausts the picture's meanings; it is not just any interchangeable *trompe l'oeil* we are staring at, after all, but one whose power to startle, shock, and amuse even now is imbricated in and complicit with a whole repertoire of classist and sexist themes through which a past generation's sense of beauty/propriety/value and ugliness/degradation/horror was constructed and maintained.

I think of that drawing now, of the way it works and the ideologies on which it draws, because *The Businessman* and *Fiskadoro*, the two books I want to describe and discuss here, offer us a similarly ambiguous, complicated pleasure. A doubly ambiguous pleasure, more specifically: first, insofar as the power of both derives from their distinct but related strategies for effacing the boundaries between order and nightmare, laughter and horror; second, insofar as those effacements, and the vertiginous slides they effect in us, from delight to dread in turn, are symptomatic of our own entanglement in an ideological web of themes and discourse we have come to describe as the postmodern. This essay began with the curious powerful mixture of delight and discomfort, *jouissance* and revulsion, which both these books touched off in me; then it took on a more decided shape as I came to see how readily and appropriately the strange representations and deranged plottings they offer us may be understood as celebrations of the Kristevan semiotic, refusals of any steady border between the impure flux of abjection and the sanitized oedipal zone of ordered, isolate subjectivity, under the sign of the (male, white, bourgeois) ego. My claim for these texts, in short, is that they offer us something like the taste of a certain poststructuralist, feminist utopia: or, if you like, they provide us with an embodiment of some of postmodernism's most fundamental utopian themes.[1] (And if, as I strongly suspect, Thomas Disch and Denis Johnson, our two novelists, are unaware of the theoretical discourses in which this utopianism has been expressed by Barthes, Kristeva, Cixous, etc., then so much the better!) But having set forth and, I hope, persuaded you of that claim in the descriptions that follow, it is my first reaction to these depictions, that initial queasiness, to which I shall return, and from which I hope to pry some theoretical and political conclusions at last.

Before we enter into the descriptions that follow, though, a word of defense and apology is in order. Novels are, after all, hardly the dominant form of cultural expression and representation in our time, and, accordingly, unlikely to be the raw material from which the newest, sharpest, most cutting-edge analysis of the postmodern condition is to be worked up. Indeed, what follows assumes that most readers of this and other essays on postmodern culture and politics are as ignorant of Disch's and Johnson's fiction as those authors are of poststructuralist theory; it will therefore be necessary to quote from and describe each of these books at some length, merely to get their particular, peculiar flavors across to you. To justify such retrograde choices, I offer two lines of defense: first, the slightly perverse argument that the very marginality of the novel within the ensemble of contemporary cultural forms and practices *enhances* the salience and symptomaticity of the representations of postmodern structures of feelings as we find them here—even, as it were, in these two *books*, of all things; second, that the disadvantage of necessarily extensive quotation is at least to some extent offset by the fact that books are directly quotable in print, in a way that films, video, and the Westin Bonaventure quite obviously are not.

And yet it may be that the best introductory terms of comparison for Thomas Disch's *The Businessman: A Tale of Terror* come from film, after all; certainly it has less in common with other books I've read (except for others by Disch himself) than with movies like *Ghostbusters* or *An American Werewolf in London*, which offer something like the same dialectically subversive mixture of comedy and horror it provides. The basic joke, you will recall—and source of horror as well—in those films is precisely the grotesque coincidence of the terrifying and the banal: as in *Werewolf*, for example, whenever Jonathan's undead friend shows up in a new stage of putrefaction to find out how things are going, what's happening in his friend's sex life, and when he's going to kill himself or get himself killed so that his rotting pal can fully die and depart in peace;

or in *Ghostbusters*, most notably when the fiendish arch-devil nemesis finally arrives on the scene, stumping gigantically up Central Park West in the guise of the Sta-Puff Marshmallow man. So, too, it is in Disch's "tale of terror", in which a demon halfling assumes the guise of a cocker spaniel, a robin, and an all-American boy named Jack, one way into paradise leads up through the main escalator of the Sears Building on Lake Street in downtown Minneapolis, and, as we shall shortly see in more detail, personal dissolution and heavenly bliss are attainable through a kind of ecstatic fusion with a red-and-white potholder held magnetically to the front of the fridge.

Yet such playfully random minglings of the banal with the horrific and sublime do not begin to suggest the full extent of Disch's blithe transgressiveness, which also shows up in both *The Businessman*'s pointedly unconventional plotting and in the smooth irreverent shifts in voice and diction from high formality to dumbbell chattiness. These features have always characterized Disch's style, but here are taken to new extremes. One has, in fact, only to read the jacket copy (written by Disch himself) for the hardcover American edition to see both features abundantly in evidence, together with the minglings of terror, wonder, and the most banal, commodified quotidian life just described:

> Murdering your wife might not sound all that difficult, and in the case of Bob Glandier it was dead simple. Agenda: fly to Las Vegas, enter the Lady Luck Motor Lodge, strangle, get back on the plane to Minnesota, and resume life as an upper-echelon executive. What came afterward was not so simple.
>
> Still in the grave when the novel opens, and none too pleased, Bob's wife Giselle can foresee that she will be obliged to haunt him. There isn't much else to think about in her situation. Quite inadvertently, Giselle's mother, Joy-Ann, releases her daughter's spirit one day, the only casualty being that she loses her own life in the process.
>
> While Giselle is out discovering how unpleasant it is to haunt her husband, Joy-Ann arrives in Paradise (not to be confused with "Heaven," which is the next stage along and designed along less mortal, more "Looking-into-the-face-of-God" lines). Joy-Ann meets Paradise's coordinator, the famous nineteenth-century actress Adah Menken, who explains the use of "Home Box Office," where events of your own and your relatives' lives can be played in any order. Adah and Joy-Ann can see that they have a lot of intervening to do to sort out the evil that began at the Lady Luck Motor Lodge.
>
> The ghost of poet John Berryman plays a major—often heroic—role in this drama, which is just as well because at the time he meets Giselle he has become thoroughly bored with suburban séances (his dyslexia making him particularly hopeless at Ouija boards). Elaborate hauntings lie ahead for Berryman and Giselle, transmogrifications and, above all, a battle against the force which will turn a white Scottish terrier and a heron into killers—not to

mention a rather engaging little boy who will soon be known as "Charlie
Manson writ small."

How a novel can at once be so lighthearted and so utterly terrifying is
something only Thomas M. Disch can answer. *The Businessman* is like *The
Exorcist* in a playful mood. The living, the dead and the indeterminate form a
cast of characters who interact in a fashion that is disarmingly logical. "Who
would have thought that the afterlife had so many rules?" asks Berryman.
Many murders and unspeakable horrors later, it seems oddly clear that terms
could never have been struck with the businessman any other way.[2]

Except perhaps for the patently mendacious claim that the actions
depicted in the course of the novel are "disarmingly logical"—so much so
that by the novel's end it is "oddly clear" why things had to happen the
way they did—all this is perfectly true to the way *The Businessman*
actually sounds and works. Unlike other postmodern authors, who have
sought to loose narrative from the double-hinged grip of the proairetic
("what happens next?") and hermeneutic ("what's the point?"), as Disch
himself has done in earlier work (his *334*, just reissued in paperback, is
nothing less than a structuralist masterpiece, the novel of late-capitalist
urban life as *combinatoire*), here Disch destroys the plot from within, as it
were, by so multiplying its codes and proliferating and entangling its
narrative lines and characters as to render plot a diffuse, zany blur. His
heroine, Giselle, dead and rotting as the novel begins, becomes a barely
sentient tree three-quarters of the way through the book, and effectively
disappears, as indeed does the businessman of the book's title, fat
murderous Bob Glandier, for much of the time. Meanwhile, the play of
codes around what the jacket copy calls "the living, the dead and the
indeterminate"—all the random rules of the afterlife for communication
between, possession of, and even sexual relations with the still living—
proliferates and mutates so constantly and arbitrarily, in the midst of so
much frenzied action, that as Adah Menken at one point tells Giselle's
dead mother Joy-Ann, "There's no time to get into the theory of what's
real and what isn't." (p. 110) No more time than there is, in effect, to
think about the codes and discourse at work on the billboards flashing by
on the beltway into the city, or on the torrent of thirty-second spots that
rush past during station breaks on the tube.

And this comparison with the rapid, fluid discourse of the TV
commercial, simultaneously sophisticated in technique and allusiveness,
and crude or even infantile in its basic appeal, fits as a way into the
workings of Disch's style as well. As he himself has described it
elsewhere, it is "a prose that slides by quarter-notes and leaps by octaves;
lyric outbursts leading to deadly banalities; details dwelt upon at inexplicable length and whole masses of exposition disposed of at a shrug; and
always the feeling of the whole not quite balancing, of the narrator being

quite mad and at the same time completely ordinary."⁵

Is the jacket copy I have quoted above sufficient evidence of the accuracy of this self-description? Perhaps not: so here are three passages, each concerned with one or another of the manifold climactic actions or outcomes of *The Businessman*'s woolly plot. In the first, a passage to which we will later have occasion to return, the dead Giselle, released now from the task of haunting her husband Bob Glandier, is able at last to enter into the rapture of the red potholder for which she has yearned so long:

> When she touched it, the barking or crying grew louder. The tip of her finger tingled. The sensation spread through her body in waves, and then her body altogether disappeared, and she had entered the space she had so many times before sought to enter and failed: a pattern of crossed lines, an immense red-checked veil that parted now to reveal another veil, identical to itself, towards which she fell as towards a net. But the net parted, or she passed through its interstices, and the pattern was repeated, mindlessly, meaning-lessly, again and again, until the white spaces within the red lines gradually darkened, like a twilight that slowly deepens to night. From time to time she would hear the barking of the dog, and then there was a larger darkness and a deeper silence and sleep closed around her like a blanket being tucked into place by a gigantic hand. (pp. 196–7)

Note the smooth slack languor of the additive sentences depicting this ecstasy; the faded, *recherché* quality of the twilight/darkness imagery, which begins as a simile and then, in the next sentence, slides over into a truth ("a larger darkness"), which itself provides the occasion for an even more wholeheartedly clichéd and bathetic figure of speech ("like a blanket being tucked into place ..."); the curious hush, simultaneously reverential and insipid, that hangs over the passage as a whole.

Now watch the equivalent play, though differently staged, between the elevated and the banal in this description of Bob Glandier's grisly end, as the demon halfling and spawn that has dogged his trail throughout the second half of the novel now leaps into his dead wife's rotting corpse at the funeral home and tricks Glandier onto the moving belt leading into the crematorium:

> Glandier's screams, as he was pulled by his necktie down the metal-rollered incline beyond the double doors (in much the same way a carton of canned goods enters the basement of a supermarket), could not be heard above the hymn's joyous conclusion. The doors closed behind him, and for a moment all was blackness. Then through the grating of the grille on which he lay he saw the hundred blue flames of the crematorium winking on, row upon row, as his wife's grinning, fleshless mouth rose towards his to seal their union with a final kiss. (p. 276)

Here, of course, the joke is the apparently tossed-off comparison lying embedded in parentheses at the heart of the otherwise elegantly periodic sentence that opens the paragraph and establishes its official high-toned horror: a kind of casual aside which nonetheless lingers through the faintly stale, elevated syntax ("for a moment all was blackness") and diction ("to seal their union with a final kiss") that follow, blunting the conventional intentions and effects of such high style with its low-life presence, idly planting a trace-image of the half-dead life of commodified production and consumption at the heart of the horror. But this element or register of the numb, the stale, the commodified, is capable at other moments of all but completely overwhelming the elevated and/or sacred altogether. Consider the following, when Adah Menken and John Berryman (or their souls, anyhow) are found in the middle of an otherworldly landscape called the Spiritual Mississippi, and are picked up by Jesus himself in a dirigible

> at least as large as the mother ship that lands on Satan's Bluff at the end of
> *Close Encounters*. Its vast bulk was given over to a complicated array of
> blinking lights that alternated the single, cheery exclamation
>
> SAVED!!
>
> with explosions and geysers and pinwheels of shimmery color, each of them
> an advertisement and a promise of heavenly bliss. (p. 281)

Traditionally, as Rosemary Jackson has argued, the literature of the gothic and fantastic works by recontaining the defiled and/or demonic psycho-social elements it first released: the ghosts are exorcized, the transgressors punished or destroyed, the endless maze or heap of evil circumstances replaced by the orderly rule of the rational, the forces of darkness by the forces of light.[4] For Jackson, and even more decisively for Julia Kristeva in her *Powers of Horror*, those defiled, demonic elements at the core of the text of horror have their source in the oedipal drama at precisely that moment when the oedipal subject is fully separated and distinguished from a mother-figure who must henceforward be feared and despised as the *abject*: the dangerous mire in which the order of the oedipal symbolic collapses and sinks, where the monstrous, perverse, polluted and abominable reign; the place, within patriarchy, of despised femininity itself, conjured up in the horror text only so that it may be all the more decisively mastered and forcibly expelled by its close.[5] One definition of the *feminist* text of horror would then be a text which refuses such closure, which valorizes and leaves unrestrained the free-floating play of the abject elements released from the Ego's grip; but another, arguably just as valid, might be the text which simultaneously observes and subverts conventional resolution, and in so doing erodes the demarcation between abject and subject, the pre-oedipal and oedipal, feminine and masculine itself, so intrinsic to patriarchal order and rule. And if the latter, is not *The Businessman* itself as I have been describing it above, with all its randomly proliferating rules and codes, its sliding, deco-pastiche style, parodic resolutions, and diffuse, floating excess of character and plot, precisely an example of such a text—the text as "that uninhibited person who shows his behind to the Political Father," in effect?[6]

Many readers whose data banks are sufficiently well stocked with key lines from the canonical texts of poststructuralist critical theory will realize without checking the last footnote that I have shifted over from *Powers of Horror* to *The Pleasure of the Text*, from Kristeva to Barthes. And when we do, we find *The Businessman* waiting to greet us as well, this time as *le texte de jouissance*, the "text of bliss: the text that imposes a state of loss ... that unsettles the reader's historical, cultural, psychological assumptions, the consistency of his tastes, values, memory, brings to crisis his relations with language"; the text "we read ... the way a fly buzzes around a room: with sudden, deceptively decisive turns, fervent and futile"; the text in which "the opposing forces are no longer repressed in a state of becoming: nothing is really antagonistic, everything is plural," and in which "I [the blissful reader] pass lightly through the reactionary darkness."[7]

Or, while we're at this marshalling of banners, why not note as well the degree to which *The Businessman* enlists as well and as gleefully in Hélène Cixous's campaign against the repressive hegemony of the unitary (i.e., male, oedipal) subject and the "fetishization of 'character'" which is the chief expression of that hegemony within literary-aesthetic ideology? " 'I'," Cixous writes, "must become a 'fabulous opera' and not the area of the known. Understand it the way it is: always more than one, diverse, capable of being all those it will at one time be, a group acting together, a collection of singular beings that produce the enunciation. Being several and insubordinable, the subject can resist subjugation."[8] We will have occasion in the closing section of this essay to return to that last sentence and consider more closely its adequacy as a prescription for a radical politics. For now, I merely want to suggest that in *The Businessman*'s swirl of metamorphosing characters, including the dead, the sort-of-dead, and the sort-of-alive, we have a quintessentially postmodern text which meets these feminist-poststructuralist demands as well; what more could Cixous wish for than a text in which the ostensibly principal characters (one of whom, as I have already mentioned, becomes the spirit of a tree) are displaced from any central hold or stable position in the book's actions by a welter of other entities, several of whom are capable, under the capricious, volatile "rules" of the afterlife, of assuming

the shape of a frog or a dog or a statue of a black jockey or of the Virgin
Mary, to name only a few of the changes *The Businessman* puts its
"characters" through? Indeed, given these qualities, plus its curious style
and wandering, loopy plot, could we not nominate Disch's novel for
consideration as a "woman-text" in Cixous's terms: one, that is, "which
gets across a detachment, a kind of disengagement, not the detachment
that is immediately taken back but a real capacity to lose hold and let go
[which] takes the metaphorical form of wandering, excess, risk of the
unreckonable"?[9]

I have introduced these quintessentially poststructuralist definitions,
assumptions, and problematics just now, and quoted from them at
length, not merely because of their uncanny relevance to *The Businessman*, but because of the equivalent but quite different ways in which
many of them seem to apply to Denis Johnson's *Fiskadoro* as well, yet
another contemporary American novel written by a man who probably
knows nothing about poststructuralist critical theory. With this novel,
however, rather than beginning with promotional copy[10] let us start with
the opening paragraph, which introduces the strange, disembodied,
unplaceable narrative voice that floats in and out of the rest of the book.

> Here, and also south of us, the beaches have a yellow tint, but along the Keys
> of Florida the sand is like shattered ivory. In the shallows the white of it turns
> the water such an ideal sea-blue that looking at it you think you must be
> dead, and the rice paddies, in some seasons, are profoundly emerald. The
> people who inhabit these colors, thanked be the compassion and mercy of
> Allah, have nothing much to trouble them. It's true that starting a little ways
> north of them the bodies still go on and on, and the Lord, as foretold, has
> crushed the mountains; but it's hard to imagine that such things ever went on
> in the same universe that holds up the Keys of Florida. It strains all belief to
> think that these are the places the god Quetzalcoatl, the god Bob Marley, the
> god Jesus, promised to come back to and build their kingdoms. On island
> after island, except for the fields of cane popping in the wind, everything
> seems to be asleep. (p. 3)

Here is an opening in which the conventional introductory tasks of
spatial and temporal placement are as much flouted as observed. We are
referred to the Florida Keys, all right, whose landscape and atmosphere
are described at some length; but where is the "Here, and also south of
us" from which this narration is launched? Similarly, though we might
correctly suspect from the reference to Bob Marley and to massive
destruction that the events to be depicted in the course of the novel are
set in a post-apocalyptic future, the opening paragraph suggests the
narrative which follows will be a retrospective one, or that, in other
words, the narration is moving between two indeterminable planes of

futurity: an earlier, originary time from the unnamed narrator's point of view, from which the actions to be recuperated and recounted come; and a second future, the future-present of the narration itself, set within the context of a new, polyglot civilization (as evidenced by the apparently equally weighted references to an Aztec god, a Rastafarian reggae superstar, and the son of God in the Christian faith) whose dimensions and character remain as unknowably mysterious to us as they are taken for granted by the narrator him(?)self.

The equivalent of the dissolute forces of the swirling spirit-world in *The Businessman* as assault forces on the settled order of conventional space-time in classical narrative is thus in *Fiskadoro* post-apocalyptic futurity itself; the splintered, fragmentary story it has to tell, we are informed by the narrator, is set "in a time between civilizations and a place ignored by authority" (p. 12), in a spatio-temporal suspension between nuclear holocaust behind (and north) of the Florida Keys, and the emergence of a new religious kingdom and order sometime later, somewhere else. And throughout the rest of the book the narration's sudden, inexplicable point-of-view shifts from character to character and slack, oblique plotting work together to maintain that sense of suspension and drift. The boy Fiskadoro, title character and, according to the narrator in his/her indeterminate future, something of a hero-to-be as well ("Fiskadoro, the one known to us best of all, the only one who was ready when we came," p. 12) is, like Glandier and Giselle of *The Businessman*, absent from the book much of the time, as attention and point of view shift over to a number of other characters, chief among whom are Mr Cheung, manager of the Miami Symphony Orchestra, such as it is, resident of and one-time mayoral candidate in Twicetown (a.k.a. Key West in pre-apocalyptic nomenclature), and his grandmother, half-British, half-Chinese survivor of both the fall of Saigon and the Holocaust, now over a hundred years old, "the oldest person on earth." (p. 12)

Each of these characters lives an almost totally anomalous, non-synchronous relationship to the present world of part-objects, fragments, and squashed language which they all tangentially inhabit. Fiskadoro, when we first encounter him, is awash in adolescent transition to adulthood, uncertainly situated in an oedipal sexual constellation of the primitive fishing village of Army (once, in our time, a military base, presumably) where his mother and family live, the sketchy boro of Twicetown where Mr Cheung lives, and the night beaches, where Fiskadoro dances around fires set in radioactive oil drums together with the tribal people who come out of the swamps after dark. Mr Cheung, in turn, is devoted to conserving the few ill-matched scraps of history and knowledge—the names of the states, a demotic version of the

Declaration of Independence, the classical music he refers to as "the blues", his grandmother herself—he has been able to shore up and stash away: "History," he thinks, "the force of time—he was aware he was obsessed in an unhealthy way with these thoughts—are washing over us like this rocknroll. Some of us are aligned with a slight force, a frail resistance that shapes things for the better—I really believe this: I stand against the forces of destruction, against the forces that took the machines away." (pp. 122–3) But for the old woman, Grandmother Wright, who behaves "as if she forgot everything as soon as it happened" (p. 32), the end of the world began "on the day when her father took his life" (p. 72) and has not ceased happening—not with her flight from Vietnam, nor with the nuclear holocaust, nor any other event—ever since: "Whatever it was, it was happening now, today, all of it, this very moment. This very moment—*now*, changing and staying the same—was the fire." (p. 125)

In addition to being centered around a protagonist rendered as a unitary subject, a relatively unproblematic and evolving Ego-Ideal in effect, the traditional novel opposed by Barthes and Cixous to the "text of bliss" or "woman-text" offers us a coherent accumulation of represented experience, tagged and ordered for ready consumption. In the decentered, gelatinous universe of *Fiskadoro*, however, aside from the tenuous circumstances tying the characters together (through Mr Cheung, significantly enough, as both the old woman's grandson and Fiskadoro's sometime music teacher and would-be mentor), any sense of narrative development is undercut and diffused by the constant, oblique shifts in chronology and point of view, into a complex and covert thematic music of memory leading up to and washed away by the undertow of loss, forgetfulness, and oblivion. In fact, the two main events of the novel both begin with the death of a father—Grandmother Wright's father's suicide when she was still a girl in Saigon; Fiskadoro's father's drowning at sea. Both are recounted only retrospectively, and both end in a loss of memory and identity so complete as to constitute simultaneously a life lived absolutely in a pure present tense and a death of the self. Fiskadoro flees from "the border of this black country [the ocean] where his father lived" (p. 112) into the swamps, in pursuit of a young black swamp-woman—into what seems at first, in other words, a quintessential landscape of the unknown, the feminine, the Kristevan abject:

> She was gone into nothing, but he knew how to follow her steps as certainly as if he carried a map—there wasn't any way to go but down. Below the level of the dune the wind was stuck. It was like being swallowed alive. The air choked him; and he recognized the odor—it was hers; she smelled like the swamps, like her birthplace and her home. To follow her over the dunes and

out of earshot and eyesight of his people, his head spinning and his throat blocked with the honey of tears, was not to know whether he would live or die. Don't look what I'm doing! he begged the dark sea. (p. 114)

Yet, if there is already something not quite sufficiently stable or conventional about this ocean/swamp opposition as a figure for the oedipal split between phallic Father and feminine Abject—the sea is, after all, the element in which Fiskadoro's father Jimmy has drowned, and is also, in conventional poetic and psychoanalytic imagery, precisely an image for pre-oedipal immersion in the omnipresent Mother—what follows Fiskadoro's flight complicates and muddles this psychic landscape even more. For the swamp itself, we will learn retrospectively, many pages later, becomes the site of a male initiation ritual which fails—and is, perhaps, intended to fail—to deliver Fiskadoro to the order of the Symbolic as much as it succeeds. Mistaken by the people of the swamp for a young man of their tribe who in reality has drowned in the surf— mistaken as a new body carrying the same soul, that is—he is swept along into a complex initiation rite in which the drugs he is given first endow him with total recall of his entire life, and then—at somewhere near the same moment that he subincises his own penis with a sharp rock— obliterate his memory completely: "His head was a blank, he felt no pain. Now he was like other men." (p. 185)

If this is Fiskadoro's induction into masculinity, then, it is a perversely non- or even anti-oedipal one: as one of the novel's minor characters, a drifting smuggler, trader, and con-man named Martin puts it later, "I think . . . all what they have to remember back for the ceremony, es a lotta trash. Not important. The old fathers just only want the boys to forget. When es all done finish, the boys don't even know they name." (p. 163) So Fiskadoro is, by this abjection-subjection, plunged into a non-linguistic perpetual present in which "every time he looked at something, it came up before his eyes for the first time, unexplained and impossible to understand" (p. 185) and in which, once he is back home in Army again, even his mother, Belinda, is only a body discovered lying nearby at night, something to feel for, touch, and probe until she smacks him away. Eventually, thanks in part to Mr Cheung's ministrations, Fiskadoro's short-term memory will return to some extent; but even then, in the closing pages of the book, "Fiskadoro didn't know what his teacher was talking about, as he hardly ever knew what anybody was talking about." (p. 217) Still, as even Mr Cheung realizes and admits in the same scene, that very incomprehension and oblivion are also a source of strength. "You'll be a great leader," Cheung prophesies; "You've been to their world and now you're in this world, but you don't have the memories to make you crazy." (p. 217)

Such oblivion, moreover, is the same endpoint Grandma Wright reaches in her perpetual replay of her nightmarish flight from Saigon and the helicopter crash that follows it, as a result of which the young girl Marie Wright must float in the sea for something over two days and nights, long after almost everyone else around her has drowned:

> By sunset she was only a baby, thinking nothing, absolutely adrift, waking to cough and begin crying, drifting and weeping, sleeping and sinking, waking up to choke the water from her mouth and whimper, indistinguishable from what she saw, which was the gray sky that had no identity, interest, or thought. This was the point when she reached the bottom of everything, when she had no idea what she'd reached or who had reached it, or even that it had been reached. (p. 220)

Only in such a state of perfect oblivion can she be saved; just as only now that he has been disburdened of his history, his language, and his past, is Fiskadoro capable of leading the way into the new future that, at the novel's close, might just be coming towards all three of them through the haze over the sea—"a white boat, or was it a cloud." (p. 220). Characteristically, we never find out which; instead, in the novel's closing paragraph, the line between what lies behind, and what looms ahead, between memory and oblivion, life and death, is further blurred as the point of view shifts to Grandmother Wright, who is either still remembering, or seeing what is there in the actual present, or perhaps dying at last: "Nodding down into a nap beneath the canopy of her memories, she jerked awake and saw the form again in the early mist of the second morning and the third day—a rock, a whale, some white place to cling to, sleep, and breathe. And in her state of waking, she jerked awake. And from that waking, she woke up." (p. 221).

This descriptive analysis of Fiskadoro's themes and workings thus leads towards a conclusion similar to the one we have already reached apropos of The Businessman. Here is a novel, after all, which not only subverts the fixed categories and conventions of classical narrative—stability of narration, specificity and rationality of space-time, unitary characterization, and the developmental linear trajectory of plot—but which takes up the problematization and dismantling of bourgeois-oedipal constructs of identity, continuity, and eventfulness as its very subject matter. A novel, moreover, in which even the one character who still stands up for those retrograde notions admits the appeal of (as Deleuze and Guattari might put it, to invoke yet two more French post-structuralist theorists[11]) the new, unrestricted schizoid self, awash in its desiring flows, freely floating in the warm, amniotic currents of the Kristevan or Barthesian semiotic, untethered by memory to any fixed sense of the self: "There was something to be envied in that," thinks Mr Cheung, oblivion's ineffectual antagonist, in the presence of Fiskadoro's new non-self. "In a world where nothing was familiar, everything was new. And if you can't recall the previous steps in your journey, won't you assume you've just been standing still? If you can't remember living yesterday, then isn't your life only one day long?" (p. 192)

The question is for Mr Cheung a more-or-less rhetorical one; it expresses a fantasy of what seems to him at the moment a kind of blissful state he can imagine yet, given his attachment to continuity, culture and history, cannot share. It is at just this point that I want to urge the same question as well, together with a set of crude questions of my own. How does it sound, this blissful state of being, this perpetual schizoid present, this rapture Fiskadoro enters on the other side of his subincision, and *The Businessman*'s Giselle finds passing in and through the potholder towards her final incarnation as the spirit of a tree?

> Thinking was no more than a kind of tune she could hum or not hum as she chose.... There was something so pleasing about having no thoughts at all. Rather like swimming under water, but without the need to hold her breath. Yet in a way she *was* thinking. Even this slow, subaqueous drift of dim pleasure was a *kind* of thought, a tree's thoughts, a way of swaying in the breeze and going nowhere. (*The Businessman*, p. 211)

If those postmodern texts do, as I have argued so far, offer us an incarnation, an embodiment, a *taste* of something like the radical utopia an ostensibly feminist and anti-capitalist poststructuralism has marked out theoretically for us, does our readerly experience of such moments unambiguously tempt us to deconstruct and disseminate ourselves (if we have not yet already done so), to pass through the potholder, take the swamp-people's drug, become tree spirits ourselves?

These are rhetorical questions, of course, rude provocations against which, unless I tread with care, rather more substantive objections than merely those against my lack of tact might be raised. So let me hasten to say that I do not consider any of the representations afforded us by these novels, or, for that matter, any of our reactions to those representations, however clear, ambiguous, or complex they might be, to originate in some never-never land out beyond ideology, in untrammeled, unmediated Experience itself, on the firm solid earth of the Real. Nor, as is perhaps already clear, do I believe that poststructuralist theory emanates from any such transcendental zone. Yet to admit the inherently ideological nature of all such representations, reactions, and arguments, including my own here, need not and should not lead to any glib dismissal of them as *mere* ideology: not if the ideological (and discursive) arises only in conjunction with active social practice, specific collectivities and institutions; not insofar as given ideological discourses do irrefutably have their effects, make their marks quite literally upon the world.

It is in this sense, then, and with these caveats in mind, that even in this post-Althusserian age we can still follow up Frank Kermode's dictum that "Fictions are for finding things out; and they change as the needs of sense-making change."[12] What does it mean, then, that we have on the one hand what is by now a veritable legacy of theoretical texts, concepts, and arguments which criticize classical narrative and the unitary bour-geois self in the name of heteroglossia, dissemination, decentering, the flux of the semiotic, and a new, post-oedipal, non-unitary subjectivity which "[b]eing several and insubordinable . . . can resist subjugation" (Cixous); and on the other, these two postmodern novels, with their representations and embodiments, their *trying-ons*, I want to say, of just such radical states of being-in-flux—trying-ons which, in turn, excite in us an ambivalent, fearful delight, a blend of *jouissance* and revulsion at best? With what social practices, institutions, collectivities are these various inherently ideological discourses and reactions aligned; what kinds of social practice, institutions, collectivities do they reflect, prophesy, reinforce?

A full genealogical working out of these questions would obviously require an argument many times the length of the present chapter. Rather than attempt it, then, I shall instead try to formulate some necessarily tentative and, I hope, provocative propositions and over-lapping suggestions, as a starting-point for theoretical and political work which lies before us to be done. One central aspect of that work, as I imagine it, would involve taking up the question of the socio-historical field in which our current structuralist and poststructuralist ideologies *of* the relations between ideology and subject-formation first appeared and took their present shape; first in the work of Althusser, and subsequently in that of Barthes, Kristeva, Cixous, and, in Britain, their squads of *epigoni* in and around the film journal *Screen*. I do not mean to denigrate or besmirch the value of much of that work; indeed, it seems to me that Althusser's conception of the subject as the site of intersection of a whole overdetermined welter of ideological discourses and appeals which keep it pinned, as it were, in place, has produced a large and important space for new political strategies and theoretical work. But what strikes me now, almost twenty years after the famous essay on Ideological State Apparatuses,[13] as the most historically symptomatic feature of that influential work, is the emphasis Althusser lays within it on the spurious *unity* of the effectively interpellated subject. This emphasis, combined with his quite exclusive concern with Ideological *State* Apparatuses— with interpellation exclusively as *subjection*, in other words, into docile worker, happy consumer, obedient citizen—helped to open the way to a virtual equation between unified subjectivity and subjugation, and a corresponding valorization of the decentered or disseminated subject, in the erstwhile radical work that followed that essay through the 1970s and well into the present decade.

I call it historically symptomatic because this emphasis and the equation that was subsequently piled on its back are most suspect as founding assumptions of an understanding of the nature of the subject, and of ideological subjection, within the First World metropoles of late capitalism. Here it seems, at least for us (an *us* I mean to specify further shortly), that the problem to be worked through and, ultimately, politically strategized is precisely that of the *dis*unified and *de*centered subject, of a vast array of ideological apparatuses, from advertising to education, politics to MTV, which work as much to *dis*articulate the subject as to interpellate it, which offer not the old pleasures of "self-understanding," of knowing and accepting our place, but the new delights of ever-shifting bricolage and blur. "This," writes John Brenkman, "is the double tendency of late capitalism and its culture—to make the subject's separation in the object consumed the core of social experience, and to destroy the space in which proletarian counter-ideologies can form. . . . Capital cannot speak, but it can accumulate and concentrate itself in communications media, events, and objects which are imbued with this power to turn the discourses of collective experience into a discourse that resembles intersubjectivity as seriality."[14]

There appears, then, to be something almost nostalgic about the Althusserian emphasis on the spurious unity of the ideologically interpellated subject, a nostalgic or regressive component in its opposition to a mode of subjection whose time is passing or past. In this respect, Althusser's work on ideology in the ISA essay shares with the events of May 1968 (to which it is said to constitute a sympathetic response) a curious, ironic complicity with the disarticulating forces of consumer capitalism's perpetual present. As Regis Debray himself has said in retrospect of the May 1968 events: "We set our sails for Mao's China, and ended up in Southern California." This complicity then deepens in much of the poststructuralist work that follows in the wake of that originary moment, and becomes a significant element in the utopian forms and projects that work attempts to describe. The point remains always "to *uncouple* and *disrupt* the prevailing array of discourses through which subject identities are formed";[15] the goal is the uncoupled, disrupted self, the "woman-text" or "fabulous opera" described by Cixous, melting in a broth of Barthesian *jouissance*. Or perhaps, as at least one post-Marxist, poststructuralist critic seems to suggest, that goal has already been reached, that world is ours right now.

So we discover that we live in a world where, by choice or circumstance [?!], we have all become experts. We confront and use signs—clothes and hairstyles, radio and tv programmes, newspapers, cinema, magazines, records—that, circulating in the profane languages of habitual sights and sounds, have no obvious author. And in the end, it is not individual signs, demanding isolated attention, but the resulting connections or 'bricolage'— the style, the fashion, the image—that count.[16]

It is the horror of such a heaven, within such a bliss, that the post-modern novels of Johnson and Disch touch off in us, by allowing us to try on such a paradisiac state of being somewhere near, or beyond, the asymptotic line towards which the magical mystery tour consumer capitalism urges us: towards Fiskadoro's passage through a post-nuclear, post-oedipal bricolage landscape to a state of pure presentness and receptivity, a life that is "always one day long"; towards Giselle's passage through the potholder, its pattern repeating "mindless, meaninglessly, again and again," towards a "slow, subaqueous drift of dim pleasure . . . a tree's thoughts, a way of swaying in the breeze and going nowhere." Or, less ambiguously still, towards Mrs. Hanson's perception of her own life within the postmodern metropole of Disch's *334* as a pure "pastime":

> Not a game, for that would have implied that some won and others lost, and she was seldom conscious of any sensations so vivid or threatening. It was like the afternoons of Monopoly with her brothers when she was a girl: long after her hotels, her houses, her deeds, and her cash were gone, they would let her keep moving her little lead battleships around the board, collecting her $200, falling on Chance and Community Chest, going to jail and shaking her way out. She never won but she couldn't lose. She just went round and round. Life.[17]

Yet the negative assessment of the poststructuralist project and its postmodern utopia I have delivered so far is too harsh, too global, and too simple as it stands; accordingly, it needs to be qualified and complicated in at least two directions, albeit ones I can only very briefly indicate here. First of all, I want to insist again on a point I have argued more extensively elsewhere: that postmodernism (and, *a fortiori*, post-structuralism, its foremost philosophico-theoretical expression) is not most valuably or accurately understood as some essential secretion of late capitalism *tout court*, and still less as a set of discourses and practices without its own social subject or home base.[18] That home base or epicenter still seems to me to be what has been called the professional-managerial class of the developed west, situated as it is in contradictory relation to both Capital above and Labor below (and, increasingly, beyond) its own ever-enlarging realm, ranks, and ken, and both author and primary target audience for most postmodernist work, mainstream (that is, including even more TV commercials, at least by now in the US) and avant-garde.[19] Extrapolating from that structure of feeling we call postmodernism beyond the boundaries of this admittedly large, hetero-geneous, unevenly developing, and ambiguously placed class, as if everyone in the west were uniformly subject to its rhythms, raptures, and horrors, seems a neat way of sidestepping or foreclosing all the important political questions about how both postmodernism and the PMC can be mobilized and radicalized: that is, with what other discourses, practices, and social subjects they may be linked up, in what ways, and towards what ends. Either postmodernism is everywhere, saturating the universe of white corporation lawyers, single mothers on welfare, and black (ex)factory workers alike, like the residues of car exhaust that can now be found even on the nether slopes of Everest, in which case we can at best only wait for the revolutionary trumpet to sound somewhere in the Third World at some unknowable future date; or, if postmodernism is simply a new kit of discourses and practices, we are free to incorporate them too now into our own endless, jaded bricolage games as the skilled, hip consumers we are. Either way, the truly political difficulties and possibi-lities that arise from postmodernism and our own position within the present mode of production are quite successfully evaded and obscured—and will, accordingly, be picked up and worked through politically by other powers from "the reactionary darkness" Barthes invites us to "pass lightly through."[20]

My second qualification comes from a quite different direction: from feminism. Or, more specifically, from a position within feminism from which the poststructuralist attack on the bourgeois oedipal subject, and hostility towards any normative concept of the unified self, make a great deal more political sense than I have so far been willing to grant them here. It is not merely that the grand unity (or myth thereof) of the oedipal is, notoriously, constructed against and through the counter-construction of a dominated and abject Feminine non-self as its assym-metrical Other; it is, as Denise Riley has recently argued, that the category "women" itself has throughout history been put to work by both men and women in conjunction with a bewildering array of other categories (especially, she suggests, those of "the social" and "the body") to forward an equally wide variety and spectrum of agendas. "Women," she writes, "is a simultaneous foundation of and irritant to feminism, and this is constitutionally so":

Indeed the trade-off for the myriad namings of "women" by psychologies, politics and sociologies is that at this cost "women" do become a force to be reckoned with. But the caveat is that none the less the risky elements to the processes of consolidation in sexed ranks are never very far away; the collectivity which distinguishes you may also be wielded, if often unintentionally, against you.... The dangerous intimacy between subjectification and subjection needs careful calibration.[21]

Against the background of such historically justified suspicion, the hostility of poststructural feminists like Cixous towards any stable identity or name for "woman", and advocacy of a resistant, mercurial subjectivity-in-slippage, become, to a great extent, *strategically* comprehensible. Yet it still bears noting that the efficacy of such strategic refusals to name, identify, consolidate, is strictly limited to resistance. Radical *transformation*, by contrast, whether towards feminism or socialism, requires more than disruption, uncoupling, slipping away; it requires precisely the construction of new *collective* subjectivities and communities capable of purposive action towards shared ends and goals. As Terry Eagleton puts it, at the close of his largely sympathetic exposition of Kristeva's work:

> Nor is the dismantling of the unified subject a revolutionary gesture in itself. Kristeva rightly perceives that bourgeois individualism thrives on such a fetish, but her work tends to halt at the point where the subject has been fractured and thrown into contradiction. For Brecht, by contrast, the dismantling of our given identities through art is inseparable from the practice of producing a new kind of human subject altogether which would need to know not only internal fragmentation but social solidarity, which would experience not only the gratifications of libidinal language but the fulfillments of fighting political injustice.[22]

My concluding intention here, though, is not to back a Marxist modernism against a postmodern feminism, and issue a rousing, nostalgic, and ultimately futile endorsement of Brecht over Kristeva. It is rather to call for a recognition of precisely the separation that *does* exist for us—as socialists, as feminists, as members of the PMC—between "dismantling" and "producing"—a recognition that should not only be accompanied by a discontent with the inadequacy of the former strategy alone, as I have been using the powerful, delightful and disturbing embodiments of postmodern bliss provided us by Disch and Johnson to argue here, but followed up by a project of historical self-understanding as well. With a properly historical and materialist understanding of the social origins of postmodernism and poststructuralism within late capitalism and consumer society, and of our own specific place within, and equivocal, complicitous fascination/revulsion with both this structure of feeling and the particular social universe which is our own, we might be able to move on to the real strategic task of constructing new political subjectivities and wills, among ourselves and together with others. Without that understanding, though—and this is my final vulgar provocation—we will be condemned to recycle our fascination/revulsion in essay after essay, conference after conference, anthology after anthology on postmodernist culture and the delirious, horrifying, decentered subjectivity we live with, love, and revile: to stage and restage, as left intellectuals, our own version of the passage through the potholders to our own earned oblivion in a doubtful paradise, a heaven where, as Talking Heads' David Byrne sings, "nothing ever happens," and in which we will deserve no better than what we—eventually, incessantly, *ad nauseam*—get.

(*1987*)

NOTES

1. See E. Ann Kaplan's discussion of feminist possibilities for a utopian postmodernism in "Feminism/Oedipus/Postmodernism: The Case of MTV," in *Postmodernism and Its Discontents* (London: Verso, 1988).

2. Jacket copy for the first hardcover edition of *The Businessman* (New York: Harper and Row, 1984). Subsequent page references are to this edition.

3. *Fundamental Disch* (New York: Bantam Books, 1981), p. 379.

4. *Fantasy: The Literature of Subversion* (New York: Methuen, 1981), p. 3.

5. See Julia Kristeva, *Powers of Horror*, trans. Leon S. Roudiez (New York: Columbia University Press, 1982), passim; and also Barbara Creed's insightful discussion, "Horror and the Monstrous-Feminine: An Imaginary Abjection," *Screen* 26, 2 (Spring 1987), pp. 47–68.

6. Roland Barthes, *The Pleasure of the Text*, trans. Richard Miller (New York: Hill and Wang, 1975), p. 53.

7. Ibid., pp. 14, 31.

8. "The Character of 'Character'" trans. Keith Cohen, *New Literary History* 5 (1974), p. 387.

9. "Castration or Decapitation?" trans. Annette Kuhn, *Signs* 7, 1 (1981), p. 53.

10. Though the copy on my paperback edition of *Fiskadoro*, significantly enough, also shuffles through both "high" and "low" culture to come up with its comparative terms. Note, for example, the blended references to canonical literature and contemporary popular culture in these excerpts from (respectively) *The New York Times* and *Washington Post* puffs quoted on the paperback's cover:

Wildly ambitious ... the sort of book that a young Melville might have written had he lived today and studied such disparate works as the Bible, "The Waste Land," *Fahrenheit 451* and *Dog Soldiers*, screened *Star Wars* and *Apocalypse Now* several times, dropped a lot of acid and listened to hours of Jimi Hendrix and the Rolling Stones.

He [Johnson] is a wonderful storyteller, and if at times *Fiskadoro* seems a mixture of Samuel Beckett, Philip K. Dick, and *Road Warrior*, that is only to his credit.

All subsequent page references are to this edition (New York: Vintage Contemporaries, 1986).

11. See, for example, *Anti-Oedipus: Capitalism and Schizophrenia*, trans. Robert

Hurley, Mark Seem, and Helen R. Lane (New York: Viking, 1977).

12. *The Sense of an Ending: Studies in the Theory of Fiction* (New York: Oxford University Press, 1966), p. 39.

13. "Ideology and Ideological State Apparatuses," in *Lenin and Philosophy*, trans. Ben Brewster (New York: Monthly Review Press, 1971), pp. 127–86.

14. "Mass Media: From Collective Experience to the Culture of Privatization," in *Social Text* 1 (Spring 1979), pp. 100–1, 105.

15. Tony Bennett, "Text and history," in Peter Widdowson, ed., *Re-reading English* (New York: Methuen, 1982); emphasis mine.

16. Ian Chambers, *Popular Culture: The Metropolitan Experience* (New York: Methuen, 1986), p. 12.

17. *334* (New York: Carroll and Graff, 1987), pp. 169–70.

18. See " 'Makin' Flippy-Floppy': Postmodernism and the Baby-Boom PMC," above. But interested readers should also check out Richard Ohmann's descriptive analysis of the cultural hegemony of this class with regard to literature and literary studies in the second half of *English in America* (New York: Oxford University Press, 1973)—an analysis which can and should now be extended to other cultural fields and media as well.

19. The term originates in Barbara Ehrenreich and John Ehrenreich's classic essay of the same name, which can be found most readily in Pat Walker, ed., *Between Labor and Capital*, (Boston: South End Press, 1979), pp. 5–45. The other essays in the collection, responses to the Ehrenreichs' piece, are also worth noting insofar as they are indicative of the debate which has followed, in which there has been little outright disagreement with the Ehrenreichs' basic contentions, nor much of any real engagement with them, either. Instead, the attempt has been to bury the analysis and the pressing political problems it sets before the American left in a thicket of cranky terminological squabbles and arcane, academicized split hairs.

20. *The Pleasure of the Text*, p. 31. But another word or two is due, if only in this note, on the nature and social origins of some of the elements of that "reactionary darkness" in these two books. I owe to my friend Sohnya Sayres the observation that *Fiskadoro* and *The Businessman* both admit and fend off the ideological challenge of resurgent religious discourse—*Fiskadoro* through the aestheticized detachment of its high poetic style, *The Businessman* through its elaborate undermining of any conventional boundary between the sacred and secular and/or banal, its intransigent, blithe wackiness. In *Fiskadoro*, moreover, this operation is specifically tied to the promise and anxiety of the rise of another, presumably non-white and non-western, civilization following the self-destructive collapse of this one. Is it not possible, then, to understand both these books as homoeopathic medicine for the PMC, introducing and defusing potentially threatening discourses arising from other races, classes, and quarters outside our own compound? Or, to put the same point slightly differently: from whose point of view do such discourses appear as "reactionary darkness" more or less by definition, a darkness which must one way or another be sufficiently diluted so that *we* can "pass lightly through" it without undue discomfort or sense of threat?

21. "Does Sex Have a History? 'Women' and Feminism," *New Formations* 1 (Spring 1987), p. 44.

22. *Literary Theory: An Introduction* (Minneapolis: University of Minnesota Press, 1983), p. 191.

PART IV

Plot Devices in the Occupation

INTRODUCTION/SETTING, PREMISE, FIRST PRINCIPAL

The first scene establishes the situation. So we begin with these two in particular speculating as to when the Occupation might have actually begun.

One of them we will call Paul. A white male in his early- or mid-thirties, with features and habits unremarkable enough that it would make little sense to take up space in the attempt to conjure them up succinctly, meaningfully here. Owned a good record collection, though—good enough, especially where what he called "classic stuff" (meaning late forties, early-to-mid-fifties bop) was concerned, that we start with his moment of hesitation beside the Garrard changer, with an early Miles Davis LP halfway out of its sleeve.

His intention had been interrupted; or, more precisely, had veered away in a new and temporary direction. What he had originally wanted to do was listen to "Green Dolphin Street." Most of all to that exact moment when on the heels of Miles's muted tactful solo Coltrane's sax grabs the tune like a pair of big hands, half-hugging half-throttling it. As his eyes ranged over the old familiar rows of records on their shelves, Paul was at first idly, pleasantly struck by various specific memories of playing this particular cut for various close friends and lovers in various places over the years. Then he was assailed by an equally pungent but less happy thought. When he ran back over any one or all of these same memories he was for the first time aware of just how much his friends' and/or lovers' capacity to recognize the fully classy beauty of such great jazz moments rested on their access to a pool of sophisticated yet benevolent detachment, an essential "cool" which by now could only be remembered, not reassumed. Which was in turn, he realized, why he himself wanted to play that cut now: not to listen to the music really, not even to get back that "cool," but to keep its memory, trap the slightest borrowed hint of its lost fragrance in his nose. For there was no such loving irony available now, not in these grim times. Not since the Occupation had set in, though "Occupation" is not how he himself sees it yet.

ACTION (1)

"Amy?" he called, this being the name we give the other one. "When did things get this bad? Or when did you first know they were?"

REACTION (1)/COMPLICATION, SECOND PRINCIPAL

Arguably a cryptic question, all the more so since she was in the next room at the kitchen table, paging through an L.L. Bean catalogue, and so had no way of knowing what he was doing, how his actions had just prompted it. Yet after two full years of cohabitation and to some extent innately, their rapport was such that she could at least begin her movement towards an answer almost immediately. She closed the catalogue on two pages of thermal socks, thinking how the great thing about L.L. Bean was in spite of the fact that she would probably never buy anything from there in her whole life (the catalogue came for this place's last occupants, she just hadn't forwarded it), they could make you half-interested in descriptions of anything, even things like long under-wear and socks. Maybe that came from giving every indication of taking it all very seriously. So in a way she was close to his point after all, which was how their relationship worked. "Pretty different questions," she called back. "Which do you mean?"

Paul turned on the amp, a JVD, and put on the record, which began to play "Green Dolphin Street," the cut he had wanted, first one on Side 2. He could see her point, there was a difference, though not one he cared much about. As a matter of fact, he had become indifferent to the whole subject, thanks to the mood which had just slid suavely over him even before Miles's entrance set the tune, with Evans's first spare gestural chords. It made him wrinkle up his nose to think that even though that sour moment a minute ago was past and proven decisively wrong, you could still get there, to the heart of this song in spite of all the shit of these last few years or so—even so, he had thrown out the question, she had picked up on it, it would have to get played out now.

The rules of relationships must be observed, she was already here in the front room with her serious face uplifted, awaiting his reply. What he really wanted was just to keep swaying, stay inside the song, but no chance.

"Don't care," he said with half-shut eyes, barely glancing at her. "Which do you want?"

BACKGROUND

A plot device can be practically anything as long as whatever it is, it either gets the story moving or at the very least keeps it up. A piece of toilet paper, a little square of it, can be a plot device if someone blows his/her nose on it or does something else that somehow sets loose a bunch of other important events down the line, ironic (because you use this particular brand, some South American peasant will die) or otherwise (a coded message is on one particular sheet, the person blowing his nose is a spy). Our job is supposed to be to employ such plot devices to shape and execute plots that seem to happen just like that, naturally, because things are the way they are. Common sense is what the world calls wisdom, said some of those Salada tea bags when they used to come with sayings on them, a few years back now. Look at it this way and it becomes clear. Characters are plot devices too, inevitably, naturally. Anyone who keeps the story moving is.

ACTION (II)

"When was the OPEC oil blockade?" she said, shuffling to the music herself: "73, 74? Anyway, I was still in California with Don, it was right at the end of that mess. We were having these arguments every night over nothing. He kept telling me I ought to start as a trainee at Intel in basic programming, he could get me in no sweat. I think back on it now, it wasn't such a bad idea, but at the time it felt like an insult. I said to him, What do you think I went to college for? His replies to this question went to smutty from snide over time. Then up in the city some madman was running around murdering random people, blacks or whites, I can't remember which, and there was a garbage strike. We would get done fighting and go to bed and I would stay awake half the night thinking strange, anxious thoughts about how glad I was we didn't have to live up there. I realize now that even this in its strange way was a sort of happiness. I was after all just 22. What I meant to get to, though, I would get up after these nights in the morning around 5:30, still pitch black,

and go out running in this park across the street next to the El Camino
Real which is this shitstrip running from the city south, down through
the Bay. But I got scared of running round and round this dinky little
park in the dark, there were winos hanging out in the bushes back in
there and I started thinking what would happen if they got it together to
jump out at me or something, so I started running up the El Camino
itself instead. This was back during the OPEC blockade, remember that?
Late 73, early 74?"

REACTION (IIA)

"Green Dolphin" was over by this time. "Round Midnight" was on.
"Early 74," he said, nodding. "That's right."

ACTION (II), CONT.

"I was running past these lines and lines of cars," she said. "You can
imagine what normal commuter traffic's like in a place like that anyway,
but this was ridiculous. The stations on the strip were only open for gas
from 6 to 7, sometimes less, and people were ready to kill for it. I was
running past one set of headlights after another. Nobody yelled at me,
nothing happened, all you could hear were the engines overheating,
brake plates scraping in unison, wearing out together. I went past
stations with fistfights, men in very nice suits slugging it out between
their facing Lincolns, right in front of the pumps. Other stations where
there were these nice young gas jockeys, just kids really, packing guns in
holsters on their belts. Maybe it was just me but things seemed so
completely unreal, so weird, it was like you had to know after this it
would never be the way it was again. I could be wrong, I mean I have no
way of knowing for sure if I thought that or not at the time, but it feels
like I did. Or at least could've, anyway. What about you?"

REACTION (IIB)/CRISIS

He was stunned into silence. He could make no reply. The music seemed
far distant from him though the record still turned and the noise
still emerged from the secondhand Fischers mounted symmetrically on
either side of the room's long wall. As far into its mood as he had
travelled, this tale of alienation, social fragmentation, youth and
premonitory shortages had dispelled it utterly. It seemed so moving, so

bleak yet so right he could hardly believe it had actually happened to someone he knew, much less to his own lover Amy, standing so simply across from him, smiling as a girl in a ballet recital might smile, taking her bows. Nothing like that ever happened to him, ever would. For one thing, she seemed to have had far more lovers, to have taken in general more risks. It was something he both loved and hated in her. When he tried to summon up the memory of any equivalent experience he might have once had all he could think of instead was a somewhat famous World War II photograph of a balding Frenchman with a horsey face standing in the crowd that had gathered to watch the Nazis enter Paris, weeping uncontrollably. And in this way the conception of these bad times as an Occupation occurred to him quite naturally, inevitably, given his character. "Sometimes I feel like we're living through an Occupation," he said, watching to see if she would realize just how serious he was, despite the way Miles had brightened up just now as if to mock him. Her smile faded, she nodded sagely, somberly, and walked into his arms as, with equivalent naturalness, he remembered something else, a line of poetry from college which he added right out loud, it seemed so right. "Let us be true to each other, love," he said, and let it hang in the air for a while. Then it seemed like he ought to say something else besides. "If I'm right and this really is like the Occupation it's the only way we'll get through." And the way her head found its place in the hollow between his shoulders and chest it was like she was answering him, I know, you're right, I know. Though you could hardly tell that kind of thing for sure. Which was itself part of the problem these days. One of its symptoms, anyway. Yet still, even so——

ADDITIONAL BACKGROUND

"A contradiction between an integrated capitalist system and a capitalist system which has destroyed its basis for stability." The half-million dollars from Mobil Oil to the country's non-communist parties. The electric needle fine enough to fit between the teeth, smuggled into the country in the U.S. diplomatic pouch. The fungus which grows on the hands of those whose job it is to spray the country's fruit with the chemicals, day after day. The 500,000 tons of bombs dropped on the country between 1969 and 1973. The 5000 people in the stadium weeks after the coup, still being beaten, slashed, lined up along the wall and shot, and the eyes of the women who etch the circuits, burning out blind, plus the recurring headaches from the acid solution that fills the long rooms with its fumes. The first beauty contest ever held in the country, a Revlon makeup kit and mirror for first prize. The country's solemn promise to reduce your assembly costs by sixty percent, minimum. The chief condition on the IMF loan to the country, an immediate hike in the pricing of basic commodities, coupled with a wage freeze. The swastikas on the walls of the interrogation rooms, the former dictator's jeep bazooka-ed to bits in a side street, the American supporters butted away from the helicopters by the Marines, the helicopters in pieces, burning in the desert sands, the woman in flames in her trailer, protesting the budget cuts. The boys in the river had it coming, the way they laughed at us on the way back from their soccer game, laughing at our uniforms, our rifles, our boots. "Contradiction between an integrated capitalist system and a capitalist system which has destroyed its basis for stability," and no one he knows can make any serious additions to their collections any more, what with records at $8 a crack.

TRANSITION

Next morning, they rise. Shower. Shave legs (hers), face (his), don appropriate clothing. Breakfast. Low, functional dialogue throughout. Emerge together just after eight. Separate shortly thereafter, so that now they are at work.

DEVELOPMENT/NARRATION, WITH FLASHBACK

The bank she works in we will say has been open for fifteen minutes already, so that makes it 10:15. The northwest corner of an intersection formed by two beltways back in the sixties. A branch office, actually. Across the road, a standard strip center dating back to the sixties too. A 7-11, a package store, a laundromat, a Persian restaurant with about two months to go. Five restaurants since she first came to work here, which means in the last three years. Italian, Mexican, Laotian, Chinese and now this. It has smoked glass windows like polarized lenses you can't ever possibly see through. No one ever goes in there, not even from the laundromat next door. Back here where she works in the bank they make up one-liners about what really goes on over there. The tellers do it, Hal the manager does it, she has done it herself even right in front of new accounts, even back when they had them sometimes. You leave it vague, leave it up to the person to think what he wants. You laugh but it's no joke, in fact it's nothing, just a way of passing time. Her main job is to handle new business accounts, of which there are none until the restaurant folds again and the next one starts up, in another two, three months. In her private opinion it would go if some Greeks took it over, made it into a Greek restaurant. Gyros, souvlaki, spanikopitas, dolmades, etc. Just a hunch but it feels right. With this recession on, so many people out of work some days only five, six people come in, an average of one an hour. She could understand if this were some kind of a retail store, but why banks? Whatever the logic, however it works, there are days, many days when she envies the tellers what little action they get. Though she is on salary and they are on wage. Though she has a desk in a roped-in section, across the lobby from them. A cut-glass vase on the desk, with a fresh rose in it daily, dropped off by some florist the bank pays by the month. One week she threw out every one from Tuesday on, drained the water from the vase, watched the edges brown, the petals drop from the Monday one on the smooth desktop, smooth floor. If the manager noticed he didn't say, if the two tellers saw it they weren't talking, and since there were no new accounts that was basically it. At least half the time, though, she got along fine. Went out with the tellers for lunch every so often, played up to Hal when necessary, sometimes just to keep him from blowing his brains out, he got so depressed. This place would be the next to go, any day now, Hal said when he got that way. Looked as busy as she had to, wore good clothes, looked presentable and pleasant. Though half the time, if the truth be told, she was thinking about something else. Right now, at this minute, Paul's riff on the Occupation last night. He'd seen some famous movie about it, the whole point of which was apparently how the overwhelming majority of the people in France once the Nazis came in kept on doing whatever they did. Hanging out at night in bistros, buying baguettes at the grocery store, tilling the earth if they were peasants, picking up where they left off. Every so often apparently the Gestapo came in and rounded up some people—mainly Jews, probably—and for a while after people would get upset. But then for the most part they just let it drop. And the most amazing thing about the movie he said was the way it made you feel like that too, given how incredibly long it was, something like three hours at least. You'd get worn down and just stop watching then something would happen, you'd see or hear something awful and realize how the same thing you saw in the movie was happening to you. The more he talked about it the more excited he got. She was washing her face, brushing her teeth, listening over the water the best she could. That must be it, he said, snapping his fingers the way he did when he'd just thought something he wanted you to know. Think about your expectations ten years ago, right? Think about what they are today. See what I mean?

At the time she hadn't wanted much to think about what he was saying, regardless. She wanted him to get into bed, she was cold. Well, who are the Nazis today then? she said as he turned out the light.

So he had to explain to her how analogies like this went only so far, all this one showed was how amazing it was the way people, including himself, could ignore the really heavy changes coming down in our society these days. Which was true; which was absolutely right. So should she keep floating like this ad infinitum? Or give in and go back, with a loan if she had to, and get that M.B.A.?

DEVELOPMENT (II)/SCENE, WITH EPIPHANY

Paul too was at his desk, examining the contents of his brown metal in-bin, structuring events and activities in what was left of his daily eight hours in what we learn to think of as the public realm, when suddenly his co-worker Carl Oxenhandler appeared in the doorway.

"Hey," Carl said. "Wanna see something?"

Paul shrugged. "Yeah, sure," he said.

They went together down the hall. Paul was conscious of how businesslike, masculine, effectual they looked. Knowing when and how to keep your mouth closed, jaw set, maintain a brisk stride, look purposeful, it was that way everywhere. As long as you kept your distance on it, you were okay. Oxenhandler he guessed was of the same opinion, but had terrible b-o. Famous for it around the office, unbeknownst of course to him. Halfway through the morning, already Oxenhandler trailed his dying animal scent. Couldn't help but like the guy, but my god.

What the company called offices were basically just partitioned spaces whose side and front walls stopped two-thirds of the way up. All the same, Oxenhandler acted like he had entered his very own castle. Took off his suitcoat, threw it on the kind of plastic side table you get at Pier 7 or some other discount store, yanked his tie away from his throat. Momma, what a smell. He was also visibly, audibly excited, grinning and breathing hard. One-handed, he reached over and picked up a battered beige box from the desk. Paul realized he had never before noticed how big, how massive Carl's mitts were. He was aware as well of how the silence between them was mounting, becoming itself a source of something like tension. A flitting miraculous image of Carl onehandedly extracting something from the box, killing him with it. Snub-nosed .38. Smith and Wesson. Ridiculous. Mentally he checked his own smile, making sure it was still safely on nonetheless. The box was levelled at his chest. A brick-shaped rocket. No. "Take a look at this!" said Carl, thrusting it closer yet.

Paul took hold of the box with his two little paws. Cradled it against his chest with one, lifted the lid with the other. Oxenhandler loomed over him with that awful stench, starting to laugh before he could tell anything. What was it with this guy, anyway?

What there was in the box was wrapped in newspaper. His fingers unwrapped the pages, pushed them aside. A beat-up pair of shoes. Oxenhandler's job in fact was in footwear returns. This was a pair of shoes, old shoes in an old shoebox. Workboots it appeared, if you wanted specifics. He stared down at them, trying to fix their nature, catch the joke. Maybe just how old they were, could that be it? "Howdja get these?" he said, slyly grinning, accenting the second word.

"Pick 'em up," said smirking Oxenhandler. "Turn 'em over and look at the soles."

He took the workboots out of the box, noting their surprising weight. Their bumpy sides and tops had a worn, oiled texture that felt to his touch like aged, weathered skin—like the way he imagined, presumed such skin would feel. He turned the boots over and for an instant or so noted only the discrepancy in patterns of wear on the soles. All along the left sole, whorls of concentric circles, intricate as an impossible tattoo, while on the right the instep still seemed fresh from the factory, untouched. Then he saw what manufacturer's error had brought this to pass, saw simultaneously the pitiful figure of an old, worn, grizzled workman of some kind actually putting such boots on, actually wearing them. A wave of hot embarrassment swept through him from head to toe. Suddenly he wished to be alone with these boots, with their mute but eloquent testimony. The effect of knowing Oxenhandler's eyes were on him at this moment was unpleasant and intense.

When he looked back up, he had at first no idea what showed on his face. Oxenhandler was laughing again, shaking his head back and forth, patting his forehead with the palm of his huge left hand. There were tears of mirth in his eyes. Yes, mirth. "Can you believe that shit?" he said.

"It's hard to believe," Paul said. "I'll grant you that."

"Boys down in the warehouse had it sent up. They'll do that with something like this, something genuinely weird," Carl said. "I'll tell you though, I've never seen anything like this."

"I should say not," said Paul.

"Came back from Missouri," said Carl. "Some farmer, odds are. That's how I picture it at any rate."

"Amazing," Paul said. "Incredible."

There was a pause. Oxenhandler got over behind his desk and shook his head a few more times with his smile gone, his eyes dully focused on a paperclipped mass of forms. "Well," he said. "Well, I thought you'd get a kick out of it at any rate."

"Yeah," said Paul. "Well, yeah, sure."

Oxenhandler shook his head once again this time with a rueful distant look, as if already nostalgic for the moment just gone by. Then he put his sports coat on again. Carefully Paul put the maimed boots back in the box, folded the newspaper around them again, replaced the lid. He set the box on the edge of the desk, next to Carl's grey metal in-bin. By now Carl was back to his work, eyeballing the forms, making little checks and notes here and there. At the sight of him working in his black vinyl chair Paul again experienced a mild terror, but of a different source and quality from that of the moment before, more immediate and more superficial. He realized how much time they had just pissed away, screwing around with those boots. He felt his own worthlessness, having not yet today done a damn bit of work. Was that how Oxenhandler felt too, why he was buckling down like this with Paul still in the room? Was this something he could ask Oxenhandler about?

He had backed up to the doorway. "Guess I better get back myself."

"Take care," said Carl tonelessly without glancing up.

On the way back he tried to calm down. Kept his face impassive, effectual, all the way down the hall as the various thoughts slid and bounced. The quarterly report due Friday, the stacks of figures, the adjustments over an extended period of time of both left and right feet to an item of footwear whose right sole has been stitched on at what appears to be a 30° slant off the horizontal, the numbers at the bottom of the column, ridges and contusions on the toes, the continuous pain one would think hour after hour, day after day and the obvious question of why whoever it was—this farmer, this plant worker, whoever he was, wherever the hell in Missouri—had not thought to return them sooner, had worn them so damn long. Heard of "quiet desperation," but this was ridiculous. Feels that same dislocated sadness and anxiety, though in this context, at this moment walking back up the hall under its even lighting and within its steady temperature does not recall what he said last night about the Occupation. Certain connections must remain repressed, certain insights must stay local. It would have been too clever, too pat, the wrong thing to have done. As he re-enters his own cubicle he notices that unbeknownst to him at some point his nose must have unstopped itself, he is back to normal breathing now that Oxenhandler's odor is no longer around. He settles down in his brown vinyl chair, turns his attention to the first set of figures on the top pages on his desk. Still smiling occasionally, shaking his head, although against his will. Back at work, in what we have learned to think of as the public realm.

CLIMAX

As a plot device you still have some options, at least up to a certain point. Given daily life for most of us, though, it is pretty hard to believe any more in those stories where you get to be the primary character in a plot that centers on what happens to you personally, or on who you "really" are. When you go from one thing, thought, or mood to another the way songs go by on the radio, one ad follows the last on TV, so many thousands starve to death every minute, so many millions spent on arms every minute of every day, it sort of knocks out your chances of being a richly developed character with a certain consistent set of attitudes and behavior patterns which in turn implies some sort of essential inner self which is so distinct and irreplaceable that we all ought to be interested in whatever happens to you. Almost nobody in his/her right mind believes that story any more, so that leaves us with two other stories instead. The first one more-or-less like most of this piece, like Paul and Amy, like this sentence on and on until something happens from outside to end it or it runs out of steam and just stops. The other more directed, more of a line—albeit one that starts out sketchy and halting, a very faint line that starts and stops; gets broader and thicker, then fades, moves forward again; etc. We are not far enough along this line to know much about the kind of story that will come to us someday from moving with it, following it out. But we know what it will sound like, what its opening premise will be. We lost until we won, this story will say. We took from them at last what they have always taken from us. Now we write our own story—or words to that effect. Who knows what comes next, after that?

DENOUEMENT

Many years later. One succeeds, one fails. Amy has gone on, is in possession of her M.B.A. Currently close to retirement, in fact, from a comparatively well-paying position as a marketing analyst within an international electronic and chemical firm best known to the general public in what is still atavistically considered this country as a producer of household appliances, toasters and the like, plus various synthetic fibers commonly used to make clothing, whereas in point of fact its main products and source of profits now as always are weapons systems, and subcomponents of weapons systems assemblies. Is aware of this in hazy ways known to us all. Somewhat troubled by unpleasant memories. All behind her now but still, the entrance lobby of the Business School turned into a blackened mouth by the bombing, rolls of barbed wire, first sight of the New Police Force standing guard in their initially disturbing regalia. Who could possibly do such a thing, something this stupid, this senseless, was the world going crazy, what would happen to my schedule, tuition, will things ever be normal again. Or that crisp October day years later with the crowd outside the office tower waiting as they had all fall that year for the moment when the employees all got out of work then surging like liquid over the barricades like a full cup and then past the guards, coming at them long before they could get in the company vans where they could have fanned their brows and shaken their heads, sadly, even to some extent sympathetically, and relaxed with a drink on the away back home, the horrible onslaught instead of all those people, ragged, dirty, multiracial, shouting and sobbing, and yes even laughing as their hands reached out for you, for you, to do things to you. Then the announcement from the gunship, yes: ultimatum in electric monotone. Then the moment when you actually prayed, Dear God let me out of this, get me out of here safe back home and I will never. Then a blank; then the first shots. Still happens sometimes, in your dreams: blackened mouth, clutching hands, frozen prayer, plus a few other things from here and there, picked up out of the corners of your eyes as you move by, even now. Yet now, years later, her daytime mind dwells on pleasanter things when it dwells. Old loves, all nice in retrospect. A more or less normally happy childhood. Satisfaction of having lived a full and arguably productive life. Nostalgia, poignance, loss, coping with the inevitable encroachment of the dark. Questions of death's finality, purpose, experiential feel. Wishes she'd travelled more, stayed married to the one after Paul, had at least one more child but who could afford it, paid less attention to the damn company. Still likes to look at catalogues, considers her skin her best feature, still ruddy and smooth as a child's people say after all these years of her life. Likes to sit in the wicker rocker with the cat called Paraguay, and watch TV. Strokes the cat's soft fur, under its throat. Feels the soft motor purr against the back of her hand, closes her eyes in the moment's repose, plenitude. Sorrows and joys of a lifetime, perhaps of human life itself. Considers herself amazingly lucky, in all. Then jumps as the program breaks for an ad, the volume goes inevitably up, Paraguay growls and jumps off. Paul, meanwhile, one way or another has met an unhappier fate. Strange how many possibilities stream from the simple premise that his true talents remain untapped. Say he stays at the same job the rest of his life, puts little in, less out. Gradually grows more and more insensitive and bitter, not to mention less well paid. Things with Amy fall apart. Other lovers follow. Feels ambivalent towards the success of others like Oxenhandler, moving up and sometimes out to other companies. Ditto towards the blacks moving in, moving up from the warehouse, into the neighborhood where his apartment still is. Glad to see them getting what he clings to thinking of as increased opportunities, aware that the neighborhood is no longer special or interesting, is in fact going downhill the same way the company is where there is nobody to shoot the shit with now, just as there is no one for a long time in what we learn to think of as his private life to play those records for, discuss his movies, think his thoughts out with. Loses his hair, develops a paunch, gets half-drunk at night by himself, goes to bed mumbling about the niggers, finds himself feeling more and more pissed off at how the country is falling apart, finds himself in front of the TV cheering the new protective measures put in action by the New Police Force on the 11 o'clock news. Comes to feel that everyone else's cynicism is somehow in advance of his own. Identifies with the guards on the corners, learns to disregard their youthful, patronizing smiles. Marries someone he meets in a bar, a chronically frightened keypunch operator he can feel superior to, and does. Moves to a larger apartment with her, an all-white street with community guards whose ranks he joins, along with the Republican Party he votes for the rest of his life. Helps organize the first funding drive for the first bunker in his area, foregoes and forgets all those scraps of poems from college, fills his wife with five kids raised as good Americans the old-fashioned way. Or: eventually loses his job, has to let go of his apartment, runs slowly out of work and money, finds himself out on the street. The next five to ten years basically spent scrounging for jobs, food, etc. One day falls into his first demonstration, scooped up by the crowd sweeping over the sidewalks, up the street, and realizes that now he does look just as dirty and ignorant and nonwhite as them, so moves along shouting and singing whatever it is they have chosen to shout or sing until the cops and guards move in to break things up and he trips and falls as the crowd scatters, some throwing things and some not and the next thing he knows the guards are looking down on him, two guards, one maybe his age and one much younger. There are shots in the distance, but down on the sidewalk where he is it is suddenly very quiet. This is it, the trouble he has been waiting for all his life. The effect of having it here at last is so familiar it is almost comic. He smiles up at the guards, especially the one his age, the one in fact who seems to look like him, who perhaps is hip to the irony too. Simultaneously he is aware that no one else is on the street, that his gym bag of clothes and belongings is gone, that his nose-bleed has stained the collar of his last half-clean shirt. Or perhaps all this happens instead later on, when he gets caught by the plainclothesmen coming out of the brownstone he has been squatting in the last six months or so with ten or twelve others, a multiracial group part of the larger rabble. Or perhaps the one who looks like him is a plainclothesman, not a guard. Perhaps he has actually joined the Resistance, and been caught up in a daring raid. Would that mean his talents were tapped after all? Perhaps the prods they use when they go to work on him are made by the corporation Amy works for. Would that be too easy an irony? Perhaps he calls up all the jazz and poetry he can remember just to get him through the pain, perhaps he thinks of his former loves, including Amy. Then we could show how this works for a while, then doesn't, how love and art and song only get you so far, we could demonstrate this in graphic detail and leave it at that, letting each reader draw his/her own conclusions. We could conclude by exploring any one of these scenarios. Or would it be better just to leave this story entirely, start another one up instead?

(1982)